Reader and media praise for earlier editions

It is a great framework to distinguish between nutcase ideas and solid possibilities, and in some cases to turn the mad ideas into something that could work.

Max Aitken, serial entrepreneur

Teaches entrepreneurs and business owners how to avoid mistakes that many make.

Start Your Business *magazine, June 2010*

The New Business Road Test has been the most valuable piece of advisory material I have come across. Whatever else I recommend to my clients, owning and reading your excellent book is highest on the list.

Ian J R Wilson, Principal, Ian Wilson Associates, Edinburgh

We combine creativity/idea generation workshops with a feasibility analysis course – based on John Mullins' *The New Business Road Test* - and it's just wonderful for critical thinking, embracing ambiguity, encouraging fast failures, and mixing imagination with formal technique. Indeed, this is a capstone class for our Professional MBA. It's also a joy to teach, if rather chaotic at times, and the students adore it, too.

Professor Sarah Dodd, Hunter Centre for Entrepreneurship, University of Strathclyde

Some entrepreneurs might wonder why such a codified framework is needed to replace instinct and they won't find this book has a great deal to offer. But for most of those considering a new venture, thinking such as this offers a smart way to quickly assess what might and might not work.

Director *magazine, July/August 2010*

Provide[s] a reality check for anyone poised to jump into a new venture without thinking. Readers will enjoy discovering the nuggets of wisdom embedded in the case studies.

Financial Times, *July 2003*

We've never met but I love your book *The New Business Road Test* – I can honestly say it has done more for my businesses than 10 years of hard graft did.

Matthew Slight, Founder, Love Tea

I want to take this opportunity to express my appreciation and admiration for your approach to analysing new business opportunities using the seven domains you so eloquently describe in your book. While there have been a number of books written on this subject, it is rare when this subject is treated in such a practical manner.

Gerry Lemberg, Chairman, Silver Fox TeroVentures

Extremely valuable for entrepreneurs and small business owners alike.

David Kelnar, Greatvine.com

I have made a real breakthrough in my first year and started to win a number of contracts. John's book really helped me to understand my business model and evaluate the risk of setting up on my own, in a style that was easy to read and understand.

Martin Costelloe, Rowan Landscapes

John Mullins is a distinguished figure in the global entrepreneurial community.

David Giampolo, Chief Executive, Pi Capital, London

I have found the framework useful in both analysing plans that we receive and structuring info memos that we write.

Richard Allen, Principal, 101Capital Limited

John Mullins's *New Business Road Test* provides the entrepreneurial equivalent to the proverbial 'sleeping policeman' on the Sunday drive: the necessary jolt of reality for those hanging on to the belief that value is created on a computer spreadsheet or a fancy PowerPoint presentation.

Professor Benoit Leleux, IMD, Lausanne, Switzerland

A mandatory step required before turning business ideas into business plans.

Federico Sarti, I3P incubator, Torino, Italy

I have read a lot of business books, however yours is the only manual that seems to offer a plan of action. ... I was alarmed to realise how much I didn't know about target markets.

Patrick Stewart, Managing Director, Central AV

My students are telling me how much they like your book for inspiration, but also for its pragmatic and practical perspective.

Professor Larry Plummer, University of Colorado

I have realised the common errors that after seemed so obvious yet no other books have really highlighted them. I think we are on the right track with our past experience and some expert advice from talented people as yourself.

Heather Bonte, Managing Director, Cultivating Minds

This is the book you should read before you even think about starting a new business.

Richard Stutely, Author, The Definitive Business Plan

As a successful entrepreneur in the satellite communication industry for the past 18 years, we were developing a new business idea for commercial launch and happened to talk with John Mullins. His book provided an overall check for our business plan and we were able to patch many holes. An excellent book providing an all-round framework for new and established entrepreneurs.

Sanjay Singhal, President/CEO, Sintel Satellite Services, Inc., New York

Whilst reading your book I found myself jotting ideas down and organising my thoughts. You have provided me with half a dozen sheets of paper full of scribbles and diagrams which between them feel like a very 'rounded' view of my business. We have been running for 18 months now, and it seems time to write a tentative business plan. Your book has provided a very welcome helping hand towards that plan.

Tim Craine, Managing Director, London Development Research

I am a Canadian entrepreneur who is having the profitable experience of reading your *New Business Road Test* book. Thanks for writing a terrific (and very sobering) book.

Christian Thwaites, President (Corporate Development),
FORPAC BioSciences, Vancouver, BC

I have added your book to my own entrepreneurship curriculum and I regularly give it to entrepreneurs we advise and in which we invest. I would like to thank you for penning such an important tome.

Vic Sarjoo, Chairman and CEO, Radical Funds, New York

I use your book regularly to assess the opportunities that come across my desk and it has been very useful in qualifying out of things that I might have wasted time on previously.

Jeremy Renwick, Kubernetes Ltd, Oxfordshire, UK

I picked up the current *HBR* and read the case about 'Good Money after Bad'. But most of all I picked up the trail to your book, *The New Business Road Test*. What a 'eureka' moment I had. Your comments and seven domains just sharpened up our thinking several very large notches.

Dave Sutherland, Retrievall Inc., Ontario, Canada

A much needed and invaluable resource for both entrepreneurs and line execs. I have spent part of my career working with people trying to start and/or grow companies, and the hardest part of pushing the rock uphill is the effort to convince them to do the hard work in that micro-market quadrant to identify the customer pain and develop the real solution to a customer's problem, rather than focusing on the 'build it and they will come' mentality. As someone who both writes and reviews business plans, I now have an important resource to hand to people rather than just shaking my head in frustration or repeating myself endlessly.

Mark Pfeifer, business planning expert

Pearson

At Pearson, we have a simple mission: to help people make more of their lives through learning.

We combine innovative learning technology with trusted content and educational expertise to provide engaging and effective learning experiences that serve people wherever and whenever they are learning.

From classroom to boardroom, our curriculum materials, digital learning tools and testing programmes help to educate millions of people worldwide – more than any other private enterprise.

Every day our work helps learning flourish, and wherever learning flourishes, so do people.

To learn more, please visit us at **www.pearson.com/uk**

The New Business Road Test

What entrepreneurs and investors should do *before* launching a lean start-up

Fifth edition

John Mullins

 Pearson

Harlow, England • London • New York • Boston • San Francisco • Toronto • Sydney • Dubai • Singapore • Hong Kong
Tokyo • Seoul • Taipei • New Delhi • Cape Town • São Paulo • Mexico City • Madrid • Amsterdam • Munich • Paris • Milan

PEARSON EDUCATION LIMITED
KAO Two
KAO Park
Harlow
CM17 9NA
United Kingdom
Tel: +44 (0)1279 623623
Web: www.pearson.com/uk

First published 2003 (print)
Second edition published 2006 (print)
Third edition published 2010 (print)
Fourth edition published 2013 (print and electronic)
Fifth edition published 2018 (print and electronic)

ISBN: 978-1-292-20839-8 (print)
       978-1-292-20840-4 (PDF)
       978-1-292-20841-1 (ePub)

British Library Cataloguing-in-Publication Data
A catalogue record for the print edition is available from the British Library

Library of Congress Cataloging-in-Publication Data
A catalog record for the print edition is available from the Library of Congress

10 9 8 7 6 5 4 3 2 1
21 20 19 18 17

Cover design by Two Associates
Cover image © petovarga/iStock

Print edition typeset in 9/13pt Stone Serif Std by 30 by SPI Global
Printed by Ashford Colour Press Ltd, Gosport

NOTE THAT ANY PAGE CROSS REFERENCES REFER TO THE PRINT EDITION

Contents

Why read this book?

Every year there are 2 million entrepreneurs in the UK actively engaged in starting a new business. Many of their ventures will never get off the ground. Of those that do, the majority will fail. There are more than 15 million entrepreneurs in the USA doing the same thing. Most of their ventures will fail, too. Of the many lean start-ups, most are soon gone. Of those who seek funds from business angels or venture capitalists, fewer than 1 per cent will be successful in raising the money they seek.

This picture of entrepreneurship is not a pretty one. The odds are daunting, the road long and difficult. Why, then, according to the Global Entrepreneurship Monitor, were a stunning one of every 12 adults in the UK – and one in seven in North America – actively pursuing entrepreneurial activities in one way or another in 2016? And why are so many individuals around the world getting involved in angel investing? In a word – opportunity. Opportunity to develop an idea that seems, at least to its originator, a sure-fire success. Opportunity to be one's own master – no more office politics, no more downsizing, no more working for others. Opportunity for the thrill, excitement, challenge and just plain fun inherent in the pursuit of entrepreneurial ventures, from either side of the deal table. I know, because I've been there, too.

❝ most opportunities are not what they appear to be, as the business failure statistics demonstrate ❞

But there's a problem. Most opportunities are not what they appear to be, as the business failure statistics demonstrate. Most of them have at least one fatal flaw that renders them vulnerable to all sorts of difficulties that can send a precarious, cash-starved new venture to the scrapheap in a heartbeat. An abundance of research makes it clear that the vast majority of new ventures fail for opportunity-related reasons:

- market reasons – perhaps the target market is too small or simply won't buy;

- industry reasons – it's too easy for competition to steal your customers;

- entrepreneurial team reasons – the team may lack what it takes to cope with the wide array of forces that conspire to bring fledgling entrepreneurial ventures to their knees.

How can a mere book help you meet this challenge?

The research underlying this book (see the Appendix 'Research methodology') suggests that the serious entrepreneur or early-stage investor who wants to beat the long odds – who wants to work harder and smarter to beat the competition – should pause in their haste to embark on a lean start-up, write that great business plan, compose a pitch deck, or invest in a start-up. Yes, I'm referring to *you*. Before setting out or putting pen to paper, you should step back and give the opportunity with which you are infatuated a road test. Examine the seven crucial domains of attractive opportunities that this book illuminates and brings to life. Find, if you can, the fatal flaw lurking in what looks like an attractive opportunity. If you're an entrepreneur, your prospective investors will be looking for that flaw, so you'd better have looked first.

Why bother?

But why shouldn't a would-be entrepreneur – or a prospective investor in an early-stage venture, for that matter – simply skip the seven domains road test this book advocates and proceed directly to preparing a business plan, or better yet, just starting the business or writing a cheque? There are three key reasons.

- First, this book enables entrepreneurs and investors alike to avoid impending disaster. For most entrepreneurs, that's the likely outcome – sad to say – according to the business failure data. Preparing a customer-driven feasibility study based on the seven domains – a concise memo addressed to oneself, really – affords you a chance to opt out early in the process, before investing the time and energy in preparing a complete business plan or heading down what may be a dead-end road. Identifying the critical flaw early can save weeks or months of time that might be wasted on a fundamentally flawed opportunity.

- Second, for opportunities that do look promising, the feasibility study builds a foundation for and jump-starts the start-up process. It provides a clear, customer-focused vision of why the proposed venture makes sense – from market, industry and team perspectives, viewed independently and collectively.

    ❝ the feasibility study jump-starts the start-up process. ❞

- Third, most business plans are not worth the paper on which they are printed. Put simply, as today's lean start-up movement is demonstrating, business plans and business planning are vastly over-rated. In my view, far too much time is spent crafting business plans in excruciating detail and far too little time is spent getting *real* data from *real* customers about *real* (probably prototype) products. A customer-driven feasibility study together with a credible and focused plan for answering unanswered questions is likely to be of far more value in many situations than a lovingly crafted – but hopelessly naïve and unfounded – business plan. But more about this subject in the rest of the book.

By ensuring that all aspects of the opportunity are examined, a seven domains road test reduces the risk of entering a venture that simply has no chance. What entrepreneur wants to be the next contributor to the sorry statistics of business failures? And what investor wants to lose money in such a venture? Surely not you. Simply put, a road test enhances the chances of starting a successful business that attracts both customers and capital.

Further, from a societal perspective, doing the seven domains homework – *before* writing and pitching business plans or getting the leanest of start-ups underway – can reduce the waste of precious entrepreneurial resources now devoted to the pursuit of fundamentally flawed opportunities. Entrepreneurs are the drivers of the global economy. Their firms create the new jobs and offer role models for others to follow. Let's be certain that today's entrepreneurs and early-stage investors – including you! – are working on ventures that have at least a fighting chance of success!

Who should read this book?

Principally, this book is for serious, opportunity-focused entrepreneurs and those who support them.

- People who are dying to get out of the big, stifling, inflexible businesses where they work today to strike out on their own. People who have identified one or more opportunities that might just be the ticket out, but who need a way to test them. People who want to run their own business and benefit from the significant upside potential that could bring them economic freedom.

- Entrepreneurs already running a start-up who are finding the challenges more daunting than they had imagined. Perhaps they are wondering whether their chosen path is a good one.

- Engineers and inventors with ideas or technologies that can spawn something more than just a new product.

There are four other groups, too, that can benefit from *The New Business Road Test* and its seven domains analysis.

- Investors – whether family or friends or business angels or even newcomers to venture capital – who want to sharpen their skills and bring more than their money to the entrepreneurial table. Independent, clear-sighted advice from investors is more valuable to entrepreneurs than the money they bring.

- General managers, new product managers and business development professionals in businesses now mired in stagnant performance or – worse – in an unforgiving industry. They know their companies must find attractive new markets and develop successful new products in order to grow. Business as usual won't cut it. But how, they wonder, can their company be made more entrepreneurial?

- The growing legion of advisers, consultants and others, all working to create better entrepreneurial ecosystems where they live and work.

- University faculty and mentors and staff at the growing number of accelerators and boot camps, all teaching aspiring entrepreneurs how to assess opportunities or write their first business plan or launch a lean start-up. For faculty and such supporters, there's even a website to provide wide-ranging resources: www.newbusinessroadtest.com.

What are these people – perhaps you are one of them – doing today? Some are spending every waking moment looking for an opportunity to join the ranks of today's growing entrepreneurial culture or to invest therein. They're spending weekends at lean camps, hackathons or start-up boot camps in search of the right spark, the right idea, and the right partners with whom to get started on what they hope will be a promising venture. starting a new venture.

❝ if you are serious about *succeeding* in your new venture – not simply starting one – this book is for you ❞

Others are already engaged in conceiving or starting a new venture. Still others have recently done so, but the path to success remains unclear. Whichever of these types of entrepreneur, would-be entrepreneur, or early-stage investor you are, if you are serious about *succeeding in* your new venture – not simply starting one – this book is for you. It will help you avoid the disaster that's waiting to happen to the majority of new ventures. Yes, even to yours.

What will be the result of reading this book?

Entrepreneurs or investors having an opportunity in hand – whether it's still in the planning stages or already navigating the turbulent waters that early-stage ventures must sail – will reach one of three conclusions after finishing this book and putting their opportunity through the new business road test.

■ Perhaps the most common outcome will be that the fatal flaw(s) will be uncovered. 'Whew! I'm glad I didn't bother pursuing or investing in *that* idea' is the likely sigh of relief. The disaster that would have ensued is now avoided, and all the time and energy – and money, too! – that would have been invested in a fatally flawed idea can be invested more productively in a better one. Those already in a new venture who reach this conclusion can plot a way to change the direction of the business – or sell it – before disaster strikes.

■ Another common outcome will be that flaws that are identified can be fixed. Opportunities are malleable, and the entrepreneur is often able to reshape an opportunity to improve its attractiveness by:

  - targeting a different market;
  - offering a different product or service than the one originally planned;
  - playing at a different level in the value chain – as a distributor rather than a manufacturer, for example;
  - adding skills or relationships to the entrepreneurial team that were missing in the original conception.

  Opportunities can evolve, and the thought process outlined in this book hastens and strengthens that evolution. The sooner the pivots – the ones based on solid evidence, of course – occur, the better.

■ A third possible outcome – the happiest, but most rare – will be that your seven domains analysis finds no fatal flaw. No matter how hard you look. Better yet:

  - your homework identifies a real problem that someone – your prospective customer – has, and you offer a solution that's better, faster or cheaper than current solutions;
  - your proposition stands a chance to establish sustainable competitive advantage with a business model that works in economic terms;
  - the market is large enough to make the effort worthwhile;
  - the industry is sufficiently attractive;
  - your entrepreneurial team has what it takes to succeed.

  The best news about this kind of outcome is that, in jump-starting the start-up process, the seven domains homework provides the evidence-based research foundation for a persuasive and compelling pitch.

Why John Mullins? What does a business school professor know about starting an entrepreneurial business?

This book brings together, from a single author, the hands-on, done-it-before experience of a three-time entrepreneur with the research expertise found among faculties at only a handful of the world's leading business schools. Put simply, I've practised what I preach and I have the entrepreneurial badges and scars to prove it. I've learned the way most entrepreneurs learn, from both failure and success.

I served as vice-president in the early high-growth days at a then young company with great casual clothing stores called Gap; I founded Pasta Via International and took it public before market and technological changes took our company down; I pioneered chimney-type charcoal starters for American barbecue enthusiasts. I've served on the boards of fast-growing entrepreneurial companies in the USA, the UK, Europe and Asia. From all these experiences and from the extensive research effort that underlies this book, I have drawn insights that deliver powerful lessons from which every entrepreneur – and many investors, for that matter – can learn.

As a professor at London Business School, where my entrepreneurship colleagues and I – many of us successful entrepreneurs in our own right – develop world-class entrepreneurs and train and provide talent for the venture capital industry, I am well positioned to have written what I hope you will find is an accessible and eye-opening book. Once you have read it, I believe you'll agree with me that ignoring even *one* of the seven domains can be a road map to entrepreneurial disaster. Entrepreneurs and investors who start their venture without putting their idea to the new business road test do so at their peril!

> **ignoring even *one* of the seven domains can be a road map to entrepreneurial disaster**

But the insights that drive the book's lessons aren't just my own. Far from it. They are the result of a series of interviews with venture capital investors, business angels and experienced entrepreneurs, alongside the extensive and detailed case study research into the fabulous entrepreneurial stories that comprise the heart of the book.

Why a fifth edition?

The previous fourth editions of *The New Business Road Test* were rousing successes, not only in the English-speaking markets where the book was first introduced, but also in translations into numerous other languages. 'But are the case histories still current?' I wondered, as the book reached more than a dozen years in print.

I've also observed and been a part of what one might call the lean start-up movement, a global phenomenon that is changing the way people think about and start new ventures. Many entrepreneurs are probably asking 'How do this book and its opportunity assessment tools and ideas fit into today's lean start-up landscape?' This new edition provides some answers.

But that's not all. Of course, this new and fully updated edition brings each and every case history up to date, adding an important and timely 'What happened' to each of the stories. This edition also makes explicit the attention given to the identification of key risks in each of the seven domains and to their prominence in a customer-driven feasibility study. In Chapter 5, following a pattern we set in the fourth edition, greater weight has now been given to the *economic* sustainability of one's new venture, alongside the sustainability of its *competitive advantage*. This greater weight reflects recent attention given in the entrepreneurship literature to how best to think about and develop business models that can actually work – *before* setting forth on an entrepreneurial journey. To reflect this balance, the lower right-hand corner of the seven domains framework has been relabelled as *competitive and economic sustainability*.

Next, given that many of today's most exciting entrepreneurs are harnessing the power of the internet in building their ventures, I also wanted to populate this fifth edition with more such companies than were on the map way back in 2003 when this book's first edition was published. From little-known companies like ThirdLove, Fuhu (already come and gone!) and Luxy Hair, to blockbuster unicorns like Groupon (a unicorn no longer!) and the high-flying Twilio, today's dot.com entrepreneurs will find plenty of highly relevant case histories, both successes and failures, from which to learn in this new edition.

Perhaps equally noteworthy in this edition, though, is the addition of a new chapter, Chapter 17: Have you got what it takes? In this new chapter, you'll read about the mindsets and behaviours that characterise many entrepreneurs. If you are an entrepreneur or an aspiring one, you may find it insightful to see whether your mindset and behaviours match up with what you read therein.

Finally, to take advantage of the power of technology, I've again linked this fifth edition to my *The New Business Road Test* app for your smartphone or tablet. In today's digitally driven world, many readers – perhaps you – will be reading this book on an iPhone, a Kindle, a Samsung Galaxy, or some other mobile device not even invented as I write in early 2017. As you are out in the marketplace searching for or assessing an opportunity that you hope will be good enough to become your next start-up, the app will make it easy to assemble evidence for your road test wherever you are. The app is keyed to the book – and the book to it – on a chapter-by-chapter basis.

To clarify the structure of the book, it's made sense to present this edition in two parts. Part 1 (Chapters 1–10) contains everything you'll need to know to road test your new business idea, while Part 2 (Chapters 11–18) provides you with the practical toolkit to carry out your road test.

In 30 seconds or less

This book helps serious entrepreneurs and early-stage investors avoid impending disaster. It puts front and centre a key question that far too many entrepreneurs and investors fail to ask, 'Why *won't* my idea work?' It shows entrepreneurs what to do *before* they write a great business plan, prepare a pitch deck or embark on a lean start-up, to enhance their chance of winning both customers and capital and actually achieving their entrepreneurial dreams. And it reveals the seven key issues that astute investors examine *before* they invest. Intrigued? Read on.

JWM April 2017

About the author

John Mullins is a veteran of three entrepreneurial ventures and a professor at the London Business School, where he teaches and studies entrepreneurship, venture capital, and the management of rapidly growing businesses. His students have started more than 200 new ventures, of which an overwhelming majority are still in business. He is a frequent and sought-after speaker and educator for audiences in entrepreneurship and venture capital.

John holds a BA in Mathematics from Lehigh University, an MBA from the Stanford Graduate School of Business, and a PhD in Marketing from the University of Minnesota. He is the author or co-author of four other books, including the widely acclaimed *Getting to Plan B: Breaking through to a Better Business Model*.

His most recent title, *The Customer-Funded Business: Start, Finance, or Grow Your Company with Your Customers' Cash,* was named one of five 'not-to-be-missed books' for 2014 by *Fortune* magazine. It challenges the all-too-widely held assumption that among an entrepreneur's first and most important tasks is that of raising investment capital. Its material provides the foundation for John's Massively Open Online Course (MOOC), *How to Finance and Grow Your Startup – Without VC* on Coursera.org, which has reached more than 25,000 viewers from around the world.

Author's acknowledgements

For the ideas that have coalesced into this book, there are more people who deserve thanks than there are stars in the Milky Way splashed across the midnight sky in Colorado, where most of this book's first edition was written in the summer of 2002 and where this fifth edition was crafted in early 2017. But two people stand out. First is John Bates, my friend and colleague at the London Business School, whose clear thinking and entrepreneurial insights and instincts inform many of its pages. John's access to the venture capital community in the UK was instrumental in the research that underlies the book's first edition. Without it, the book simply would not exist. Thank you John, and Wendy too. Second, Suzanne Stoller uncovered and researched the original set of companies whose case histories – successful and otherwise – would bring to life the lessons of the seven domains. Her opening vignettes in each chapter make the book more engaging and readable, and her humour and intellect made the work more fun and engaging. Many thanks, Suzanne! But the case histories have moved on, and my thanks go to Elizabeth Philp for conducting the painstaking research in autumn 2012 and again in winter 2017 to bring each of the case histories up to date and help me uncover, critically examine and bring to life some new ones.

At the heart of the book, informing the research that led to the seven domains model, are some two dozen venture capitalists, angel investors and entrepreneurs in the UK and USA who shared their time and candid insights with me. If the ideas in this book make a difference in how the current generation of aspiring entrepreneurs and early-stage investors fares, it is these thoughtful men and women who deserve the thanks. Most of the good ideas are probably theirs. Any errors in fact or interpretation are, of course, mine. Thanks, too, to Grant McCracken's *The Long Interview* for teaching me how to interview them.

To my students who, over the years, helped these ideas grow, many thanks for challenging them as they took shape in our class discussions. Just like opportunities, ideas can be shaped. The very best thing about being a teacher is how much one learns, especially when one is exchanging ideas with the many entrepreneurs I've come to know so well from the world's largest and most robust network of entrepreneurs, the Young Presidents' Organization, and its vibrant cousin for younger and earlier stage entrepreneurs, the Entrepreneurs'

Organization. To my teachers of a lifetime – my late parents Jack and Alice Mullins, the late Larry Cummings, and many, many more – who taught me to always ask questions and helped me learn how to think clearly in search of answers, this book is but one manifestation of my thanks to you all.

My readers and I owe thanks to everyone at Pearson, especially my editors Stephen Partridge, Linda Dhondy, Liz Gooster, Nicole Eggleton and Eloise Cook, whose gentle candour and careful work have made every edition more readable. To the many entrepreneurs and investors who have used and commented on the seven domains framework as its form and its application have emerged over time, thanks, too. There are fewer factual errors and fewer erroneous insights thanks to all of you.

I would be remiss if I did not thank my family – Donna, Kristina and Heather – for embracing both our temporary move from our home in Colorado to the PhD programme at the University of Minnesota more than 25 years ago and my move to London Business School in 2001. I'm one of those fortunate people who loves his work, but I couldn't do it without your support.

Conducting research like that which forms the basis of all five of the book's editions takes both time and money. Thanks go to the University of Denver's Daniels College of Business for financial support and for the sabbatical that took me to London to begin the research, and to London Business School for providing both my livelihood since 2001 and generous research support, which permits and encourages me to write. Thanks, too, to the Marketing Science Institute, whose research grant was crucial in the early stages of the initial research. Likewise to my friends and incomparable colleagues at London Business School, who from the beginning supported, believed in and helped with this project. It remains a genuine pleasure working with all of you.

I and the entire entrepreneurial ecosystem also owe a huge vote of thanks to several recent authors whose work, taken collectively, has debunked the business plan as the centerpiece of entrepreneurial practice. The first edition of this book, way back in 2003, may have been among the first chinks in the armour, but there are more chinks now, and anyone who reads this book will want to read one or more of the others that have contributed so much to entrepreneurial practice. In chronological order, then, let's give thanks to Steve Blank (*The Four Steps to the Epiphany,* 2005), my co-author Randy Komisar (*Getting to Plan B,* 2009), Alex Osterwalder and Yves Pigneur (*Business Model Generation,* 2010), Eric Ries (*The Lean Startup,* 2011), and, back to Steve, with Bob Dorf (*The Startup Owner's Manual,* 2012).

Finally, to tomorrow's entrepreneurs, whose passion and dreams will make this a better and more humane world for all of us, thanks in advance for your entrepreneurial inspiration, vision and efforts and for the jobs and economic development you provide. If this book helps you in any way, please tell me about it. If it doesn't, please tell me that too. I'd love to hear from you.

John Mullins
London, April 2017
jmullins@london.edu
http://faculty.london.edu/jmullins
www.newbusinessroadtest.com
www.coursera.org/learn/startup-financing-without-vc

Acknowledgements

We are grateful to the following for permission to reproduce copyright material:

Text

Epigraph on page 3 from William P. Egan II in 'Venture capital has gone from one unreality to another', Knowledge at Wharton, http://knowledge.wharton.upenn.edu, with permission from William P.Egan II; epigraph on page 27 from *The Effective Executive*, 2nd revised edition, Butterworth-Heinemann Ltd (Drucker, P. 2007) p. 27, Copyright (c) 2007 Elsevier; epigraph on page 77 from Warren Buffett quoted in Herb Greenberg, 'How to avoid the value trap', *Fortune*, 10 June 2002, p. 194; epigraph on page 103 from *Inc*, August, pp.48–51 (Collins, J. 2000), with permission from Jim Collins; Chapter 14 adapted from the work of Robert McGowan and Paul Olk, University of Denver, Reproduced with permission; Chapters 15 and 16 adapted from *Marketing Management: A Strategic Decision Making Approach*, 8th edition, McGraw-Hill Companies, Inc (Mullins, J., Walker, O.C., Boyd Jr, H.W 2013), Chapters 6 and 7, Copyright (c) 2013 McGraw-Hill Education; Chapter 17 adapted from 'The counter-conventional mindsets of entrepreneurs', *Business Horizons*, 60, pp. 597–601 (Mullins, J. 2017), Copyright (c) 2017, with permission from Elsevier.

Part 1

Road test your new business idea

1

Our opportunity: why will or won't this work?

You may have capital and a talented management team, but if you are fundamentally in a lousy business, you won't get the kind of results you would in a good business. All businesses aren't created equal.

Long-time venture capitalist William P. Egan II[1]

Passion! Conviction! Tenacity! Without these traits, few entrepreneurs could endure the challenges, the setbacks, the twists in the road that lie between their often path-breaking ideas – opportunities, as they call them – and the fulfilment of their entrepreneurial dreams. The very best entrepreneurs, however, possess something even more valuable – a willingness to wake up every morning and ask a simple question about their nascent opportunity: 'Why will this new business work when most will fail?' Or, to put it more realistically, 'What's wrong with my idea, and how can I fix it?'

They ask this simple question for a very simple reason. They understand the odds. They know most business plans never raise money. They know most new ventures fail. Most of all, they don't want to end up starting and running what Bill Egan would call a 'lousy business', one that consumes years of their energy and effort, only to go nowhere in the end. Despite asking this crucial question every day, their passion remains undaunted. So committed are they to showing a reluctant world that their vision is an accurate one that they want to know before bad things can happen why they might be wrong.

If they can find the fatal flaw *before* they write their business plan or *before* it engulfs their new start-up, whether lean or otherwise, they can deal with it in many ways. They can modify their idea – and pivot to a better version – thereby shaping the opportunity to better fit the hotly competitive world in which it seeks to bear fruit. If the flaw they find appears to be a fatal one, they can even abandon the idea before it's too late – before launch, in some cases, or soon enough thereafter to avoid wasting months or years in pursuit of a dream that simply won't fly.

Better yet, if, after asking their daily question and probing, testing and especially experimenting for answers, the signs remain positive, they can embrace their opportunity with renewed passion and conviction, armed with a new-found confidence that the *evidence* – not just their intuition – confirms their prescience. Their idea really is an opportunity worth pursuing.

Tools to answer the question 'Why will or won't this work?'

Just as most car buyers take a road test before committing to the purchase of a new vehicle, so serious entrepreneurs and street-smart investors run road tests of the opportunities they consider. Each road test resolves a few more questions and eliminates a few more uncertainties lurking in the path of every opportunity.

❝serious entrepreneurs run road tests of the opportunities they consider❞

This book provides a road test toolkit that any serious entrepreneur or investor can use to resolve these questions and eliminate these uncertainties *before* writing a business plan and *before* getting started on a path to nowhere. It addresses the seven domains that characterise attractive, compelling opportunities. It recounts the vivid case histories of path-breaking entrepreneurs who understood these domains, to their enduring advantage. Perhaps more importantly, the book brings to life the less happy stories of other entrepreneurs whose opportunities ran foul of one or more of the seven domains and who, as a result, failed to achieve their goals. Learning from failure is something most successful entrepreneurs do well. As many entrepreneurs put it, in talking about their battle scars, 'If I can make each mistake only once, I'll be in good shape.' The common as well as some not so common mistakes are here in this book for all to see.

What this book is and what it is not

This book is *not* about how to write a business plan. It's about what to do *before* you write your business plan, and before you embark on a lean start-up and its series of hypothesis tests leading to possible adjustments. If you're a budding entrepreneur, its purpose is to help ensure that your venture has a better chance to compete for the time and attention – and hopefully the money – of the financiers and other resource providers you will approach, be they the three Fs (family, friends and fools, as the saying goes), angel investors, bankers, venture capitalists or prospective partners or employees. Or even your prospective customers, as we explore in some detail in Chapter 12! If you're one of those investors, my purpose for you is to help you avoid at least some of the errors commonly made in investing in early-stage ventures. You surely don't want those mistakes to offset the gains from the best of your deals.

This book doesn't just tell the story of one entrepreneur's route to glory – there are already plenty of books in that category – for it's grounded in solid research into what characterises attractive opportunities across a wide variety of market and industry settings (see the Appendix). This research brings together insights gleaned from leading venture capital and angel investors and successful serial entrepreneurs. Their insights apply equally to high-potential ventures and to lifestyle businesses that can enable an entrepreneur to be his or her own boss and get out of the corporate rat race.

It's also not a book about the personalities and traits of successful entrepreneurs, for an abundance of research has made clear that successful entrepreneurs come from all walks of life, from all strata of society.[2] The sources of their opportunities, however, do show some patterns, which we examine later in this chapter.

“this book is not about how to get rich quickly”

Finally, this book is not about how to get rich quickly. And it's not for those who want to start a business – any business – over a weekend. It's about how serious entrepreneurs and their investor partners – whether embarking on a new start-up or building something new within the confines of an existing organisation – can prepare a solid foundation for the development of an enduring business that creates and delivers value for its customers and owners alike. There's nothing more fun in business than doing this, and the results are well worth the effort, as any successful entrepreneur will attest.

So what *is* this book? It's a map for the opportunity-assessing, opportunity-shaping process. It provides a useful framework – the seven domains – to lay a solid foundation on which to build a business plan or to create a successful entrepreneurial venture.

Opportunity assessment and shaping in today's lean start-up world

The lean start-up movement has burst onto the entrepreneurial scene and is revolutionising the way many entrepreneurs think about starting their ventures. Drawing on the work of Steve Blank, Eric Ries and others,[3] the central notion is that before investing lots of money into a venture that's based on numerous untested and highly precarious assumptions, it makes more sense to think flexibly at the outset and invest fewer resources – staying 'lean' as the lean start-up moniker indicates – to begin systematically testing the most crucial assumptions to see whether they make any sense. If the assumptions prove erroneous, then you 'pivot' – altering the strategy, without abandoning your vision, as Eric Ries defines the term – and use what you've learned to work your way toward a better strategy that's more viable.

While the lean approach doesn't work for all kinds of start-ups, it holds great promise for many of today's new ventures, especially for the technology-enabled internet and mobile ventures that many readers of this book are probably contemplating. You'll find several compelling case histories of such ventures – some successful, some not – between the covers of this book. But, as the next section points out, not all markets or industries are equally attractive settings in which to launch a start-up, whether lean or otherwise. And you or your entrepreneurial team are probably better placed to start some kinds of ventures than others, if you're honest about it. Hence there are some crucial steps you should take *before* launching your lean start-up to ensure that the opportunity you plan to pursue – in lean fashion, perhaps – is one that's really worthy of your time and effort.

The seven domains of attractive opportunities

At its heart, successful entrepreneurship comprises three crucial elements: markets, industries and the one or more key people who make up the entrepreneurial team. The seven domains model (Figure 1.1) that drives this book brings these elements together to offer a new and clearer way to answer the crucial question that every aspiring entrepreneur and every early-stage investor must ask themselves every single morning: 'Why will or won't this work?' The model offers a better toolkit for assessing and shaping market opportunities[4] and a better way for entrepreneurs or entrepreneurial teams – and investors, too – to assess the adequacy of what they themselves bring to the table as individuals and as a group. The model also provides the basis for

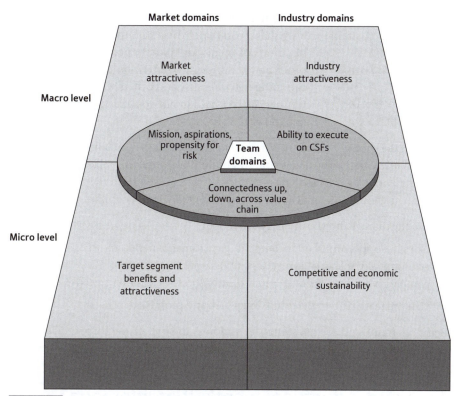

Market domains **Industry domains**

Market
attractiveness

Industry
attractiveness

Macro level

Mission, aspirations,
propensity for
risk

**Team
domains**

Ability to execute
on CSFs

Connectedness up,
down, across value
chain

Micro level

Target segment
benefits and
attractiveness

Competitive and economic
sustainability

figure 1.1   The seven domains of attractive opportunities

what I call a customer-driven feasibility study that entrepreneurs may use to guide their assessments – *before* they invest the time and effort in writing a business plan or getting started in earnest.

At first glance, the seven domains model appears simply to summarise what everybody already knows about assessing opportunities. So it does. Upon more careful scrutiny, however, the model goes further to bring to light three subtle but crucial distinctions and observations that most entrepreneurs – not to mention many investors – overlook:

■ markets and industries are not the same things;

■ both macro- and micro-level considerations are necessary: markets and industries must be examined at both levels;

■ the keys to assessing entrepreneurs and entrepreneurial teams aren't simply found on their resumés or in assessments of their entrepreneurial character.

Moreover, the model's seven domains are not equally important. Nor are they additive. A simple scoring sheet won't do. Worse still, the wrong combinations of them can kill your venture. On the other hand, sufficient strength on some factors can mitigate weaknesses on others. Good opportunities *can* be found in not-so-attractive markets and industries.

> **good opportunities *can* be found in not-so-attractive markets and industries**

As the model shows, it is made up of four *market* and *industry* domains, including both *macro* and *micro* levels, and three additional domains related to the entrepreneurial *team*. These seven domains that emerged from my research address the central elements in the assessment of any market opportunity.

- Are the market and the industry attractive?
- Does the opportunity offer compelling customer benefits, an economically sustainable business model as well as a sustainable competitive advantage over other solutions to the customer's needs?
- Can the team deliver the results they seek and promise to others?

Before examining these questions, let's address the first of the three crucial distinctions, that between markets and industries.

Markets and industries: what's the difference?

A market consists of a group of current and/or potential customers having the willingness and ability to buy products – goods or services – to satisfy a particular class of wants or needs. Thus, markets consist of buyers – people or organisations and their needs – not products.

> **markets consist of buyers, not products**

One such market, for example, consists of businesspeople who get hungry between meals during their workday. We'll call this the market for workplace snacks.

> **an industry consists of sellers**

An industry consists of sellers – typically organisations – that offer products or classes of products that are similar and close substitutes for one another. What industries serve the market for workplace snacks? At the producer level, there is the salty snack industry, the confectionery industry and the fresh produce industry, to name but three. There are also industries providing the distribution of these products to workplaces, including the supermarket industry, the restaurant industry, the coin-operated vending machine industry, the coffee bar industry and so on. Clearly, these industries offer varying bundles of benefits to hungry workers. Some of these industries are more attractive than others to would-be entrants seeking to serve the workplace snack market.

Why is the market–industry distinction important? Because judgements about the attractiveness of the *market* one proposes to serve may be very different from judgements about the *industry* in which one would compete. This should not be – but often is – surprising, for the questions asked to assess market attractiveness are different from those for industry attractiveness, a point easily obscured when words like 'sector' and 'space' are used indiscriminately or carelessly in the opportunity assessment process. (Does the user of these terms mean 'market' or 'industry'? See Case Study 1.1.) So, if market and industry attractiveness are both important, how should each be assessed?

---

case study 1.1

A lesson learned from the dot.com crash

In the late 1990s, entrepreneurs stumbled over one another in a mad race for first-mover advantage in the dot.com space. But what did they mean by 'space'?

Did they mean the *market* of individuals and organisations who would use the internet for shopping, information, communication and other purposes? In hindsight, we now know that this market was and is extremely attractive: it was growing fast and would soon include most segments of the population, as the so-called digital divide shrunk rapidly.

Or did they mean *industries*: internet service providers, social networks, e-tailers, e-publishers and so on. In hindsight, we now know that some industries on the Web were and still are unattractive, because numerous new competitors can enter easily, differentiation is difficult to establish and competitive advantage is hard to sustain with competitors only a mouse-click away.

As entrepreneurial efforts, business plans and venture capital followed like lemmings from business-to-consumer to business-to-business to peer-to-peer models in the late 1990s, it soon became clear that, while many of these models served potentially attractive *markets,* they were situated in not very attractive *industries* in which to compete. Unfortunately for the many dot.com entrepreneurs whose ventures failed, the recognition of this crucial distinction came too late.

▶

> As time has healed some of the internet wounds, significant numbers of
> attractive internet opportunities have emerged. They share in common
> many of the attributes – attractive markets and industry settings, clear
> customer benefits, sustainable competitive advantages, business
> models that work, all delivered by capable management teams – that
> characterise many of the pre-dot.com case histories in this book. As
> we now know, the internet, while perhaps not the change-the-world
> phenomenon in as many ways as was predicted at the turn of the
> millennium, is alive and well!

Is the market attractive? Macro and micro considerations

All else being equal, most entrepreneurs and most investors would prefer to
serve attractive rather than unattractive markets, of course. How might such
market assessments be made? My research showed that assessments must
be made at both macro (broad, market-wide) and micro (particular to a specific segment, one customer at a time) levels. The macro/micro distinction is
important, for the assessment questions differ.

Macro level

It is actually quite straightforward to conduct a macro-level market assessment. One first assesses – usually by gathering secondary data from trade
publications, the business press and so on – how large the market is. Market
size can be measured in many ways – the more the better. Measures include:

- number of *customers* in the market, say for workplace snacks;
- the aggregate *money spent* by these customers on the relevant class of
  goods or services, in this case workplace snacks;
- the number of *units* of relevant products or usage occasions, such as
  workplace snacks, bought annually.

One also collects recent historical data, to ascertain how fast the market has
been growing, together with any available forecasts about how fast it is likely
to grow in the future.

The investors and entrepreneurs we interviewed in researching this book concurred with this view:

We want to know the size and growth rate of the market, so that if the product catches on, we should have a substantial upside.[5]

HH, UK

We want to know that the overall market opportunity is big, and we have to be able to demonstrate that the market size of this particular offering is robust.

TP, USA

One then assesses broad macro-environmental (macro for short) trends – demographic, sociocultural, economic, technological, regulatory and natural – to determine whether things are likely to get better or worse in the future.[6] Do the trends favour the opportunity, or will the entrepreneur be swimming against a powerful tide?

I think that being able to assess, spot, and maybe even create trends is very big – a key to decision making. There are many problems that don't have solutions yet. Just look at the cell phone . . . As you know, in many countries today, the penetration of mobile telephony now surpasses the penetration of desktop or wireline phones.

CM, USA

The broad, macro-level market assessment is important to both entrepreneur and investor, for both take risk in investing years and investment capital in an idea that, in the end, may not be substantial enough to be worth all the time and effort. It's important to know whether the opportunity is a substantial one, serving a large and attractive market, or a niche opportunity with limited potential. Either may be acceptable. It depends on the entrepreneur's and the investor's aspirations. It is also important to know which way the tides are flowing. Thus, reaching a clear conclusion about market attractiveness is critical. But this macro-level assessment – done at the 30,000-foot level, so to speak – is only half the market domains story. It is essential aerial reconnaissance and a good look at the road ahead, but for the full picture you need observers on the ground.

Micro level

No matter how large and fast-growing a market may be, entering it in the face of other competition is likely to be difficult, since customers are probably already satisfying their needs – though perhaps not optimally – in some way. In this sense, there's no such thing as a new market in customer terms. Aspiring entrepreneurs who say 'We have no competition' are simply naïve. Thus, most successful entrepreneurs, rather than targeting the entire

❝aspiring entrepreneurs who say 'We have no competition' are simply naïve❞

market, identify a much smaller segment of customers *within* the overall market. The micro-level market assessment involves asking four key questions relevant to such a segment.

- Is there a target market segment where we might enter the market in which we offer the customer clear and compelling benefits, or – better yet – resolve their pain at a price he or she is willing to pay?

- Are these benefits, *in the customers' minds,* different from and superior in some way – better, faster, cheaper or whatever – to what's currently offered by other solutions? Differentiation is crucial. With the possible exception of niche markets in which small entrants can safely fly 'below the radar' of competitors, the vast majority of me-too products fail.

- How large is this segment, and how fast is it growing?

- Is it likely that our entry into this segment will create a stable platform that will facilitate entry into other segments that we may wish to target in the future?

This new service concept is turning the existing business model in the market on its head, making it a cost-effective alternative in a market that hasn't been properly serviced in the past. Customers are lining up for it.

JS, UK

How can these questions be answered? Most commonly, a combination of first-hand primary data (gleaned from talking to or surveying prospective customers) and secondary data (data collected previously and available on the internet or in libraries or from other sources, to determine segment size and growth rate) can deliver the understanding that both entrepreneurs and investors need.

❝ many aspiring entrepreneurs make the mistake of examining only the macro-level ❞

As we shall see later in this chapter, many aspiring entrepreneurs – not to mention many early stage investors – make the mistake of examining only the macro level. This behaviour appears to be especially common in technologically driven firms. Through failing to identify the first customers who will buy – almost by name – and why they would benefit,[7] and in ignoring how entry into this segment might create one or more options for growth into other market segments,[8] they risk pursuing a dead-end path on two counts:

- without differentiated benefits, most customers won't buy;

- without a pathway to growth, most investors won't invest.

Most market segments are simply too small to sustain a high-growth business for very long, although such segments may be quite attractive to entrepreneurs seeking to establish niche-market or lifestyle businesses that fly 'below the radar' of larger competitors and grow more slowly. The story of Nike's entry and subsequent growth in the athletic footwear market demonstrates the importance of the micro-level assessment of market attractiveness (see Case Study 1.2).

---

case study 1.2

Nike wins at the micro level

The story of Nike's origins is now a familiar one. Phil Knight, a distance runner, and his track coach Bill Bowerman used Bowerman's wife's waffle iron and some latex to develop a running shoe for distance runners that was lighter (benefit: faster race times), had better cushioning (benefit: fewer shin splints and stress fractures from miles and miles of training) and had superior lateral stability (benefit: reduced chance of ankle sprains caused by running on uneven terrain).

At the macro level, the market for athletic footwear was stagnant at the time. Most people had only one or two pairs of trainers and saw no need for another. From a micro perspective, however, distance runners loved Knight's and Bowerman's new shoes, and the new company's success in the distance running segment led to later successes in tennis, basketball and other sports that have made Nike one of the world's leading brands.

In opportunity terms, what Knight and Bowerman saw initially was a chance to offer a demonstrably superior product that customers – elite distance runners – would prefer and pay for, one that could then lead to similar success in other sharply targeted footwear niches. Their sport-by-sport advance across the formerly stagnant athletic footwear market, accompanied by astute marketing that made high-priced athletic shoes a fashion item, led to that market's stunning growth (how many pairs of different athletic shoes are in *your* wardrobe today?) and to Nike's leading position in today's athletic footwear industry.

Is the industry attractive? Macro and micro considerations

Just as serious entrepreneurs and sensible investors prefer to serve attractive markets, so they also prefer to compete in industries in which most participants are successful and profitable, rather than in industries where many firms struggle to survive. They also prefer to compete on the basis of some sustainable advantage that their competitors do not enjoy, and with a business model that won't soon run out of cash. How might these crucial judgements be made?

Macro level

Michael Porter, in the late 1970s, identified the forces that determine industry attractiveness.[9] These forces – five of them – are powerful determinants of the overall profitability of any industry, not a bad thing for an aspiring entrepreneur to know:

- threat of entry;
- buyer power;
- supplier power;
- threat of substitutes;
- competitive rivalry.

Assessing these forces and any ongoing or likely future changes therein lies at the heart of a macro-level assessment of industry attractiveness.

So, how should a five forces analysis be done? What should be its outcome? The aspiring entrepreneur first identifies what industry his or her new business will be in – retailing, food manufacturing, software, or whatever. Doing this is not a trivial exercise. Industries can be defined broadly or narrowly, as we shall see in Chapter 4.

The entrepreneur or investor then asks a series of questions (discussed in detail in Chapters 4 and 14) about each of the five forces to determine whether that force is favourable or unfavourable on balance. The more forces that are favourable, the more attractive the industry, and vice versa. As it turns out, most industries are not very attractive. Would-be entrepreneurs should note that severe problems on just one force can be enough to tip the balance, so the weighing must be done in a thoughtful manner. Identifying such problems in advance enables the entrepreneur to craft plans to deal with them, or to abandon the opportunity altogether, if the problems are too severe.

❝ most industries are not very attractive ❞

Once all five forces have been assessed, the key outcome is to reach a clear conclusion about the attractiveness of one's industry. This step is crucial to the overall assessment of your opportunity, and it is one issue that professional investors always examine. If necessary, admit that your industry just isn't very attractive. Note, however, that all is not necessarily lost if the verdict is unfavourable. Other factors elsewhere in the seven domains analysis may compensate for these concerns.

As in the case for the macro-level assessment of market attractiveness, gathering secondary data is necessary here, but such data tell only part of the story. Additional, first-hand industry knowledge or primary data are usually required to develop a clear understanding of how the industry works and how it is changing.

We research where the industry is heading and what factors are affecting it. We want to know that the industry is here to stay and that it's not about to be replaced by technology.

JS, UK

One might imagine that a macro-level assessment of industry attractiveness would be sufficient, provided the micro-level market assessment has indicated that customers want to buy what the new entrant offers. For entrepreneurs who seek to build small but stable firms serving narrow market niches, this may sometimes be true. For more growth-oriented entrepreneurs and for most early-stage investors, however, there's another important piece of the puzzle: the micro level.

Micro level

Even if customers like what the prospective new entrant offers and most firms in its industry are successful due to favourable industry structure, a new venture is not likely to grow over the long term if the initial advantage it brings to its customers cannot be sustained in the face of subsequent competitors' entry, or if its business model lacks economic viability. Thus, identifying and assessing the competitive and economic sustainability of the proposed venture is necessary to fill in the micro-level industry piece of the opportunity assessment puzzle.

How might these micro-level industry judgements be made? Assessing the sustainability of the proposed venture requires examining, in relationship to its competitors, the proposed venture itself – whether a new firm or a venture within an existing firm. The goal is to determine whether certain factors are present that would enhance the ability of the venture to sustain any advantage that it might have at the outset, without quickly running out of cash. These competitive and economic factors are the following.

■ The presence of proprietary elements – patents, trade secrets and so on – that other firms are unable to duplicate or imitate.

- The likely presence of superior organisational processes, capabilities or resources that others would have difficulty duplicating or imitating.[10]

- The presence of an economically viable business model – one that won't quickly run out of cash! This factor, in turn, involves a careful look at some more detailed issues:

  - revenue, in relation to the capital investment required and margins obtainable;
  - customer acquisition and retention costs, and the time it will take to obtain customers;
  - contribution margins and their adequacy to cover the necessary fixed cost structure to operate the business;
  - operating cash cycle characteristics, i.e. how much cash must be tied up in working capital such as inventory, how quickly will customers pay, and how slowly may suppliers and employees be paid, in relation to the margins the business generates.[11]

Information on the economic structure of most industries can be found from published sources such as the Risk Management Association's *Annual Statement Studies,* available in most business libraries and on the internet, e.g. the Risk Management Association's website, www.rmahq.org

Aspiring entrepreneurs who plan to compete based on price should note that building a business by giving away your products for less than they cost to acquire or produce is not a sustainable strategy in the long run, as numerous dot.com entrepreneurs learned in the turn-of-the-millennium dot.com bust. Another economic viability issue often overlooked is this:

Too often entrepreneurs fail to understand how long it will take (and thus how much capital) to actually close a sale, no matter how good the opportunity looks.

RJ, UK

It's worth noting here that first-hand experience in the industry makes all the difference in addressing these issues. Entrepreneurs who know the territory will have the necessary answers. Those who don't must find people who do. Adequate answers for most of these issues are not likely to be found on the internet. If the entrepreneur doesn't have such experience, then they must obtain it from others. Picking up the phone and calling industry experts can help, and it helps build your network, too, a topic we address further later on.

❝ first-hand experience in the industry makes all the difference ❞

The point addressed by the micro-level assessment on both the market and industry sides is that even in generally attractive markets and industries – such as financial services and pharmaceuticals – not all new ventures succeed. Favourable industry conditions at the macro level are not a panacea. Positive results from your investigations into these micro-level conditions are typically far more important.

Can the team deliver?

When pressed to name the single most important factor in their investment decisions, many of the investors we interviewed said, simply, 'Management, management and management.' But we learned that assessing 'management' involves more than judging character and reading CVs. Our research identified three domains relating to the entrepreneur or entrepreneurial team itself, and we include any investors therein. Examining these domains is necessary in order to complete the opportunity assessment task.

- Does the opportunity fit the team's business mission, personal aspirations and risk propensity, and does all of that align with that of a prospective investor?

- Does the team have what it takes, in a human sense – in experience and industry know-how – to deliver superior performance for this particular opportunity, *given its critical success factors,* i.e. those factors that, done right, almost guarantee superior performance, even if other things aren't done so well; or done wrong, will have severely negative effects on performance, regardless of doing other things right?

- Is the team well connected up, down and across the value chain so it will be quick to notice any opportunity or need to change its approach if conditions warrant?

Let's take a look at each of these final three domains.

The team's business mission, personal aspirations and risk propensity

For a variety of reasons, individual entrepreneurs and investors come to the opportunity assessment task with certain preconceived preferences, often defined in terms of:

- markets they wish to serve (Nike's founder, Phil Knight, an athlete himself, wanted to market to athletes);

- industries in which they are willing to compete (for Knight, athletic footwear);

- their own aspirations (how big a venture; how soon, if at all, do we wish to exit; are we committed to this opportunity, or are we buying an option to see whether it pans out?);

- risks they are willing to undertake (with how much money; how certain must we be of a successful venture; must we have control, or are we willing to share it?).

Opportunities that do not match these preferences will be seen as unattractive, even though other observers having different sets of preferences and dreams might view them more favourably.

We've turned down opportunities because they didn't meet our criteria for investing, and sometimes they go on to do well with another firm. But when you change your threshold, you let in a lot more false positives. Your level of scrutiny should be exactly proportional to how much risk you are willing to take on in bringing in deals that may actually turn out to be bad. False positives are what you worry about, not false negatives.

TP, USA

The team's ability to execute on the critical success factors

The backgrounds and prior experiences brought to the venture by particular entrepreneurs and investors make them better prepared to execute on some sets of critical success factors than on others. Understanding the critical success factors relevant to a particular opportunity and the industry within which it will compete, and matching them against the team's ability to perform on them, is among the most compelling questions most investors ask in assessing opportunities. Entrepreneurs should do the same.

“understanding the critical success factors is among the most compelling questions”

We really dig into the management team. We want to be totally confident that this team can deliver on the promises they have made. We do that by looking at their experience, by assessing how well they understand their industry and their customers. We want to know about their leadership in terms of the CEO and the heads of engineering, R&D and marketing. Probably those were the most important functions for this opportunity.

OD, USA

I don't mess with products or markets I don't know how to read.

PB, UK

Entrepreneurs who fail to assess accurately whether they and their team have what it takes to execute on the critical success factors they will face take a huge personal risk – beyond the business risk they already take – if they seek external capital. It is all too common for venture capital investors who like an opportunity to tire of the team they first back and bring in a new one at the first sign of trouble. Losing their companies is not something most entrepreneurs are keen to do.

The team's connectedness up, down and across the value chain

A favourite saying among venture capital investors is: 'I've made more money on Plan B than I ever made on Plan A.'[12] In other words, the ability to combine tenacity with a willingness to change course – sometimes due to changes in the marketplace, fortuitous or otherwise – can make all the difference. Thus, good luck can help a new venture, but those best

❝I've made more money on plan B than I ever made on plan A❞

prepared to take advantage of good luck are those whose leading-edge information connections enable them to respond to market changes quickly and adroitly. Entrepreneurial teams should ask how connected they are, both up and down the value chain – with suppliers and customers – and across their industry to address this concern. How can they get connected if they are not? One partial answer: network, network, network.

We had three products when we entered the business, and we thought we knew their order of importance in the marketplace. We lost the market for what we thought would be our biggest product, and things looked really bad. But we had an outstanding board that brought to the team a lot of experience and partnerships and connections. One of our salespeople told a story about a customer's interest in our third product, a network interface card. The board seized upon the story and talked to some people that knew. It turned out that the board had spotted an early trend, and this is where we made all of our money. Without a doubt, the thing that carried us through was the quality of the team and all of its connections.

HH, UK

By assessing themselves with respect to the three *team* domains as part of their broader opportunity assessment efforts, entrepreneurs and entrepreneurial teams gain in three ways.

■ If the team needs to be strengthened to better suit an otherwise promising opportunity, the best time to do so is *before* writing a business plan and *before* seeking seed capital. Doing this early enables the venture to benefit from the talents, insights and perspectives of the team's new members.

■ Viewing investors as part of the team also builds trust and can reduce the risk investors perceive in the venture, since many investors like to help build the team. Entrepreneurs who are willing to admit they don't have all the skills required often rate highly with the investor community.

■ If external funding is to be sought, then pitching an inadequate team is not only likely to be unsuccessful but also undermines the credibility and reputation of the team members, thereby hampering their ability to raise capital in the future. Get the team right first, then pitch. You'll need to make a convincing case that the team will be able to deliver the results it seeks and those it promises to investors and other stakeholders.

These benefits are important, even for entrepreneurs in emerging industries who may not appreciate the need for well-developed connections. (For more on this topic, see Case Study 1.3.)

---

case study 1.3

What about entrepreneurs bearing new paradigms?

A visionary entrepreneur can change the world, or at least some part of it. They may be tempted to say, 'Our new paradigm changes everything. The old rules no longer apply.' But is this true?

The not very pretty record of dot.com ventures at the turn of the millennium suggests that entrepreneurs pitching new paradigms must understand clearly the realities of the old ones. Otherwise, they risk being blindsided by market or industry forces they fail to foresee, or facing critical success factors they are ill prepared to address. Including both old- and new-paradigm people and perspectives on the entrepreneurial team is one way to ensure that this does not happen.

Putting the seven domains model into action

Using the seven domains model requires a considerable amount of data. Mere opinions that an opportunity is attractive will not suffice and will destroy the credibility of the aspiring entrepreneur in the eyes of others. How, then, should an entrepreneur or investor obtain and interpret the necessary data?

In Chapter 10, we address this question in some detail. For now, however, let us note that some of the data the model calls for can be obtained quickly from secondary sources: trade and other business publications in the library or on the internet, government reports and so on. Typically, though, an abundance of primary data – from interviews, observation, surveys of prospective customers and/or industry participants, or market experiments – are necessary for the two micro-level assessments making up the lower row in the model and for understanding the industry's critical success factors. So, build a simple mockup or prototype, pick up the phone or get out of the building and get some feedback! Make the connections up, down and across the value chain that any entrepreneurial team will need to fully assess your opportunity and to run a successful venture.

As for interpretation (and as was noted earlier in this chapter), using the model is not a simple matter of constructing a score sheet that adds scores for the seven domains. The domains are not additive and their relative importance can vary. Thus, a simple checklist will not suffice. The wrong combination of factors can kill your new venture, and enough strength on some factors can mitigate weaknesses on others. We address these situations in Chapter 9. For now, however, if a checklist is not sufficient, then how should anyone who completes a seven domains analysis draw conclusions about what it means?

Why *won't* this work?

Along the seven domains path, concerns inevitably crop up – a risk list, in a sense – that may have potentially fatal flaws that can render one's opportunity a non-starter. The key task in answering the crucial question 'Why won't this work?' is to find that major flaw that cannot be resolved, the opportunity's Achilles' heel. Thus, the crucial things to look for on the downside are elements of the market, industry or team that simply cannot be fixed by pivoting or shaping the opportunity in a different way.

> **find that major flaw that cannot be resolved, the opportunity's Achilles' heel**

If flaws that cannot be fixed are found, then the best thing to do is to abandon the opportunity at this early stage and move on to something more attractive. Persisting with a fundamentally flawed opportunity is likely to have one of two outcomes, both of which are unpleasant.

■ *Best case:* The best and most likely outcome is that experienced investors or other resource providers – suppliers, partners and so on – will identify the flaws that you have ignored and refuse to give you the resources you need, even if you have gone to great lengths to craft a business plan or a pitch deck that papers over these flaws. Fortunately for you, their refusal will save you the agony of investing additional months or years of your life in actually running a lousy business, though your efforts in preparing and pitching your business plan will have been wasted. The harsh reality is that this is the case with the vast majority of business plans, for the opportunities they seek to pursue are fatally flawed. Most business plans should have been abandoned before they were written. Fortunately, most aspiring entrepreneurs now understand that writing a business plan – which is almost always about a well-loved but unlikely-to-succeed Plan A – is not the first thing they should do.[13]

- *Worst case:* The second, though less likely, outcome of pursuing a fundamentally flawed opportunity is that, in spite of the flaws, you are able to secure the resources you need and actually start the business. At some point, the flaws will rear their ugly heads, and you'll need to scramble to recast the business before it goes under. Some readers of this book may find themselves in this unhappy predicament today. It's not a pretty place to be.

The simple fact is, though, that inherent in virtually every entrepreneurial opportunity are some key flaws or risks that merit considerable attention. The seven domains analysis helps identify such risks wherever they lurk, and makes them salient enough to both entrepreneur and investor so they are not ignored.

So, 'Whose job is it to conduct a seven domains analysis of a prospective opportunity?' you might ask? 'Is this the entrepreneur's job, or is it the investor's?' Actually, unless you're a swashbuckling risk-taker who cares little about outcomes, you'd *both* better do it for the reasons already pointed out in this chapter. Indeed, in all of my own angel investing activities, I always bring a seven domains perspective to the table, front and centre. This allows me to quickly rule out opportunities that are not up to par, and spend my time on opportunities for which the upside looks great and the key risks appear manageable and worth taking.

Why *will* this work? Can the opportunity be shaped?

The good news in all this is that opportunities are not static. They can be shaped and developed in many ways. Potentially fatal flaws are there to be fixed. You can choose a different target market, one more receptive to the proposed offering. The product offering can be adapted to make it better fit what the market needs. Decisions can be made to pursue the opportunity at a different level in the value chain – as a distributor, rather than as a retailer or a manufacturer, for example – if a different industry setting would be more hospitable. Finding

❝ potentially fatal flaws are there to be fixed ❞

additional individuals who can help the team deliver on the critical success factors or who bring appropriate connections up, down or across the value chain can strengthen the entrepreneurial team.

All of these approaches to reshaping but not abandoning your opportunity are what the lean start-up movement calls pivots: changes in strategy *without* a change of vision.[14] If your opportunity turns out to be one you decide merits no further pursuit, however, don't fool yourself by calling this a pivot. Simply abandon it and move on.

Mapping a route to your dreams

Completing the seven domains road test provides the light to see through the fog of uncertainty that surrounds every opportunity. It enables the entrepreneur and investor to make the necessary pivots to reshape the opportunity so that it becomes worth pursuing – *before* writing a business plan and *before* launching a lean start-up. Most likely, your initial conception of your opportunity isn't quite optimal. It can probably be improved. This book provides tools for doing so and for identifying and guiding the initial pivots your venture – whether a lean start-up or otherwise – is likely to require.

In this chapter, I've provided an overview of the seven domains framework and shown how it can protect entrepreneurs and investors against pursuing ill-advised ventures that are fatally flawed, and how it can help entrepreneurs to achieve their dreams. In the next seven chapters, taking each of the seven domains in turn, the book relates the case histories of successful entrepreneurial heroes from around the world whose businesses exemplify 'getting it right' in seven domains terms. Each chapter also examines one or more case histories of entrepreneurs who violated the precepts of that domain – and paid the price. To complete each of these chapters, I draw on the research that underlies this book to outline what investors look for in each of the seven domains. And I summarise the powerful lessons the case histories offer to aspiring entrepreneurs who hope to avoid the mistakes of others who have ventured down the entrepreneurial path before them.

Then, Chapters 9 and 10 bring it all together. Chapter 9 shows how the seven domains can work together to spring traps that wary entrepreneurs should look out for in their own opportunities and shows how and where attractive opportunities can be found in stagnant or otherwise unattractive markets and industries. It also points out the kinds of opportunities that are particularly well suited to niche-market entrepreneurs – those who hope to build a fly-below-the-radar business that they can operate for many years or pass on to their children.

Chapter 10 examines where the best opportunities usually come from and addresses the practicalities of conducting the necessary market research and preparing the evidence-based forecasts that are so crucial in the development of any new venture. Chapter 10 also outlines the steps that aspiring entrepreneurs should take in writing a customer-driven feasibility study for their own opportunity. Such a study – a short memo to oneself, really – captures and clarifies the conclusions of the seven domains road test. It provides a clear, customer-focused vision about why the proposed venture makes sense (or not!) – from market, industry and team perspectives. Best of all, it takes the entrepreneur halfway home in preparing a compelling business plan or pitch deck, thereby jump-starting either a business planning process or a lean start-up journey and ensuring it rests upon a firm foundation.

In the second half of the book, in Chapters 11 through 17, we put some of the tools you'll need for your opportunity assessment journey into your toolkit, and we link those tools to the *New Business Road Test* app for your smartphone or tablet, about which there's more information below. So, read on and enjoy the ride!

A tool for when you are out and about: *The New Business Road Test* app

If you're like most entrepreneurs, assessing your opportunity is a day and night effort. You just never know where a crucial morsel of information will come from, and we want you to be ready to record it whenever and wherever that happens. So we've built a dandy little app for your smartphone or tablet that enables you to keep track of your notes, links to pertinent online content, and interviews you conduct as your seven domains research unfolds. It's got places to keep track of the risks you identify ('Why won't my idea work?') and of your judgements of the attractiveness of each of the seven domains as those judgements evolve. Cool! As one well-known marketer of credit cards used to say, 'Don't leave home without it!'

2

Will the fish bite?

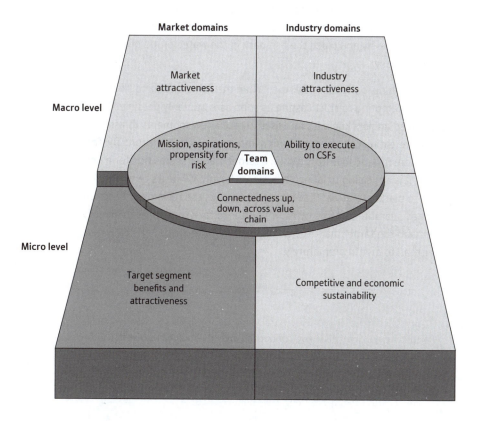

It's a crisp July morning in Lewistown, Montana, where you are on holiday. You wake up at 5:30 a.m. to overcast skies (perfect for fly-fishing) and nothing on your calendar but a date with the brown trout on the Upper Missouri River. Within an hour, you find your way to one of the most pristine fishing spots in the western USA. Wearing your waders, and sporting a vest full of home-tied flies, you trudge along the banks until you reach the perfect spot. About ten yards away is a pod of what must be 30 or 40 trout, feeding contentedly on the morning's hatch. And these are not small fish. By the looks of their mouths, they must be a good 20 inches long.

Having spent enough time on the river, you know these fish are smart. They won't bite at just anything. So, you take a few minutes, checking the air and the surface of the water to figure out what they are eating. Instead of hastily casting your line with the Royal Coachman fly from your last fishing trip, you sit down on a rock and carefully attach a mid-sized Caddis fly. After casting five or six times, you feel a tug at the end of your line and proceed to fight a strong and able brownie for three exhausting minutes. With your forearm throbbing, you finally pull this 21-inch beauty out of the water. Its colours are magnificent. You unhook the fly and place the fish back in the water, proud of your first catch of the day.

When fly-fishing, patience is a virtue. When the fish are feeding like mad, it is all too tempting to start casting as soon as is humanly possible. But experienced anglers know it's far wiser to take a few moments to assess what the fish are eating than to start fishing impulsively with the wrong fly. The same is true for and investors. When a target market seems ripe for a new venture, it is appealing to launch a business hastily. While it's tempting to go quickly to market to attain first-mover advantage, the rewards of haste are by no means guaranteed. More often, it's better to take some time to identify and understand the target market, figuring out what the customers really need, rather than to dive in prematurely.

Do customers matter?

The customer . . . is the ultimate reason for whatever the organization produces.

Peter Drucker[1]

As Peter Drucker says, it's all about customers. Without customers, there can be no business. Without satisfying what the customers want or need, or – better yet – resolving their pain, there will be no customers. It's simple, really. So, why do most aspiring entrepreneurs, when asked about the businesses they hope to start, begin with words like these:

■ 'We provide . . . '

■ 'Our new product is . . . '

■ 'With our new technology . . . '?

It's not about *you*. It's not about your revolutionary products or services. Successful entrepreneurial ventures are about serving customers and their needs and resolving their pain. Not just any customers. Target customers. It's about providing differentiated benefits that are so compelling that customers abandon their allegiance to former providers and give their business to you.

❝it's not about *you*. It's not about your revolutionary products or services❞

But you've already got an idea for a new business, and you know it's a good one, or you probably wouldn't be reading this book. 'Of course customers will buy it!' you argue. 'It's much faster (or better, cheaper, or whatever) than what they're using now.' While you may be right, the chances actually are, based on the accumulated learning of generations of entrepreneurs who have gone before you, that you are either *not quite* right, or perhaps even dead wrong! And as most early-stage investors will tell you, more money gets made on Plan B (or C or D or Z) than ever gets made on Plan A.

So, before you get too far into the book, whether you're an entrepreneur with an opportunity in hand or an investor conducting due diligence, I suggest you turn to Chapter 11, where you'll learn about a powerful interviewing technique that will show you how to find out what you don't know you don't know about your new venture idea. Or more to the point, how to learn what you don't know you don't know about what customers *really* could use in the small bit of their lives that your venture proposes to target. Yes, you've read these sentences correctly – you need to learn what you *don't know* you don't know.

When you return here from Chapter 11, you'll be all set to dig into the lower left quadrant in the seven domains model. Why begin here, as opposed to one of the other quadrants? Because it's worth listening to Drucker. Because without target customers whose needs you satisfy, the rest of the model doesn't matter very much.

As you learned in Chapter 1, there are four crucial questions you need to ask to understand your specific opportunity in micro-market terms. These questions are repeated in Box 2.1. The answers you are looking for, however, will vary depending on the kind of venture you hope to build.

---

box 2.1

Four crucial micro-level questions about target markets

1   Is there a target market segment where we might enter the market in which we offer the customer clear and compelling benefits, or – better yet – resolve the customer's pain, at a price he or she is willing to pay?

2   Are these benefits, *in the customers' minds,* different from and superior in some way – better, faster, cheaper or whatever – to what's currently offered by other solutions?

3   How large is this segment, and how fast is it growing?

4   Is it likely that our entry into this segment will facilitate entry into other segments that we may wish to target in the future?

If your dream is to build a high-growth venture that will put you in Richard Branson's or Mark Zuckerberg's league some day, you'll need to answer 'Yes' to the first two questions, 'Large, fast-growing' to the third and 'Very likely' to the fourth. If, on the other hand, your dream is to build a simple and satisfying lifestyle business that flies below the radar of major competitors, then a small target market with limited scope for expansion may be just fine. The local fly-fishing shop in Lewistown, Montana, is just such a business, and those who are stuck in the big-city rat race may well envy its proprietor.

In this chapter, we examine the case histories of three companies that have achieved some measure of success largely because of their ability to understand and capitalise on the needs of carefully defined target markets. And we take a more cursory glance at an early-stage business having a so-called two-sided market, something we're all seeing more of these days in our increasingly internet-driven world. We also examine a failure story, as we can often learn as much from failure as from inspiring success.

First, we look at NTT DoCoMo, the Japanese company that found a whole new market for mobile phones with its iMode service. Next, we go back in time to the USA more than 30 years ago, where, in a then-novel approach to beer marketing, Miller pitched its new, low-calorie beer to beefy, 20-something sports spectators. In doing so, Miller created an entirely new product category – light beer – that now wins a huge share of the American beer market.

Finally, we look at the competitive advantage that two entrepreneur–athletes gained from their initial entry into the niche market of elite distance runners. Today, their company, Nike, serves almost every segment of the athletic shoe market, each with carefully targeted products and creative marketing that have made Nike one of the world's best-known brands.

We then examine the other side of the coin and turn to the troubles of OurBeginning.com, a company that thought it knew who its target market was but spent large amounts of cash for promotion in media not well suited to that target. The results, as it turned out, did not exactly ring wedding bells.

Before wrapping up the chapter, we take a brief look at BeautyBooked and the challenges it faced in building both sides of its two-sided market. Finally, we close by considering the investor's perspective and we examine the lessons learned in Chapter 2. We consider how entrepreneurs can use these lessons to determine whether their opportunity makes sense from the target customer's perspective. Will the fish bite? Without an affirmative answer to this crucial question, an entrepreneur has little to offer, either to customers or to investors.

iMode delivers what Japanese mobile phone users want

How many companies can boast of acquiring nearly 20 million customers in just two years?[2] Not many! The ones that are capable of such rapid market penetration must be doing something right. In the case of Japan's NTT DoCoMo's iMode, the company had conceived a product with carefully targeted appeal. Launched in February 1999, Japan's wireless phone service iMode had signed up nearly 20 per cent of the total Japanese population by the middle of 2001, or 25 per cent of the population between the ages of 15 and 64.[3] Even more impressive, in just two years the company became the most widely used mobile internet service in the world.[4] iMode's success in the wireless market is an example of how important it is to have a product that offers clear and compelling benefits to a carefully targeted market.

> " iMode's success in the wireless market is an example of how important it is to have a product offering clear and compelling benefits to a carefully targeted market "

iMode's target markets

In 1999, the Japanese population numbered 126 million. Of this 126 million, only 12.2 per cent of the population had internet access,[5] compared with 39 per cent of the US population, 21 per cent of the British population and 23 per cent of the Korean population. In a study conducted by AOL and Roper ASW, 69 per cent of Japan's online population said the internet was essential to everyday life, but 29 per cent said that dial-up telephony costs were the biggest obstacle to internet access.[6]

While seemingly behind the times with respect to internet access, mobile phone use in Japan was more prevalent than in many other industrialised countries. At the end of 1999, 44.5 per cent of the Japanese population had mobile phones, compared with 40 per cent in the UK and 31 per cent in the USA. In a country where dial-up telephone access was expensive and consumers were obsessed with media – from information about stock quotes to comic strips and weather reports – Japan was ripe for an inexpensive wireless data service that targeted carefully defined segments of users with what they needed, any time, any place.

One target market that intrigued Takeshi Natsuno, Executive Director of NTT DoCoMo, included consumers interested in the financial markets and their own personal finances. To appeal to this group, iMode developed relationships with the banking industry: 'Of the more than 700 content partners we have, 320 are banks,' said Natsuno.[7]

Another target market comprised customers with an eye for comics. To serve this segment, iMode contracted the publishing firm Shueisha to provide weekly comic strips for a monthly fee of 300 yen (less than £2) for the transmission of a weekly comic strip. The toy company Bandai sold *charappa* or cartoon characters. For less than £1 a month, subscribers received a different cartoon image on their phone every day. By February 2000, Bandai had 400,000 iMode subscribers.[8] As Natsuno said, 'The success of iMode is because we adjust our site to Internet users.'[9] The only disadvantage of the product was its transmission speed of 9.6 kilobytes per second.

The price was right

With its slow transmission speed, iMode knew it was not in its best interest to charge customers based on the amount of time spent on the Web. Instead, iMode priced its services based on the amount of information downloaded, not the connection time. The pricing format was reasonable. Emails cost 1 yen (5p, or 8 US cents) per 20 Japanese characters (40 roman letters). Downloading still images cost 7 yen (4p), checking share prices cost 26 yen (14p), and transferring funds from bank accounts cost 60 yen (33p). While some of iMode's content providers charged a flat monthly fee, others were free of charge.[10] In 1999, iMode charged a basic monthly fee of 300 yen (£1.60) and a packet fee (based on the volume of data sent or received) of 0.3 yen (2p) per 128 bytes of information. iMode was also sure to price its phones reasonably, comparable to a normal mobile phone.[11]

Not only was the price low, but also the billing method was convenient for users. Instead of paying iMode for service fees and paying the content providers for subscription fees, iMode customers received one monthly bill with all of their mobile charges. 'The iMode system has made m-commerce (mobile commerce) a reality in Japan by introducing information billing systems that attach charges directly onto telephone bills,' said Natsuno.[12]

Suppliers have needs too

NTT DoCoMo's insight into the needs of its content providers was an important contributor to its early success. By taking care of the customer billing, iMode made business easy for content providers, who were hesitant to sell online because handling the billing was a large and expensive burden.

❝iMode made business easy for content providers❞

The company also kept a firm grip on its business, controlling all aspects of the iMode service. DoCoMo required its content providers to create wireless content from the ground up, specifically generating content to fit the mobile phone format. DoCoMo's success lay not in its technology, which actually was not state-of-the-art, but in its ability to bring together and control all these pieces and thereby deliver content that its target customers wanted.

Results

NTT DoCoMo created iMode at a time when the Japanese market for mobile phones was reaching maturity and users were in need of new services. Its foresight and customer understanding led to impressive initial results:

- 4.5 million subscribers in iMode's first year of operation;[13]

- 50,000 new customers each day over the next two years;[14]

- by May 2001, iMode had 22 million subscribers, approximately 20 per cent of Japan's population,[15] making DoCoMo's domestic customer base twice the size of its closest rivals.

In 2003, after four years of red-hot growth, iMode faced a two-pronged challenge: fighting off rivals that wanted a piece of iMode's market and sustaining the growth. With iMode maintaining its dominance in Japan, management decided to take its offering overseas through licensing agreements with local telecom operators.[16] Could iMode duplicate its success abroad, or was it strictly a Japanese cultural phenomenon? Its key target was Europe, where mobile penetration was also reaching maturity.

By the middle of 2004, overseas iMode subscriber numbers had grown to 3 million, on top of more than 46 million subscribers in Japan.[17] But competition and cultural differences made the going in Europe more difficult. Despite having secured partnerships with some of Europe's leading mobile operators, such as KPN (Netherlands), O2 (UK and Ireland), Bouygues and Orange (France), and E-plus (Germany), iMode did not enjoy the growth it had experienced in Japan. By the end of 2011, all of these operators had stopped supporting iMode.[18]

Though the newly updated 3G networks in Europe made iMode even easier to use, the iMode technology itself didn't. iMode required handsets and content specifically designed for iMode, not compatible with other widely used mobile operating systems provided on the majority of handsets in Europe. In the UK, for instance, mobile operator O2 sold only 12 types of handset supporting iMode technology, compared to 240 types supporting other internet browsers. In Europe, as the mobile industry matured, the customer simply had many more easily accessible options both in handsets and content. On 4th November 2016, DOCOMO announced that of its six iMode handsets, all but one would be discontinued as stock runs out. Having peaked at nearly 50 million users in 2009, iMode users had fallen to 17 million by the end of September 2016. Translating success from one region to another – from Japan to Europe, in iMode's case – is often more difficult than it looks! And maintaining that success in the face of new competition is even more difficult!

American beer drinkers see the Lite

To revolutionise an industry is a goal most companies can only dream of. For Miller Brewing Company, its decision to introduce light beer in 1975 had exactly this kind of impact. Barely on the radar in 1975, light beers made up only 1 per cent of beer consumption in the USA. By 1994, they accounted for 35 per cent of all domestic beer sold in the USA, some $16 billion in sales.[19] Miller Lite, the brand that built the light beer category, was credited for this monumental shift in consumer purchasing. How did Miller make this happen?

Miller's achievement can be attributed to two simple principles: segmented marketing and saturation advertising to reach the target market. Through consumer research, Miller realised there was a beer-drinking market segment of young men who were interested in a lower-calorie beer.[20] This appeal for lower-calorie beer stemmed from trends towards health and fitness in the 1970s. As we saw in Chapter 1, trends like these can have powerful effects on demand. The beer market was no exception. And, unlike what had been assumed previously, men were just as interested in light beer as women were. In this section, we examine how Miller identified a new target market for its beer, how it appealed to that new market and the results of its efforts.

❝trends can have powerful effects on demand❞

A new target market

There were a number of trends occurring in the mid-1970s. First, a nationwide health kick was in the works.

Led by maturing baby boomers and fitness fanatics, Americans were breakfasting on less bacon and fewer eggs, forgoing the lunchtime Scotch, and seeing a lot more sparkling water and chicken breasts at dinnertime. The new abstinence was touching the lives of so many people that it created havoc in some very large industries, including the beer industry. For marketers of products spurned, or favoured, by increasingly health-conscious Americans, abstinence was either a problem of historic proportions or a magnificent opportunity.[21]

Second, in 1975, of the 76 million strong baby boomer population, nearly 20 million were in their mid- and late-twenties.[22] The result of these two trends was a large but changing beer-drinking demographic, one increasingly concerned with its health.

Realising that its customer demographics were changing, Miller took action, conducting extensive consumer research to determine how best to appeal to its evolving target market. The research results were like music to Miller's ears, despite the fact that brewers overall were suffering (along with distillers of hard liquor) from declining per capita beer consumption as health and fitness trends took hold.

The beer-drinking generation was made up predominantly of men – no change there – in their mid-twenties, a segment quite different from the late-teens/early-twenties males who had traditionally attracted the lion's share of beer marketers' attention. The beauty of this demographic was that it was quite large (some 10 million in 1975) and it was growing. There were still 20 million male baby boomers yet to reach the legal drinking age. And all evidence suggested that the trend towards health and wellness would not be short-lived. If Miller could brew and market a beer that would appeal to this somewhat older, more health-conscious segment of the beer market, then the opportunity looked attractive. But would real men buy light beer?

Reaching its target market

Miller's goal from the onset was making light beer a mainstream, acceptable choice for young, macho, albeit health-conscious, men. To appeal to this target segment, Miller focused its advertising predominantly on sports. As Miller's Alan Easton said, '. . . the sports fan and the beer consumer are essentially the same'.[23] Miller's research also showed that this group of once-in-shape athletes was growing up and out of sports participation. Increasingly, they were becoming spectators whose beer guts replaced rippling six-pack abs. As Easton commented, 'Once you're into the demographics of sports, you are also into the total demographics of beer drinking. You get them all, from the couch-potato spectator to the high- action, participating jocks – joggers, softball players, bowlers.'[24]

But how could a beer company promoting something as prissy as low-calorie beer attract this testosterone-fuelled group? Miller's answer is now legendary. When they introduced Miller Lite in 1975, they had the wit to hire famous ex-athletes to endorse it in hilariously funny television commercials. Beefy ex-jocks, like football player Bubba Smith, who tore the cover off a Lite can, demolished the idea that real men didn't drink light beer.[25] And, like Miller's target market, the athletes in the ads were all somewhat past their prime. 'We try to choose the sort of guys you'd love to have a beer with,' said Bob Lenz, the ad executive who conceived the Lite campaign.[26] The idea was to show that low-calorie beer appeals to a man's kind of man.[27] The clear message was that this brew was not for sissies.

Sparkling results in a flat beer market

Throughout the 1950s and 1960s, two brewers, Anheuser-Busch and Joseph Schlitz, had dominated the American beer industry. In 1970, the fragmented industry had comprised 10 major brewers accounting for 69 per cent of the country's beer production, and consumption was as flat as a day-old beer. Miller ranked seventh, with a 4 per cent share.[28] But then things changed.

- By 1977, following its hugely successful introduction of Miller Lite, Miller had jumped from seventh to second place among US brewers and was threatening the long-time leader, Anheuser-Busch.[29]

- By 1980, light beers accounted for 13 per cent of total US beer shipped, with Miller Lite the runaway leader.

- One year later, Miller Lite became the third largest selling beer in the USA after Budweiser and Miller High Life. Selling 12.5 million barrels, Miller Lite had more than 50 per cent of the low-calorie beer market.

- In 1985, Miller Lite, originally a brand extension, for the first time outsold its parent, Miller High Life, to become the company's flagship brand.[30]

Miller's insights years earlier about trends in the American beer market had borne fruit beyond its wildest dreams. The target market Miller had spotted – consumers concerned with health and fitness who didn't want to give up their beer – had proven far larger than Miller had imagined. 'Americans' taste appears to be turning lighter,' said Peter Reid, editor of *Modern Brewery Age,* an industry publication, in 1997. 'Five of the top 10 beers are light and those are the only ones showing any kind of growth.'[31]

Light beer, once a niche product, had grown to 35 per cent of domestic beer consumption. Fast-forwarding to 2012, five of the six top-selling American beers were light beers, with Miller Lite having slipped to third in that category, coming in fourth overall.[32]

Sadly for Miller and the other major makers of light beers, however, another revolution in the beer industry had been gaining momentum since the early 1990s. Craft beers, brewed in small facilities by artisan brewers, had been steadily gaining a foothold in the beer market, especially with the younger beer consumer that Miller had abandoned. By 2015, the craft brewers' share of the overall US beer industry reached 12 per cent and the number of breweries in the US reached 4,269, of which an overwhelming 99 per cent were small independent breweries.[33]

Needless to say, no market sits still for 40 years. Consumers' tastes change. The major American and international beer makers have taken notice, and have begun buying up some of the most successful craft beer makers, a development much unloved by the craft brewers' previously loyal customers.[34] The craft beer trend has even reached China, the world's largest beer market, where the big global brewers like AB InBev are pitching the craft beers they've acquired in America, like Chicago's Goose Island, to Chinese consumers.[35] It seems they don't want to be left behind yet again!

Nike: running away with the athletic market

Anyone's shortlist of the world's leading brands would surely include Nike, the global icon for the athletic set. Anyone under the age of 20 probably thinks Nike has been around since the beginning of time, but in reality the story of Nike is little more than 50 years old. While today's consumers know Nike as a broad-based athletic footwear, equipment and clothing company, Nike's beginning was rooted exclusively in shoes for elite distance runners.

As we saw briefly in Chapter 1, the story of Nike provides a compelling case study of how a company entered one target market, then used its success therein as a springboard to expand into other segments. Here, we look in greater depth at Nike's entrepreneurial roots, at how the capabilities Nike developed in running shoes enabled the company to expand into other market segments, and at how a company started on a mere $1,000 investment became one of the world's best-known brands.

❝how a company started on a mere $1000 investment became one of the world's best-known brands❞

One waffle iron plus two entrepreneurs equals better shoes for distance runners[36]

It was 1964, and Phil Knight was still thinking about the business plan he had developed for a class assignment at Stanford's Graduate School of Business. Knight's plan had argued that there was an opportunity to build a business around American-designed, Japanese-made shoes for distance runners. Knight, a former distance runner at the University of Oregon with a 4:10

personal best in the mile, and Knight's former track coach at Oregon, Bill Bowerman, thought the German-made shoes everyone wore at the time were too expensive. More crucially, in their view the German shoes weren't really designed with the unique needs of distance runners in mind.

Distance runners, especially elite distance runners like Knight and others whom Bowerman was coaching, had different needs in athletic footwear from other athletes, different even from sprinters who did most of their running on tracks. Distance runners ran several miles every day, often more than 100 miles a week. Most of these miles were run on dirt trails, whose uneven surfaces and the occasional rock led to sprained ankles, or on country roads, where the miles and miles of pounding could lead to shin splints or stress fractures of the bones in the feet, ankles and legs.

Bowerman, a lifelong tinkerer and innovator, believed distance runners could benefit from shoes that provided greater cushioning (against the repetitive impact from the miles and miles of training), that gave better lateral stability (to protect against ankle sprains), and that were more flexible and lighter than the shoes then on the market (to improve his runners' race times).

Knight's work at Stanford had shown him that athletic shoes could be sourced from factories in Asia at costs that were low enough to compete favourably with the dominant German competitors. The question, then, was how to design a shoe that would meet distance runners' needs. The now legendary answer was found in Bowerman's kitchen, where, with his wife's waffle iron and some latex, he created the waffle sole, which, together with a lightweight nylon upper, would revolutionise the running shoe.

Knight, by then with a day job as an accountant, and Bowerman chipped in $500 each to form a new company, Blue Ribbon Sports, that would import Bowerman-designed shoes made by Onitsuka Tiger in Japan. There was no angel investor, no venture capital and no inkling of the potential that lay ahead. In 1964, Blue Ribbon Sports sold about 1,300 pairs of running shoes, generating a mere $8,000 in revenues. During their first five years in business, Knight's ageing station wagon could be found at track meets all over California and the Pacific Northwest, where Knight peddled his shoes to an increasingly accepting market. As runners wearing Tigers won more and more races, word spread. By 1969, with the business having grown to 20 employees and a handful of retail outlets, Knight quit his day job and began to devote all his energies to the growing business.

> **ⁱin 1964, Blue Ribbon Sports sold about 1,300 pairs of running shoes, generating a mere $8000 in revenues**

Creating a brand

At the US Olympic trials in 1972, Blue Ribbon Sports introduced its Nike brand after a dispute led to the break-up of the relationship with Onitsuka Tiger. In the 1972 Olympic marathon that soon followed, four of the top seven finishers wore Nike shoes. By 1974, after ten years of effort, the Nike shoe with the waffle sole had become America's best-selling training shoe. Nike was on the map at last, and in 1978 Blue Ribbon Sports changed its name to Nike.

One segment leads to another

By the mid-1970s, Nike had developed some capabilities that would serve it well. It had mastered low-cost outsourced production, using factories in Asia that could produce the innovative shoes created by Knight's designers. These designers had learned how to build relationships with elite athletes to identify their footwear needs, and design shoes that would not only contribute to better performance but also protect them from injury. Knight and his team realised that these capabilities could now be applied in other athletic shoe segments to develop high-performance shoes tailored specifically to the needs of each sport.

In 1978, tennis great John McEnroe signed with Nike, and tennis became another growth business. That same year, the Boston Celtics and the Los Angeles Lakers began wearing Nike's new basketball shoes. By 1983, Nike had expanded its offerings to include apparel as well as shoes. In 1985, a promising rookie basketball player named Michael Jordan signed a deal with Nike for a new line of basketball shoes based on the air-cushioned technology developed by Nike for its running shoes. Air Jordan shoes became the envy of every American teenager, as Jordan became the best player ever in basketball.

Soaring results

By 1985, after 20 years in business, Knight's and Bowerman's little company reached the billion-dollar mark in worldwide sales, and Nike was acknowledged as the technological leader in the athletic footwear industry. Though it stumbled for a time in the late 1980s, as Reebok won the aerobics market with sleek, stylish shoes that consumers preferred to Nike's clunky, more functional designs, Nike regained its touch by renewing its focus on the customer, and understanding both the psychological and functional benefits that its brand offered.[37] Its progress continued, as it widened its product lines to include more apparel, in addition to

> **❝❝ by 1985, Knight's and Bowerman's little company reached the billion-dollar mark in worldwide sales ❞❞**

footwear. It made inroads into golf and football (soccer, to the Americans in Nike's Oregon headquarters), and ramped up its lifestyle and fitness offering for women. In 2012 Nike was named one of the most digitally savvy companies around, thanks to new high-tech offerings that helped athletes track their performance.[38] As Kenny Tomlin, CEO of Rockfish Interactive, a digital agency, put it, 'They embraced how digital can create entirely new business models for them while simultaneously enhancing their offline business.'

'We're leading the transformation of sports retail,' said Heidi O'Neill, Nike's President of Global Direct to Consumer. 'Powered by immersive digital trials and in-store experts, this store is about elevating every athlete's potential.' Adds tennis champion Serena Williams, 'It's great to see the everyday athlete getting the same personalized treatment from Nike that I've enjoyed over the years.'[39] By embodying in its culture the play-to-win competitiveness and determination that world-class athletes embrace,[40] Nike's performance has continued to soar, with revenue reaching a record $32.4 billion in its fiscal year ending May 2016.[41] Focusing on meeting the unique needs and the aspirations of athletes in one sport after another, and playing to win, has served Nike very well.

OurBeginning.com's marketing bomb

Choose the correct answer to this question:

A company that shells out over $5 million on four television ads in one day:

(a) is large and very profitable

(b) has a consistent revenue stream

(c) has a marketing budget the size of Coca-Cola's

(d) has a significant amount of cash on hand

(e) has almost no other cash on hand.

If you chose (e), you would be correct, referencing OurBeginning.com's audacious marketing endeavour during Super Bowl XXXIV in early 2000. The story was not uncommon in the dot.com era, when many companies spent inordinate amounts of investors' money on poorly targeted marketing campaigns. The results of such campaigns were typically mediocre results and a waste of crucial cash.

Having seen in this Chapter 3 examples of companies whose successes were based in large part on getting it right in micro-market terms – the stories of iMode, Miller Lite and Nike – we now examine the case of a company that got it wrong.

It's the story of a company that failed to focus its efforts on a clearly identified market segment. In this section, we consider OurBeginning.com's offering, we identify who its target market was, we examine its decision to advertise during the Super Bowl, which enjoys the single largest television audience each year in the USA, and we discuss its results.

The offering

Launched in early 1999 by Michael and Susan Budowski, OurBeginning. com took its first order in March 1999. Susan was a wedding planner. Michael had started several successful businesses of his own. Based on Susan's experience with wedding planning, the site was originally designed to meet couples' needs for wedding invitations: 'We launched the original OurBeginning.com site with a focus on weddings – providing the Internet's largest selection of invitations, as well as a focus on convenience and personalized service.'[42]

Once the customer decided on the style, design, paper and wording, he or she could place an order. OurBeginning sent the orders to outside printers, who printed and shipped to customers under the OurBeginning label. Boasting that its invitations were 10–30 per cent cheaper than those from retail stores, the company was, according to an early press release, the 'first Internet resource for selecting and purchasing high-quality wedding invitations online'.[43] OurBeginning.com also included a number of other services, providing suggestions about invitation wording, advising on invitation content and allowing friends and family to look at the invitations before placing an order.

Target market

By focusing on weddings, OurBeginning had a very specific target market. Customarily in the USA, women and their mothers plan the wedding, including choosing the wedding invitations. In order to use OurBeginning's site, customers needed access to the internet. Thus, the company's target market was quite specific – women planning a wedding who had access to the internet. In 1999, there were approximately 2.4 million weddings in the USA, a rate of 8.3 weddings per 1,000 adults.[44] At the same time, approximately 55 per cent of the US population of marrying age had access to the internet.[45] Thus, the size of OurBeginning's target market was approximately 1.3 million women in 1999.

The marketing plan

To increase brand awareness and generate sales, OurBeginning developed a marketing strategy. The key element would be three pre-game advertisements and a fourth one during the Super Bowl football game on 30th January, 2000. The total cost of this effort, including $1 million to create the ads and another $1 million to beef up the site to handle the planned increase in Web traffic, would be $5 million. In Michael Budowski's view, these ads would 'put a turbocharger in the company', and would create a database of some 5 million customers: 'It's the largest captive audience of the year,' said Budowski.[46]

This statement, of course, was true. In 2000, approximately 130 million people would tune in to watch Super Bowl XXXIV. But, how many of those 130 million viewers were interested in purchasing wedding invitations? Of those 130 million, 45 million were women.[47] What percentage of these 45 million was planning a wedding? If there are 8.3 weddings per 1,000 adults (including both men and women, or 16.6 weddings per 1,000 women), then of the 45 million women viewers (assuming conservatively that they are all adults, a significant overstatement), there were perhaps about 750,000 weddings in the works among this audience. With an interested audience of such a small size, how effective was this $5 million marketing decision?

Results

In January, the company reported 284,049 unique visitors to its site, an average of about 10,000 per day. What kind of response did its Super Bowl advertising generate?

- Traffic on the company's site jumped by 82 per cent on the Monday following the Super Bowl.[48]

- In February, after the ads aired, the site had 510,730 unique visitors, more than a 50 per cent increase to be sure, but far less than the 5 million-strong customer list Budowski had hoped to build.

- By March, however, the number of visitors plummeted to 92,292.[49] One of the reasons for this sharp drop-off was that there is no consistent relationship between advertising spending and lasting brand awareness for dot.com companies, according to a study by Greenfield Online, an internet marketing research company.[50]

How much did the increased traffic spend with OurBeginning.com? In the first quarter of 2000, visitors to its site spent a total of $510,000.[51] While this was a 350 per cent increase in revenues from the previous quarter, the figure pales in comparison to the $5 million it took to generate the increased sales. If an average OurBeginning customer spent, say, 20 per cent less than the reported industry norm of $350 on invitations, i.e. $280,[52] then there were approximately 1,800 customers in the first quarter of 2000. Thus, put another way, the company spent about $2,800 to acquire each customer, or ten times what the customer spent, and probably 20 times the gross margin achieved on each sale. Suddenly, these results don't look as impressive. Perhaps the Super Bowl wasn't the most efficient way to reach OurBeginning's target market.

To be fair, its Super Bowl advertising netted OurBeginning additional press coverage, including 450 press mentions and more than 100 broadcast hits.[53] These side benefits enabled OurBeginning and its agencies to put a brave face on its results. But awareness and business results are two different things.

By June 2000, OurBeginning had a watchful eye on its dwindling six-month cash reserve and was reducing its marketing expenses.[54] By the beginning of 2001, the company was still not profitable and had revised its marketing strategy significantly. The marketing budget for 2001 would be $1 million, a small share of its budget the previous year. When asked about advertising in the 2001 Super Bowl, Budowski said he would 'merely be a spectator'.[55] By 2002, however, the Budowskis had become spectators not just of the Super Bowl but of the wedding invitation business *per se,* with their site having been quietly taken over by an already established, traditional printer of wedding invitations. Details of the transaction were not publicly disclosed.

Why did OurBeginning.com fail?

There were probably several reasons, including the fact that the business model Budowski conceived simply was not viable, a topic we address in Chapter 5. But the crucial flaw appears to have been a lack of understanding of who its target market really was and the unfocused marketing effort that ensued.

What investors want to know

Not every entrepreneur needs investors to get started. As we saw earlier in this chapter, Phil Knight and Bill Bowerman each contributed $500 to get their business rolling, and then nursed it for years until it reached a sustainable level. Theirs was a lean start-up ahead of its time. For many entrepreneurs, however, raising money appears essential, whether from family and friends or from more established sources, such as banks, business angels or venture capital investors. Doing so typically requires the entrepreneur to prepare some kind of business plan or pitch deck, so the would-be investor can ascertain the likelihood of at least getting their money back and hopefully earning an attractive return on the investment. Such a proposition must, at its heart, be driven by the lessons of this chapter.

If you are an investor reading this chapter, what do investors like you – arguably the most important audience for such a plan or pitch – want to know from a micro-market perspective?

- First and foremost, investors don't want to know about your ideas or products – they really couldn't care less about you and your idea, at least at the outset. They want to know about the customer pain that your offering will resolve. No pain, no gain. If you can identify the customer pain, *then* their attention will be piqued.

- Alternatively, for some business-to-consumer opportunities, investors will settle for consumer delight. Making a previously mundane experience into something delightful – the Starbucks experience compared to an old-fashioned coffee shop, for example – is another, though often more difficult, way to go.

- Investors want to know who the target customer is who has the pain, or will receive the delight, and they want evidence that the target customer will buy what's to be offered at a price that works for you.

We ask, 'Who will be your first ten customers – names and addresses, please – and who will be your largest customer in five years?'

JT, LONDON

The biggest shortcoming of the business plans we see is the complete absence of market research. Dreams of demand just won't do. Hard evidence is what attracts our money.

IC, LONDON

Any entrepreneur pursuing a business-to-business opportunity who cannot answer these questions – for business-to-consumer marketers, names and addresses are not relevant, although the same clarity of purpose is still needed – simply won't raise the money in today's demanding funding markets. The days when entrepreneurs could scrawl a dot. com business plan on the back of an envelope and raise millions from eager investors are long gone.

❝ any entrepreneur who cannot answer these questions simply won't raise the money ❞

But mere words and blind faith are not enough. Evidence is what counts. What sort of evidence do sensible investors require? Marketing research is good. Better, though, are actual sales or customer commitments based on some sort of market test – using a prototype, perhaps, or even a test on eBay. A little market experimentation can go a long way towards instilling investor confidence, not to mention, of course, your own! In fact, what investors love more than anything is ongoing customer traction that's already been demonstrated. That's why many astute entrepreneurs are building customer-funded business models, in which the initial cash the company needs is provided by customers so eager for what the new company offers that they're willing to pay for it, sometimes in advance, whether on Kickstarter or in other settings. We explore these kinds of models in more detail in Chapter 12.

The clear lesson here is that the entrepreneur must be painstakingly clear about who makes up the target market that he or she seeks to serve, and they must show tangible evidence that the customers in that market will buy. Why will they buy? To obtain benefits other solutions don't offer – faster, better, cheaper and so on. Without benefits – without pain relief or delight – there will be no customers. Without customers, there will be no business.

Lessons learned

While world domination may be their ultimate goal, most successful entrepreneurs start with a single, sharply targeted market, often a niche that's really quite small. How are such markets defined? In simple terms, there are three good ways to do so, as described in Box 2.2. Many new ventures succeed

---

box 2.2

Three ways to define market segments

1 By *who* the customers are, i.e. in demographic terms (age, gender, education, income, etc.). For business-to-business opportunities, demographics refer to the industry in which the customers do business, plus firm size and other firm characteristics.

2 By *where* the customers are, i.e. in geographical terms.

3 By *how* the customers behave, i.e. in behavioural or lifestyle terms. For business-to-business opportunities, behavioural segmentation specifies differences in how the products are used. For example, makers of pumps serve a broad variety of market segments, depending on what is to be pumped (liquid or gas, high or low viscosity, etc.) and the conditions under which the pumping occurs (e.g. the cold temperatures under which oil is pumped from wells in the Siberian tundra versus the hygienic conditions in a dairy facility).

> Different market segments have different needs, thereby calling for different solutions. Entrepreneurs are renowned for finding new ways to segment markets that they serve, often behaviourally, thereby creating new segments that they can dominate.

because their founders see a new way to segment and target an existing market, often in behavioural terms. Doing so enables the entrepreneurial venture to target a behaviourally defined segment with benefits suited uniquely to that segment, benefits not offered by existing solutions.

Whether you are an aspiring entrepreneur or an early-stage investor, it is not enough to hope there is a market for your product. In order to understand your opportunity in micro-market terms and to demonstrate that your customers will really buy, it is essential to become intimately familiar with the needs of the target segment or segments most likely to purchase your product. Embarking on a lean start-up is one way to gain the familiarity you need. Better yet, you'll want actual sales or purchase orders or letters of intent for your still-hypothetical product, before you get started.

Knowing why customers will buy comes down to benefits, because customers buy benefits, not features, a distinction many entrepreneurs fail to understand. Benefits are the lead actor. Features are simply the supporting cast – a mere delivery system for the benefits customers seek. What do we mean by 'benefits'? Benefits are the often-measurable end-use consequences of using the product – the pain relief – as opposed to some physical attributes of the product itself. The waffle sole and nylon upper of Bill Bowerman's early running shoes were features – tangible product attributes – but that's not why runners bought his shoes. They bought them for protection from injury while training and because, when wearing them, they ran faster. These benefits differentiated the shoes from others and made the sale.

Lessons learned from iMode

As the iMode case history demonstrates, DoCoMo's new service was an instant hit because of its designers' intimate familiarity with the Japanese market on a segment-by-segment basis. Identifying clearly who its target markets were allowed the company to offer an internet-access mobile phone service that appealed to a large number of customers. DoCoMo segmented its markets behaviourally and designed offerings of different downloadable information for each segment: those interested in financial markets, comic strips, cartoons and so on. The iMode story also provides an example that answers the often-asked question, 'Which must come first, the idea (or technology) or the customer need?' In iMode's case, internet and communications technology created the possibility of delivering information to mobile customers, any time, anywhere.

> **❝it's not so important whether recognition of the need comes first, or whether the technology comes first❞**

The application of those technologies to the particular set of consumer needs that iMode targeted then followed. Thus, it's not so important whether recognition of the need comes first, or whether the technology that makes new things possible comes first. Either route can be successful. What's crucial, though, is that, at the end of the day, there's a clear target market, a genuine customer need, and that what the company offers satisfies that target market's need in a way that's faster, better, cheaper or otherwise more beneficial – again, benefits, not features – than other solutions.

Lessons learned from Miller Lite

Entrepreneurial behaviour, as the Miller Lite story shows, can occur within established firms, as well as in nascent start-ups. In a brutally competitive industry serving a stagnant market, Miller Brewing Company needed to find a way to grow. The company used consumer research to determine whether and where there was an unfilled or under-served need. Miller identified a large and growing market segment, the 10 million, 20-something male baby boomers interested in low-calorie beer.

Thus, before introducing its light beer, Miller knew it had a sizeable target market with needs that were not served currently by other brewers. Unlike iMode, which segmented its market behaviourally, Miller identified a demographically defined market segment, although it used its customers' affinity for sports, a behavioural factor, in further targeting its marketing effort. Given the powerful demographic surge that lay ahead – with 20 million male baby boomers yet to reach drinking age – the segment had attractive potential for growth as well. As we shall see in more detail in the next chapter, demographic and other macro-trends can lead to the creation of new market segments waiting to be served by entrepreneurs whose customer insights uncover unserved or under-served needs that others have overlooked.

The Miller Lite story also shows that market niches sometimes turn out to be far larger than an entrepreneur might originally anticipate. From the 10 million males in its original target market, the light beer segment grew to encompass one-third of US beer consumption 20 years later – a $16 billion market. For entrepreneurs – especially those having resources more limited than Miller's – niche markets aren't bad places to begin.

Lessons learned from Nike

From Nike, we've seen how entry into one segment, if successful, can lead to success in additional segments. The additional value that such a successful entry offers can constitute an important part of the value that entrepreneurs bring to investors who back them. Understanding these options and articulating them effectively can help entrepreneurs pitch the upside of what they propose to investors, thereby making their opportunity more compelling.

Unlike the Miller Lite story, where the entrepreneurial behaviour took root in an established firm, Nike's story began with two runners passionate about running. And unlike iMode, where the technology came first and made the concept possible, in Nike's case the venture was driven by customers' needs, needs that Knight and Bowerman, as runners themselves, knew intimately.

Nike learned its trade in one segment, elite distance runners, clearly a niche market then and now. There it built crucial capabilities:

- the art of understanding the needs of such athletes;
- the engineering of products that appealed to these athletes;
- the business of sourcing these products in low-cost offshore manufacturing locations;
- the ability to build relationships with high profile athletes;
- the marketing savvy to build on the performance of these athletes to attract interest from the rest of the athletic pyramid.

Nike then used these capabilities when entering other segments. In almost every segment it entered, Nike won the match.

Nike's segment-by-segment success raises several questions that entrepreneurs should ask.

- What can I learn from this first market segment that will allow me to make waves in additional segments?
- What other segments exist that could benefit from a related offering?
- Can we develop capabilities that are transferable from one segment to another?

By answering these questions, entrepreneurs can identify additional value in the opportunity at hand – value that lies beyond the market targeted originally. As the Nike case history shows, that extra value can be more than small change!

Lessons learned from OurBeginning.com

It is one thing to identify a target market; it is another thing to market effectively to this segment. OurBeginning may have had a good sense of who its target market was, but the company made decisions about how to reach this segment that reflected a lack of understanding about target marketing. And when men placed a whopping 35 per cent of its early orders (do men buy most wedding invitations?), it might have given careful thought to the implications of this figure.[56] Was the marketing reaching the real target market? As the Monday morning quarterbacks noted and more savvy marketers would have foreseen, 'You're a stationery company, focusing on etiquette and customer service – not exactly the market that watches the Super Bowl.'[57]

Thus, for both entrepreneurs and those who invest in early-stage ventures, understanding one's target market is a good start, but it requires effective execution, as we'll explore further in Chapter 7. Without clearly articulating one's target market up front, that execution is very likely to miss the mark. And, of more immediate concern to entrepreneurs about to launch a lean start-up or prepare a business plan, without a clear definition of the target market, the entrepreneur won't know which doors to knock on and no sensible investor will invest.

The new business road test: stage one – the micro-market test

- What customer pain will your offering resolve? Or what kind of mundane customer experience will you replace with a delightful one? How strong an incentive do customers have to give you their money? Will the fish bite at a price that works?

- Who, precisely, are the customers who have the pain or will be given delight? Do you have detailed, accurate and current information about who they are, where they live or do business, or what they do?

- What differentiated benefits does your offering provide that other solutions don't?

- What evidence do you have that customers will buy what you propose to offer?

- What evidence can you provide to show that your target market has the potential to grow?

- What other segments exist that could benefit from a related offering?

- Can you develop capabilities that are transferable from one segment to another?

- Based on the evidence you compile in answering the above questions, what key micro-market risks remain, to which early attention should be given?

THE NEW BUSINESS ROAD TEST

If you open your *New Business Road Test* app for your smartphone or tablet, you'll find the above checklist reproduced there, along with note-taking and recording features that let you keep track of evidence you find – from observing or interviewing potential customers or users, for example – as you are out in the marketplace. The app also asks you start tracking the risks as you identify them, tabulating them for later reference, once you are ready to set your mind to finding ways to mitigate or eliminate them. No rose-coloured glasses, please! Recall Chapter 1's key question that you should be addressing in doing so: 'Why will *or won't* my idea work?'

3

Is this an attractive market? Competitive and economic sustainability

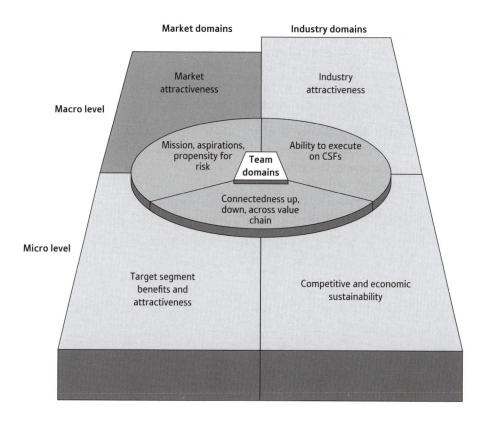

Market domains

Industry domains

Market attractiveness

Industry attractiveness

Macro level

Mission, aspirations, propensity for risk

Ability to execute on CSFs

Team domains

Connectedness up, down, across value chain

Micro level

Target segment benefits and attractiveness

Competitive and economic sustainability

After years of searching for your dream car, a 1950s' Austin Healey, you happen upon a mint-condition 1956 100 series BN2. With the exception of its price tag it is perfect. Pillar-box red exterior. Leather seats. A dashboard more vintage than the car itself. With the money you saved over the past year, you hop on a plane to Las Vegas, ready to enjoy the desert sun and win yourself enough money to buy the car. Sure, you could have gone to a nearby casino on a riverboat or to an Indian reservation, but the jackpots are bigger in Las Vegas.

When you walk into the casino, you are entranced by the commotion. Readying (or steadying) yourself for a day of gambling, you sit down at the bar for a quick shot of vodka and a glass of freshly squeezed orange juice. At the bar, you notice a blank lottery ticket sitting in front of you. The payback in this game called Keno is enormous. For a small price of $7, all you need to do is pick seven numbers. If all seven numbers are included in the 20 selected during the lottery drawing, your winnings are $77,777. Not a bad return on an investment – if you hit the right numbers, of course. Your other gambling choice is a bit less rewarding. You sit at the bar and calculate how long it might take you to win $77,777 at the blackjack table. Your realisation is that $77,000 is more than a day's work when playing blackjack under the very best of circumstances. Choosing games in Las Vegas is a bit like choosing markets, you reflect. Choose the right game – or the right market – and the payoff can be huge. But the size of the possible payoff isn't the only thing to consider.

Knowing that the odds of picking all seven numbers correctly in Keno are about 41,000 to 1, whereas you have about a 50 per cent chance of winning a hand in blackjack, which game do you choose?

Do markets matter?

> There is a tide in the affairs of men, which, taken at the flood, leads
> on to fortune . . . We must take the current when it serves, or lose our
> ventures.
>
> William Shakespeare[1]

Most entrepreneurs and all thoughtful investors consider both risk and reward when starting or funding an early-stage venture. As we have seen, the odds against hitting the jackpot as an entrepreneur can be nearly as daunting as those in Las Vegas or Monte Carlo. One way to mitigate the long odds, as we saw in Chapter 2, is to make sure you've identified an attractive market segment, one where the customers, according to evidence you've gathered, are almost certain to buy what you'll offer. But let's pause to ask some more questions.

- What if you are offering clear and compelling benefits to a carefully targeted market (as NTT DoCoMo did with iMode)?

- What if (like the 10 million young, diet-conscious, beer-drinking men that Miller identified) you have plenty of customers willing to buy your new product?

- What if the segment you'll initially target is likely to take you naturally into other segments (as did Nike's distance runner segment)?

Is it time to launch your lean start-up, write your business plan, or prepare your pitch? No. Not even close.

❝having a target market whose customers are likely to buy is like table stakes❞

As we'll see in this chapter, I've only scratched the surface in giving you the tools you need to assess your opportunity. One domains down, six to go. Having a target market whose customers are likely to buy is like table stakes. It gets you into the game, but it's by no means the end of the story. Thus, the next piece of the game we'll examine is the upper left quadrant of the seven domains model, the attractiveness of the market at the macro level.

As Chapter 1 showed, one of the best ways to improve your odds for success – apart from serving an attractive target market segment – is to seek to do business in a market that's attractive in a wider sense. As we saw in Chapter 2, the assessment at the micro (or the target segment) level involves looking very closely at your target market to make sure that you offer clear and differentiated benefits to a clearly defined group of customers. Here in Chapter 3, as we deal with assessing markets at the macro level, we view your market from 30,000 feet, rather than one customer at a time.

What you are looking for here is big enough to be seen from the air and you'll need some distance – a macro perspective – to understand what you're looking at. What you want to find is evidence of market size and market growth, both today and tomorrow. Doing so involves asking the three key questions listed in Box 3.1. Chapter 13 provides a market analysis worksheet for digging into these questions in more detail, and it highlights the importance of reaching an overall conclusion about market attractiveness at the macro level, once you've gathered the evidence necessary to answer the questions.

---

box 3.1

Three crucial questions about markets

1   Is your market large enough today to allow different competitors the opportunity to serve different segments without getting in each other's way?

2   What are the predictions for your market's short-term growth rate? (In the absence of other information to the contrary, the recent rate of growth in your market may be the best available predictor of growth in the near future.)

3   What are the predictions for your market's long-term growth rate? (This is likely to be influenced heavily by macro trends: economic, demographic, sociocultural, technological, regulatory and/or natural.)

In asking these questions as an aspiring entrepreneur or as a potential investor, you must know what you want. If you take a long-run perspective and your aspirations include building a large and lasting venture that creates value over time, then you'll be concerned with the answers to all three questions. If you plan to exit quickly, selling your business and perhaps moving on to another one, or you plan to build a small business in a protected market niche, then questions 2 and 3 might be less crucial for you.

In this chapter, we examine the case histories of three entrepreneurial success stories driven largely by the attractiveness of the market in macro terms. First, we travel to California to examine the story of Twilio, one of the early 21st century unicorns and now a high-flying publicly held company, that's bringing effective and inexpensive communications solutions to apps and Web pages everywhere.

We then see how the tide of growing demand for natural and organic foods propelled Whole Foods Market into the front-runner position in a rapidly growing segment of the American supermarket industry.

Finally, we discuss how EMC, a data storage company, succeeded in tracking and anticipating technological trends for more than 25 years, though not without some bumps in the road, outperforming its competitors and just about every public company in the USA for much of that time.

On the other side of the coin, we examine the story of Thinking Machines, a supercomputer company whose failure can, to a large degree, be attributed to insufficient market size. Despite its founders' hopes, Thinking Machines simply couldn't find a large enough market to sustain its ambitions.

To conclude the chapter, we explore the investors' perspective on market attractiveness, we examine lessons learned, and we consider how you, as either an entrepreneur or an investor at any stage of the entrepreneurial life cycle can use these lessons to determine whether your overall market is attractive in macro terms. Will you find yourself swimming against the tide? Or, like a sailor with the wind at your back, will you benefit from a favourable breeze?

Twilio goes after the telecom giants

Shortly after founding Twilio with two friends in 2008, Twilio CEO Jeff Lawson had an opportunity to introduce his new company at a networking mixer in San Francisco. He didn't want to simply *talk about* what Twilio did, however. He wanted to *show* what it did.

In front of an audience of 1,000 people, while Lawson began telling his story, he wrote a few lines of code that his tech-savvy audience easily understood to create a conference line, open an account and secure a phone number, to which he asked everyone in the room to dial in. It was a mob conference call! With a few more lines of code, Lawson then used the Twilio app to thank the crowd for dialling in. As all the mobile phones in the room started buzzing, the crowd, many of whom were software developers, went wild.[2]

Riding a wave

Before starting Twilio, Lawson already understood that the cloud – an array of giant servers that enabled software to reside centrally and inexpensively, instead of on one's own server – represented the future of the software industry. "We are riding the grand adoption of the cloud," says Lawson.[3] A veteran of two earlier start-ups plus a 15-month stint in the early days of Amazon Web Services (AWS), a leading purveyor of cloud technology, Lawson believed the cloud would make it vastly easier and faster for software developers to get software built, and at far less cost, too. Instead of writing all the code their software would require, they would simply stitch together building blocks already hosted in the cloud.

> **We are riding the grand adoption of the cloud**

Surmising that communications would be a suitable arena to target – after all, communications had been essential to his earlier start-ups – Lawson and his co-founders developed a prototype communications tool and launched it on AWS. Developers loved it, and soon Twilio had its first customer, a service called PhoneMyPhone.com, which consumers could use to call and locate their mobile phones when they were lost between the sofa cushions.[4]

Twilio's proposition to the developer world was simple. It initially offered basic communication functions – 'dial', 'play, 'record', and so on – which developers could bolt onto the internet applications they were developing.[5] Twilio worked in the background to connect these functions to the global telecommunications infrastructure, across numerous telecom carriers and around the globe. In essence, Twilio permitted developers to add voice and texting capabilities to their applications by simply adding a few lines of code.[6] No carrier contracts, no phone numbers, no hardware, nothing. It just worked.

And another wave

Before long, it became clear that developers by the thousands were writing applications for the rapidly growing number of iPhones and other smartphones. Lawson jumped on the trend. With Twilio, any developer could easily add voice and text messaging – and later, video and chat, too – to whatever they were developing. Take Uber, for example. When I call an Uber to take me to the airport, the driver and I are able to communicate directly, without having to disclose our phone numbers, a security risk that some passengers would not care to take. Trek Medics offers access to emergency services in countries like Haiti and Tanzania, where services like 911 in the USA do not exist. The ubiquitous What's App, and more prosaic companies like Walmart, Coca-Cola and Alaska Airlines are customers, too. Department store retailer Nordstrom even uses Twilio as the basis for a concierge service that connects its sales associates with customers.[7]

As Twilio investor Fred Wilson put it, way back in 2010, 'We believe that one way to build a large network of web users is to build something that makes developers' lives easier. And Twilio does exactly that. It masks all the complexity of telephony into a finite number of API calls that web developers can use to build apps quickly and easily.'[8] By mid-2015, Twilio's community of registered software developers passed the 500,000 mark,[9] aided by the more than 500 developer events and hackathons in which the company had participated in 2014. It even convinced one of its investors to create a $250 million seed fund to invest in start-ups that used the Twilio platform.[10]

How large is Twilio's opportunity?

Blogger Nick Hughes says Twilio is all about disruptive innovation. 'It's the difference between the electronic typewriter, which improved the typewriter,' he says, 'and the word processor, which supplanted it. AT&T is the typewriter. Twilio looks to be the word processor.'[11] So, just as the growth of the Web has disrupted the movie and music industries, could telecommunications be next?

At its recent growth rate, Twilio could hit a $1 billion run-rate in revenue in late 2018, up from $167 million in 2016, according to one observer.[12] In Lawson's view, huge portions of telecommunications are poised to move from hardware – copper wires, switches, switchboards, and so on – to software. Lawson sees telecom services as a trillion-dollar market. As the telecom world becomes increasingly mobile-centric, cloud-enabled and developer-driven, Lawson says there's plenty of room for growth, with plenty of room for multiple players to thrive. 'We are absolutely just getting started,' he says.[13]

Quite a ride

In 2016, after having raised half a dozen rounds of venture capital along the way, Twilio raised another $150 million in an initial public offering (IPO) in June 2016 at $15 per share. The stock took off, reaching a high of about

$71 per share in September, before sinking sharply on the heels of news that Twilio would offer another $400 million in shares, more than 85 per cent of which were to be sold by major shareholders taking advantage of the run-up in Twilio's price.[14] By November, the roller-coaster ride had calmed down, and Twilio settled in at around $30 per share, still double its IPO price.[15]

It would be myopic to attribute Twilio's success to simply catching and riding some potent waves: first the cloud, then smartphones and apps. As the company's case history shows, Lawson and his team have continued to innovate, and have managed to serve multiple market segments very well. Will they be able to continue to stay abreast of consumers' and B2B customers' evolving communications needs and of technological trends that make new solutions possible? Time will tell, but given the lofty valuation that Twilio enjoys, its shareholders seem to agree with Lawson that the company is, indeed, just getting started.

Tofu and toothpaste: the rise of Whole Foods

In the USA in 1980, retail sales of organic products totalled just $178 million, and natural and organic products and foods appealed to just 2 per cent of the population.[16] The market for natural and organic foods was a small one, thought John Mackey, owner of Safer Way, a small health-food store in Austin, Texas.

But Mackey had noticed that his customers were asking more and more for natural foods and organically grown fruits and vegetables, so he figured the market would grow. Mackey joined hands with Craig Weller and Mark Siles of the Clarksville Natural Food Grocery to form what would become the first Whole Foods Market. The new store would serve a relatively tiny clientele: an eclectic group of vegetarians, macrobiotic dieters and others whose diets included a variety of supplements with near-unpronounceable names – ginkgo biloba, echinacea and others that collectively formed an entirely new lexicon for the three grocers. Like other 'mom-and-pop' organic shops elsewhere, the store was friendly, intensely concerned with its products' purity and very expensive.

Happily for the three entrepreneurs, consumers were more numerous and more responsive than Mackey and his partners would have predicted in their wildest dreams. In its first year, their small 10,500-square-foot store sold $4 million of natural products and organic foods.

Whole Foods' subsequent expansion from small-town natural foods grocer to a $15 billion grocery store chain is not just a fairy tale. It is a story of real-life market savvy. In a class of their own, Whole Foods' executives not only understood consumer demand for natural and organic products; they also knew what else drove Americans' supermarket purchasing patterns.

Understanding the trends

The decade that followed was the beginning of the nutrition movement in the USA and, soon thereafter, in the UK and elsewhere. 'The word "nutrition" was launched into the headlines more than in any previous decade,' according to Elaine McIntosh, a biologist and writer on nutrition.[17] Sparked by increasingly widespread interest in health, food companies began to introduce more products that claimed to have less fat, fewer calories and lower cholesterol, while at the same time providing more nutritional value such as fibre, vitamins and minerals. This trend augured well for Mackey and his partners, and for others who saw these developments.

When organic supermarkets started springing up in the 1980s, their proprietors figured that the aisles would be populated by a nation of granola eaters happy to pay a substantial premium for the halo of purity. They were wrong. Americans remained a nation of committed junk-food eaters even while welcoming organic foods to the table. Further, there were limits to the premiums consumers were willing to pay for organic foods, and they were unwilling to give up any of the conveniences of shopping in large stores that stocked everything from tofu to toothpaste.[18] So, what did Mackey and his team do to meet consumers' desires?

❝ They were wrong. Americans remained a nation of committed junk-food eaters ❞

For starters, they built larger stores. With an average store size that soon reached 26,000 square feet, the stores offered chemical-and preservative-free foods, organic produce, hormone-free meats, cruelty-free cosmetics and ecologically friendly household products. Each store had at least one aisle of nutritional items for homeopathic and alternative healthcare. But, unlike the old niche stores, Whole Foods Markets were not ascetic: you could buy beer and wine as well as non-organic produce, foods with refined sugar, and even household cleaners – of the environmentally friendly kind, of course.

When the so-called home meal replacement market started growing in the 1990s, Whole Foods responded by selling quick entrées, side dishes, soups, rotisserie-grilled items, sushi and sandwiches, all of which were made fresh daily with natural ingredients from around the store.[19] They even added tables where customers could sit down and eat. A McKinsey & Company survey soon found that one of the dominant eating places for baby boomers aged 35–54 and mature middle-aged consumers aged 55–64 was the supermarket prepared-food section.[20] Prepared foods became one of the fastest growing and most lucrative elements of Whole Foods' business.[21]

Whole Foods also responded to its customers' growing interest in information by offering printed and Web-based information to help shoppers maintain a healthy lifestyle. The company also had an entire section of its website devoted to health issues and references.

Tasty results

As demand for natural and organic foods and products grew, so too did Whole Foods. The natural products market reached $25 billion in sales in 2000 and the organic industry was growing at a rate of 20–24 per cent per year.[22] By 2015, US organic product sales had reached $43.3 billion – the fourth year running that growth had been in double digits.[23] Whole Foods garnered a whopping $15.4 billion, now with stores in the USA, Canada and the United Kingdom.[24] For Whole Foods it has been quite a ride.[25]

- From one store in 1980 to ten stores in 1991, Whole Foods Market grew to 117 strong by 2001, with the help of several acquisitions financed by an initial public offering along the way.[26] It accomplished this feat in two ways. First, it kept pace with the growing interest in natural foods and products. Second, it drove demand for these products by offering consumers conveniently located, well-designed stores and an enjoyable shopping experience.

- In 2000, Whole Foods customers forked out an average of $826 per square foot, compared with the number-two natural-foods chain Wild Oats' $538, far outpacing average supermarket sales of $487 per square foot.[27]

- The recession of 2008–09, however, provided a new set of challenges for the retailer sometimes referred to as 'Whole Paycheck'. Despite continuously growing sales figures reaching nearly $8 billion in its year ending September 2008, comparable-store sales fell in 2009. Mackey and his team were forced to reduce spending and lay off staff, as well as limit store expansion.[28] They set to work on shedding their luxury image through initiatives such as 'value tours' to highlight good deals and good value items in stores.

■ By 2012, it was clear that sales at established stores were defying the still tepid economy, rising 8.2 per cent in its fiscal third quarter. Co-CEO Walter Robb said, 'In an economic environment that is proving to be difficult for many retailers, we are thriving'.[29] For the same period, profits were up 32 per cent.

■ By 2015, sales growth slowed as natural and organic products became more widely available, making life competitively more difficult. To counter this, Whole Foods introduced its '365' store concept, aimed at the more budget-minded millennials. The new concept featured, along with lower prices, an environment that is, in John Mackey's view, 'hip, cool and tech-oriented'.[30]

Catching the natural and organic foods wave and riding it early had served Whole Foods well. Amazon's Jeff Bezos noticed, and Amazon acquired Whole Foods in 2017. So, too, did Paul Lindley of Britain's Ella's Kitchen, whose story is told briefly in Case Study 3.1.

---

case study 3.1

Ella's Kitchen: making kids' eating healthy and fun[31]

In 2006, Paul and Alison Lindley were facing a bit of a challenge in getting their six-year-old daughter Ella to eat. In his Caversham kitchen, Lindley started concocting blends of natural and organic fruits and vegetables that were fun, colourful, and fit the family's on-the-go lifestyle. Quickly realising that there might be a market for his tasty creations – which Ella loved! – Lindley soon moved his fledgling operation out of his kitchen and into a couple of beautiful barns in South Oxfordshire.

Ella's Kitchen baby and toddler food pouches – filled with all-natural purees of organically grown fruits and vegetables – began finding their way into the homes of almost any British family with young children about. Organic smoothies in four kid-friendly flavours – the red one, the green one, the purple one and the yellow one – followed, as did a range of toddler-sized fruit snack bars and a host of other products.

Lindley then expanded internationally – after all, eating should be fun, tasty, and cool for kids, no matter where they live. In 2013, Ella's Kitchen was acquired by Hain Clestial, a leading American marketer of natural foods and beverages. Since then, it has been awarded

▶

certification as a B Corporation, recognition that it meets rigorous standards of social and environmental performance.[32]

The trend toward natural and organic foods has been as attractive a wave to ride for Ella's Kitchen as it's been for Whole Foods. And numerous other organic and natural entrepreneurs are riding the same wave!

EMC: matching technology to customers' changing needs

There are no better markets than technology markets for examining what happens when wave after wave of high-tech disruption washes up on every beach. Michael Ruettgers, former CEO of EMC, a data storage company, uses an analogy of 'a surfer spotting, catching, and riding successive waves, each one representing an opportunity created by a disruptive technology, new market, or new business model'.[33]

> **❝radical and continuous change is a simple fact of life in any technology-based business❞**

Radical and continuous change is a simple fact of life in any technology-based business. Why can some companies keep pace with such change, reinventing themselves and their technologies to keep customers happy and competitors at bay, while others come and go as one-hit wonders? And what lessons can such companies teach budding entrepreneurs about assessing opportunities based on the next high-tech breakthrough?

EMC is hardly a household name. The company, founded in 1979, managed brilliantly for more than two decades to keep pace with the changing needs of its customers brought about by the changing capabilities of the computer software and hardware solutions it employed. During the 1990s' bull market, EMC's 84,000 per cent stock price increase was the best in the US market, outperforming better-known companies such as Dell and Cisco. In 2001, however, another round of change hammered EMC's margins and market share. For the first time in more than a decade, EMC posted a loss for the year, losing $508 million on sales of $7.1 billion. Its once-hot stock plummeted to $7.20 in 2002, a loss of more than 90 per cent of its value since its peak in September 2000.[34] But EMC wasn't down for long, as we'll soon see. First, though, let's examine the EMC story from its earliest days.

Spotting a market – decentralised minicomputers

In August 1979, Roger Marino and Richard Egan opened shop. The two computer industry veterans were intimately familiar with the corporate computing landscape. They saw that companies were moving away from mainframe computers to minicomputers, resulting in an increasingly decentralised minicomputer marketplace.[35]

Business needs were driving the trend. Minicomputers and workstations enabled department managers and individual engineers to control their own projects and accomplish time-sensitive business tasks more effectively than centralised IT departments. With less centralised computing, data storage moved from the mainframe in the corporate data centre to decentralised servers and workstations. Egan and Marino realised that with such decentralisation, there would be a growing need for additional memory for the rapidly proliferating number of minicomputers.[36]

In response, the two concentrated on selling add-on memory for minicomputers. Their first product, introduced in 1981, was a 64-kilobyte memory board, developed for Prime Corporation. Sales for this board reached $3 million in 1982 and $18.8 million by 1984. The company soon sold improved memory capacity for minicomputers to customers like IBM, Hewlett-Packard, Wang and Digital Equipment. By the time of EMC's initial public offering in 1986, the company reported net income of $18.6 million on $66.6 million in sales.[37] Not bad for a five-year-old start-up in pre-internet time!

Market two – data storage

By the late 1980s, the memory business was becoming one of high volume and low margins, unappealing economics for a company like EMC accustomed to fat profit margins. To compound the problem, EMC was suffering from quality problems and was losing money. 'The quality of our products makes me puke,' said new Executive Vice-president for Operations Michael Ruettgers, having distributed airsickness bags to top executives to make his point graphically.

> **Ruettgers distributed airsickness bags to top executives to make his point graphically**

So in 1989, with Ruettgers' promotion to President and Chief Operating Officer, the company changed its focus from memory and memory enhancement to data storage. EMC pivoted before pivoting was cool! As Richard Egan recalled, 'We realized that [EMC] could reach a big but underpublicized market: disk storage.'[38] The trend towards decentralised computing had generated huge amounts of new data, all of which had to be stored somewhere. EMC entered the storage market with the introduction of a mainframe-compatible solid-state disk subsystem, the Orion.[39] Orion's compatibility with a variety of IBM and other mainframes, coupled with its speed, allowed EMC to continue to grow.

Market three – open storage

Technology shifted again in the mid-1990s. By then, most large companies had a number of different computer systems, most of which couldn't communicate effectively with one another. Data were everywhere, except, as it often seemed, where they were needed. Now CEO, Ruettgers realised 'There was a desire to consolidate data storage, but it would require a reliable storage system able to communicate with the variety of computers that usually exist within an organization.'[40] Ruettgers spent over $1 billion developing software that would make its storage units compatible with many types of servers.

With the introduction of its Symmetrix 5500 in 1994, EMC introduced the first platform-independent storage system, capable of simultaneously supporting virtually all major computer operating systems.[41] In 1995, EMC overtook its competitors, becoming the data storage leader, with a 41 per cent market share, up from just 5 per cent three years earlier.[42]

Market four – networked data storage

By the mid-1990s, distributed computing had become unmanageable, notwithstanding EMC's efforts to support centralised but open data storage architectures. Complicating matters was a growing tension between centralisation and decentralisation of computing power, data storage and IT systems management.[43]

EMC's answer was networked information storage, whereby far-flung data storage systems of various kinds could communicate with a company's typically far-flung network of servers.[44] EMC's enterprise storage networks wove together the hotchpotch of storage, switches, hubs and servers into a coordinated infrastructure that central IT departments could manage and scattered users running different operating systems on different platforms could use.[45] As new EMC President Joe Tucci asserted, the Symmetrix 8730 'is the industry's best-performing, most functional, most reliable, most scalable and by far most open enterprise information storage architecture'.[46] Of the 14 largest makers of servers worldwide, eight sold EMC units with their computers.[47]

Market five – along comes the internet

Every time an internet surfer purchases a book from Amazon, buys stock online or clicks on a banner ad, data are created that must be stored and tracked. For a data storage company like EMC, the advent of the internet was a veritable gold mine.[48] But EMC almost missed the internet party. 'In our business, only a few large companies provided the majority of data storage, so we focused on com-

❝EMC almost missed the internet party❞

panies with more than $500 million in revenue, 150 people in the IT department, and so forth. But suddenly there were companies with little or no revenue who were poised to immediately buy as much storage as some of our largest customers,' said Ruettgers. 'The Internet wave turned out to be much bigger and faster than we thought. It could have crashed over us.'[49]

Realising the size of this emerging new market for data storage, EMC focused its efforts not just on its usual Fortune 500 companies but also on smaller internet companies. EMC posted a record year in 2000, with sales of $8.9 billion and prospects for $12 billion in 2001.

What goes up must come down

In early 2001, the dot.com bust made the bottom drop out of high-tech, and EMC was hit hard. The market for data storage fell off a cliff:

- EMC's sales in the third quarter of 2001 fell by 47 per cent;
- the company posted a $1 billion loss in 2001, including one-time charges;[50]
- by 2002 EMC's revenues had fallen 40 per cent in two years to just $5.4 billion, and its stock price had plummeted from $100 to $4.[51]

Tucci, having taken the CEO's baton from Ruettgers in January 2001 when everything looked rosy, was faced with reinventing the company once more. Once again, EMC was up to the challenge. Tucci slashed prices, cut costs and strengthened relationships with EMC's customers.[52] With a rising tide of data sloshing its way through most businesses, Tucci also saw that the storage game had changed. 'I want to solve your information needs, not your storage needs,' Tucci says. '[We want to be a company] you can't live without.'[53]

. . . and up again!

Embarking on an aggressive stream of acquisitions, Tucci transformed EMC into an end-to-end data management solutions company, a strategy that worked. Once again, EMC was a growth machine, with revenues reaching $14.9 billion in 2008, up 12 per cent over 2007, and earnings up 7 per cent. But in the first quarter of 2009, amid a faltering global economy, sales slipped, down nearly 10 per cent from 2008, and EMC was considered takeover bait.[54] As always, EMC soon recovered, posting record sales and earnings in 2012.[55]

Then, however, EMC went on an acquisition spree, shoring up its position in cloud computing and security technology and posting full-year revenue growth of 18 per cent in 2011. 'The market is now saying EMC is likely to be a consolidator and not a consolidatee,' said Tucci.[56]

In September 2016, EMC joined forces with Dell Technologies in a stunning merger to form the world's largest privately controlled technology company. The new company, Dell EMC, blends Dell's go-to-market strength with small business and mid-market customers with EMC's strength with large enterprises. Michael Dell, chairman and CEO of Dell Technologies, explained the rationale for the deal. 'We are at the dawn of the next industrial revolution. We have the products, services, talent and global scale to be a catalyst for change and guide customers, large and small, on their digital journey.'[57]

Thinking Machines: I thought I had a market . . .

There is no question that bright people founded Thinking Machines, a supercomputer maker in Cambridge, Massachusetts. The company's founder Danny Hillis was, at the time, a graduate student at the Massachusetts Institute of Technology's Artificial Intelligence Lab.[58] For his thesis, he conceived of what is known as a massively parallel processing (MPP) computer. His idea was simple but ingenious. Unlike a regular computer that has one processor working on one piece of data at a time, parallel machines have thousands of processors working on data simultaneously.[59]

❝his idea was simple but ingenious❞

As Hillis said, 'Instead of trying to do one thing fast, a parallel processor does a lot of things at once.'[60]

Even folks like MIT's artificial intelligence guru Marvin Minsky supported the concept of starting a company that develops and sells MPPs.[61] How, then, is it possible that a company with such bright people, working on what seems to be such a clever idea, could last only 11 years before filing for bankruptcy?

A brief history of Thinking Machines

Started in 1983 with lofty ambitions but no clear business plan, Thinking Machines had two goals: to find a way to develop artificial intelligence software programs without worrying about university research funding, and to manufacture and sell supercomputers based on MPP technology. Market? Who cares?

The company was off to a running start when, in 1984, it won a $4.5 million Defense Advanced Research Projects Agency (DARPA) contract to build supercomputers for the US defence industry. With the money from DARPA, Thinking Machines developed its first MPP machine. The 5-foot-square box with flashing red lights called Connection Machine number one (CM-1) was completed in 1985 and had a $5 million price tag.[62] CM-1 had limited appeal. Its only real application was artificial intelligence, and its only buyer was DARPA. Fortunately for Thinking Machines, DARPA bought seven machines.

In 1986, Thinking Machines launched CM-2. Unlike CM-1, the newer model was able to run FORTRAN, the then-standard science computer language, and was therefore more appealing to a wider community of scientists.

With its wider appeal, Thinking Machines sold CM-2 machines to Los Alamos National Laboratory, American Express, NASA and others,[63] and by 1989 the company had sold 35 CMs, booking profits of $700,000 on $45 million in revenues.

In 1991, Thinking Machines announced its newest model, the CM-5. Like the earlier CMs, the CM-5 used anything from 32,000–64,000 processors. In techno-speak, it had teraflop capabilities, capable of performing a trillion calculations in a second. With a much more reasonable starting price of $750,000, the goal was for the CM-5 to have even broader appeal, attracting businesses as well as the scientific community. Though Hillis claimed it had the highest 'theoretical' performance of any supercomputer ever made, there was just one problem. The CM-5 was actually slower than its predecessor, the CM-2.[64]

Later in 1991, the *Wall Street Journal* uncovered a scandal between DARPA and a number of technology companies, Thinking Machines being one of them. Over the course of their seven-year relationship, DARPA had subsidised the sale of 24 CMs – sometimes offsetting the entire purchase price

– translating into $55 million or 20 per cent of Thinking Machines' lifetime revenues.[65]

The party ended quickly. With the end of a cushy era of government subsidies, Thinking Machines found itself selling its CMs on a level playing field. No longer protected from its competition, the company went head to head with the likes of Intel, Kendall Square Research, MasPar Computer and nCube. By 1992, with products that just wouldn't sell, the company reported a loss of $17 million for the year. Not long later, Thinking Machines filed for bankruptcy protection under Chapter 11, the US equivalent of insolvency in the UK.

Why did Thinking Machines fail?

While Thinking Machines did last a decade, it was not because the company had a solid footing in the supercomputer market. Rather, the company stayed afloat almost entirely because of the fortuitous, albeit somewhat scandalous, relationship it had formed with DARPA. Without DARPA, the market for MPPs was not big enough to keep Thinking Machines in business.

The root of Thinking Machines' problems can be found in both micro- and macro-market domains. In micro-market terms, it neither identified nor understood its target market. Rather than examining its market, understanding the needs of its prospective customers and then building a machine, Thinking Machines built powerful computers and hoped they would appeal to someone. As one of the company's research directors, Lew Tucker, remarked later, 'Our charter wasn't to look at a machine and figure out the commercial profit. Our charter was to build an interesting machine.'[66]

In macro-market terms, the bottom line was that Thinking Machines' interesting machines were not interesting to a big enough market. For the academic community, the CMs were far too expensive and few academics needed such power. For most applications, PCs or workstations were more than sufficient.

For the corporate community, CMs were more technology than was needed. Even for the biggest corporations, the market for computers with the CM's power was very small. Buying a CM was like using a sledgehammer to kill a fly. According to Gartner Group Vice-president Howard Richmond, 'The key is industrial acceptance, and industry does not do grand challenge applications. It makes automobiles and engines and other mundane things.'[67]

The only real market for CMs consisted of that part of the scientific community involved in solving 'grand challenges' like decoding the human genome.[68]

> **there were few such grand challenges on the radar, and even fewer entities to fund them**

But there were few such grand challenges on the radar, and even fewer entities to fund them.

What went wrong? With no clear understanding of market size or market needs before launching the company – or afterwards, for that matter – Thinking Machines had little chance of success.

Numerous dot-com businesses have suffered a similar fate for similar reasons even these days. Do we really need an Uber-for-everything?

What investors want to know

As we saw in Chapter 2, not every entrepreneur wants or needs investors. Some investors – like the three Fs: family, and some friends and fools – don't really need returns on their investments, although they'll

> **aspiring entrepreneurs should not mistake such expressions of love for confidence in the venture, nor should they treat them as affirmation of their opportunity's merit**

be happy if they get them. While they *hope* for returns, the real motivation for most of this group is to support someone they love. Aspiring entrepreneurs should not mistake such expressions of love for confidence in the venture, nor should they treat them as affirmation of their opportunity's merit!

Most other investors – business angels and venture capital investors – invest in order to achieve returns on their investments. Knowing that most new ventures fail, they expect spectacular returns on the best of their deals in order to make it worth their while to bear the significant risks they know are involved, and to pay for the deals that go bust! What sort of returns do such investors require?

A successful venture capital portfolio might, at the end of its life, have one or two in ten of its investments hit the jackpot, returning ten or one hundred times their investment or more. Two or more may return their capital,

> **fewer than 10 per cent of VC funds that actually deliver such returns!**

but little more. The remaining deals – the outright lemons – lose the firm's entire investment. It's not a pretty picture. On the other hand, if the one or two good deals are good enough, then a successful fund (that is, the fewer than 10 per cent of VC funds that actually deliver such returns!) earns an overall 20 or 30 per cent annual return over the typical ten-year life of the fund, enough to reward the partners handsomely and to make the pension funds and others who provide their capital happy indeed.

Given this picture, what sort of return do you suppose a venture capital firm seeks from each deal it invests in? A typical rule of thumb is at least ten times their investment over, say, six to ten years, a figure that amounts to something like a 60 per cent *annual* return on their investment, at minimum. Some angel investors might be happy to invest in deals with returns projected at only half this level. But what does all this have to do with market attractiveness at the macro level?

Do you know any (legal) business that returns that kind of money year after year? Invest ten pounds or ten dollars, return six, again and again? No, neither do I. The only way venture capital investors can get the kind of returns they require is for the business to grow so fast that it becomes worth far more tomorrow than it is worth today. They then sell the business, either to another company or to the public in an initial public offering. This kind of growth doesn't happen in niche markets, for there simply isn't the market potential to make it happen. Large markets are required. Nike did well in running shoes, but the overall athletic shoe market provided the scale that enabled Phil Knight and his team to grow the business substantially. Similarly, as we've seen earlier in this chapter, Twilio is disrupting a telecoms industry that Jeff Lawson thinks serves a trillion-dollar market.

Thus, if you are a would-be entrepreneur seeking capital to start your company, or if you are an angel investor seeking to generate attractive returns, market attractiveness – in macro terms – is a big deal indeed.

We need to know whether the opportunity has the potential to be big – in other words, scale.

RJ, UK

A large and growing market is not the entire story, by any means, but an opportunity lacking such a market is unlikely to be funded by professional investors. Why? Large and growing markets offer two things that investors like. First and foremost, large and growing markets offer the opportunity to build a large company, one worth much more tomorrow than today. That's good for returns. Equally important, large markets offer the chance for multiple players to be successful, each serving a different segment, perhaps in a different way. That's good for reducing risk, because it offers multiple pathways to success.

Lessons learned

We've seen why large and growing markets are important to investors and, in turn, to those who pursue high-potential opportunities through venture finance. On the other hand, if your purpose in becoming an entrepreneur is to build a business that you can control and run for a long time, without having to worry about bosses, boards of directors or others looking over your shoulder – except bankers, perhaps – then market attractiveness may work in reverse. Large, growing markets invite competitors – not exactly what you had in mind.

For you, a small and perhaps stable market or market niche – too small for the big guys to worry about – may be far more attractive. And, who knows, that niche may grow, as John Mackey happily discovered with Whole Foods. Unless you have intellectual property or other assets that can protect you from the competition that larger, faster-growing markets usually bring on – an issue to be addressed in Chapter 5 – then a smaller market where you can fly low, under the competitors' radar, may be more attractive.

So, whether you are an entrepreneur or an investor, what have we learned from the case histories we've studied in Chapter 3?

A lesson learned from Twilio

In 2008, when Jeff Lawson and his partners started Twilio, could they have foreseen the explosive adoption of smartphones and the app economy that followed soon thereafter? Perhaps not. But they did foresee the potential that cloud computing would offer, and that opportunity offered plenty of juice to get started. A key lesson for both entrepreneurs and investors is that, once a solid foundation has been built to serve one market, the lessons learned and capabilities built therein can provide the impetus and foundation for serving market number two. We've seen this phenomenon play out not only with Twilio, but also with Nike in Chapter 2 and EMC in this Chapter 3.

Lessons learned from Whole Foods Market

The story of Whole Foods Market provides dramatic evidence of the power of macro trends to create opportunities that savvy entrepreneurs can capitalise on. Such trends – in this case, sociocultural ones – create groups of customers having needs not served well by incumbent companies. The trend towards health and nutrition that began in the 1980s is still going strong, and it continues to create opportunities for entrepreneurs in every country where the trend has taken root, as we have seen with the UK's Ella's Kitchen. There, organic and other natural foods now comprise one of the fastest-growing categories in the food industry, and conventional supermarkets and others are responding to take advantage of this trend. Understanding today's macro trends is one key to discovering where tomorrow's entrepreneurial opportunities will lie. For those looking for a way to leave the corporate nest and start an entrepreneurial venture of their own, thinking carefully about macro trends can provide the impetus to make such a move possible.

> ❝Understanding today's macro trends is one key to discovering where tomorrow's entrepreneurial opportunities will lie❞

Lessons learned from EMC

For its first 20 years, EMC rode wave after wave in the high-tech world, successfully identifying and pursuing one opportunity after another. These opportunities, like those pursued by Twilio and Whole Foods Market, were driven largely by macro trends – technological ones, in this case – that created an unending cascade of new needs for data storage and related products. They then repeated that pattern each time they hit a rough patch, which ultimately delivered the high-profile merger with Dell. In an interview at the end of 2000, Michael Ruettgers identified several key practices that had enabled his company to ride the waves for ten years without being swamped.[69] These practices, some of which extend beyond the macro-market focus of this chapter, hold useful lessons for entrepreneurs assessing and pursuing their own opportunities.

- *Lesson 1:* Speed to market matters, even if all the bells and whistles are not fully in place, a practice that according to Ruettgers was, 'frustrating for engineers, who typically want to refine and refine to ensure that a product is perfect before letting it out the door. But left in their hands, a product might be released too late to catch the wave – if it ever leaves the factory at all.' But Ruettgers tempered this lesson with the next one.

- *Lesson 2:* Sell the early versions to low-profile customers in out-of-the-way locations rather than to high-profile customers where failure can be costly. As Ruettgers put it, it's like 'having out-of-town tryouts for a Broadway show'. It's not a bad idea for early-stage ventures to iron out the bugs and better understand customers' responses and real needs. Doing so can also be a precursor to raising capital, providing hard evidence – as opposed to a mere forecast – that customers will indeed buy.

- *Lesson 3:* Spend time with prospective customers. 'I talk with about 500 customers and prospects a year, which accounts for maybe 20 per cent of my time,' says Ruettgers. 'They can provide unexpected insights.' Ruettgers' conversation in the early 1990s with the Chief Information Officer of John Deere reinforced EMC's hunch that there was a real need for consolidated data storage in large companies. Some entrepreneurs think the way to perform due diligence on their opportunity is to surf the Web for market and industry data. Doing so is an important start and helps to quickly assess market size and growth rate and identify macro trends. But it's the tip of the iceberg, really. So, pick up the phone or hail a taxi, and build your customer network. It will pay great dividends.

■ *Lesson 4:* Be clear about what business you are in. In a word, focus. 'I think our focus on a single business actually helps us stay ahead of the curve. In some respects, this runs counter to what I learned in business school, where the prevailing wisdom was to diversify,' said Ruettgers. 'But our single-minded focus creates a special lens through which to view and interpret customers' current and future needs.' Budding entre- preneurs should remember how limited their resources are, in terms of time, attention, money and people. It's usually far better to focus on doing one thing exceptionally well than to spread one's efforts all over the map. For entrepreneurs, such diversity increases risk, rather than mitigating it. Focus. Focus. Focus!

Lessons learned from Thinking Machines

It's perfectly fine for the product idea – rather than the customer need – to come first, to then be followed by the necessary work to identify a market that needs what might be offered. We've seen how such a strategy was successful, at least for a while, for iMode in Japan. But Thinking Machines never really took the sec- ond step. They never really identified who the market was for the machines they would offer, and thus they never really understood what those customers needed.

This error is all too common for technology-driven opportunities, where the entrepreneurs' love for the technology can blind them to real market needs. As we saw in Chapter 2, without custom- ers there will be no company. Without benefits, there will be no customers. Identifying who the target customers are and understanding their needs are important first steps. A key element in doing so, as William Shakespeare noted in intro- ducing this chapter, is riding the tide of macro trends and taking the current where it leads. Equally important, though, as we've learned in this chapter, is to assess how many customers there

> **❝identifying who the target customers are and understanding their needs are important first steps❞**

are and how much customer spending there is – market size – and how fast these numbers will grow. Thinking Machines ignored all these steps, to their eventual peril.

The new business road test: stage two – the macro-market test

- What sort of business do you want? One with potential to become a huge business, or a small 'lifestyle' operation servicing a niche market? Without answering this question first, you cannot assess for your particular opportunity the meaning of the others below.

- How large is the market you are seeking to serve? In how many ways have you measured it?

- How fast has it grown over the last one/three/five years?

- How quickly will it grow in the next six months or two/five/ten years?

- What economic, demographic, sociocultural, technological, regulatory or natural trends can you identify that will affect your market, and what effect, favourable or otherwise, will these trends have on your business?

- Based on the evidence you compile in answering the above questions, what key macro-market risks remain, to which early attention should be given?

This information can be found from secondary sources – library materials or information from the internet – and from primary sources too. What information on market trends can you glean from talking to your potential customers, suppliers or competitors?

Finally, are you seeking venture capital? If your market's not huge and/or growing rapidly, then forget it.

THE NEW BUSINESS ROAD TEST

If you open your *New Business Road Test* app, you'll find the above checklist reproduced there. As you surf the Web or talk to experts to find macro-market data on market size, growth rates and trends, you'll find places to keep track of links to your online sources or record what you glean from your conversations or interviews. But don't forget that your task isn't simply to *gather* market data; it's to *make judgements* from what the data tell you, whether that's good news or bad. So be certain to make note of any key risks, and to then indicate your tentative conclusion about the overall attractiveness of your market at the macro level, as that conclusion evolves. Without drawing any conclusion, you risk fooling yourself later on.

4

Is this an attractive industry?

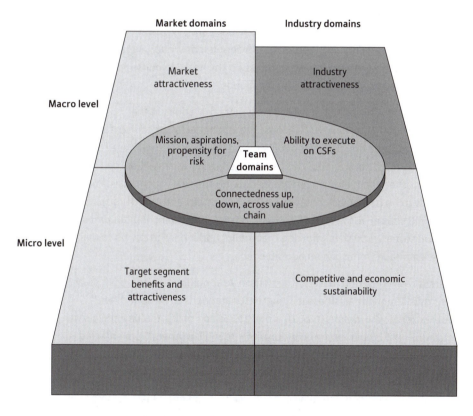

Your name is Thomas Collins – Tommy to your friends. You are ten years old. You live in a suburb of a city in the Midlands where your family has lived since well before you were born. It is a quiet and safe neighbourhood of mid-sized homes. While the neighbourhood was at one time a haven for young families, it has evolved into a community comprised predominantly of retirees.

This leaves you and your brother with only a few neighbourhood pals and a lot of surrogate grandparents.

For the past two summers, you have spent your time building a profitable lemonade business. Your lemonade stand is made of a folding card table and a large piece of poster board attached to a wooden post, admittedly not very fancy. Your lemonade recipe is your grandmother Mary's award-winning combination of lemons, sugar, water, ice and a splash of orange juice.

You have a pretty good set-up. Each Monday, your mother goes to the local grocery store to do her weekly shopping. You put in your request for lemons, cups, sugar and orange juice, and you store all of your materials in the unused refrigerator in the garage. Your mother is proud of her entrepreneurial child and does not mark up the cost of goods. To date, she has always been a very reliable supplier – providing you with sufficient lemons, cups, sugar and orange juice each Monday afternoon. Mum tallies up the cost of your supplies and requests payment when you receive the goods.

With a neighbourhood full of retired folks, very few adults in the neighbourhood work nine-to-five jobs. This is wonderful, of course, for your business, as there are plenty of people taking walks every day. These retirees are, for the most part, middle class – finally enjoying their well-earned pensions. The grandparent-aged adults dote on the few young faces. Yours happens to be particularly cute – with lots of freckles and two chubby cheeks. While you squirm at the thought of having your cheeks pinched ten times a day, you suffer through it, knowing that adults find it hard to say no to a glass of icy lemonade from such an adorable face.

There is really only one reason other kids in your neighbourhood don't start their own lemonade businesses. That reason happens to be your older brother Terry, who weighs in at 10 stone at the age of 13. You pay him a small retainer – just 10 per cent of your profits – to inhibit others from entering this profitable industry. Your retainer has been well worth it. No kids in your neighbourhood have dared to start a lemonade business.

All in all, you have done quite well for yourself. At the end of last summer, you purchased a brand new mountain bike, and this summer you are saving up for an iPad. While you attribute your good fortune to Grandma Mary's recipe, Terry's domineering presence and your chubby cheeks, the reality is that you have found yourself in a great industry – one that allows you to prosper quite profitably.

Good industries, good businesses

When a management with a reputation for brilliance takes on a business with a reputation for bad economics, it's the reputation of the business that remains intact.

Warren Buffett, noted investor[1]

Why is the lemonade stand industry so good to Tommy? As we saw in Chapter 1, industry attractiveness is determined in large part by the five forces – threat of entry, supplier power, buyer power, threat of substitutes and competitive rivalry – so let's take a look at them in Tommy's case.

Threat of entry

With only some lemonade and his stand – made out of a folding card table and a large piece of poster board – there were no significant start-up costs that would deter others from entering Tommy's industry. This is not a knowledge-intensive industry. Just about anyone can figure out how to make lemonade: no barrier to entry here, either. And, at present, Tommy has no protection for his intellectual property – recipes cannot be copyrighted or patented. However, Tommy's big older brother – who takes a 10 per cent cut of all proceeds – is responsible for scaring off competitors. So far, he has done a tremendous job. Terry's presence really does put a dampener on anyone's decision to enter this industry, in his and Tommy's neighbourhood at least. There appears to be little threat of entry.

Supplier power

Mum buys lemons, cups, sugar and orange juice from the supermarket each week, and does not take a cut on these raw material sales. Not only that, but Mum is also pretty fair, asking that Tommy pays for his raw materials upon receipt. Fortunately, the local supermarket carries plenty of lemons, cups, orange juice and sugar, so Tommy never has to worry about a back order. If for some reason Mum didn't want to be his supplier any longer, Tommy is sure that one of his elderly neighbours would gladly fill in on similar terms. All told, the power of suppliers to Tommy's industry is weak, which is favourable for his industry – lemonade stands.

Buyer power

Tommy's customers, the grandparent-aged people who dote on the few young kids in the community, have a decent amount of disposable income and seem to enjoy hydrating themselves with fresh lemonade. With no other lemonade stands in the neighbourhood, Tommy's friendly neighbours have no way of switching to another fresh lemonade provider within walking distance. These buyers are content with the status quo and exert no pressure on sellers like Tommy to change his operations or lower his prices. The power of lemonade buyers is weak. That's good for his neighbourhood industry.

Threat of substitutes

Those who need a caffeine fix can always head to Nancy Lipton's iced tea stand a couple of streets away. Her prices are competitive with Tommy's. Some people are carrying water – either bottled or tap – or fruit drinks on their neighbourhood walks these days. The reality is that many substitutes for Tommy's product do exist. This is the biggest downside for his industry, but so far his winning smile seems to keep the customers coming back.

Competitive rivalry

Thanks to Terry, there are no other lemonade stands in Tommy's neighbourhood. If there were, they would be unlikely to offer better prices than Tommy's. The local grocery store does, however, offer freshly squeezed lemonade, but at a much higher price. That said, Tommy has been selling *Tommy's Own* lemonade for two summers now, and the brand has begun to catch on. Terry's reputation, coupled with the lack of many other children in the neighbourhood, makes this competitive landscape fairly barren. Little rivalry is good news for lemonade stand operators like Tommy.

Overall assessment of industry attractiveness

The five forces analysis indicates that Tommy's industry is quite attractive, as four of the five forces are favourable. The only unfavourable one – threat of substitutes – does not seem severe. Tommy has chosen a good industry in which to play, which undoubtedly helps Tommy's profitability.

In reality, few industries are quite as attractive as this scenario, nor is any industry nearly as neat, simple and easy to analyse. Let's turn our attention to the real world, where we examine industries that are by no means as attractive or simplistic as the one in which Tommy competes. But first, there's the matter of industry definition to attend to.

Defining your industry

Is Tommy Collins in the lemonade stand industry or the wider food service industry? Is easyJet in the airline industry or the transportation industry? Is Ball Corporation in the aluminium can industry or the packaging industry? You cannot assess your industry, of course, without first identifying the one in which you will compete.

❝you cannot assess your industry without first identifying the one in which you will compete❞

The real question here, for entrepreneurs and investors alike, is whether it's better to define your industry narrowly or broadly. Defining industries narrowly has some merit. It can clarify your focus as to who the principal competitors are, which helps in assessing competitive rivalry. Doing so also can help you think clearly about differentiation, an important issue, as we saw in Chapter 2. EasyJet competes with Ryanair, British Airways, Air France and so on. But a narrow industry definition can, if you are not careful, make it easy to overlook relevant substitutes, which, in some industries, are crucially important. Ball Corporation must worry about glass, paper and plastic packaging companies in addition to other aluminium can makers, for example. In wooing its leisure traveller customers, easyJet must consider rail and the car.

Defining one's industry broadly also has merit, for it brings substitutes – glass and plastic packaging makers, for Ball for example – directly into the rivalry assessment. Doing so may decrease your chance of being surprised by substitutes that might otherwise be overlooked. A broad industry definition also makes it easier to consider changes in your offering that might enhance its marketability. Viewing his industry as food service, Tommy might decide to add cookies to his lemonade stand. On the downside, viewing things too broadly may lead to a lack of focus. In cash-starved entrepreneurial start-ups, focus is essential. There simply aren't enough resources to do very many things well.

"in cash-starved entrepreneurial start-ups, focus is essential"

So, what's the answer? There isn't an easy one. It's generally worth thinking both broadly and narrowly. The key point, though, is that your industry, as well as other substitute industries, consists of other sellers – not customers, not products – of goods or services that meet the kinds of customer needs that you hope to satisfy.

Does your industry matter?

In Chapter 2, we saw that selling what customers want to buy is important to entrepreneurial success – no great surprise. In Chapter 3, we examined the implications of large, growing markets and smaller niche markets, both of which can be attractive to entrepreneurs, and perhaps their investors, under different circumstances. But most of the time, having a product that customers want to buy and an attractive market are not sufficient to build an entrepreneurial venture over the longer term. That's the case because some *industries* just aren't very attractive – the profitability of most companies in these industries is mediocre and, in the worst industries, the failure rate is uncomfortably high.

"having a product that customers want to buy and an attractive market are not sufficient to build an entrepreneurial venture over the longer term"

As we saw in Chapter 1 and again in the lemonade stand example, industry attractiveness is best assessed using Michael Porter's[2] five forces framework. The key questions are listed in Table 4.1. Chapter 14 addresses each of the five forces in greater detail, and notes the importance of reaching an overall industry assessment once all of the forces have been analysed. After all, you really want to know how attractive – or not – your industry is if you are intending to enter it, whether in a lean manner or otherwise! Note also that an industry analysis and the judgement that flows from it have little to do with *your* company, *your* strategy or *your* products, no matter how wonderful they may be from a market or competitive advantage perspective. Even if you decide to enter your industry, you probably won't materially impact its structure or attractiveness, at least not any time soon, despite your fondest intentions!

Table 4.1   Five macro-level questions to assess your industry

The five forces	Questions to ask	Answers that entrepreneurs want to hear
Threat of entry	Is it easy or difficult for companies to enter this industry?	Entrepreneurs planning a very quick exit are happy if it's easy to enter (so they can get in). Those hoping to build more enduring ventures prefer high barriers to entry (so others cannot easily follow).
Supplier power	Do suppliers to this industry have the power to set terms and conditions?	Entrepreneurs prefer weak supplier power.
Buyer power	Do buyers have the power to set terms and conditions?	Entrepreneurs prefer weak buyer power.
Threat of substitutes	Is it easy or difficult for substitute products to steal my market?	Entrepreneurs prefer little threat of substitutes.
Competitive rivalry	Is competitive rivalry intense or genteel?	Entrepreneurs prefer little competitive rivalry.

Based on all five forces, what is your overall assessment of your industry? Just how attractive or unattractive is it?

In this chapter, we examine the case histories of two industries, both of which have seen extensive entrepreneurial activity in recent years. First is the global pharmaceutical industry, an industry that has for many years had the reputation of being enormously profitable and having a very favourable competitive climate. Is it still so attractive? Read on. We then look at the so-called daily deals industry, which, despite vast infusions of venture capital, has suffered from a far less attractive competitive landscape. In both examples, we use the five forces model to assess industry attractiveness. Finally, we take a brief look at industry attractiveness in the dot.com world, where many of today's aspiring entrepreneurs hope to play.

The pharmaceutical industry in the 1980s

In the 1970s and 1980s, the average profit margin (as a percentage of revenues) of the Fortune 500 pharmaceutical companies was two times greater than the median for all industries in the Fortune 500.[3] Each drug introduced between 1981 and 1983 'made at least $36 million more for its investors, after taxes, than was needed to pay off the costs to develop it . . . Such profitability was two to three percentage points greater than for comparable industries, even after factoring in the risks of new drug development.'[4] Nearly two decades later, in 1999, the industry was still a star. The pharmaceutical industry ranked at the top in all three of *Fortune* magazine's measures of profitability: return on sales, return on assets and return on equity.[5] What made the global pharmaceutical industry so profitable for so long? Why has its profitability remained so strong, and will the industry remain so attractive?

Threat of entry

For an entrepreneur, high barriers to entry make it more difficult to launch a venture. But happily, for those who are somehow able to enter, these same barriers serve to protect their ventures once they have joined the party. Thus, while barriers to entry can be considered

❝barriers serve to protect their ventures once they have joined the party❞

obstacles for the entrepreneur, they also serve to keep competitors out of the industry. A number of barriers mute the threat of entry into the pharmaceutical industry. These include barriers both financial and intangible in nature, ranging from high fixed costs to stringent intellectual property protection. Let's look in some detail at conditions in the pharmaceutical industry in the 1980s.

Heavy expenditures on research and development were (and still are) required for the arduous processes of drug discovery, development, manufacturing, and approval through the various regulatory bodies, such as the Food and Drug Administration (FDA) in the USA and the Commission on Human Medicines in the UK.[6] The process of developing a drug was time-consuming, expensive and precarious. During the 1980s, it took an average of 12 years and $194 million to bring a drug to market.[7] And the long and tedious process, which included research and development, clinical trials and government approval, did not guarantee favourable results, as more than 50 per cent of all development dollars were spent on products that never reached the market.[8] The sheer size of an investment like this, coupled with the great uncertainty of whether there would be a payoff, was a powerful barrier to deter those who might have entered the industry.

Research and development were not the only exorbitant costs. Sales and marketing costs were also substantial, as pharmaceutical companies spent large sums promoting their drugs to hospitals and doctors. To compete effectively against the industry's leaders, a new company had to spend millions of dollars annually on large salesforces and other marketing and promotional activities.[9]

Substantial as these financial barriers were, they paled in comparison to the protection that governments placed on intellectual property. Companies generally won patents for their new drugs. These patents were issued on either the drug's chemical structure or its method of manufacturing or synthesis. This highly favourable competitive environment, in which drug companies obtained patents to protect them from rivals, meant that competitors were effectively blocked from manufacturing and marketing drugs with the same chemical composition for 17 years, which equated to between 8 and 12 years once the drug actually got to market.[10]

The result? In terms of threat of entry, the picture of the pharmaceutical industry in the 1980s was clear. Entry barriers were extremely high, resulting in little threat of entry, a very favourable condition for industry incumbents and for new pharmaceutical start-ups that could find a way to enter.

Supplier power

Pharmaceutical companies were flooded with raw material suppliers anxious to sell to such a strong and profitable industry. In 1982, there were over 12,000 chemical companies in the USA alone.[11] Their products had long shelf lives, most were readily available from numerous sources and were bought largely on the basis of price and delivery.[12] These conditions left the chemical suppliers with little power to set the terms and conditions under which their raw chemicals were sold to the drug companies. From the drug companies' point of view, supplier power was virtually non-existent.

❝from the drug companies' point of view, supplier power was virtually non-existent❞

Buyer power

How would you like to be in an industry where your buyers are uninformed about your product and almost 100 per cent insensitive to its price? Not only that, but imagine that there are few if any substitutes for your product, and that using it may be a matter of life or death for your consumer. These were, for the most part, the circumstances prevailing in the pharmaceutical industry through the 1980s. The industry enjoyed an almost powerless group of buyers. Drug companies reaped the benefits of unaware doctors who were partial to prescribing brand-name drugs to obtain the most medically effective solution, regardless of price; price-insensitive patients who did not care about the cost of their prescription medications; ill-informed consumers who blindly trusted their doctors'

❝the industry enjoyed an almost powerless group of buyers❞

treatment suggestions; and few alternatives to prescription drugs.[13] The weakness in buyer power contributed significantly to the profitability of the pharmaceutical companies.

These companies also benefited from consumer trends in Europe and North America towards health and nutrition. Consumers were increasingly eager to do whatever it took to become or stay healthy. Further, consumers had the luxury of being indifferent to drug prices because most of them did not pay full price for their medications. Rather, through the 1980s in most developed countries, government agencies, insurance companies or employers paid the patients' prescription drug bills. And without easy access to information on medications, customers had little say in their treatment plans.

Threat of substitutes

Until the mid-1980s, the global pharmaceutical industry was largely unthreatened by substitute products. If a patient was ill, they took the medicine the doctor ordered. Patent laws prohibited companies from replicating others' brand-name drugs for as long as 17 years, and other regulations deterred the development of chemically equivalent generic drugs. For most conditions treatable by prescription drugs, there simply were no substitutes for the medications the doctors prescribed.

Competitive rivalry

The pharmaceutical industry of the 1980s was populated by hundreds of companies, though none had more than 5 per cent market share. There were two main reasons the pharmaceutical industry was so fragmented.

- Different companies focused on entirely different classes of drugs. These classes included cardiovascular treatments, antibiotics, central nervous system therapy, gastrointestinal treatments, etc.

- The industry's growth rate made it easy for companies to grow without taking share from one another. There was little pressure to expand beyond one's niche, given abundant opportunities for growth therein.

The result of this fragmentation was that most firms had few direct competitors. The lack of direct competition allowed drug companies to raise prices as they pleased. Couple this lack of competition with a weak threat from

❛❛the industry experienced little dissent when raising prices❜❜

substitutes and little buyer power, and the industry experienced little dissent when raising prices to meet profit objectives. Competitive rivalry was almost non-existent.

Summary of industry attractiveness in the 1980s

The result of these industry conditions was impressive profit growth through the middle of the 1980s. With significant barriers to entry, docile suppliers, powerless buyers, almost no threat of substitutes and little rivalry, the pharmaceutical industry in the 1980s was just about as perfect an industry as one could imagine. Given its attractiveness, the industry attracted the attention of genetic and molecular biology scientists and the venture capital community, who saw its appeal and thought their revolutionary approaches to drug therapy could attract enough money to overcome the formidable entry barriers the industry enjoyed. They, too, wanted to join the party!

Thus, as scientific advances in biotechnology took hold, numerous entrepreneurial companies like Genentech and Amgen were founded to commercialise new scientific breakthroughs. Genentech, the first biotech firm to have commercial success, developed a protein that broke up blood clots. Amgen's molecular biology used recombinant DNA to produce erythropoietin, a hormone that increases the supply of red blood cells in anaemic patients under treatment for cancer and other diseases. By 2000, erythropoietin was generating $2 billion in sales and another $3 billion in licensing revenue for Amgen.[14] Both of these new entrants fared very well.

- Genentech went public in 1980, and by 2001 its shares had appreciated 2,700 per cent since its IPO. In 2004, Genentech earned $785 million in profits and its market capitalisation of $83 billion surpassed that of Merck, the longtime pharmaceutical giant.[15] In 2009, Roche, the Swiss pharmaceutical powerhouse, bought the 44 per cent of Genentech that it did not already own for a whopping $46.8 billion, some 22 times expected 2010 earnings and a market capitalisation of $106 billion for Genentech. Analysts hailed the acquisition as the best of 2009's big drug deals.[16]

- Amgen shares, first offered in 1983, soared more than 16,000 per cent by 2001.[17] In 2004, Amgen earned $2.4 billion.[18] Growth continued steadily and by 2008, Amgen's earnings reached $15 billion.[19]

Was the pharmaceutical industry an attractive industry in which to play? The venture capitalists that backed Genentech, Amgen and other companies like them have not been disappointed, in spite of the fact that the biotech segment of the industry has remained unprofitable as a whole.[20] Saddled with the enormous costs of developing new drugs and the lengthy and uncertain processes required to test new drugs for safety and efficacy, and lacking the cash flow that the older drug companies enjoy from their earlier blockbuster drugs, most biotechs' roads have been much more difficult. But for Amgen, Genentech and a few others whose early discoveries hit the charts, the high entry barriers were worth tackling.

Thus, for entrepreneurs who can marshal the resources to overcome high barriers to entry – and who have something to sell that customers want to buy – attractive industries like pharmaceuticals can be rewarding places to play.

The pharmaceutical industry in the twenty-first century

Alas for the drug makers, industries are not static places. Like the rest of the business world, industries are dynamic, subject to ever-changing environments. The pharmaceutical industry has not remained quite as cushy as it once was. Let's look at what has changed.

Threat of entry

Starting in the mid-1980s, the barriers to enter the pharmaceutical industry began to show cracks. New legislation made it easier for generic drug companies to enter the market. In the USA, the 1984 Hatch-Waxman Act, which changed the rules for generic drug manufacturers, reduced the barriers to generic entry. Instead of having to prove the generic drug's safety and efficacy, the Act required companies only to prove their formulas were equivalent to that of the brand-name drug. The subsequent growth in generic drugs was profound. By 1996, generic drugs accounted for more than 40 per cent of pharmaceutical prescriptions.[21] In 2003, the Food and Drug Administration (FDA) introduced further regulations limiting the ability of patent-holders to delay the onset of generic competition, so the market share held by generics began to grow even more.[22]

> **in the mid-1980s, the barriers to enter the pharmaceutical industry began to show cracks**

Aside from the influx of generics, the pharmaceutical companies also saw a wave of biotechnology competitors enter their industry – Genentech and Amgen had been good role models – suggesting that economies of scale meant less than they used to, and that barriers to entry, while still high in absolute terms, were dropping, thanks in part to the availability of venture capital.[23] Further, the biotech companies' new science-focused research model, known as rational drug design, stood the traditional approach to drug discovery on its head. These drug companies worked backwards from known disease biochemistry to identify or design chemical 'keys' to fit the biochemical 'locks' of that disease.[24]

The result of these changes? Barriers to entry crept lower, increasing the threat of entry and making the industry somewhat less attractive.

Buyer power

Beginning in the mid-1980s, three developments gradually began to increase the power of the pharmaceutical industry's buyers:

∎ the growing strength of managed care in the USA, the industry's largest market;

∎ increased pressure from governments, especially in Europe;

∎ a better-informed patient population.

The American transition from an insurance-based healthcare system to one of managed care changed the dynamics of the pharmaceutical industry dramatically. By 1993, 80 per cent of the US population was covered by managed care organisations (MCOs), compared with 5 per cent of the US population covered in 1980. These MCOs typically provided full coverage for prescription drugs. But, because of their sheer mass, these institutions had considerable bargaining power with drug companies, and exerted downward pressure on drug prices.[25] Thus, while patients maintained their price insensitivity for drugs, their healthcare payers were far more price-sensitive.

To further increase drug-price awareness in the American medical community, health maintenance organisations (HMOs) set up formularies (lists comparing the prices and benefits of various drugs). HMOs regularly updated these formularies, deciding which drugs to endorse. If the HMOs did not approve a certain drug, then doctors affiliated with the HMO could not prescribe it. Of course, it is not surprising that HMOs favoured the less expensive generic drugs over brand-name drugs. In 1995, a *Medical Marketing & Media* article claimed: 'Pharmaceuticals appear headed for commodity status, pushed by generics, formularies, and other cost pressures.'[26]

The American HMOs were not the only ones putting downward pressure on drug pricing. European governments established price controls, limiting prices at which prescription drugs could be sold.[27] In the UK, a new government agency, the National Institute for Clinical Excellence (NICE), was established to determine the cost-effectiveness of drugs before the National Health Service (NHS) would pay for them, and the Drug Tariff capped prices at which the NHS would reimburse dispensing pharmacists for individual medications.

In addition, by the turn of the century, the coming of age of the internet generated approximately 100,000 health-related websites and online pharmacies. Empowered with more information, patients became more knowledgeable and, consequently, more powerful. And, with new legislation that now permitted prescription drug advertising in the USA, patients there began taking a more active and knowledgeable role in their medical decision-making.[28] Similarly, in the UK it was estimated that by 2011, one in seven people was buying prescription medication online, severely reducing the influence of the doctor, who had been the established sales channel of pharmaceutical firms.[29]

❝buyer power had increased❞

Other sources of buyer power also emerged. In 2009, 'comparative effectiveness' studies proposed by the Obama administration mandated drug comparison trials that would reveal whether a specific name brand drug truly had a better effect than a cheaper generic drug: a welcome test for consumers and HMOs, but not for drug makers.[30] In 2016, CEO Heather Bresch of Mylan, a specialty pharmaceutical company, was called before the US government to explain a 500 per cent price increase for its EpiPen, and in the UK, Pfizer was fined £84.2m for overcharging the NHS.[31] Taken together, these events suggested that governments were beginning to take drug pricing seriously. As a result of these and other pressures, buyer power increased considerably. The result of this increase in buyer power was additional downward price pressure on prescription drugs.

Threat of substitutes

Not only were direct competition from generic drugs and better access to information impacting the industry, but trends towards more natural therapies also led consumers to try substitutes for prescription drugs. Exercise, nutrition and herbal remedies all began to take market share from the prescription drug makers.

Competitive rivalry

Throughout the late 1980s and the early 1990s, rivalry in the pharmaceutical industry increased. Given the new pressures described above, traditional drug companies felt the pressure to consolidate to take advantage of economies of scale.[32] By choosing to merge, rivalry among the top firms increased, as their areas of expertise began to overlap.

Additional rivalry stemmed from the flood of more science-focused drug discovery firms. While some biotechs were purchased by the large drug companies, others such as Amgen became strong competitors in their own right.[33] Unlike the drug companies, biotechs were not burdened with high overheads, and some possessed superior product and disease knowledge in their chosen segments.[34] Rational drug design enabled them to discover new therapeutic compounds more quickly and more efficiently than before.[35] While traditionally these biotechs had discovered new drugs and then sold their discoveries to established drug companies, this pattern seemed to be changing. Some began not only to discover but also to develop and market their own drugs.[36]

The reduced barriers to entry of generic drugs also exacerbated the industry's competitive rivalry, with the global generics market predicted to reach $35 billion by 2020.[37] Making matters worse, the pharma industry overall was expected to lose $215 billion in sales due to patent expirations between 2015 and 2020.[38] Thus, the pharmaceutical industry found itself with a whole new set of competitors, some of which were more agile and science-focused, some lower-priced.

❝the pharmaceutical industry found itself with a whole new set of competitors❞

Summary of industry attractiveness in the early twenty-first century

How has the industry fared in light of these developments? A study by the US Congressional Budget Office concluded that, 'since 1984, the expected returns from marketing a new drug have declined by about 12 per cent, or $27 million in 1990 dollars. That decline has not made drug development unprofitable on average, but it may have made some specific projects unprofitable.'[39]

The changing industry environment has had a clearly measurable impact on industry profitability. In 2000, the pharmaceutical industry ranked as the most profitable industry in the USA, with a return on assets of 17.7 per cent.[40] But by 2005, the industry had fallen to ninth position on the *Fortune* magazine list of most profitable industries, with a return on assets of 10.3 per cent, down more than 40 per cent in just five years.[41]

From 2006 through to 2009, the industry's average return on assets ranged between 10.5 and 11.5 per cent.[42] Despite its challenges, however, the pharmaceutical industry has held up remarkably well. In 2016, the return on assets for the biotechnology and drugs industry was 13.47 per cent, second only to tobacco, according to CSI Market, a provider of financial information and analysis.[43]

> **"while not consistently as attractive a place to compete as it had been earlier, the pharmaceutical industry remained more attractive than most"**

While not consistently as attractive a place to compete as it had been earlier, the pharmaceutical industry remained more attractive than most. Why?

- Threat of entry remained comparatively low, despite the incursion of generic drug makers and biotech firms. Starting a pharmaceutical company isn't nearly so simple as, say, starting a restaurant or an airline.

- Buyer power had increased – a genuine problem.

- But suppliers to the industry still lacked power – good news.

- Substitutes such as exercise, nutrition and herbal medicines were no match for many prescription therapies for cancer and other life-threatening illnesses.

- Competitive rivalry, despite some challenging factors, remained relatively modest, as the drug companies, having common interests, sought to protect their traditionally high profit margins.

Thus, the pharmaceutical industry remained an attractive place to play, far more so than most industries, including the daily deals industry which we examine next. Will this continue to be the case, or will the pressure of these trends erode the industry's attractiveness further? Only time will tell.

The daily deals industry

In late 2008, when many recession-pressed small businesses were struggling and many consumers were watching their pennies, a new way of shopping was launched. Groupon, the first daily deals website, used the buying power of its groups of customers as an incentive for small businesses to create time-bound special offers. Groupon founder Andrew Mason took the company from a tiny start-up to a multi-billion-dollar valuation in less than three years, raising six rounds of venture capital along the way.[44] Groupon became the fastest company to be valued at $1 billion (it was among the earliest 'unicorns'),[45] raised some $700 million on NASDAQ in November 2011, and earned a $17.8 billion market capitalisation in the eyes of eager investors in its post-IPO bounce.[46] It was the largest IPO by an American internet company since Google's IPO in 2004.

It appeared to consumers and investors alike that Groupon had uncovered a vast new *market* for sending 'daily deals' to consumers' email inboxes.

> **But was the daily deals *industry* robust enough to prosper in the long-run?**

Indeed, it had. But was the daily deals *industry* robust enough to prosper in the long run? Let's examine the industry's five forces and see what we can learn.

Threat of entry

Groupon executed its business model exceedingly well. It hired armies of salespeople to knock on small businesses' doors, offering them an opportunity to bring in (supposedly) new customers at a one-time discount price – 50 per cent off lunch, next week only, if you pay now! Groupon was paid by the consumer's credit card when the deal was purchased online, remitting payment to the merchant (less Groupon's cut, of course) in a series of installments over as many as 60 days, once the deals had been redeemed. Alas, the model was too good to be true and too easy to copy.

A huge number of similar sites followed globally, most notably LivingSocial in the USA in 2009 and the Chinese site Meituan in 2010. It was easy to do. Any entrepreneur could knock on doors in their own geographic area, write some code, and, 'Voila!' they're in business. And with Groupon's astonishing growth, investors were all too eager to back them in hopes of duplicating Groupon's apparent success elsewhere. LivingSocial managed to raise a total of $928m over nine rounds between July 2008 and February 2013.[47] With this kind of funding available for copycat players, the threat of entry proved to be exceedingly high – bad news for the industry!

Supplier power

One strong daily deal could make the difference between failure and success to a struggling small business, or so the owners of such businesses thought, especially a new one looking to make its mark; merchants were queuing up to join in. The visibility that a promotion gave was seductive. Even though a business typically had to give 50 per cent of the selling price back to Groupon or any other daily deals website, the no-cash-up-front method of gaining new customers made it seem worth it. The merchants, the key suppliers to Groupon and its copycats, weren't going to quarrel with the terms. And, as small businesses, they had little power to argue anyway. Supplier power was not a problem.

Buyer power

In the early days, in any new geographical area, consumers came in droves, eagerly anticipating tomorrow's daily deal and its discount. They tried things that they had been wanting to experience – a new restaurant here (or perhaps a deal at their neighbourhood favourite), a new hair salon there – even a deal on laser surgery to correct their vision. They experimented with different brands instead of sticking to their usual brand or treated themselves because the price was just too good. Thus buyers, who had no power anyway, were certainly not complaining about saving money.

Threat of substitutes

Alas, as the novelty wore off, customers soon tired of opening and considering the growing flood of daily deals, reverting to their usual behaviour. How many daily deals do *you* want to peruse in your inbox?

❝How many daily deals do *you* want to peruse in your inbox?❞

Brand loyalty and habit trumped new experiences. Traditional shopping with its regular sales – either brick-and-mortar or online – was enough to satisfy customers, who found many other things to do with their time and money. Thus daily deals industry was not the only place where consumers could get good deals. The threat of substitutes was very high.

Competitive rivalry

Very quickly, the daily deal industry found itself saturated with competitors, many of whom had received VC investment. Market leaders like Groupon and LivingSocial, flush with boatloads of venture capital, began to buy smaller companies in order to access new geographies and eliminate their growing competition, but this consolidation presented new challenges, as there were multiple well-funded competitors competing to buy the smaller operators, driving up costs.

Meanwhile, on the ground, the daily deal players were competing with one another to sign up merchants, too. But the merchants were discovering that the one-time offers were not bringing in new repeat customers. Worse, the low margins they earned on the daily deals meant their profitably was suffering. And slow payment by the daily deal providers was hurting their cash flow. The result? Many merchants simply stopped signing up.

The industry unravels

By the end of 2012, Groupon's stock plummeted to around a quarter of its IPO level and questions were being asked over the longevity of its business model. In early 2013 founder and CEO Mason was fired. Technology consultant and prominent Groupon critic Rakesh Agarwal noted, though, that Mason's departure was little more than a symbolic gesture, as the company's structural challenges remained in place.[48]

After having undergone significant expansion through acquisition, Groupon began to reduce its market presence, from 47 countries at the beginning of 2015 to 15 countries by the end of 2017.[49] In November 2016, Groupon bought its largest competitor, LivingSocial, for an undisclosed sum. It was reported that the 'acquisition consideration is not material'[50] and some have speculated that Groupon bought LivingSocial for less than $20m,[51] an ignominious end for a company into which investors had poured $928 million. The daily deals industry has whimpered to a shadow of its former self, as the survivors scrambled for new ways to do business that did not depend on daily deals.

Summary of industry attractiveness: daily deals

Virtually no barriers to entry. A substantial threat of substitutes from other sources of deals, from brick-and-mortar retail sales to flash sales websites to Overstock.com. And overwhelming competitive rivalry. Is anyone surprised that daily deals companies did not fly for long?

At least in the industry's early days, the *market* for daily deals appeared vast. At the micro level, too, a global economic downturn was putting the squeeze on consumers' wallets, and daily deals offered at least some relief. As time went on, however, consumers grew tired of the email clutter and merchants lost interest. Thus, what had appeared to be an attractive market soon slumped. The real killer, however, was the industry, which was structurally unsound.

Industry attractiveness in the dot.com world

In today's dot.com world, it's easier than ever to start a new business. Write or assemble some code, design a website, and off you go, or so the story goes at the plethora of start-up weekends and hackathons that are all the rage! There's a considerable amount of truth to this perspective, because it is both easy and inexpensive to get started in virtually any online business today. But do you really want to compete in any of the numerous industries where this is possible?

Consider the flash sales industry, where web-based merchants like Vente Privée, Gilt Groupe and others offered discounts on various kinds of merchandise – from designer apparel to fine wine – but for only a limited time and in limited quantities. Sadly, and to the considerable disappointment of their VC backers, they've fared little better than their daily deals cousins, with plummeting valuations, business failures and fight-to-survive consolidation all over the map. 'What about taxi-hailing services, such as Uber and MyTaxi?', you might ask. Or food delivery, or travel websites such as Airbnb, or the spate of subscription business that arose in 2012 and 2013 in almost any category imaginable?

If you are considering starting or investing in a new venture like any of these, I suggest you run a five forces analysis before you get too excited, and see what you think about their industry's long-term prognosis. Will some of them suffer a fate similar to daily deals and flash sales? Whatever your analysis foretells, however, does a bad industry always mean you should abandon your dot.com idea? Not necessarily, as we'll see. It is possible, of course, to build a successful and valuable dot.com company, as Twilio's Jeff Lawson, Amazon's Jeff Bezos and Facebook's Mark Zuckerberg, among others, have shown. Perhaps you can, too. But given the daunting conditions in most dot.com industries, successes like theirs are outliers, not the norm.

What investors want to know

A common myth is that investors invest in good ideas and good management teams. If you're an early-stage investor, there's probably an element of truth for you in both parts of this statement. The essence of venture capital investing, according to Silicon Valley investor Bob Zider,[52] is this: "The reality is that [venture capitalists] invest in good industries – that is, industries that are more competitively forgiving than the market as a whole.'

> **❝The reality is that [venture capitalists] invest in good industries❞**

What Zider's statement means, in five forces terms, is little threat of entry (i.e. high barriers to keep future competitors out), weak supplier and buyer power, little threat of substitutes (thereby limiting competition from other industries) and little competitive rivalry. Since these are crucial issues to investors, entrepreneurs who intend to seek capital at some point would do well to have invested some time and effort to understand them fully for the industry they propose to enter.

Most institutional investors have already made clear and conscious decisions about the industries they will and will not invest in. Many go so far as to make this information public in various venture capital industry directories or other guides, and often on their websites.[53] If the industry you want to enter with your new venture is one that a particular investor has already identified as within their scope, then the chances are good that they will already know a great deal about the industry, perhaps far more than you do. Thus, doing your industry analysis homework, using the lessons of this chapter, can help you establish your own credibility as one who understands the game you seek to play.

Lessons learned

In this chapter, we've looked in detail at two industries, one quite attractive, with profits to show for it over the long term, and the other a killing field, where few new entrants prospered or survived. What can entrepreneurs learn from these industry analyses? The first and foremost lesson of this chapter is that markets and industries are different things. Don't confuse them! When you see an attractive *market,* don't get so enamoured of it that you forget to ask whether the *industry* is one in which you want to compete. As Warren Buffett noted at the outset of this chapter, the characteristics of the industry are likely to outweigh your prowess as an entrepreneur.

Lessons learned from the pharmaceutical industry

As the pharmaceutical industry example shows, regulatory issues can have powerful effects on industry attractiveness and the profitability of the firms that it comprises. Where regulation makes it difficult for competitors to enter and compete, and other forces are also favourable, it may be worth an entrepreneur's trouble to find a way in, as the biotech companies have done. Many of the long-established players and some biotech newcomers have prospered.

The pharmaceutical industry example also shows that high barriers to entry are good. Love and cherish them. And, once you get in, work to keep the barriers high. The same is true of weak buyer and supplier power, and of little threat of substitutes, as we've seen here. While changes in some of these forces have detracted from the drug industry's overall performance, the industry remains, in comparison to many others, an attractive place to play.

> **❝high barriers to entry are good. Love and cherish them.❞**

Finally, entrepreneurs and investors alike should note that industry performance data, like those cited in this chapter for pharmaceutical industry performance, are readily available in business libraries in most developed economies. It's well worth a look at such data in the early stages of assessing an opportunity. If an industry is a poor performer overall, you should take a critical look at your opportunity to ask why you expect it to fare differently. Without a persuasively positive answer to this question, I would suggest moving on to something more attractive.

Lessons learned from the daily deals industry

Following the 'get big fast' strategy that Amazon employed in its early days, numerous other venture capital-backed companies have sought to apply such a strategy, in part to counter unfavourable industry structure, including a high threat of entry. The thinking here is that the winner will take all, and the followers will lose. While winners have done well in broad-based e-commerce (Amazon), social networks (Facebook), and in some other internet-based industries, a 'get big fast' strategy cannot offset deeply unfavourable industry structure or a market that soon tires of what's being offered, as we've seen here with daily deals and flash sales, to name but two such cases.

Thus, putting in the time and effort to understand the attractiveness of your industry today and its likely attractiveness tomorrow is an essential activity that is too often overlooked. One of the most common causes of new venture failure I observe is getting blinded by the attractiveness of a large or fast-growing market, and ignoring a deeply unattractive industry structure. The lesson for would-be entrepreneurs? Attractive markets are one thing. Attractive industries are quite another! I should also flag a similar caution with regard to buyer power and supplier power, though these issues were not the source of the daily deals industry's problems. Many entrepreneurs and investors have been trained to consider entry barriers in assessing their opportunities, but they often overlook the other four of the five forces, especially these two. Ignore them at your peril!

The final lesson from the daily deals fiasco is this. A large and fast-growing market enjoying predominantly favourable macro trends along with a market segment that's eager to buy, as appeared to be the case for the early days of daily deals, is not sufficient justification for pressing the 'start' button on your new venture if you're hoping to build or invest in a business that lasts. Such conditions may support a 'get in and get out quickly' strategy, if you can get out before others recognise the competitive difficulties that may soon arise, if the industry structure is unattractive or if other domains pose additional challenges. So, please, repeat after me: 'An attractive market is not a sufficient reason to press "Start"!'

Can one make money in an unattractive industry?

The lessons of this chapter are sobering. The unfortunate reality is that most industries are not nearly as attractive as the pharmaceutical industry, although many are better than daily deals or flash sales. But can one make money in unattractive industries? Can *you* make money in a business of the kind Warren Buffett described at the outset of this chapter – one with a reputation for bad economics? The story of Ulta, in Case Study 4.1, and its success in another difficult industry, retailing, suggests that sometimes you can. We further examine this question in Chapter 5.

---

case study 4.1

Ulta: saving women time[54]

The highly fragmented retailing industry has long been a poor performer overall, ranking poorly on return on assets and noted for its high failure rate. But Ulta, founded in 1990 by a group of former chain drugstore executives, bucks the norm. Its roomy stores, most of which are located in outdoor strip shopping centres, offer a vast selection of cosmetics, fragrances and salon services – hair styling, eyebrow trims, and more – to suburban American women. It sells everything from mass market brands to high-end cosmetics, and professional hair products, too. 'The core idea', recalls Terry Hanson, a co-founder, was 'to save women time.'

Why has Ulta, which in less than three decades in business has grown to more than $4 billion in sales, become the largest beauty-specialist retailer in the US? 'They are relatively hip for a specialty retailer, and they have products you can't get anywhere else if you want to be different,' says Bloomberg Intelligence analyst Seema Shah. Adds Edward Jones & Co analyst Brian Yarbrough, 'They have allowed people to buy both mass and prestige, as well as get salon, brow and other services which historically would have been done at multiple locations.' In addition, Ulta's loyalty programme, Ultamate, whose more than 20 million members deliver a remarkable 80 to 90 per cent of the company's sales, gives Ulta's merchandisers the information they need to effectively target customers and tailor the product assortments they want to buy, store by store.

Fortuitously, perhaps, in an age where major shopping malls are struggling in the face of online competition and many brick-and-mortar retailers' sales are soft if not down, Ulta's closer-to-home strip-mall locations have become an asset. In sharp contrast to the current meltdown among department stores, Ulta stands out. 'There is nothing wrong with strip malls if Ulta has a nice presentation, traffic, training, and experience', says up-market cosmetics giant Estee Lauder's CEO Fabrizio Freda.

Will Ulta's distinctive strategy and loyal customer base enable it to continue to thrive in the hotly competitive retailing industry? Investors seem to think so, having boosted Ulta's share price by 38 per cent in 2016, four times higher than the S&P 500 index's gain.

The new business road test: stage three – the macro-industry test

- What industry will you compete in? Define it carefully.
- Is it easy or difficult for companies to enter this industry?
- Do suppliers to this industry have the power to set terms and conditions?
- Do buyers have the power to set terms and conditions?
- Is it easy or difficult for substitute products to steal your market?
- Is competitive rivalry intense or genteel?
- Based on all five forces, what is your overall assessment of this industry? Just how attractive or unattractive is it?
- If your industry is a poor performer overall, are there (based on the lessons of Chapters 2 and 5) persuasive reasons why you'll fare differently? If not, consider moving on.
- Based on the evidence you compile in answering the above questions, what are your key macro-industry risks, and how – if at all – might they be mitigated?

THE NEW BUSINESS ROAD TEST

If you open your *New Business Road Test* app, you'll find the above checklist reproduced there. As you surf the Web or talk to experts to find macro-industry data to assess each of the five forces, you'll find places to keep track of links to your online sources or record what you glean from your conversations or interviews. But don't forget that your task isn't simply to gather industry data; it's to make judgements about what the data tell you, whether that's good news or bad. So be certain to make note of any key risks, and to then indicate your tentative conclusion about the overall attractiveness of your industry at the macro level, as that conclusion evolves. One key factor that brings many new ventures to their knees is brutal *industry* conditions, despite what may be – as was daily deals, at least at its outset – an attractive *market*.

Competitive and economic sustainability: how long can we dance?

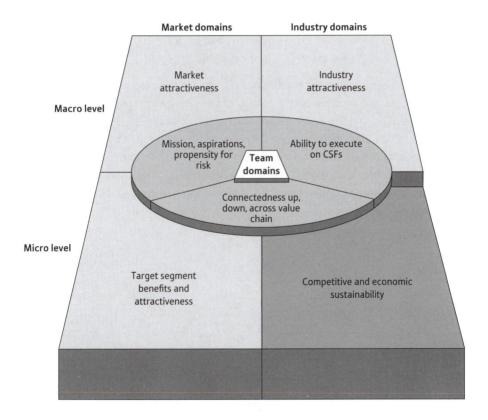

It is 2016, and you and your best friend Simon have just returned to the USA from a holiday in England. While you were there, you did your best to quaff a pint or two of every British beer you could find. The pubs were far more interesting than the museums, in your view, and the robust taste of English bitters made the American beer – even some of the craft beers, like IPAs and ambers – back home seem lifeless in comparison.

You and Simon decide it is high time someone started selling real British-style beer in the USA, hearty brews like the bitters and ales you enjoyed across the pond. You've dabbled for years at making beer at home, and your friends have always told you just how terrific they taste. With your taste buds to create the beers and Simon's marketing experience, you are fairly certain you have what it takes to make millions in the craft beer industry. After all, craft beers have been on a roll for years.

Stop there. Had you and Simon chosen to launch your own microbrewery 25 years earlier, by the late 1990s you would likely have crashed and burned, or at best been bought by one of your competitors as growth in craft beer consumption in the USA came to a screeching halt in 1997.[1] Fortunately, though, for the craft beer industry, it took off again.

Making craft beer is just not that difficult. And, while making a good one does take some time and experimentation, plenty of folks have accomplished such a feat. The reality is that thousands of brewing fanatics had similarly auspicious dreams of hitting it big with their specially brewed, secret-formula beer. Over 1,000 speciality brewers had had a go at it in the USA by 1996, and the craft brewing rush continues today.[2] But with literally hundreds of microbrews vying for each retailer's limited retail shelf space, it was – and still is – tough to compete.

Sustainable advantage: how long can we dance?

Best beats first.

Best-selling author and management researcher Jim Collins[3]

Why is it that some American entrepreneurs and their angel investors tried but failed to hit the jackpot in the craft beer industry? Why is it that so many restaurants fail? Most industries aren't like the pharmaceutical industry. There, most companies make money, and lots of it (as we saw in Chapter 4). But in the restaurant industry and the craft beer industry, the threat of entry is extremely high, and thus new competitors crop up every day. And there are almost countless substitutes too – numerous ways to satisfy one's hunger or quench a thirst or get drunk. As a result, the failure rate in these industries is enormous and average returns have been modest.[4]

Other industries have other difficulties. In food retailing, there's intense competitive rivalry, as competing grocers fight for this week's customers. In apparel manufacturing, there's severe buyer power, enabling the big apparel chains like Zara, Gap and H&M to dictate the terms and conditions under which they will buy. But, despite these difficulties many restaurants, craft brewers, grocers and apparel manufacturers clothing companies get along very well. Why?

despite these difficulties many restaurants, craft brewers, grocers and apparel manufacturers get along very well

The principal answers to competing in a not-so-attractive industry are found on the micro level – the lower row of the seven domains model. In Chapter 2, we saw the importance of selling what your target customers want to buy. At the outset of a new venture, doing so can sometimes offset the difficulties inherent in an unattractive industry. If customers flock to your offering because it's faster, better or cheaper, then you'll be off and running.

The hard part, though, is sustaining that initial advantage, since offering superior benefits at the outset is not sufficient to build an entrepreneurial venture that can last over time. Imitation occurs quickly in most industries, both from existing competitors and from new entrants, so initial advantages can disappear in a heartbeat. What many large companies do best, in fact, is act like fast followers, letting entrepreneurial firms like yours take all the risks entailed in bringing innovations to market, and then stealing the show with their superior firepower.[5] Thus, for aspiring entrepreneurs, a second key to competing in not-so-attractive industries is whether factors are present that will enable the company to *sustain* its initial advantage over an extended period of time.

> **❝first-mover advantage is most often a myth❞**

The widely talked about first-mover advantage is most often a myth. As management researcher and best-selling author Jim Collins puts it, 'Best beats first' almost every time.[6]

Establishing competitive and economic sustainability , as we saw briefly in Chapter 1, involves several issues, which are addressed in Boxes 5.1 and 5.2.

---

box 5.1

The keys to competitive sustainability

An initial competitive advantage arises when the offering provides differentiated benefits to customers that – in the *customers'* minds – are better, cheaper or faster than those offered by competitors. Such an advantage is likely to be sustainable when:

■ there are proprietary elements – patents, trade secrets and so on – that other firms are not likely to duplicate or imitate;

■ there are superior organisational processes, capabilities or resources that others would have difficulty in duplicating or imitating.

---

box 5.2

The keys to economic sustainability

The economics of a business become sustainable when the company's business model is sufficiently robust so as to not run out of cash. Economic sustainability rests largely on the following factors:

■ revenue is adequate in relation to capital investment required and margins obtainable;

■ customer acquisition and retention costs and the time it will take to attract customers are viable;

■ contribution margins are adequate to cover the necessary fixed cost structure;

■ operating cash cycle characteristics are favourable, including factors such as these:

  – how much cash must be tied up in working capital (inventory or other) and for how long;

  – how quickly customers will pay;

  – how slowly suppliers and employees can be paid.

In this chapter, we explore the twin concepts of competitive and economic sustainability – what it takes for an entrepreneurial company to sustain its advantage over the long term, without running out of cash. First, we look at three stories about competitive sustainability. With strong patent protection, the British pharmaceutical company Glaxo (now GlaxoSmithKline) found itself in a sustainably profitable situation with its drug Zantac – not surprising, given what we learned in the previous chapter.

Nokia, the once fast-growing Finnish mobile phone giant, utilised hard-to-copy organisational processes to continuously innovate, staying a few steps ahead of its competitors for many years. As we'll see from the Nokia story, though, rarely does competitive advantage last forever. Smartphones from Apple, Samsung and others did them in. Third, though EMI's invention of the CAT scanner made waves in the medical world, its competitive advantage didn't last. Insufficient patent protection coupled with inadequate organisational processes and resources made the company's initial advantage unsustainable.

We then look at three companies that demonstrate the principle of economic sustainability – if the business model isn't sustainable, you'll run out of cash.

Internet auctioneer eBay, one of the longest-running dot.com success stories, proved to have one of the most compelling and robust business models of any Web-based company. Finally, in an archetypal dot-bomb story, we examine online grocer Webvan's business model to understand why the company went under, and we contrast Webvan's story with that of Bristish grocery retailer Tesco, whose very different foray into selling groceries on the Web has gone very well.

To conclude this chapter, we explore investors' views on competitive and economic sustainability, we examine the lessons learned and we consider the likelihood that the industry you'll enter is probably not as attractive as pharmaceutical drugs.

❝the industry you'll enter is probably not as attractive as pharmaceutical drugs❞

Whether you are an aspiring entrepreneur or an early-stage investor, this closing discussion provides insights for how you can assess whether your opportunity has what it takes to become sustainable, from both competitive and economic perspectives, even if your chosen industry isn't so attractive.

Zantac – protected and profitable

One in ten adults develops a stomach ulcer at some time in his or her life, a sizeable target market with clearly defined pain in need of relief.[7] In the late 1970s, the leading anti-ulcer medication was SmithKline Beecham's Tagamet, but researchers at Glaxo, the British pharmaceutical firm, had developed a new and chemically different drug in the same class as Tagamet. Both drugs reduced the secretion of stomach acid, thereby allowing the ulcer to heal.

With a huge market in its sights, Glaxo wanted to be sure it offered doctors and their patients a clear advantage over Tagamet. The drug that Glaxo developed and patented was Zantac, introduced in Europe in 1981 and in the USA in 1983. Glaxo's pitch to prescribing physicians was that Zantac was new, had fewer side-effects and was more convenient to take – twice each day, rather than four times a day – than Tagamet.[8]

Glaxo shareholders wanted to know that these advantages could be sustained for long enough to reap sufficient rewards for the R&D investments already incurred. The answer, as we've already seen in this industry, was patent protection.

Winning a patent

Glaxo won a 17-year US patent in 1978 and secured FDA approval to market Zantac in 1983. With patent in hand, Glaxo decided to price the new drug at a 20 per cent premium to Tagamet.

So, how did Zantac fare?

▦ Just three years after it received FDA approval, Glaxo's sales of Zantac reached $1 billion, making it the largest-selling prescription drug in the world.

▦ By 1989, Zantac had far surpassed Tagamet, winning 53 per cent of the market for prescription ulcer remedies compared with Tagamet's 29 per cent.

▦ In 1994, Zantac generated $3.6 billion in sales, $2.1 billion of that in the USA.

▦ By 1995, 240 million people worldwide had Zantac prescriptions.[9]

By then, however, Zantac's patent was about to expire, and generic manufacturers would be ready with copycat drugs at far lower prices. But Glaxo wasn't finished with Zantac just yet.

Glaxo had prepared itself for the day when Zantac no longer had proprietary protection from generic imitations. To improve its chances of discovering another winning drug, the company had increased its number of research scientists from 2,000 in 1986 to 5,000 in 1989, funded in part from the profits Zantac generated during the life of its patent.[10]

But betting on new drugs wasn't all that Glaxo did. Any product that delivers genuine value to 240 million customers and enjoys 12 years without imitation is going to develop a very powerful brand. But even a powerful brand won't be enough to protect you when chemically identical products become available at a fraction of the price – especially when the purchasing decision for prescription drugs is taken not by the consumer but by increasingly price-conscious insurance companies and governments. So, in 1996, as Zantac's patent expired, Glaxo won FDA approval to market a milder version of the drug called Zantac 75, available over the counter without prescription. Ulcer sufferers could now purchase a milder version of the drug themselves. Even if an identical generic product became available for a lower price, many consumers were probably less likely to trust an unbranded generic over the powerful and trusted brand of Zantac.[11]

The Zantac case history offers a specific example of why the pharmaceutical industry is so attractive and shows that the music need not stop when the patent expires. Zantac's outcomes – resulting from a superior product that enjoyed 12 years of patent protection and was difficult to imitate – were good for Glaxo employees, good for Glaxo shareholders, and good for patients, who benefited not only from Zantac's ulcer relief but also from subsequent products that the drug's success made possible. Zantac's sustainable advantage is a straightforward story, one that's been repeated frequently in the pharmaceutical industry. Our next case history is considerably more complex.

Nokia: innovator extraordinaire

Nokia, a company that takes its name from a small river outside the Finnish city of Tampere, began life in 1865 as a wood pulp and paper producer. Over its history, it has manufactured rubber boots, tyres and television sets and generated electricity. Nokia found its way into telecommunications in the early 1960s. Since then, over more than 50 years, Nokia developed and refined its telecommunications focus, and by concentrating on mobile communications it became the world's ninth most valuable brand in 2008. Alas, by 2012 it suddenly plunged to number 192 in the global rankings, as the smartphone revolution took its toll.[12] Encouragingly, though, by 2017 Nokia once again was reinventing itself, this time as a telecom network service provider.[13]

Let's examine Nokia's rise and fall in mobile communications:

- In 2000, Nokia sold 128 million phones, with sales of $26.1 billion and pre-tax profits of $5.25 billion;

- By August of 2001, Nokia had 35 per cent of the worldwide mobile phone market, with almost three times the volume of its nearest rival Motorola;

- Further, Nokia's margins were dramatically better than those of its competitors: Nokia's 20 per cent pre-tax margins – about $28 per phone – put Motorola's 2 per cent margin – less than $3 per handset – to shame;[14]

- Despite having missed the consumer trend towards clamshell phones in the early 2000s, Nokia's 2004 market share of 30 per cent was still more than double that of arch-rival Motorola;[15]

- for several years thereafter, Nokia remained the leader in supplying low-cost phones to emerging markets like India, its second largest market where it held around a 30 per cent share, down from 50 per cent earlier, and Africa – two regions where most of the world's growth in mobile telephone subscribers lay.[16] But low-cost upstarts in China were giving Nokia a run for their money at the low end of the market, putting pressure on profit margins there. And at the high end, smartphones and tablets from Apple, Samsung and others soon ruled.

No source of competitive advantage lasts forever. Nokia's certainly didn't. Its smartphone products failed to catch on and by June 2012, it had lost its position as the world's biggest phone maker, announced 10,000 job cuts and issued its second profit warning in nine weeks. It soon closed its only remaining factory in Finland[17] and in 2013, agreed to sell its mobile phone business to Microsoft.[18]

❝No source of competitive advantage lasts forever❞

How did Nokia thrive for so long in this admittedly cut-throat industry, in which most competitors have fared less well? 'Superior processes,' says telecom expert Andrew Tausz.[19] 'Namely, processes that allow for and encourage innovation.' Nokia's support for innovation came in two key areas: people (and the capabilities they bring) and corporate venturing.

Acquiring capabilities

In any technology-focused company, having the right human capital is a necessity. Not only did Nokia need clever people with experience and creativity, but the company also looked for people who fit within Nokia's culture. Because the knowledge and capabilities they needed were not available at home, in a country of only 5 million people, Nokia had to attract and develop skills from abroad.[20]

Nokia's human resource policies and processes played a vital role in attracting the best and the brightest. The company's human resource management included a rigorous and extensive interview process and team-based compensation methods. The company's culture, including the organisation's structure, learning environment, team focus and job flexibility, also contributed to Nokia's human resource acquisition and retention.[21]

The result, according to Dan Steinbock,[22] whose book chronicles the Nokia revolution, was that Nokia acquired 'the most technologically savvy individuals in all of Scandinavia'. Put simply, Nokia was a great place to work. Nokia's human resources policies and culture worked with its structure and organisational processes to keep new ideas alive.[23]

Exceptional organisational processes

Innovation is imperative to staying afloat in the business world, especially in high-tech businesses. But promoting innovation in a large company can be cumbersome. For Nokia, like other growing organisations, the challenge that faced the company was how to stay innovative as it grew. 'You can't force people to be innovative; you can foster it, encourage it, nourish it, but you can't force it,' said Nokia's Senior Vice-president for Corporate Communications Lauri Kivinen.[24] 'It's a spirit of trying to think outside the box, trying to look around the corner, trying to imagine the outcome of a chain of developments,' says Kivinen, who adds there is no secret formula to the company's success. 'It has to be something that is nurtured all the time; you allow people to make mistakes, allow people to take bold moves, you try to spread energy.'

But talk is cheap. It's easy to *say* your company will remain innovative, but how did Nokia really do it for so long? Processes were its key, and some of Nokia's key processes were those in the Nokia Ventures Organisation (NVO), the company's formal approach to fostering, encouraging and nourishing innovation. The NVO was created to develop new business opportunities that fell outside the current focus of Nokia's core businesses.[25] The NVO sought to develop both internally generated projects as well as external projects. Once ideas were developed, either they were moved into one of Nokia's business units or they were sold.

> **❝it's easy to *say* your company will remain innovative, but how did Nokia really do it?❞**

To implement such a strategy, the NVO had a collection of corporate venturing tools and capabilities. In particular, there were four specific initiatives for driving innovation and developing new businesses:

- the Insight & Foresight group identified disruptive technologies and developed new business models for Nokia;

- the New Growth Businesses group took business ideas and made them a reality, transforming them into sustainable businesses;

- the US-based Innovent was a team that collaborated with external entrepreneurs to offer expertise and resources that helped clarify their visions and could accelerate the process between concept development and commercialisation in emerging areas of interest to Nokia;

- finally, the organisation's Nokia Venture Partners (NVP) raised capital from Nokia as well as from external investors to invest in mobile telecommunications and related start-ups.

Processes tough to imitate

Nokia's innovation processes were unique to its culture and difficult to imitate. The NVO allowed the company to concentrate on its core businesses while simultaneously nurturing innovation as efficiently as a smaller company. Further, with an organisation like the NVO, Nokia could alter its innovative processes easily. If the company felt it should concentrate on internally developed ideas, then the NVO could direct funds to internal projects. On the other hand, if Nokia wanted to look outside the company for ideas, then the NVO could direct monies elsewhere. This kind of flexibility is difficult to establish and maintain in most large, international companies.

Competitive sustainability can result from superior organisational processes and capabilities, as the Nokia case history demonstrates. But if its processes and capabilities were so good, what prompted Nokia's sudden decline? Some observers say Nokia stopped doing those things that made it successful in the first place. It failed to respond to the changing market; it stopped innovating; it didn't anticipate the competition; and it lost focus on execution.[26] Or maybe Nokia was good, but Apple and Steve Jobs were even better.

That Nokia then transformed itself from a mobile communications company in 2012, with a market capitalisation of $5 billion, into a company that provides technologies to connect people and things, with a market capitalisation of nearly $40 billion at the end of 2016, demonstrates its ability to use its organisational processes and capabilities to change its focus yet again.[27] Nokia certainly wasn't down for long!

So far, we've seen in this chapter how proprietary protection of one's intellectual property and superior organisational capabilities and processes can lead to sustainable competitive advantage at least for some time, though not forever. Sounds easy, right, as long as you don't have to contend with Steve Jobs? So what else can go wrong?

EMI – advantage lost

The British firm EMI had long been considered a technology pioneer, having developed the first commercial television system that the British Broadcasting Corporation (BBC) adopted in 1937. EMI had product lines in advanced electronics and in the movie and recording industries, where its success with artists such as the Beatles, the Rolling Stones and other top recording artists put it in a strong financial position as it entered the 1970s. Concerned, though, about the fickle nature of the music business, EMI decided to extend its technological prowess and encourage innovation that might lead to opportunities outside of its current businesses.[28]

Godfrey Hounsfield, an EMI senior research engineer, had been carrying out pattern-recognition research. This research and subsequent clinical work showed that something called computerised axial tomography (CAT) could generate and display a cross-sectional view of the human body or parts thereof. Hounsfield's discovery, which was subsequently hailed as the most significant advance in radiology since the X-ray and would go on to win a Nobel Prize in 1979, led to EMI's 1973 entry into the medical products industry.[29] In its first three years, EMI won a 75 per cent share of the global market for scanners, generating £42 million in revenue and £12.5 million in pre-tax profits. The future looked bright.[30]

As the EMI story went on, however, things quickly unravelled. Despite first-mover position in the large and lucrative US radiology market with a cutting-edge product that hospitals needed, and despite patents to protect Hounsfield's technology, within six years EMI had lost its market leadership position. By year eight, it had dropped out of the business entirely. How could such a promising start have gone so wrong?

❝how could such a promising start have gone so wrong?❞

Patent protection

EMI secured patents on its technology, but patent protection only covers that which is patented. As we saw with Zantac and Tagamet, where Zantac's slightly different chemical composition enabled Zantac to go to market despite Tagamet's earlier patent, EMI's competitors went to work. General Electric Company (GE), the leading producer of conventional X-ray equipment, began a crash programme to develop a similar scanner, without infringing on EMI's patents.[31] Others did likewise. By late 1974, competing CAT scanners hit the American market. In 1975, GE announced its CAT scanner, which it began shipping in mid-1976. EMI's patents had not provided an enduring defence.[32]

Competitors were not only finding their way into the scanner market; they were also finding ways to make improvements in scanner technology. Initially, EMI's scanner had a speed advantage over its competitors. But competitors' machines soon leapfrogged EMI's speed; some could even scan the entire human body, whereas EMI's scanner scanned only the head. In response, Hounsfield developed a second-generation machine, the CT 5000, which offered improved image resolution and could scan the entire body.[33] Would a better machine save the day?

Organisational capabilities and processes

EMI's competitors, all established medical equipment makers, enjoyed significant experience in manufacturing medical products, had established marketing channel access and capabilities, as well as service and support systems, and benefited from an in-depth understanding of the hospital system in the USA, the largest market for scanners.[34] GE, for example, at the time of its scanner introduction in 1976, had a 300-person salesforce and a service network of 1,200 people.

EMI had to learn and develop all these capabilities from scratch. The challenge proved too great. EMI, besides lacking sufficient patent protection, lacked the organisational systems, processes and capabilities to compete with its better-established rivals. In 1978–79, plagued by production problems and technical bugs in its scanners, EMI's performance tumbled and its scanner business lost $23.5 million pre-tax. EMI sued GE for patent infringements, but it was too little, too late. The debacle was so severe that EMI was forced into a merger with Thorn Electrical Industries Ltd in December 1979. Thorn EMI then agreed to settle the lawsuit by selling GE the scanner business for a pittance.[35]

❝in six short years, EMI had gone from an innovative leader in a huge and growing market to exiting the business entirely❞

In six short years, EMI had gone from an innovative leader in a huge and growing market to exiting the business entirely. Why?

- Its patent protection proved insufficient.
- It failed to build the necessary organisational processes and capabilities to enable it to compete with its better-established competitors.

EMI had an undisputed advantage at the outset. But it was unable to sustain it.

Can your sustainable competitive advantage last?

Clearly, most entrepreneurs and most investors who back them would prefer to invest their time and money in ventures that are competitively sustainable. And well they should. But strategy guru Rita McGrath argues that these days, globalisation, the digital revolution, and a variety of other forces are conspiring to put an end to sustainable competitive advantage as we know it.[36] She argues that today's companies should be seeking to build a *portfolio* of strategic initiatives, one following the other, that can keep it ahead of those who chase it. The case history of Nike that we saw in Chapter 2 illustrates her point.

The good news is that many entrepreneurs are well-suited to take full advantage of this reality. Coming up with new ideas and running experiments to test their viability is central to what many entrepreneurs do, as is their passion to make some part of the world better in some way. Intuit's vice president of design innovation, Karen Hanson, has a clear view about what's important in today's rapidly changing world: to 'fall in love with the problem you are trying to solve,' rather than with your particular solution, and to be comfortable iterating toward better solutions as you work toward the answer.[37]

So should you seek to build your venture in a competitively sustainable manner? Of course you should. But at the same time, you must not rest on your laurels, because competitors with fatter budgets and better market access will seek to eat your lunch just as soon as they can. McGrath argues that one element in the way forward is the kind of 'roughly right decision making' at which many entrepreneurs excel, as opposed to strategic deliberations that are 'precise but slow'.[38]

Sustaining competitive advantage, whether with patent protection like Zantac's or with McGrath's more iterative portfolio approach, is one thing, of course; doing so economically is another, a subject to which we now turn.

eBay, one internet business model that worked

We've seen in this chapter how patents and business processes can give companies sustainable advantage – a competitive advantage that lasts for years, though never forever. But there's one more piece to this important puzzle that we have not examined carefully, that of putting all the pieces together in a way that's economically viable. During the dot.com bust, countless companies went under precisely because the business models they had created were simply uneconomic. One dot.com stood out for a very long time, however: eBay. Why?

❝one dot-com stood out, however: eBay❞

eBay was founded by Pierre Omidyar in September 1995. Omidyar and his team did many things right, but the most dramatic of these was the business model they created. Table 5.1 shows how eBay's business model matches the criteria for economic viability that we saw at the beginning of this chapter.

Table 5.1	eBay's ingenious business model
Keys to economic viability	*eBay's answer*
Revenue is adequate in relation to capital investment required and margins obtainable	Plenty of revenue – customers are happy to pay transaction and other fees. Investment is modest
Customer acquisition and retention costs and the time it will take to attract customers are viable	Customers arrive by word of mouth – little marketing expense needed; no shortage of people having items to sell
Contribution margins are adequate to cover the necessary fixed cost structure	Virtually no cost of goods sold, since the customers own them, and transactions are paperless; huge contribution margins, minimal fixed costs
Operating cash cycle characteristics are favourable, including factors such as: ■ how much cash must be tied up in working capital (inventory or other) and for how long ■ how quickly customers will pay ■ how slowly suppliers and employees can be paid	Sellers pay for the listing in advance and for the transaction upon completion; no receivables to collect; no inventory, since eBay's customer – the seller – owns it

Let's direct some attention to each of these items.

Adequate revenue

eBay generated revenue by way of various fees and commissions. 'It's a very clean model. There are not many risks,' said eBay's Chief Financial Officer Rajiv Dutta.[39] To start with, eBay charged an insertion fee based on the opening price of the merchandise. Sellers paid between $0.30 and $3.30 per product listed on eBay's site. An additional fee was charged to those interested in a ten-day auction option. Other fees were charged if a seller wanted to promote their own auction. eBay also allowed businesses to auction merchandise. In this space, eBay charged fellow companies $9.95 per month to have what it called a 'store front'. For items that were not up for auction (fixed price), eBay charged its sellers another fee. And, in what was called a 'Dutch auction' scenario, where sellers sold more than one item per auction, eBay established yet another special fee.

While the fees accounted for some of eBay's revenues, commissions were its bread and butter. eBay charged a commission on each sale. The commission percentage was based on a sliding scale, depending on the sale price of the merchandise. In 2001, the company generated $300 million in commissions. In January 2002, the company raised its commission rates, or what it called its 'final value fees'. For items selling for $25 or less, the company charged a 5.25 per cent fee. For items that sold for between $25.01 and $,1000, the company charged 2.75 per cent. And for those that sold for over $1000, eBay received a 1.50 per cent commission.[40]

The best news was that sellers and shoppers were plentiful. In 1998, a mere three years after its launch, eBay had 1 million shoppers, some 600,000 items for sale and $6 million in revenues. In 2004, the company generated over $34 billion worth of transactions and generated over $3 billion in revenue.[41] No longer a site to exchange stuffed dolls, eBay users bought cars, jet planes, computers, printers, cameras and more.

> **❝the best news was that sellers and shoppers were plentiful❞**

Customer acquisition and retention costs, time to attract a customer

As good fortune would have it, more than half of all eBay users were referred by other users, which means eBay had to spend relatively little on marketing.[42] Aside from an occasional advertisement and deals with major portals like AOL to deliver customers, it cost eBay little to win a customer and even less to retain them.[43] As tech writer Rick Spence wrote, 'Last fall I fell in love with eBay . . . It's all there. I was hooked.'[44]

Adequate contribution margins to cover the fixed cost structure

Best of all, because eBay is nothing more than a series of software applications placed on servers, the actual cost of doing this business is extremely low – certainly much, much lower than the cost of running Amazon's business. eBay does not buy products that it then has to package and sell. Instead, eBay lets its sellers bear these costs. And it needs no distribution centres with all the fixed costs they entail. As *BusinessWeek*'s Robert Hof notes, 'Customers are eBay's de facto product-development team, sales and marketing force, merchandising department, and security detail – all rolled into one.'[45]

The net result of all this is gross margins above 85 per cent. True, eBay must invest in software, server technology and customer service. But factories? No. Distribution centres? No. Delivery trucks? Not one. That twentieth-century business model is an expensive one. eBay simply enables the resale of things that others own and takes a small cut of each sale.[46]

Operating cash cycle characteristics

Most entrepreneurs have to worry about how much cash they'll have to tie up in working capital like inventory, how quickly their customers will pay and how long they can wait to pay their suppliers. Not the case for eBay. Since the real transactions were carried out between eBay's buyers and sellers, eBay didn't have to worry about any of these things. Sellers paid to list what was for sale and they paid again when the transaction was done. If they didn't pay, they lost their ability to use eBay again. It's a self-policing system, and it works. These favourable cash cycle characteristics meant that once eBay got started and went public, it was able to grow without needing to raise further capital.[47]

❝it's a self-policing system, and it works❞

Sparkling results

eBay's business model offered something for everyone: buyer and seller were happy when they reached a deal, and eBay got its cut. And eBay's cut was nothing to sneeze at.

- In 1998, there were 2 million items for sale on eBay. Those 2 million items sold for $746 million, of which eBay generated $47.1 million in revenues. That came to $687,000 in revenues per eBay employee.

- By June 2005, the eBay community included 157 million registered users worldwide, with 64.6 million of them active in the previous 12 months.[48] Revenue hit $1.08 billion in the second quarter alone, up 40 per cent over the prior year, with $10.9 billion in merchandise having changed hands.

- The real story, though, was eBay's profitability. Operating income, up 49 per cent over the prior year, reached $379 million for the quarter, some 35 per cent of sales.[49]

Rivals were in awe: 'These guys have done a killer job,' admits Amazon.com Chief Financial Officer Warren C. Jenson. Financial analyst William Harnisch, President of Forstmann-Leff Associates, says eBay is one of the few companies that can sustain speedy growth even in a sluggish environment.[50]

But was Harnisch right? The economic recession of 2008 and 2009 created a few bumps in its road, though eBay pulled through and delivered impressive growth, with 2008 full-year revenues of $8.5 billion growing to $14 billion by the end of 2012. Sadly for eBay, however, internet auctions stopped being quite so attractive to consumers, and revenues for 2013 plummeted to $8.3 billion, a whopping decrease of 41 per cent. They have remained around this level ever since.[51]

eBay has had to deal with the problems of a maturing business: its core auction offering has been in decline and the growth market of full-priced ecommerce sales is highly competitive,[52] not least because it pitches eBay directly against Amazon. eBay's annual report for the 2016 fiscal year stated its problem bluntly: 'To compete effectively, we will need to continue to expend significant resources in technology and marketing. These efforts require substantial expenditures, which could reduce our margins and have a material adverse effect on our business, financial position, operating results and cash flows and reduce the market price of our common stock and out-standing debt. Despite our efforts to preserve and expand the size, diversity and transaction activity of our buyers and sellers and to enhance the user experience, we may not be able to effectively manage our operating expenses, to increase or maintain our revenue or to avoid a decline in our consolidated net income or a net loss.'[53] There's an important lesson here: having an attractive business model is no panacea if customers decide they have better places to shop.

> **❝There's an important lesson here❞**

Webvan's unsustainable business model

We have seen how eBay's business model allowed it to have positive cash flow almost from day one, and to maintain it for many years, even in the face of a global economic downturn. Having examined that model, we know that internet-based companies can be profitable. So, why was it that so many dot.coms were unable to survive? For many, the business model was simply not economically viable. Some sold bulky bags of pet food, delivered to the consumer's door for prices far less than the cost of the delivered product. Others spent more on acquiring customers than those customers would ever be worth. Perhaps the most striking example of a dot.com business model that simply was not viable was Webvan, whose demise would cost investors more than $1 billion.

Webvan's idea

In 1997, Louis Borders, a successful entrepreneur in book retailing, saw what he thought was an opportunity to revolutionise American grocery retailing. Borders believed that, by using automated warehouses and computerised scheduling software, he could let customers order groceries on the internet and have them delivered to their doors at no more cost than if they picked them up at the supermarket.[54] Given his previous track record, Borders was able to attract investment capital from a star-studded roster of blue-chip investors, including Benchmark Capital, Sequoia Capital and Goldman Sachs.

In June 1999, Webvan took its first grocery order in the San Francisco Bay area. The company offered customers access to 24-hours-a-day, 7-days-a-week online grocery ordering. Webvan promised to deliver orders within a 30-minute window, allowing customers to pick a convenient time to receive groceries. For consumers, the story was attractive. No more weekly trip to the supermarket. No more waiting in long lines at the checkout. No more fighting the crowd to select the freshest peaches. Let's take a look at how the business model matches the criteria for economic viability (Table 5.2).

Table 5.2 **Webvan's business model**

Keys to economic viability	Webvan's answer
Revenue is adequate in relation to capital investment required and margins obtainable	Huge up-front investment to build high-tech distribution centres; US grocery retailing is a very low-margin business; *requires lots of customers spending lots of money per order to overcome*
Customer acquisition and retention costs and the time it will take to attract customers are viable	Widespread publicity during the dot.com boom means everyone knows about Webvan; *but will they switch? How compelling are the benefits?*
Contribution margins are adequate to cover the necessary fixed cost structure	Ordinary grocery stores benefit from customer labour to select and take home the groceries; *Webvan must incur these labour costs itself, narrowing contribution margins*
Operating cash cycle characteristics are favourable, including factors such as: ■ how quickly customers will pay ■ how quickly suppliers and employees must be paid ■ how much cash must be tied up in working capital (inventory or other) and for how long	No major problems here – customers pay immediately with credit cards, suppliers offer terms; inventory turns quickly, but spoilage can be a problem

Revenue in relation to capital investment and margins

Webvan's initial capital investments were enormous. The company's 300,000-square-foot distribution centres were the most automated in the world. 'Infrastructure is everything,' said David Cooperstein, an analyst with Forrester Research in Cambridge, Massachusetts. 'To do online sales the right way rather than the rush-to-market way, they need to develop a very complex distribution system.' In groceries, profit margins 'are so tight you need to figure out where the leverage is', said Cooperstein, adding that Webvan had determined that the leverage was in distribution. To make these investments pay, Webvan would need either large numbers of customers spending large amounts per order or great margins. Read on.

> **Webvan would need either large numbers of customers spending large amounts per order or great margins**

Margins in the US grocery business

In the American grocery business, returns on sales of 2 to 3 per cent were considered healthy.[55] One per cent returns were not uncommon. The business works on very high volumes at razor-thin margins. Unless customers were willing to pay substantially more for Webvan's convenience – an unlikely prospect – or unless customers would spend more online than they spend the old-fashioned way – also unlikely given America's traditional weekly trips to the supermarket – then the only route to economic viability would have to be through significant productivity advances. Hence, the highly automated warehouses.

Obtaining customers at affordable cost

With all the fanfare surrounding the dot.com boom, everyone knew about Webvan and other online grocery retailers. But would customers switch? Would they trust Webvan to deliver only ripe peaches, not hard ones? If the green beans weren't fresh, would they arrive anyway, instead of perhaps broccoli for tonight's meal, as one might decide in store? Would one out-of-stock item render tomorrow's dinner plan unworkable, necessitating a trip to the store anyway?

From Webvan's perspective, would enough customers switch their shopping to Webvan to make the huge investments worthwhile? Webvan did $13 million in sales in 1999, its first half-year. By the end of 2000, its San Francisco customer list had grown to some 47,000 households, with fourth-quarter sales totalling $9.1 million. But orders averaged only $81, short of the $103 Webvan's plans required. And sales volumes were far short of what an ordinary high-volume supermarket would generate, despite the far higher capital investment.[56] Online grocery retailers like Webvan had to overcome die-hard shopping habits and a preference among some people simply to squeeze their own melons. In addition, price was a factor for many budget-conscious consumers, who liked shopping for specials.[57] Worse, it was costing Webvan about $210 to acquire each customer.[58]

Contribution margins compared with fixed cost structure

As we have seen, Webvan needed either huge sales volumes or significant operating efficiencies to make its model work. Operating the facilities, marketing the company and delivering the orders were all more costly than Webvan anticipated, however. The process of fulfilling customers' orders was particularly expensive.

Order handling and fulfilment cost the company approximately $27 per order, $18 of which went directly on the delivery process.[59] In ordinary supermarkets, the customer does this work at no cost to the retailer. The company charged a $4.95 delivery fee for orders under $50, a threshold it increased to $75 in November 2000, as delivery expenses exceeded budgets. As Paul Malatesta, a University of Washington finance professor, said later, grocery delivery can work in densely populated areas where grocers offer delivery without building expensive and complicated distribution systems: 'If you have a relatively low-wage delivery person who is pretty much packing grocery boxes and riding elevators, you don't have a large capital investment. But if I have to run $100,000 trucks through the suburbs and pay a driver $25–$35 an hour, when they spend part of the day idling in traffic, that just isn't going to work.'[60]

Webvan also lacked the buying power of Kroger and other large chains.[61] Without the enormous economies of scale its competitors enjoyed, Webvan could not easily keep its costs of goods low.

Thus, high variable costs – including higher than normal cost of goods sold and delivery costs – put severe pressure on contribution margins. But this was only half the story. Keeping Webvan's high-tech distribution centres running added a significant fixed cost burden that the thinner-than-thin grocery-industry margins couldn't cover.

❝ high variable costs put severe pressure on contribution margins ❞

Operating cash cycle characteristics

Of the four keys to economic viability shown in Table 5.2, the first three looked gloomy indeed. Only the fourth key posed no real problems. Webvan got the same payment terms that other grocers received, and its customers paid when they placed their orders. Inventory turned at a respectable rate. But these cash cycle characteristics provided little comfort to offset the significant economic disadvantages Webvan faced in the first three arenas.

Results

By July 2001, after just two years in business, Webvan had spent just about all of the $1.2 billion put up by investors. Its audacious plan to reinvent grocery retailing was not going to work. Instead, on 9 July, the company closed its doors. As Miles R. Cook, a vice president at Bain Consulting, said, 'They've got an approach that's profit-proof.'[62]

On the outside, Webvan looked like a new-economy company. On the inside, it was a very old economy, with its high-cost warehouses, its fleet of vans and its labour-intensive delivery system that couldn't compete. As we've seen – and some might have foreseen – its business model simply wasn't viable.

Tesco.com – an online grocery model that works

Tesco, the leading British supermarket chain and one of the top four global grocers, launched its online service in 2000, although it had operated home delivery since 1996. Since 2000, Tesco.com has seen double digit sales growth and by 2012 was serving over 500,000 customers each week.[63] What has made Tesco.com successful?

No expensive physical infrastructure

Unlike Webvan and its high-tech but costly distribution center, Tesco based its model on its local stores, employing extra staff to select and pack goods ready for delivery. In posh areas where customers were sensitive to having a Tesco delivery van pulling up outside their house, Tesco used discreet Range Rovers. As Tesco.com has grown, it has opened a number of 'dark' stores, often using inexpensive real estate, stores that are not open to the public but exist only to fulfill online orders. Given their low costs, these stores are financially sound, even though many are operating at only a small fraction of capacity.[64]

Low customer acquisition costs

Initially, Tesco.com relied on the already broad awareness of Tesco in the UK and its access to customers through its Tesco Clubcard database. As smartphones grew in popularity, Tesco launched its own app, offering a new generation of shoppers the chance to shop conveniently, amend orders on the go and find recipe ideas.

Cost-effective IT

The Tesco.com website and its IT infrastructure are supported by Tesco's Hindustan Service Centre in India, a wholly owned subsidiary of Tesco set up in 2004 to support Tesco's online growth.[65] In its early days, Tesco.com was very focused on improving the customer experience online; over time, Tesco's engineers were able to decrease the time it takes for a new customer to complete their first order from over an hour to 35 minutes through usability work that culminated in a major site revision.[66]

Manageable gross margins

Pre-tax profit margins for grocery retailers typically run 6 to 8 per cent in the UK, versus 2 to 3 per cent in the USA, as a result of generally higher gross margins in retailing in the UK compared to the USA.[67] Fortunately, Tesco found that shoppers bought a higher-margin mix of groceries online than in stores, since they were less likely to pick up sale-priced goods. These higher margins, plus a delivery charge, helped offset the costs of picking and delivering orders. And the fixed delivery charge encouraged customers to place larger orders to make the delivery expense worthwhile.

Growth potential

Tesco.com saw the potential in online grocery shopping at a time when many analysts were sceptical due to the dot.com crash. It has benefited from the huge growth in this segment of the grocery market, with current projections suggesting that UK sales in online grocery retailing are set to hit £11.2 billion (nearly $18 billion) in 2016, almost twice the estimated value for 2011 of £5.9 billion. At the end of 2011, the online grocery market was expected to account for 3.8 per cent of total grocery spend in the UK and was projected to increase to 6.0 per cent by 2016.[68] Of this, Tesco.com owned a hefty 48 per cent market share![69]

Will Tesco's approach work in the long run?

By 2012 Tesco.com was one of the UK's top five most visited retail websites; and more than a million UK households regularly ordered around a billion items.[70] 'Despite a challenging operating environment, Tesco.com continued to increase its online customers, even as it lost customers in its retail stores.[71]

Clearly, Tesco had hit upon a trend that was still going strong. By 2016, although there were 11 per cent of overall shoppers who would only shop online, the figure was 19 per cent in the 25–34 year-old age category. Of these, 36 per cent were shopping more frequently than they did a year before, with a move towards shopping on an 'as-needs' basis rather than the traditional weekly shop. Unfortunately, this placed pressure on Tesco.com margins, as small orders were costlier to fulfill and deliver than large orders.[72]

Undeterred, in January 2017, Tesco announced a trial collaboration with Convibo to deliver its orders to some London-based customers within an hour of it being received.[73] CEO Dave Lewis explained why. 'By behaving differently, by doing things differently,' he says, 'and by putting the customer at the centre of everything, we set ourselves up really very well for what is ahead of us.'[74]

Webvan was right that there was a bright future in online grocery retailing, but both competitive *and* economic sustainability matter. Webvan didn't get its business model right. By all indications, Tesco has.

What investors want to know

As we've seen, business angels and venture capital investors require returns far in excess of the annual returns on investment that most businesses generate year in, year out. The only way to obtain such returns is to grow the business over time and then to sell it, either to the public or to a trade buyer. But that process takes time – except in exceptional periods, like the aberrant days of the dot.com boom – typically five to seven years or perhaps several more. If you are an investor, you'll want to know that any advantage your new venture possesses will have the staying power to thrive that long. Otherwise, competitors may enter and overtake your company before an exit can be achieved.

> **investors want to know that any advantage your new venture possesses will have the staying power to thrive that long**

Competitive and economic sustainability are what ensure the possibility for a successful exit. Of course, the very notion of competitive sustainability implies that there's some sort of competitive edge you possess at the outset. From a seven domains perspective, this means that not only must your product offering resolve some customer pain (as we explored way back in Chapter 2) or offer some new kind of customer delight (as we'll see in the case of Starbucks in the next chapter), but also that in doing so your offering differs, in ways meaningful to your customer, from those of your competitors. It's better, faster, cheaper, or whatever, from the *customer's* perspective, and you have evidence to prove it. Investors will want to see that you have examined your competitors' offerings with real insight, and determined through competitive analysis how your offering meets this test.

Investors also must understand that the financial markets are cyclical. Your ability to exit successfully from a venture you've backed will depend not only on the company's performance but also more broadly on conditions in the financial markets. Is the IPO window open? Are the prices being paid for acquisitions or IPOs in your industry at cyclical highs? It's impossible to judge, when investing, exactly when the stars will align properly to permit an IPO or trade sale at an attractive price. Thus, sustainable advantage that can last until market conditions are favourable – whenever that may be – is important to investors for this reason as well.

Finally, we saw in the previous chapter that most industries are simply not as attractive as the pharmaceutical industry. Investors know that an industry that they find attractive enough to merit their investment today may change – as we've seen to some degree in pharmaceuticals – and become less attractive tomorrow, perhaps before an exit. Competitive sustainability, through patent protection or superior organisational processes, capabilities or resources – and based on an economically sustainable business model that protects a company from running out of cash – offers significant protection against such changes and against future competition more generally. Regardless of the level of industry attractiveness, however, such protection, as we've seen, is by no means guaranteed.

Lessons learned

At the end of Chapter 4, I raised the question, 'Can an entrepreneur or an early-stage investor make money in an unattractive industry?' We've now looked at mobile phones: a great market but a tough industry that humbled the seemingly invincible Nokia. Tagamet – in one of the most attractive industries on earth – lost its market leadership in ulcer medications to Zantac. EMI lost its early market leadership in CAT scanners to GE. None of these successes was sustained forever. What are the lessons we can take from the case histories in this chapter?

Lessons learned from Zantac

Companies with strong proprietary patent protection enjoy a comparatively benign competitive environment and relative freedom to set prices at levels that generate substantial profits, profits that may be reinvested in developing future winners or simply taken to the bank. Zantac enjoyed 12 generic-free years on the market (the other five were spent getting FDA approval). By 1995, Zantac had been prescribed to 240 million people worldwide and had reaped over $3.6 billion in sales.[75] If you've got a superior product with patent protection that's not easily circumvented, it's a licence to print money.

But entrepreneurs and their investors must consider not only whether their product or idea can win patent protection. It's also crucial to know whether that protection will be sufficient to ward off rivals. Doing so typically takes a deep understanding of the technology involved as well as in-depth understanding of how one's industry works.

Lessons learned from Nokia

Entrepreneurs who build superior organisational processes and capabilities into their companies can, like Nokia, maintain sustainable competitive advantage over their current and future competition *without* patent protection, at least for a time. Nokia's processes for attracting and retaining skilled people and for managing innovation enabled the company to remain innovative and agile, even as its organisation grew quite large. Thus, one thing entrepreneurs and the investors who consider backing them should think about in assessing an opportunity is whether the opportunity offers ways in which hard-to-imitate processes and systems can be built that can keep the new firm at least a few steps ahead of its current and future competitors. Even then, however, such advantages are unlikely to last forever, as Nokia has seen.

Lessons learned from EMI

While EMI's CAT scanner was the first of its kind, the patents it received were not broad enough to ward off imitation. Don't assume that a patent means protection. Further, EMI lacked the organisational capabilities to remain at the forefront of CAT scanner technology, and its lack of medical marketing and service capabilities put it at a significant disadvantage to its more established competitors.

❝don't assume that a patent means protection❞

Within six short years, it lost its market leadership, and in eight years it had exited the market entirely.

Thus, neither entrepreneurs nor investors should assume that their superior, patented product – even one destined to win a Nobel Prize – is sufficient to ensure long-term success. Zantac trumped Tagamet, and GE trumped EMI.

The EMI story is also a poignant reminder that first-mover advantage is often tenuous. Where is VisiCalc, the first spreadsheet software for PCs? Where is Osborne, the first portable PC? Both long gone. Why were Palm Pilots – then BlackBerrys – everywhere, while the earlier Apple Newton failed? Why doesn't anyone use Sinclair or Commodore computers – or Blackberrys, for that matter – any more? Most often, it takes something more than patent protection, and something more than a product or service that's new and better, to win in the long term. It takes organisational processes, capabilities and resources that can keep the business at the cutting edge. It takes a competitive advantage that lasts.

Lessons learned from eBay, Webvan and Tesco

Put simply, if your business model doesn't add up, your business won't last. If it costs you too much to do what you want to do – regardless of how innovative you are – then your business will die. eBay's economics worked for a long time, Tesco's too – though eBay appears to have lost its way with consumers in recent years. Webvan's economics simply did not work. To be sure, numerous other factors, such as great execution, helped eBay and Tesco. Similarly, poor execution probably hastened Webvan's demise. Given its model, however, Webvan's case history suggests that its demise was probably inevitable.

> **❝if your business model doesn't add up, your business won't last❞**

An economically sustainable business model is not a panacea, as we've seen with eBay, but it does serve as table stakes. Without a business model that's going to work, you really cannot expect a seat at the table for very long. But discovering a business model that will really work is no simple task. In my work with many readers of this book's first two editions, I discovered that the words 'business model' seemed to mean everything and anything and nothing at all. So I set forth on a research project in 2006 to build a framework to enable entrepreneurs and others to think more clearly about business models and to develop a disciplined process for getting to a business model that's likely to actually work – and, just maybe, to reinvent your industry in the process. The fruits of that labour are found in another of my (really good!) books, *Getting to Plan B*.[76] Alexander Osterwalder's business model canvas is another helpful tool that may help you develop your thinking in this regard.[77]

So, whether you are an aspiring entrepreneur or an early-stage investor, before you get rolling on your next start-up or deal, put your opportunity through the business model rigour articulated in this chapter. If your business model doesn't make sense, as Webvan's didn't, either find a way to fix it or move on.

Building competitive and economic sustainabiliity in lifestyle businesses

Not every entrepreneur seeks external investors and not every entrepreneur has the resources to build the kind of sustainability that the likes of Zantac enjoyed. So why is it that many entrepreneurs are able to build businesses of modest size that do business quite profitably over extended periods of time – for years, decades, even generations? With limited resources, how can entrepreneurs whose intent it is to be their own boss protect themselves from voracious competitors who may one day try to eat their lunch?

Often the key for lifestyle entrepreneurs or those of modest aspirations is to fly below the competitors' radar, serving niche markets having unique needs that an attentive entrepreneur can understand and appreciate. In such niches an entrepreneur's ability to tailor what's offered and serve customers exceptionally well can build loyalty that's difficult for larger competitors to erode or dislodge.

Doing so over time typically requires exceptional customer relations and selling skills, which results in deep insights into changing customer needs that may differ from what mass marketers are likely to address. Without these skills, and without the customer loyalty that can result from their effective application, small business owners are likely to see customers jump at the first opportunity when a bigger, better-known and perhaps more efficient competitor comes calling.

Taking stock of our progress so far

We've now observed in some depth several case histories that bring to life the four market and industry domains:

■ We've seen how markets and industries differ;

■ We've seen how micro- and macro-level assessments complement one another to tell a more complete story of an opportunity's attractiveness than those told by the macro-level assessments alone;

■ We've seen how it's possible to be successful in stagnant markets and in brutally competitive industries if there's sufficient strength at the micro level, including superior benefits for target customers and a way to sustain the advantage that those benefits bring over a long period of time;

■ We've seen that time is not necessarily on the entrepreneur's side and that first-mover advantage is largely a myth.

What we have yet to examine in any detail are the three domains concerned with what many see as the heart of any entrepreneurial venture, the entrepreneur, and his or her entrepreneurial team. There's a saying among venture capitalists that – market and industry considerations aside – successful entrepreneurship comes down to three elements: management, management and management. Is this aphorism true? Is this why Louis Borders, with his strong entrepreneurial track record, was able to raise so much money for Webvan? Can investors – not to mention the entrepreneurs who seek their backing – forget all we've just seen, and simply place bets on capable, experienced entrepreneurs they choose to back? In the next three chapters, we'll take a look at these questions.

The new business road test: stage four – the micro-industry test

■ Do you possess proprietary elements – patents, trade secrets and so on – that other firms cannot likely duplicate or imitate?

■ Can your business develop and employ superior organisational processes, capabilities or resources that others would have difficulty in duplicating or imitating? Evidence please!

– In what ways, from your customers' perspectives, will your offering be better, faster, cheaper (or whatever) than those of your competitors? Where might yours fall short? Evidence-based comparison, please!

■ Is your business model economically sustainable, i.e. can you show that your company won't run out of cash quickly? That depends upon the answers to these questions:

– Will your revenue be adequate in relation to the capital investment you need and the margins you can get?

▶

- How much will it cost you to acquire and retain customers?
- How long will it take you to attract customers?
- Will your contribution margins be adequate to cover your fixed cost structure sometime soon?
- How much cash must be tied up in working capital (inventory or other), for how long?
- How quickly will customers pay?
- How slowly will suppliers and employees be paid?

■ Based on the evidence you compile in answering the above questions, what are your key micro-industry risks, from both competitive and economic perspectives, and how – if at all – might they be mitigated?

THE NEW BUSINESS ROAD TEST

If you open your *New Business Road Test* app, you'll find the above checklist reproduced there. As you surf the Web or talk to experts to find data to underpin your business model or to assess the likelihood that you will be able to make your initial competitive edge a lasting one, you'll find places to keep track of links to your online sources or record what you glean from your conversations or interviews. But don't forget that your task isn't simply to gather data; it's to make judgements from what the data tell you, whether that's good news or bad. So be certain to indicate your tentative conclusion about the sustainability of your proposed venture, from both competitive and economic perspectives, as that conclusion evolves. Without drawing any conclusion, and without putting together solid underpinning for the numbers, your entrepreneurial journey is likely to be a difficult one. Entering a market or industry without suitable sources of competitive and economic sustainability is probably a trap!

6

What drives your entrepreneurial or investment dream?

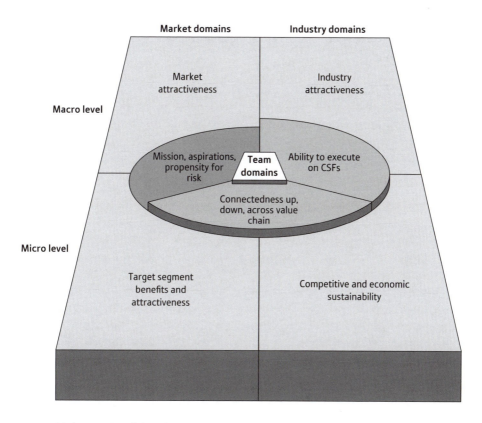

Mahatma Gandhi. Father of the Indian nation. Arguably, Gandhi did more in his lifetime for India and the Indian people than any other human being. The combination of his passion to eliminate injustice and his resolute belief in peaceful solutions led him to establish 'satyagraha' or passive resistance. He worked tirelessly throughout his 78 years for the rights of low-caste

Indian peoples, for peace between Hindu and Muslim Indians and for the independence of India from British rule.

Rather than encouraging violence, Gandhi used peaceful resistance and economic pressure to encourage favourable outcomes. To end violence, he fasted for weeks at a time. To promote independence from the British Empire, he led fellow Indians on the legendary Salt March. He encouraged Indians to spin their own fabrics rather than buy British cloth. His enduring efforts and leadership – and his dream – led to India's independence from Britain in 1947.[1]

What was it that made Gandhi successful? Gandhi was unfaltering in his mission to bring justice to the Indian people. His lofty aspirations to bring about justice for all Indians were ambitious, steadfast and unwavering. And he was willing to take enormous risks – facing imprisonment, even death – to attain such goals.

The mission, personal aspirations and risk propensity of entrepreneurs

Vivre sans rêve, qu'est ce? (What is life without a dream?)

Poet and playwright Edmond Rostand (1868–1918)[2]

It is rare to find someone as committed to a cause and as willing to make sacrifices in the name of his cause as Gandhi. Likening Gandhi's passion to that of an entrepreneur should by no means trivialise Gandhi's efforts and successes. Rather, the intensity and consistency in Gandhi's mission, personal aspirations and risk propensity provides a stirring example of what one person can accomplish.

Each successful entrepreneur brings to their venture an important set of elements that drives their entrepreneurial dream:

■ A mission that determines what kind of business to build or what kinds of markets to serve;

■ A set of personal aspirations that guides the level of achievement to be sought;

■ Some level of risk propensity that indicates what sort of risks are to be taken and what sort of sacrifices are to be made in pursuit of the dream.

Phil Knight of Nike had a mission to serve athletes and to help them deliver the best possible performance. He probably would not have been interested in an entrepreneurial venture that targeted any other market. Jeff Bezos, founder of Amazon.com, had aspirations to revolutionise the way people shop for books – and eventually nearly everything else! – and to become one of the world's largest retailers in the process. Bezos would not have been content to build a smaller business more limited in scale and scope. As we'll see in this chapter, Howard Schultz, the creator of Starbucks as we know it today, was prepared – twice – to risk a promising career to fulfil his entrepreneurial dream to 'unlock the mystery and romance of coffee. The Italians had turned the drinking of coffee into a symphony',[3] and Schultz saw an opportunity to recreate the Italian coffee bar culture in America.

The point here is that entrepreneurship – the pursuit of opportunity without regard to the resources under one's control[4] – is a very personal game. *Successful* entrepreneurship almost always requires a clear vision about what you as an entrepreneur want out of the effort. What's your mission? Do you want to serve athletic markets? Do you want to sell coffee? What level of aspirations do you have? Do you hope to be the next Phil Knight, Richard Branson or Mark Zuckerberg, or would you prefer to build a nice little lifestyle business – perhaps any business – that you can run yourself? What sort of risks are you prepared to take? Will you put your own money on the line? How much? Will you go without income? For how long? Must you control your venture, or are you willing to have a smaller piece of a larger entrepreneurial pie at the risk of some day losing control or even being tossed out of the venture you started?

> ❝entrepreneurship is a very personal game❞

Only you can decide these things, and decide you must, whether your venture will operate by today's lean principles or otherwise. Without a clear mission, your entrepreneurial efforts will be fragmented, lacking in purpose and direction. Without understanding your own aspirations, you'll be unable to articulate to others whose support you will need – for money, time, love and much more – why they should support you. Without identifying your own level of risk propensity – it's different for everyone, and in different settings, from business to skydiving – you'll be unable to demonstrate to investors, if you seek investment capital, that you are willing to share in the risks you'll ask them to take. Without sharing the risk, you probably won't raise any money. Thus your own very personal answers to the questions raised here are likely to be of considerable interest to prospective investors, too.

Equally important, the three elements that drive your entrepreneurial dream – mission, personal aspirations and risk propensity – must fit together in a coherent and cohesive way. You probably cannot aspire to greatness without tolerating some level of risk. You cannot aspire to greatness without a willingness to share at least some ownership and control, since successful entrepreneurship is, most often, a team sport. Going it alone can work for a lifestyle business, but it's unlikely to enable you to become the next Branson or Zuckerberg.

In this chapter, we examine two case histories. The first, that of the seemingly ubiquitous Starbucks, we explore in considerable depth; the second, Third-Love, we treat at a glance as its story at this time of writing is just getting started.

Howard Schultz and the coffee experience[5]

The visionary creator of what we know as Starbucks today, Howard Schultz, had a mission to bring quality coffee and the Italian coffee-drinking culture to the American public. He aspired to be a part of a company with a vision, a conscience and a powerful energy that could bring about greatness. His personal aspirations were not only to start such a company but also to bring the company to the pinnacle of prominence. To achieve these aspirations, Schultz was willing to take the personal and professional risks necessary to get there.

By 2017, Starbucks was generating annual revenues north of $21 billion and operated more than 24,000 coffee bars in 70 countries. It had grown from its roots as a speciality coffee roaster and retailer in Seattle to one of the world's best-known brands. Howard Schultz made it happen. Here is his story.

Schultz's passion for coffee awakens in Seattle

Schultz grew up a child of 'working poor' parents, as he would say later, in the Bayside Projects in Brooklyn, New York.[6] After finding his way to college on an athletic scholarship, he graduated and began his career in 1976 as a sales trainee for Xerox. After three years at Xerox and realising his indifference towards word processors and office equipment, Schultz joined Perstorp, a Swedish company with product lines in building supplies and consumer durables for the home. While selling Perstorp's kitchen components in North Carolina, Schultz again found himself less than excited about his product line. It was not until he took the position of Vice-president and General Manager of Hammarplast, Perstorp's housewares subsidiary, that he became more enthusiastic about the products he sold, stylish Swedish-designed kitchen gear.

In 1981, while working for Hammarplast, Schultz noticed that one particular retailer – a Seattle-based company called Starbucks Coffee, Tea, and Spice – consistently purchased large quantities of his drip coffeemakers. With only a handful of small stores, Starbucks was buying more of Hammarplast's coffeemakers than Macy's, New York's leading department store. Schultz wanted to know why. He flew to Seattle to take a look.

Starbucks was a coffee drinker's paradise, selling some 30 different varieties of whole-bean, mountain-grown arabica coffees – from Sumatra, Kenya, Costa Rica and everywhere – as well as high-end coffeemakers. While the store encouraged customers to taste the coffee, they did not sell coffee by the cup.

❝Schultz was hooked, and returned to New York determined to find a way to work for Starbucks❞

Schultz was enamoured with the company's coffee, and was even more impressed with the passion that Jerry Baldwin, one of Starbucks' three partners, felt towards his product: 'I had never heard anyone talk about a product the way Jerry talked about coffee.'[7] Schultz was hooked, and he returned to New York determined to find a way to work for Starbucks.

Risk number one

Over the next year, Schultz found ways to spend some time with Baldwin. He believed Baldwin's concept would sell in New York, Chicago, Boston, everywhere. And Schultz had the marketing experience and drive to help grow the business. He wanted in. At last, over dinner in San Francisco in the spring of 1982 with Starbucks' partners, Schultz thought he had won the job. But, on the phone the next day, Baldwin called with bad news: 'I'm sorry, Howard. It's too risky. Too much change.' Schultz was shell-shocked: 'I saw my whole future pass in front of me and then crash and burn.'[8] The next day, Schultz called and reminded Baldwin of his own vision for Starbucks. A day later, Schultz had the job, along with a steep cut in pay and a tiny slice of equity in the company.

In 1983, Starbucks sent Schultz to Milan for a housewares show. During that visit, he experienced the Italian coffee bar culture. This Italian ritual of drinking coffee and socialising intrigued Schultz: 'Coffeehouses in Italy are a third place for people, after home and work. There's a relationship of trust and confidence in that environment.'[9] Schultz discovered that there were 200,000 coffee bars in Italy, with some 1,500 in Milan alone. He became fascinated with the idea of bringing such a concept and culture to the USA: 'The connection to the people who loved coffee did not have to take place only in their homes, where they ground and brewed whole-bean coffee. What we had to do was unlock the romance and mystery of coffee, firsthand, in coffee bars.'[10] 'Coffee bars are the mainstay of every Italian neighborhood,' he said. 'That's what I wanted to bring back to Seattle.'[11]

❝what we had to do was unlock the romance and mystery of coffee❞

Schultz returned from Milan and pitched the coffee bar idea to the Starbucks partners. Their initial response was a resounding no. They did not want to enter into what they considered the restaurant business, not the best of industries in their view. Schultz finally convinced the partners to add a small espresso bar in their sixth store, which would open in April 1984. Within two months, the store was serving 800 customers a day, compared with the traditional Starbucks stores that averaged 250 customers a day. But even with impressive numbers to support his idea, Schultz could not convince the company's partners to try the coffee shop concept further: 'I felt torn in two by conflicting feelings: loyalty to Starbucks and confidence in my vision for Italian-style espresso bars.'[12]

Risk number two

In 1985, Schultz made one of the toughest decisions in his still-young career. He decided to leave Starbucks to start what seemed to be a very uncertain coffee bar business. At the time, coffee was a seemingly risky game. With the disclosure of health risks associated with caffeine, consumption of coffee had been falling in the USA since the 1960s, hardly the most exciting of markets.

At the time, Schultz's wife was pregnant with their first child and he needed an initial $400,000 in seed capital to open his first store and get the business started – money he simply did not have. As Schultz was planning how to raise the money, Starbucks stepped forward to invest $150,000 in Schultz's venture, and Jerry Baldwin agreed to serve on the board. Gordon Bowker, Baldwin's partner in Starbucks, also agreed to help. Shortly thereafter, Schultz received another $100,000 from a local doctor, who said, 'It appears to me that people who succeed have an incredible drive to do something . . . They spend their energy to take a gamble. In this world, relatively few people are willing to take a large gamble.'[13]

By the time Schultz's son was born in January 1986, Schultz had raised the rest of the money he needed to open the first store. His real goal, though, was another $1.25 million to open seven more stores and to prove that the idea would work on an extended scale. It took an entire year to raise all the money, during which Schultz approached 242 potential investors, 217 of whom turned him away. Over the course of a year, he raised $1.65 million from about 30 investors, enough to open eight coffee bars. Schultz said, 'If you ask any of those investors today why they took the risk, almost all of them will tell you that they invested in me, not in my idea.'[14]

> **❝Schultz approached 242 potential investors, 217 of whom turned him away❞**

Schultz opened the first Il Giornale, as his new coffee bars were called, on 8 April 1986. Il Giornale meant 'the daily' in Italian and was the name of the largest newspaper in Italy. On its first day in business, Il Giornale served 300 customers. Within six months, the store was serving 1,000 customers a day. Even with just one store, Schultz was dreaming big: 'At the time, our plans seemed impossibly ambitious. Even then, when nobody had heard of Il Giornale, I had a dream of building the largest coffee company in North America, with stores in every major city.'[15]

The first Il Giornale was not a perfect success. Schultz soon realised that Italian opera was not the preferred music of American coffee drinkers. He also learned that the shops should include seating for those customers wishing to relax and stay awhile. Learning from these mistakes, Schultz opened his next Il Giornale six months after the first in a downtown Seattle high-rise office tower. By mid-1987, there were three Il Giornale stores, and each store was generating approximately $500,000 in annual sales.

Risk number three

In March 1987, with the first Il Giornale having been open for less than a year, Jerry Baldwin and Gordon Bowker decided to sell their six Starbucks stores, roasting plant and name. Jerry wanted to concentrate on Peet's, a small chain of stores selling beans and ground coffee that Starbucks had acquired. 'As soon as I heard, I knew I had to buy Starbucks. It was my destiny,' said Schultz. But it would take nearly $4 million to do it. Having seen Starbucks struggle under an excessive debt burden when it bought Peet's, Schultz knew the new money would have to be raised through the sale of equity, in spite of the fact that it would dilute his ownership of and control over the business. Schultz looked again to investors, including those who had invested in Il Giornale and others who had passed, to raise the needed capital. His pitch to investors was one of pure passion: "How many things do people in America drink every day? Coffee is such a social beverage, a personal beverage. There's the romance of coffee, its history. We had an opportunity to utilize the relationship I saw in Italy, the safe haven of the coffee bar, and package it with undeniably great coffee and service that is completely different from most establishments in America. I mean, we can change how people start their day.'[16]

Schultz's passion for great coffee and his concept proved successful. By August 1987, at the age of 34, Schultz had raised another $3.8 million, and the original Starbucks was his.

The rest of the story

Schultz realised that taking over a company was not an easy task. His initial goals were twofold: to win the support of the existing Starbucks employees and to hire a winning team of managers. In his first meeting with the Starbucks employees, Schultz announced his mission of building a national company whose values and guiding principles they all could be proud of. Schultz had to make sure the existing employees were on board in order to move forward with his plans. He also recognised that, as his company grew, he would need to rely on the expertise of others: 'I knew I had to go out and hire executives with greater experience than I had.'[17]

❝hire people smarter than you are and get out of their way❞

Schultz did just that. He hired a number of experienced people to lead his management team. He lived by a simple philosophy: 'Hire people smarter than you are and get out of their way.'[18] Finding and retaining top people was one of Schultz's ways to lay a solid foundation for growth.

In October 1987, Schultz and his team opened the first store under the Starbucks name in Chicago. It was their first attempt away from the west coast. In the following six months, three more stores opened in Chicago. The results were less than stellar. With distribution and logistics costs added in, the cost of goods sold was much higher in Chicago than in Seattle. And, Chicagoans showed less interest in the coffee shop experience than their Seattle compatriots. In 1987, the company lost $330,000.

But those financial losses didn't faze Schultz and his team. Schultz could show investors the attractive unit economics at each store to convince them the business model was viable. Overall losses were necessary in order to invest in the people and systems necessary for his company to reach its potential. Investors could also see that the speciality coffee business all over the country, both in supermarkets and coffee bars, was becoming as hot as a freshly brewed cup of espresso.[19] Starbucks kept growing:

■ In 1988, Starbucks opened 15 new stores and developed its first mail-order catalogue, but losses grew to $764,000 for the year;

■ In 1989, the company opened more stores and lost another $1.2 million;

■ In 1990, with another 30 new stores, the company turned profitable.

By that time, the company had received three major rounds of private funding: the $3.8 million to acquire Starbucks; $3.9 million in early 1990 to finance additional growth; and $13.5 million later in 1990 from venture capital investors who saw the potential that the Starbucks story represented.

By 1992, Starbucks' revenues were rising at approximately 80 per cent per year. In June of that year, Starbucks went public, raising $29 million to support even faster growth in new stores. At the time of its initial public offering, Starbucks had 2,000 employees and 600,000 customers weekly. That year, 53 additional stores were opened, bringing the grand total of Starbucks coffee bars to 140.

By 1993, Starbucks ranked among the 40 fastest-growing companies in the USA according to *Fortune* magazine. And the company was not just a model for growth. In 1994, Schultz received an award from the Business Enterprise Trust for courage, integrity and social vision in business.[20] And the growth continued:

- In 1997, Starbucks' revenues exceeded $1 billion;
- A year later, the company had 1,500 outlets and 25,000 employees, and was beginning to sell its coffee in supermarkets;
- By 1999, stores were averaging $800,000 in annual revenue and there were 80 Starbucks stores in Great Britain and 53 stores in Japan.

In 2000, Schultz decided to cede his CEO position to his President and COO, Orin Smith. Not ready to leave Starbucks, Schultz remained as Chairman and Chief Global Strategist. At first, the company didn't miss a beat:

- by the end of 2001, Starbucks was serving 2 million customers a week from its 5,000 outlets worldwide, and had delivered 121 consecutive months of positive comparative store sales;
- that year, profits grew by 92 per cent to $181.2 million on sales of $3 billion;
- by 2002, Starbucks operated 1,200 stores outside the USA in 20 countries, up from 281 international stores in 1999.[21]

Starbucks' stock had soared more than 2,200 per cent over the past decade, outpacing Wal-Mart, General Electric and Microsoft in total return. Schultz's shares alone were worth $400 million. By 2004, Starbucks' annual revenue had passed the $5 billion mark, with comparable store sales still growing, up 10 per cent on 2004, and with overall net revenue up 30 per cent on the previous year.[22] The company ranked 11th in *Fortune* magazine's '100 Best Companies to Work For' list.[23] The lad from the Projects in Brooklyn had done quite well.[24]

Starbucks' incredible growth continued over the next four years, breaking $9 billion in revenues in 2008.[25] But all was not as well as it seemed: there was talk of over-expansion in the US, same-store sales figures were dropping rapidly,[26] and the company's long-time focus on the customer experience, the very thing Schultz had been so passionate about, was getting lost as the megabrand grew in scale.

Schultz was asked to take back the top job. His task was not made any easier by the recession, a difficult environment in which to sell $4 lattes. In 2008 and 2009, 900 locations were closed and $580 million costs were cut.[27] There was renewed focus on the customer. By 2009, operating margins began to increase, though sales continued to disappoint. 'The entire Starbucks organization is committed to continually improving our customer experience as the roadmap to renewed growth and increasing profitability. At the same time, we will continue to innovate and differentiate, two perennial hallmarks of the Starbucks brand,' said Schultz.[28]

Indeed, since 2009, Starbucks has recovered its mojo and aggressively expanded, particularly into the Chinese market, where they were the first to introduce western-style coffee shops on a substantial scale. Schultz even suggested that soon there may be more Starbucks outlets in China than in the USA. In 2017, Starbucks was set to enter Italy, the country that first inspired Schultz.[29]

Schultz's return to the helm had served Starbucks well, but all good things must come to an end. Once again, on 1st December 2016, Schultz (aged 63) announced that he would step down from being Starbucks' CEO in April 2017. He planned to retain a position as executive chairman, focusing on Starbucks Reserve, a premium offering for customers who are more exacting about their coffee and where alcohol was also served. His pride in his achievements was clear. 'Starbucks consistently outperforms the retail industry because our stores, our offerings and the experiences our partners create make us a destination.'[30]

Schultz' entrepreneurial dream has served Starbucks and its customers well over more than 35 years. Will ThirdLove's Heidi Zak and Ra'el Cohen be able to match Schultz's commitment to their own entrepreneurial dream? Let's take a brief look at what they hope to accomplish in Case Study 6.1.

---

case study 6.1

Building a bra that fits[31]

ThirdLove co-founder and CEO Heidi Zak put it simply: 'I had always dreaded bra shopping.' At a 100-woman focus group in San Francisco in 2013, Zak was hoping for new insights to aid in the development of her fledgling company's virtual bra shopping app. Instead, what she

▶

learned was that 37 per cent of all women fall between cup sizes. 'That helped explain why my bras never fit,' recalled Zak, who had alternated between two bra sizes all her adult life.

Zak was convinced that bras as a product category were in desperate need of an overhaul. After digging through LinkedIn, she found Ra'el Cohen, a designer at a high-end lingerie company, and was able to convince Cohen to come on board. 'I knew the industry was broken,' says Cohen. 'I also knew that if they could persuade someone like me to leave a good company to join them, they would be able to recruit good people and raise money.' After creating new half-size prototypes, Zak and Cohen invited the focus group women back for a fitting. 'Everyone was, like, "Finally! A bra that fits!"', recalls Zak. 'Some even got a bit teary.'

Zak's and Cohen's dream was to give a woman a bra so comfortable that she could forget she was wearing it. Their passion led to the development of several proprietary elements, including a lightweight memory foam that molded to the shape of the breast and felt like a second skin, attributes that defined ThirdLove bras. And their devotion to detail, getting everything just right – from a comfortably padded clasp to labelling that was printed-on, not sewn-on (inevitably scratchy!) – began to pay off, with monthly shipments reaching nearly 50,000 bras per month in 2016. Says Cohen, 'You wouldn't want to buy a shoe that didn't have half-sizes. Why would you want to buy a bra without them?'

What investors want to know

Some entrepreneurs, hence some lean start-ups, need no investors. They are able to pursue their entrepreneurial dreams without external capital. Others, like Starbucks' Howard Schultz and ThirdLove's Heidi Zak, cannot expect to reach their aspirations without more capital than they and the three Fs (family, friends and fools, remember?) can bring to the table. What roles do an entrepreneur's mission, aspiration and risk propensity play in attracting investment capital?

First, most professional investors – business angels or venture capital investors – have missions of their own, often driven by what they already know or what's made money for them before. Some invest in certain industries, like telecommunications or media. Some invest in certain markets, like companies serving medical practitioners. Matching your mission to their mission is critical, for only rarely will investors invest outside their chosen arenas. Had Howard Schultz chosen an initial mission of coffee manufacturing and wholesaling – as some companies did once they saw Americans' growing fascination with better coffee – instead of coffee retailing, then his investor group would probably have looked quite different. Most investors want a clear understanding of the kind of company you plan to build.

Second, professional investors' aspirations are usually quite simple – to make loads of money for themselves and/or their own investors. Doing so involves growing and *ultimately selling* the ventures they invest in – reader, take note – either to the public or to a trade buyer. The day you accept venture capital is the day you've agreed to sell your business. If your aspirations are less lofty – something that's true for many entrepreneurs – or if your dream is to run your business independently for a long time rather than selling it, then seeking investors other than the three Fs is probably not for you.

Third, professional investors understand the risks they take. They know the odds are stacked against any single venture meeting its goals. Only one or two out of every ten deals in a typical venture capital portfolio will make big money. A few more may return their capital but earn no return. The rest will probably lose most or all of the capital invested.

❝investors want to see that *you* are willing to risk your capital, just as they are risking theirs❞

Given these difficult odds, angels and venture capitalists want to know that the entrepreneurs they back will make extraordinary efforts and commitments to beat the long odds. To ensure such commitment, they want to know that you have something to lose if you fail, just as they do.

What this means, in practical terms, is that investors want to see that *you* are willing to risk your capital, just as they are risking theirs.

Typically, they measure your willingness to share in the risks by the relative amount you'll risk compared with what you have. If you don't have much money, then your cash investment can be modest. If you've already made it big once, then you'll be expected to risk some of your gains alongside the capital you ask others to put at risk.

In summary, you need to be clear about your mission, aspirations and risk propensity *before* you launch a lean start-up, before you write a business plan, and before you approach prospective investors. Approaching them sooner is a waste of time or – worse – a potential disaster. There's no faster way for investors to remove you from your leadership role than to have them discover that your and their goals are incompatible. This is far more common than most nascent entrepreneurs would believe. Building an NLO business – a nice living for the owner – is not something most investors have in mind.

What investors must consider in their own entrepreneurial dreams

In a very real sense, those who invest in early-stage ventures are every bit the 'entrepreneurs' as are the individuals they back. Thus, they, too, should give careful thought to what their missions, aspirations and risk propensities are – their own entrepreneurial dreams – when they begin investing this way.

First, it's worth pointing out that the odds of making good money as an early-stage investor are stacked against you. After all, we all know what most early-stage ventures do – they fail! And sadly, the lemons tend to ripen earlier than the cherries and plums! While I'd like to offer some research evidence to support the point I've made here, I'm afraid I cannot. Though 'research studies' reporting purported aggregate returns for angel investors appear from time to time, they tend to suffer from what's called 'non-response bias' and 'survivor bias'. That is, while those who make good money are happy to boast about (and report) their attractive returns, those who fare poorly tend to keep quiet or disappear from the early-stage investment scene altogether. Thus I put little faith in such reports. Neither should you.

Nonetheless, I continue to make angel investments, and I enjoy (and profit from) doing so. So here's what I suggest you do. First, reread the section immediately preceding this one, 'What investors want to know', and ask yourself questions similar to those I've posed therein for entrepreneurs:

- What's your mission in becoming an angel investor? Are you in it for the fun, and for the stories you'll be able to tell? Will you restrict your investing to 'markets and industries that I know and understand'? Will you join an angel club or network and follow others' leads, or carve your own path?

- What are your aspirations? Is making large amounts of money on your angel investments important to you? Or are you in the game for other reasons? Many early-stage investors seek to 'repay' today's generation of entrepreneurs with the same kind of support – financial and otherwise – that was provided for them by their own earlier angel investors. But be careful. If you're not investing in what you know and understand, the 'help and advice' you give may be less than helpful, perhaps even detrimental!

■ What sort of risks are you willing to take? I suggest you invest only money that you can afford to lose. If you fail to follow this maxim, you'll be likely to panic when the going gets tough, as it so often does, and that won't help your entrepreneurs. Will you seek to build a diverse portfolio to diversify your risk? Will you invest in lines (a series of data points providing evidence of a venture's progress over time) or dots (a slick pitch that gets you excited at a single moment in time)?

Sad to say, it's pretty sexy to be an angel investor today. Just as I don't want attractive markets to cause you or your entrepreneurs to overlook the rest of the seven domains, I don't want all the hype about early-stage investing to blur your vision.

Lessons learned

Not every entrepreneur can start a company and lead it to greatness in just 15 years. Some are good at the start-up stage and pass the leadership baton once things are well under way. Others grow their businesses slowly and steadily, sometimes taking decades to reach their dreams. Only a few can take the business all the way from conception to stardom as quickly as did Howard Schultz. What can would-be entrepreneurs learn from Schultz's story?

❝his clear sense of purpose helped him focus his energies❞

■ Schultz was clear about his mission: to build a company that brought the Italian coffee bar culture to the USA, to serve only the finest coffee and to run an organisation that valued its employees. His clear sense of purpose helped him focus his energies.

■ His personal aspirations were audacious: to build a large, prominent and profitable company that would change how Americans enjoyed their day. Simply running a few coffee shops in Seattle was not his cup of tea.

■ He was willing to repeatedly take risks to achieve his goals.

Lessons learned about mission

Howard Schultz didn't choose coffee because coffee was hot. As we have seen, American coffee consumption had been declining for years before Schultz and other espresso entrepreneurs came along and reversed its direction. He chose coffee because he was hooked. Hooked on the taste and aroma of dark-roasted arabica coffee, so different from what he had known as coffee before. Hooked on learning about coffee and different ways to roast it. And hooked on the idea of introducing the Italian coffee culture to the USA and, thereafter, the world.

Schultz's passion for coffee served him – and Starbucks – well. It helped him attract and retain committed employees like coffee aficionado Dave Olson, who came to personify the company's passionate attitude towards coffee.[32] It helped him win investors, without whom his story never would have played out. It helped him win believers among suppliers who would go on to benefit greatly from Starbucks' growth.

While for many investors the mission is simply to make money, for entrepreneurs a burning desire to make money is not enough on its own. It's almost impossible for an entrepreneur to be wildly successful in a business they don't care about deeply. Without a greater purpose than money, the battles are simply too tough to tackle simply for money's sake. As Jeff Hawkins, founder of Palm Computing and Handspring (whom we will hear about in the next chapter), says, 'Do something you believe because you believe it.'[33]

Early in his career, Schultz was successful in selling copiers and housewares, but he could never have matched what he achieved selling the coffee experience if he had tried his own venture selling, say, office supplies. Schultz's story suggests that if you don't feel passionate about your opportunity, then you might be better advised to find a venture that does light your fire. Simply looking at what's hot – whether plastics, software, biotech or whatever – isn't the answer. Nor is seeking to start a business – any old business – with an eye toward changing your plans if things don't work out. Your time and your energy are too precious to waste!

> **what makes more sense for a would-be entrepreneur – a laser-like focus on a single direction, or hedging one's bets?**

There's another mission-related aspect of Schultz's story that offers lessons to learn. At the beginning, Schultz was focused clearly on a single direction that his business would take – coffee bars in urban settings. Would-be entrepreneurs sometimes lack Schultz's single-minded mission, seeing multiple paths that they might pursue. For Schultz, his passion for great coffee could have been pursued in other ways.

Coffee speciality stores like Jerry Baldwin's original Starbucks stores were one possible choice. Roasting better coffee for the supermarket trade was another. What makes more sense for a would-be entrepreneur – a laser-like focus on a single direction, or hedging one's bets?

Experienced entrepreneurs, and seasoned early-stage investors as well, know there are two serious drawbacks to the latter approach. First, attempting multiple things with the typically scarce resources that most entrepreneurs have at hand results in doing none of them well. Less is more. It's usually far better to devote all one's energies to the most promising path. If the path turns out to be blocked, then something will likely have been learned that can identify a more promising one. Probably one of the reasons you're reading this book is that you're trying to identify just what your best path is and whether it's good enough to be worthy of placing your bet.

A second drawback is that having multiple paths in mind can detract from your ability to attract employees, investors and suppliers to your cause. If you lack the confidence and commitment to choose the best path for your business, then why should these other stakeholders get on board? Single-minded focus wins every time with these groups.

Lessons learned about personal aspirations

Different entrepreneurs have different aspirations. For some, their entrepreneurial dream is simply to make a satisfactory living for themselves and their family, or to escape the humdrum world where they work today. Others, like India's Mahatma Gandhi and Starbucks' Howard Schultz, want nothing less than to change the world in some way. There are three questions every aspiring entrepreneur should ask.

■ How big do I want this business to become – in sales, profits, number of employees, number of locations or by some other measure?

■ What role do I want in this venture: do I want to create, *do, manage* or *lead*?

■ For how long do I want to remain involved with it?

Some entrepreneurs or entrepreneurial teams have aspirations to run a business just large enough to meet certain objectives: to provide a living for their family, to provide multiple roles in which two or more partners can work, to build a nest egg of a certain size, and so on. Most such ventures, unfortunately, are probably not backable by most early-stage investors, most of whom have more expansive dreams in mind. Other entrepreneurs, like Schultz, want to build something big. In Schultz's words 'If you want to build a great enterprise, you have to have the courage to dream great dreams. If you dream small dreams, you may succeed in building something small. For many people, that is enough. But if you want to achieve widespread impact and lasting value, be bold.'[34]

Reaching the kind of scale that Starbucks has reached is not something a single individual can ordinarily do. Entrepreneurship played for these kinds of stakes is a team sport. Not every entrepreneur has the capacity, courage and willingness to do this. And with size comes complexity. Some simply don't want this sort of complexity in their business lives, or they may prefer to devote significant energies to their personal lives – family, avocations and so on. Building a fast-growing venture takes all one can give. As Schultz says, 'You have to work so hard and have so much enthusiasm for one thing that most other things in your life have to be sacrificed.'[35] It's not for everyone. Is it for you?

The question of roles is also worth some thought for every would-be entrepreneur. As small businesses grow into large ones, the roles of those who lead them must inevitably evolve. At the outset, what entrepreneurs do is *do*. Schultz roasted coffee, made espressos, raised capital and found locations for his next stores. But it simply was not possible for him to do these things himself forever. As it turned out, Schultz was happy bringing on 'people smarter than me' and letting them do what they'd been hired to do. As Schultz puts it: "There's a common mistake a lot of entrepreneurs make. They own the idea, and they have the passion to pursue it. But they can't possibly possess all the skills needed to make the idea actually happen. Reluctant to delegate, they surround themselves with faithful aides. They're afraid to bring in truly smart, successful individuals as high-level managers.[36]

But managing and delegating are not what every entrepreneur wants. If you are an architect whose work is admired, then do you want to do architecture and keep designing interesting buildings, or do you want to grow your business and manage architects and let them exercise their own creativity? It's an important choice, and one not to be taken lightly. Make it consciously, not by default.

Then there's the question of how long you want to manage or lead your business. Do you want to stay the course for many years to build your business yourself? Or are you happy to get it started, exit early if possible and move on to something else? Is it creating, i.e. the early-stage work, or the managing, i.e. the later-stage work, that turns you on? It's another choice to take seriously. What is it that you really want out of being an entrepreneur? Prospective investors will want to know!

> **"what is it that you really want out of being an entrepreneur?"**

Lessons about risk propensity

Most successful entrepreneurs do not regard themselves as risk-takers. Managers of risk, yes. But risk-takers, no. Their job is to offload the inherent risk in their ventures to suppliers, investors, landlords and whomever is willing to bear it. In their hearts, most entrepreneurs see little risk – naïvely, perhaps – given their belief that theirs is one new venture that will buck the long odds and succeed.

But, as Schultz's story points out, there are repeated risks to be taken along the way. The obvious ones include money – yours and others' – and months or years of your life and the opportunity costs of doing something else with that time. There are other risks that are less obvious. There's the risk that your investors may at some point decide that you should go. Is this a risk you are willing to bear to raise investment capital, or is maintaining control, even at the cost of limiting the scale of what you can accomplish or the resources you can assemble, a crucial factor

> **❝there are risks that are less obvious❞**

for you? And what about the risk propensity of those you love who are sure to bear some of the costs of your entrepreneurial pursuits? Marriages have been broken as entrepreneurs and their spouses fail to agree on what should be risked. Dinner with the family? The house? The security of a regular salary? What level of risk are you willing to bear? Is that level of risk acceptable for the upside your opportunity offers? As Schultz tells it:

For me, the thrill of business is in the climb. Everything we try to achieve is like climbing a steep slope, one that very few people have managed to scale. The more difficult the climb, the more gratifying the effort put into the ascent and the greater the satisfaction upon reaching the summit. But, like all dedicated mountain climbers, we're always seeking a higher peak.[37]

Risk and reward, constant companions. How much of each will you choose? What's the nature of your entrepreneurial dream? And what, indeed, is life without such a dream?

The new business road test: stage five – the mission, aspirations and risk propensity test

■ What's your entrepreneurial mission?

- – To serve a particular market?
- – To change a particular industry?
- – To market a particular product?
- – Is the passion really there?

■ What level of aspirations do you have for your entrepreneurial dream?

- – To work for yourself?
- – To build something small or something big?
- – To create? To do? To manage? To lead?
- – To change the world in some way?

■ What sorts of risk are you and are you not willing to take?

- – Will you risk a secure salary and the things that go along with your current employment? For how long?
- – Will you risk losing control of your business?
- – Will you put your own money at risk? How much?
- – Will you risk your home or time with your family or loved ones?
- – Do those you love accept the risks you'll take?

■ In what ways, if any, do your mission, your aspirations or your risk propensity add new elements of risk to the venture? How might any such risks be mitigated?

THE NEW BUSINESS ROAD TEST

If you open your *New Business Road Test* app, you'll find the above checklist reproduced there. Gaining honest insights into what's driving you to be an entrepreneur – whether in your kitchen or garage, or in an entrepreneurial role in the company where you work – and what you hope to get out of it will require reflection and introspection. In addition, it's often helpful to read about or talk with others who have travelled the entrepreneurial path before you, to benefit from what they've learned about the commitments that are necessary and the sacrifices that it can take. As you engage in this process, you'll find places in the app to keep track of links to your online sources or record what you glean from your conversations or interviews. This is the only one of the seven domains for which no judgement is required about your opportunity itself. Instead, the judgements are about you – who you are and what you want to achieve, and how that fits with this particular opportunity. But don't ignore these issues or underestimate their importance, because they provide a lens through which the other six domains must be viewed.

7

Can you and your team execute?

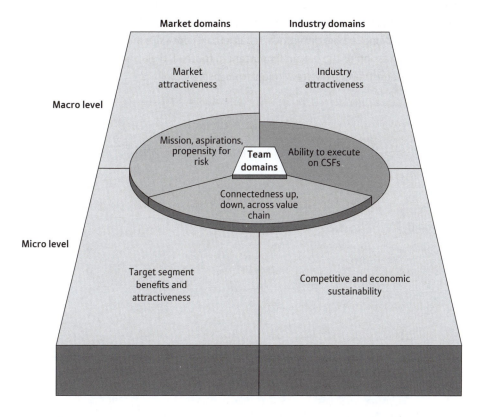

What makes a sports team successful? It depends upon the sport. For most teams, the need for talented, conditioned, well-trained athletes and a competent coaching staff are obvious requirements. Yet, beyond these fundamental criteria, no two sports have the same critical success factors.

Take, for example, basketball, football and polo. Successful basketball teams must have players with the hand–eye coordination to shoot the ball accurately. Having tall players doesn't hurt, either, of course.

On the other hand, football (soccer) is played largely with the feet, so hand–eye coordination doesn't matter very much. Agility and an ability to control the ball while keeping one's head and eyes up are critical, however.

A polo team's success depends on both the athletes and the horses. As in basketball and football, the athletes need to have a good shot, but they must also be able to make this shot while riding a horse at high speed.

In all three sports, endurance also matters – the fittest team often wins. In each of these sports, different factors are critical to success. Height and shooting ability make a big difference in basketball. Foot skills and the ability to maintain possession of the ball are important in football. Well-trained horses and skilled equestrians separate winners from losers in polo.

The sport of entrepreneurship

In the People was my trust, And in the virtues which mine eyes had seen.

William Wordsworth (1770–1850)[1]

Just as nearly every sport requires its athletes to be physically fit, so every entrepreneurial venture needs to have the fundamentals – a superior product or service, an efficient supply chain, motivated people and so on. These are the basics without which no business can survive for long. Returning to sport for a moment, all the world's top tennis players, all the footballers in the World Cup, all the runners on the start line of an Olympic marathon are superbly fit. Fitness is a basic requirement. But it takes more than fitness, of course, to win a Wimbledon title, the World Cup or an Olympic medal.

So, what separates the great athletes and great teams from the very, very good ones? The great ones are the ones who consistently meet the critical success factors for their chosen sport, whether that be speed, strength, balance, tactical savvy or whatever. An ability to execute on these critical success factors is the difference between great and almost great. As in the World Cup or on the tennis circuit, where there's significant difference in performance between the winners and those who don't place, so the same is true in the business world. In mobile phones, Nokia thrived while Motorola and others struggled. Then, suddenly, Nokia struggled, too. In athletic footwear, Nike and UnderArmour grew rapidly while the traditional athletic footwear makers just muddled along. What is it that causes such variation in performance within an industry?

We've already seen some sources of variation, such as patent protection and organisational processes and capabilities that are not imitated easily. But there's something else that can account for such differences. That 'something else' is a management team's ability to execute against the few critical success factors – no more than a handful, usually – that tend to account for much of the difference in performance from one company to another within an industry.

> **"just as in each sport there are a few key attributes that separate the winners from the losers, the same is true in entrepreneurship"**

Just as in each sport there are a few key attributes that separate the winners from the losers, the same is true in entrepreneurship. A common difference between winners and losers is that the winners figure out the factors critical to succeeding in their particular industry, and then assemble their team accordingly. The losers either do not identify these critical success factors or do not possess a team capable of delivering on them.

So, what if your industry is extremely competitive, with one or more of the five forces conspiring against you and your prospective competitors? Can you still be successful? The answer to this question is 'Yes, *but . . .* '. This chapter speaks directly to the 'but'. Even in relatively unattractive industries, at least some companies typically perform quite well. Others are left in the dust. So, the 'but' is this: yes, entrepreneurs can succeed in difficult industries, *but* they must be able to:

- Identify the critical success factors specific to their particular industry;
- Assemble a team that can execute on these factors.

Getting things right on the rest of the seven domains doesn't hurt either, as we've already seen.

In this chapter, we'll first discuss how you can determine the critical success factors for your industry, and we'll take a brief look at a dot.com business that got this right. Then we'll examine in more depth the case histories of two companies that eventually lost their way: Palm Computing, an early leader in handheld computing, and Schwinn, a long-time bicycle manufacturer. In each case, the stories identify the factors critical to success in the relevant industry and look at the degree to which the company's team – the key people in whom investors had placed their trust – was able to execute on these factors.

Thereafter, we consider what investors should look for in the entrepreneurs and entrepreneurial teams they invest in, and we examine the lessons an entrepreneur or an early-stage investor should learn from this chapter. In doing so, I remind you that the industry you may enter is unlikely to be as attractive as pharmaceutical drugs. The lessons of this chapter, in concert with those already learned in Chapter 5 about competitive and economic sustainability, can provide a way around any shortcomings your opportunity may have in industry attractiveness terms.

Identifying the critical success factors

How do I work out what the critical success factors (CSFs) are for my industry, you may ask. Are the answers found in the trade press, on the internet or in strategy textbooks? Unfortunately, no. Knowledge of the CSFs for any industry resides in the experience of those who have learned – often the hard way – which things absolutely must be done right. Whether you have such experience or you must access that of others who have it, there are two key questions to ask to identify your industry's CSFs.

■ Which few decisions or activities are the ones that, if you get wrong, will almost always have severely negative effects on company performance, even when other things are done well?

■ Which decisions or activities, done right, will almost always deliver disproportionately positive effects on performance, even if other things are done less well, or even poorly?

In retailing, the industry where I spent much of my business career, the CSFs are, as they say, location, location, location. Retailers in great locations can get other things wrong and still perform well, at least for a time. Those in poor locations, despite doing most other things right, will struggle to survive. That's how powerful CSFs are. As Starbucks' Howard Schultz said, 'Our process of site selection was enormously time-consuming, but we couldn't afford a single mistake. One real estate error in judgment would mean . . . a minimum of a half million dollars at stake.' The Starbucks team demonstrated such skills, for 'Of the first 1000 stores we opened, we opted to close only two locations because of site misjudgments.'[2]

> **❝in retailing, the CSFs are location, location, location❞**

To identify the CSFs in your industry, ask the two questions above of 15 or 20 thoughtful, successful entrepreneurs and executives in your industry. You'll get various answers, of course, but some will converge on the same few themes. That's what you are looking for.

Palm Computing: Jeff Hawkins' innovation catches on

It is rare today to sit in a business meeting and not see at least one person checking their email, calendar or contacts on an iPhone or another mobile device. While these little battery-operated gadgets have been on the market since 1993, it was not until 1996 that the concept really caught on. Introduced to the public in April 1996, the Palm Pilot was a near-instant success, selling 1 million units in its first 18 months. Palm's little invention had been accepted faster than any other computer – even faster than televisions, video recorders, mobile phones or almost any previous consumer electronic product.[3] In just two years, the company sold more than 1.5 million Pilots. What made Palm so successful, beating out the earlier Apple Newton and Microsoft Pocket PC?

Learning the hard way

The Palm story began with Jeff Hawkins, an electrical engineer and inventor who was more interested in the human brain than starting a multibillion-dollar company. In the late 1980s, Hawkins was working for GRiD Systems, a computer company in the San Francisco Bay area. It was at GRiD that Hawkins worked on pen computing. With this new technology, users could write directly on the computer screen with a stylus (it looked like a pen but contained no ink); theoretically, the user's handwriting could be recognised. The key word was 'theoretically'. The concept depended heavily on the computer's handwriting-recognition capability.

Hawkins had already developed PalmPrint, a software program that could recognise hand-printed characters. In 1989, with Hawkins' software under licence, GRiD developed and marketed a tablet computer called GRiDPad. While it was a modest success as the only pen computer available commercially, it was too big and heavy, at 4.5 pounds, and too expensive, at $2,500, for use outside the specialised markets for which it had been designed.[4]

In 1991, Hawkins set out to create a pen computer that would be more appealing to everyday consumers. He pitched the idea to Tandy, GriD's parent and the operator of some 7,000 consumer electronics stores. As Hawkins saw it, 'Palmtop computing devices will be as ubiquitous as calculators by the end of this decade . . . To get an idea of the market size for these computers, consider the possibility that most high school students, nearly all college students, and most professionals will own one. With prices starting at $200, it is entirely conceivable, and I believe likely, that 50 per cent of those people will own or use a portable handheld computer at some time in their life.'[5]

Tandy and two venture capital firms liked Hawkins' idea, and in January 1992 Palm Computing was financed with $1.3 million in exchange for 40 per cent of Hawkins' company. Hawkins' proposed product, the Zoomer, would consist of hardware and an operating system that allowed the computer to serve as an address book and a diary. Hawkins knew he could not develop the Zoomer alone, so in early 1992 he hired three talented engineers and set to work.

Hawkins and the Palm Computing team immediately faced pressures from the project's various partners. By autumn 1992, there were six partners on the Zoomer project, including Casio, Tandy, AOL and Intuit. Palm was a living example of too many cooks in the kitchen. These partners wanted everything and the kitchen sink included in the product. Palm's Engineering Director Monty Boyers said, 'They had the longest, longest list of features they wanted to put into the device. And it would not make any difference to them at all whether these things made sense or not. Our point of view was: "Gee, we don't need all these things. Let's make this other stuff work really well."'[6] With Hawkins at the helm, the Palm team tried to stave off the idea that 'more is better', focusing instead on simplicity and functionality. But the battle wasn't easy.

> ❝ **Palm was a living example of too many cooks in the kitchen** ❞

In August 1993, Apple began shipping its Newton. Palm's Zoomer followed in October. Neither of the two products was terribly successful. Of his own product, Hawkins said, 'When I personally used the product, I felt it was usable, but a lot lacking.'[7] At $700, this somewhat heavy and cumbersome handheld device was equipped with only a mediocre handwriting-recognition tool. And by then, the Palm team realised the need for PC connectivity, which the Zoomer lacked. They wanted to find a way to move data back and forth from the Zoomer to the PC.

Working quickly, Palm brought to market in November its PalmConnect, an add-on to the Zoomer that allowed information to be moved from the handheld to the PC, and vice versa. While PalmConnect was a useful and successful add-on, it did not save the fate of the Zoomer. Both the Newton and the Zoomer failed to gain momentum. After selling 20,000 units in its first two months, Zoomer's sales slowed to a crawl.[8]

What does it take to win in high-tech?

Hawkins, a tenacious sort, was not about to give up hope after the less than successful Zoomer project. The first thing he did was to strengthen his team by hiring Donna Dubinsky as his CEO. She had a proven track record of managing high-tech teams and delivering results. More importantly, her appointment also released Hawkins from a managerial role he had never wanted to play, leaving him free to concentrate on learning from the mistakes made on the Zoomer in order to develop a handheld that had real market appeal.

Hawkins and Dubinsky learned some important lessons about what it takes to be successful with high-tech innovation.

- First, they learned that developing new technology was the easy part. Many high-tech entrepreneurs could do that.

- Second, and far more important, they learned that what was crucial in the high-tech world was linking the promise of technology with genuine customer needs so that real customer problems are solved.

As we've already seen in Chapter 2, satisfying customer needs is nothing new – it's important in any industry. In high-tech, though, doing so or not doing so turns on three CSFs. Getting these CSFs wrong dooms the business. Getting them right gives it a good chance of success. What are they?

- Anticipating and understanding customers' real problems or needs – or, more graphically, the customer pain.

- Understanding deeply an area of technology and what it can and cannot deliver, both today and tomorrow.

- Finding ways to harness the technology to resolve these problems or needs. Can the customer's pain be relieved?

For high-tech ventures, sometimes the technology comes first and customer pain must be found that can be relieved by the new technology. At other times, the customer need comes first, driving the engineers to develop a solution. Either sequence works, as long as the meeting of the two – the third CSF – occurs. Let's look at each of these CSFs and see how they played out at Palm.

What did customers really need?

With Dubinsky now on board, Hawkins and the Palm team went to work on understanding what needs customers had that could be resolved by a hand-held device. But which customers?

The Palm team decided to target the growing number of PC users. Within this large market, their target was professionals who were not necessarily experts in computers but who were unafraid of technology. Refining the target market further, the Palm team focused on the segment of professionals who worked away from their offices, whether locally or at large distances. What did these mobile professionals who were comfortable with technology really want in a handheld device?

Let's ask the customers what they really want, thought Hawkins. Their answer was clear: don't try to replace our desktop computers; just replace our pocket and desk calendars. People wanted an accessory to their PCs, some means of carrying around some of the data already on their hard drives – especially contact and appointment data. Eureka! 'I realized my competition was paper, not computers.'[9]

❝let's ask the customers what they really want'!❞

Most of the PC functions that Palm had painstakingly built into the Zoomer served only to clutter the screen with options that the customer didn't need.[10] Hawkins' realisation allowed him to focus his attention on the features and functionality that his prospective customers really wanted. Instead of developing a handheld PC, Hawkins and Dubinsky pushed their engineers to design a straightforward, portable, easy-to-use organiser.

Hawkins knew what was on the drawing boards at other companies and was sure that every one of them was missing the boat. What everyone was doing was not what the customers wanted.

Peter Skillman, who worked with Hawkins as a consultant for IDEO, the engineering firm that teamed up with him on several of the Palm products, said: 'Jeff understands the user experience and instinctively knows what's important to them. He has a real empathy for customers.'[11] In other words, he was able to execute on the first of his industry's CSFs.

Hawkins identified the characteristics most important to his market. Customers required simplicity, small size, reasonable price, attractive design and connectivity: 'We knew people would want something that's reliable and intuitive and quick, very quick. Faster and easier to carry than paper. Products can do complex, sophisticated things. But the user experience has to be simple.'[12] A Forrester Research study concurred, finding that people used their handheld organisers to manage calendars and to-do lists far more than they used them for complex tasks like retrieving and sending emails.[13] 'It had to be easy to use for the average consumer,' said Hawkins, 'not a product for techno geeks, but as easy and fast to use as the millions of DayTimer and Filofax paper organizers that were sold each year.'[14]

What could (and couldn't) technology deliver?

In order to keep the product small, fast and convenient, Hawkins realised that Palm would need great handwriting-recognition technology. The problem was that, at the time, the technology was not good enough. More importantly, Hawkins, who knew this technology arena intimately (CSF number two in high-tech), knew it would not be good enough any time soon. He needed to come up with a better handwriting-recognition tool. His invention was ingenious. Instead of asking the computer to recognise everyone's handwriting, as Apple's Newton and Palm's Zoomer had tried to do – ineffectively, as it turned out – Hawkins decided to create a standard alphabet and characters that people could learn to use. He would train people in a new but easy way to write.

Graffiti, Hawkins' new alphabet, mimicked traditional Roman letters with just simple modifications. The result was a near-perfect technological solution with two key benefits. First, anyone could learn to print characters that the product could recognise, thus eliminating the handwriting-recognition issue. Second, the handheld no longer needed a keyboard, thus facilitating a smaller product.

Yet another problem with technology was the limited screen space. When writing long words or sentences, the user would run out of room on the small screen. Hawkins' solution was to have users write one letter on top of another, forcing the software (rather than the user) to display the letters and characters in sequential order. Again, Hawkins came up with an inventive and practical solution that was technologically feasible.

The team also realised the importance of data exchange between the handheld and the PC. Palm engineers wrote software that could import and export data to and from a number of desktop software programs, like Microsoft Outlook and Lotus Organizer. With this functionality, pertinent daily information usually stored on a PC suddenly became portable.

Matching the two – harnessing technology to meet customer needs

With Hawkins' criteria in mind and the key technologies in place, the Palm crew set out to develop a superior handheld organiser. The team was meticulous when it came to the product's features and functionality. They knew the machine had to be simple to operate. Keeping it simple meant fewer features. When deciding what features to include in Palm's handheld, Vice-president of Marketing Ed Colligan asked, 'Is this feature going to sell one more unit?'[15] If the answer was no, then the Palm team dropped it. Colligan's discipline was a key factor that helped execute on CSF number three. What the engineers designed would be what the customers wanted – no more, no less. In the end, the team decided on four basic features: a calendar, an address book, a to-do list and a memo pad. Palm's competitors, on the other hand, missed the boat, cramming far too much functionality into their little handhelds.

Hawkins also realised that existing operating systems wouldn't work for the simple and sharply focused device he had in mind. A better operating system was needed, and Palm's Ron Marietti was the engineer who delivered it, another instance of Palm's ability to execute on harnessing technology to meet customer needs.

While the Palm team was busy sticking to its simple features, the company did allow for software add-ons for customers who might want them. The company relied on outside software developers to provide these applications. Independent software developers could obtain a Palm software development kit and create add-on shareware and commercial programs for Palm's handheld. Anxious to get their hands on a big audience, these developers designed everything from financial calculators and video games to astrological charts and news updates.

Results – a hit from day one

Palm Computing demonstrated its new Palm handheld at a trade show in January 1996. Half of the more than 400 trade show attendees took Palm up on its $149 pre-order offer. In April of that year, Palm began shipping. *PC Computing* magazine wrote: 'The Pilot 1000 is an outstanding product: It's fast, easy to use, and inexpensive . . . If you're searching for the ultimate palm-size organizer, look no further.'[16]

The company knew it had a hit when computer columnists failed to return its review units.[17] Throughout the remainder of 1996, Palm's Pilot organiser gained popularity. By the end of the Christmas season, Palm's Pilot won over 70 per cent of the US handheld market. That year, the Pilot received 21 'best product' awards from the press, consistently beating Microsoft's handheld launched in the autumn of that year.[18]

❝the company knew it had a hit when computer columnists failed to return its review units❞

It took Palm only 18 months to sell 1 million Pilots. But Hawkins and Dubinsky refused to rest upon their laurels. To maintain momentum, Palm worked vigorously to develop newer, better versions of its handheld. Palm III hit the market in March 1997. This version was slimmer than the original Pilot, and weighed only 6 ounces. Gartner Group said, 'The product delivers exactly what existing users want.'[19] A still thinner version, the Palm V, was next. While the Palm V had no functional difference from the Palm III, it was a far more attractive product. As Hawkins said, 'The goal was beauty. Beauty, beauty, beauty. I didn't want any distraction with other things.'[20] The Palm V sold for $449, weighed 4 ounces, and was equipped with rechargeable batteries. Palm VII took a jump into the wireless world. Equipped with an antenna, it could send and receive emails and Web clippings. In 1998, however, Hawkins, Dubinsky and Colligan departed to form a new company, having struggled for years under corporate oversight that, in their eyes, limited their progress.

For a time, the rest of the Palm team continued to deliver impressive results. During its fiscal year ending May 2000, Palm reached over $1 billion in sales. During the next six months, it sold another $922 million. It had taken Palm three and a half years to sell 5 million handhelds.

But profits were another story. Amid rampant innovation across the category and fierce competition – including the new Visor from Hawkins' and team's new company, Handspring – PalmOne, the portion of the old Palm that marketed devices, had by mid-2003 chalked up nearly $900 million in losses over three very difficult years.

In October, Hawkins and team returned to Palm, bringing together Handspring's engineering and design prowess with Palm's manufacturing and sales expertise. The reunited companies launched the Treo 600 to rave reviews, as combination devices like Treo and the BlackBerry, which combined PDAs and mobile phones into a single unit, became the next must-have device for on-the-go businesspeople. In 2005, with Colligan holding the reins as CEO, Palm announced its first annual profit since 2000.[21]

Despite the positive outlook in 2005, hot new products from BlackBerry as well as Apple's iPhone and the smartphone revolution presented Palm with serious challenges in the ensuing years. By 2009, revenue was falling sharply, off a whopping 44 per cent from 2008; Palm incurred $732,000 in losses for its year ending June 2009.[22] Colligan, after 16 years at the company, stepped down from his CEO post and Palm's Executive Chairman Jon Rubinstein, an Apple veteran, took the reins. In mid-2009, Palm introduced its Palm Pre to compete with the iPhone and a new webOS operating system, again to rave reviews from technology pundits.[23]

In July 2010, Palm was taken over, presumably for its technology or its brand, by Hewlett-Packard, in a transaction which valued Palm at approximately $1.2 billion.[24] One year later, HP announced it was scrapping development of the Palm operating system, effectively consigning Palm to the scrapheap.[25] But in 2012, when Meg Whitman took the reins at HP, the operating system elements of Palm (webOS) were rescued, made open source and placed in an incubator company called Gram. By February 2013, HP had sold elements of webOS and licensed other elements to LG Electronics for use in televisions.[26] And in October 2014, HP sold the Palm trademark and other items of intellectual property to TCL Corporation, a Chinese maker of consumer electronics.[27] At the time of writing, no new products have emerged and whether the Palm brand will ever reappear remains to be seen.

What made Palm a high-tech success in its early years? Palm's success did not result from proprietary technology that was patent-protected, although Palm did win some patents and it did develop its own operating system. The story wasn't superior organisational processes that others could not match. The key element in Palm's ability to win in a business where other companies and products – including Palm's own Zoomer – had failed was the ability of the entrepreneurial team to execute on the three factors that were – and still are – critical to high-tech success. Let's recap how Palm's entrepreneurial team – Hawkins, Dubinsky and Colligan – executed on these three CSFs.

- *Understanding customers' real problems or needs:* Hawkins, Dubinsky and Colligan focused relentlessly on building the small and simple product that they knew customers wanted. 'Delight the customer, was Colligan's mantra for design decisions.[28]

- *Understanding deeply an area of technology and what it can and cannot deliver, both today and tomorrow:* Hawkins knew the limitations of handwriting-recognition technology and what it could and could not do well at the time. With Graffiti, he found a better way to resolve the technical problem.

- *Finding ways to harness technology to resolve these problems or needs:* 'He was really anal about a lot of stuff,' recalls Karl Townsend, who designed the electronics for the first Palm Pilot. 'He said, "Look, it's really important how thin it is; it's really important how the buttons feel." All the other products I had worked on, people didn't have the same passion that Jeff had, and the product then becomes a huge gigantic compromise.'[29]

Of these three CSFs, the first and third are often overlooked in technology-driven companies, where engineering elegance sometimes takes precedence over customer needs. The Palm team, however, executed superbly for several years. At the end of the day, it's execution – not design brilliance or engineering elegance alone – that counts. Hawkins and his team executed. They delivered cutting-edge products that worked and that customers wanted and would pay for – all things easy to say but difficult to do in the high-tech world. Alas, as the last several years have shown for Palm, it's become increasingly difficult to continue to do so in the face of innovative, fast-moving and capable competitors.

> **❝at the end of the day, it's execution that counts❞**

Schwinn hits the skids

We now turn our attention from a company, for a long time, that executed superbly on its industry's CSFs to a company that succumbed in the bicycle industry by failing to do so. In the USA, Schwinn is a brand that evokes nostalgia. American baby boomers remember the classic Schwinn models and reminisce fondly about riding their Schwinns around town. So, what was it that caused a venerable company with a widely recognised brand to fail? The sad reality is that the company's team did not execute on its industry's CSFs.

Before we begin the Schwinn story, let's first identify the CSFs in the bicycle industry. Sometimes, those factors depend on the nature of the strategy a company pursues. In bicycles, as in most mature manufacturing industries, there are three broad strategic approaches, as Treacy and Wiersema[30] point out.

- *Operational excellence,* i.e. 'providing customers with reliable products or services at competitive prices and delivered with minimal difficulty or inconvenience'. Such a strategy seeks to lead the industry in price and convenience.

- *Customer intimacy,* i.e. 'segmenting and targeting markets precisely and then tailoring offerings to match exactly the demands of those niches'. This strategy is focused on individualised service to each customer, based on an intimate understanding of what that customer needs.

- *Product leadership,* i.e. 'offering customers leading-edge products and services that consistently enhance the customer's use or applications of the product, thereby making rivals' goods obsolete'. Product leadership companies seek to provide a continuing flow of state-of-the-art products or services to remain at the cutting edge of their industry.

What CSFs are required to carry out each of these strategies effectively?

According to Treacy and Wiersema,[31] here's what each strategy requires.

- Operational excellence:
  - Minimise costs in every regard;
  - Optimise business processes for extreme efficiency and effectiveness.

- Customer intimacy: gather detailed information about each customer so that they may be assigned to a micro-segment in which the offering is tailored carefully to that segment's needs. Sometimes, the segmentation is so precise that offerings are tailored to market segments of one.

- Product leadership:

- Creativity, to recognise and embrace ideas that may originate outside the company;
- Optimise business processes for speed, in order to bring these creative ideas to market quickly;
- Relentlessly pursue new solutions that may render obsolete those that the company has just introduced. If anyone is to render the product leader's technology obsolete, then the product leader prefers to do so itself.

In addition to the one or two CSFs pertinent to each strategy, another CSF applies to manufacturers regardless of strategy.

■ Effective, efficient value-chain relationships: without effective and mutually beneficial relationships with suppliers and resellers, any manufacturer will face an uphill battle. From suppliers, manufacturers need reliability, quality and on-time delivery at an affordable price. From resellers, they need commitment and sell-through – a commitment that a manufacturer wins by being a reliable supplier of quality products itself.

Let's see if Schwinn executed on any of these CSFs.

A changing American market for bicycles[32]

One day in the late 1970s, a group of Schwinn engineers paid a visit to a small California bicycle factory called Fisher MountainBikes. Back in 1974, Gary Fisher had built a dozen 'klunkers', as he called them, bikes cobbled together from sturdy bike frames found in thrift shops, but fitted with the latest European parts – fancy ten-speed gears, thumb shifters, motorcycle brake levers, knobby dirt-grabbing tyres and so on. The purpose? To enable Fisher and his buddies to ride their bikes up and down the dirt tracks among the hills along Northern California's dramatic coast.

Fisher, though still not 30 years of age, now had a real company, and he and others like him were building bikes like none built before (see Case Study 7.1). The engineers from Schwinn, long the leading bicycle brand in the USA, were there to take a look at the mountain bikes Fisher had crafted, including one made from an old Schwinn Excelsior. As Fisher recalled the scene some 15 years later, 'This guy in his 50s was looking down at me like I was some jerk kid who didn't know anything. The Schwinn engineers are going, "We know bikes. You guys are all amateurs. We know better than anybody"'.[33]

It was Fisher who knew bikes, not Schwinn. As had happened in the 1970s, when Europe's lightweight ten-speed road bikes invaded the American bicycle market, and later with motocross-inspired BMX bikes, Schwinn was left in the

---

case study 7.1

Entrepreneurial newcomers remake the bicycle business[34]

In 1979, ten years after the mountain bike craze began in earnest, Gary Fisher's Fisher MountainBikes was selling 15,000 bikes annually at prices up to $1,200 each. Fisher was on his way towards being a millionaire. There were more than 5 million mountain bikes on the trails in the USA alone.[35] Fisher's was among the best-known of the new companies that had built thriving businesses from what Schwinn had overlooked. Steve Potts, at the smaller but high-priced end of the scale, offered tailor-made bikes built to order for customers willing to pay $3,400 for his signature craftsmanship.

Specialized, another newcomer, having seen the mountain bike trend and knowledgeable about low-cost manufacturing in Asia, sold a broad line of mountain bikes at half Fisher's prices. Even the European makers like Raleigh finally got into the game.

Like Phil Knight of Nike, John Mackey of Whole Foods Market and Pierre Omidyar of eBay, these entrepreneurs had changed the way consumers live and play. That's what entrepreneurs do.

---

dust. By the end of the 1980s, mountain bikes like Fisher's would account for 60 per cent of a booming American market for bicycles, and Schwinn would be on its way towards bankruptcy court. Was the Schwinn team able to execute on the CSFs entailed in any of the Treacy and Wiersema strategies in the 1970s and 1980s? Consistently not. Let's see how Schwinn fared on the success factors that characterise it.

Trouble at Schwinn

While Schwinn had been a trendsetter in the bicycle industry for 80 years, by the 1970s the family-run company had lost its ability to gauge the market. In October 1979, Ed Schwinn, aged 30, took over the presidency of Schwinn Bicycle Company from his uncle Frank V. Schwinn. At the time, Schwinn had a 12 per cent share of the American market and was by far the most trusted name in bicycles.

After just a few months in his new job, Ed decided that the long-time executives who had led Schwinn for years weren't what the company needed. In April 1980, he arrived unexpectedly at Schwinn's western sales office in

California and said to Max Scott, Schwinn's Vice-president for Sales and Marketing, 'Max, I'm here to ask for your resignation. We'd like for you to leave the company right now. You can come tomorrow to get your belongings. That's all I have to say.'[36] Marketing Director Ray Burch was also replaced. The veteran number-two man, Al Fritz, was banished in 1980 to Excelsior Fitness, a small Schwinn division selling exercise equipment. As the veterans left, in came younger family members lacking in business experience. Schwinn's old guard may have lacked the ability to develop cutting-edge products but they had presided over decades of operational excellence. Would the new team be able to match them?

The year that Ed Schwinn took over, Schwinn's Chicago factory employees voted to unionise. Rather than continue to work with his experienced but now unionised factory workers, Ed decided to close Schwinn's Chicago factory. In its place, the youthful Schwinn decided to open a new factory in Greenville, Mississippi. Things went downhill quickly from there.

As Chris Travers, one of Schwinn's California dealers, said later, 'Greenville was quickly branded as having an inferior product.' Other dealers complained that the Greenville-manufactured bikes had parts that did not fit together, wheels that weren't true or frames that had mismatched colours.

For a while, some bikes even arrived without seat posts. There were delivery issues as well. Long-time Schwinn dealer Joe Russell said, 'We just couldn't get the right bikes when we needed them.'[37] Clearly, Schwinn failed to execute on the CSFs for an operational excellence strategy and in doing so was beginning to do irreparable damage to the company's relationships with its resellers, a major shortcoming on one of the CSFs.

❝some bikes even arrived without seat posts❞

The manufacturing problems in Greenville led to significant operating losses, exacerbated by write-offs of obsolete inventory, equipment and buildings in Chicago. The severance costs associated with laying off all the Chicago factory employees also proved financially damaging to Schwinn, as did the habitually free spending of Schwinn's management team, itself a further difficulty in maintaining operational excellence. The result was that the Schwinn Company's net worth plunged from $43.8 million in 1980 to $2.7 million just three years later.

Seeking to resolve its continuing manufacturing problems, Schwinn transferred most of its production to Taiwan-based Giant Manufacturing Corp. Ed Schwinn was soon captivated by doing business in Asia, even bringing to Chicago a Chinese junk that he would sail on Lake Michigan. The odd-looking boat was a reminder to all of Schwinn's free-spending culture.

❝the odd-looking boat was a reminder to all of Schwinn's free-spending culture❞

Schwinn's globetrotting too: 'It doesn't cost that much more to eat well,' commented Vice-president of Finance John Barker, after one of his regular trips to China.

Despite the free spending on overheads, the lower Asian manufacturing costs boosted unit profit margins from losses of $5–20 per bike to gains of $20–30. Margins on Al Fritz's exercise bikes were even better, in the 50 per cent range. Sales of Fritz's new Air-Dyne exercise bikes doubled, but Schwinn's corporate team didn't believe the optimistic forecasts that Fritz was making. As a result, according to Fritz, 'We never had enough exercisers.'[38] This time it was the new management team who proved unable to deliver on the CSFs required for product leadership. Indeed, the fact that Schwinn didn't miss the exercise craze completely was due largely to the experienced Al Fritz.

In 1984, Schwinn turned its first profit in four years, earning $3 million on sales of $134 million, due mainly to the booming exercise business. By 1986, Schwinn's earnings peaked at $7 million, its best in a decade, on sales of $174 million, and it opened swanky new offices.

Schwinn's troubles go global

Alas, the good news was only temporary. Schwinn's network had grown to include suppliers in mainland China and Hungary, leading to reduced reliance on Giant, their established Taiwanese supplier, which in 1986 had been producing some 80 per cent of Schwinn's bikes. What did those decisions do to their value-chain relationships? Giant retaliated with higher prices, cutting into Schwinn's margins and forcing it to raise prices. Schwinn bikes were suddenly priced $10–20 higher than competing models. 'When people came in here and saw the price – boom, out the door they went,' said John Pelc, a Schwinn dealer for more than 40 years.[39] To compound the problem, Schwinn had quality problems once again, this time with its new Chinese supplier. Both efficiency and effectiveness had gone out the door.

❝both efficiency and effectiveness had gone out the door❞

Once again, Schwinn's manufacturing and supply problems showed up on the bottom line. In mid-1989, Controller Don Gillard came to Ed Schwinn with an analysis that showed Schwinn was losing money on bikes, and that only the Air-Dyne cash cow was keeping it afloat. Gillard was asked to resign soon after. Ed Schwinn just didn't like hearing bad news.

Meanwhile, Giant decided to expand its own brand and reduce its reliance on Schwinn. When Schwinn bought a $2 million stake in its Chinese supplier, China Bicycles Company, Giant's President Tony Lo was furious. Lo hired Bill Austin, Schwinn's recently departed marketing chief. Austin shrewdly offered dealers a better profit margin than Schwinn was offering, along with a compelling story – Giant bikes were made by the same factory that made Schwinn! By 1992, Giant would sell more than 300,000 bikes in the USA, more than half of Schwinn's 543,000.

The end of Schwinn's road

By the end of the 1980s, Schwinn was back in the red, losing $2.9 million in 1990 and $23 million in 1991, when it shut down the Greenville factory. The Air-Dyne cash cow disappeared, as its sales plunged by one-third due to lower pricing by competitors. Al Fritz, after complaining of the lack of pay rises for his division's staff, had been dismissed years earlier. By 1991, Schwinn's lenders were applying pressure once again and family members, long accustomed to fat dividend cheques, were growing restless. In 1992, Schwinn's banks began sweeping cash from Schwinn's revolving line of credit to pay overdue loans, leaving Schwinn with little money with which to pay Giant and China Bicycles. Schwinn's debt to these two suppliers ballooned to some $30 million, and Schwinn's net worth was wiped out. 'It was like being on a runaway train,' said Dennis O'Dea, Schwinn's attorney in the bankruptcy that soon followed.

❝the most respected name in the American bicycle business brought a paltry $2.5 million❞

'It was horrific.'[40] In October 1992, Schwinn filed for bankruptcy. Soon after, brand and remaining assets were sold to a group of investors. The most respected name in the American bicycle business brought a paltry $2.5 million.

Execution, not

At the beginning of this section, we identified the CSFs entailed in the strategies that Schwinn might have chosen. Let's summarise how the Schwinn team executed on the industry's CSFs.

■ Did it minimise costs? Hardly. A free-spending culture. A Chinese junk on Chicago's Lake Michigan. And a swanky new office building.

- Were business processes optimised for efficiency and effectiveness? Certainly not. Severe quality and delivery problems were recurring events.

- Were there detailed customer data for targeting small or expanding segments? None. We saw no evidence of any attempts to tailor the offering to meet small segments' individual needs.

- Creativity and a willingness to accept new ideas like mountain bikes and bring them to market quickly? No way. From all appearances, Schwinn's leadership appears to have been about as backward-looking as a management team can get.

- What about organisational processes? Relentless pursuit of new solutions? Were they geared to speed, to support a product leadership strategy? Except for Air-Dyne, Schwinn's days as a product leader were long gone.

- Value-chain relationships? Cutting out a reliable supplier? Supplying its dealers with faulty products. Inadequate product delivery. Not exactly what most observers would call effective execution.

Sadly, the Schwinn story is a textbook example of 'management missteps, global mishaps and the pitfalls sometimes found in family-owned businesses by third- and fourth-generation executives'.[41] There are lots of phrases one could use to describe the Schwinn debacle, but effective execution on CSFs is not among them.

What investors want to know

Do investors care about execution? Absolutely, they do. It's what keeps them awake at night. It's the best protection they have after they've made a decision to invest in a nascent entrepreneurial venture. Once they've made the decision to invest in your venture, your ability to execute on your CSFs is the best – maybe the only – protection they have for their money. No wonder they'll fixate on it before they settle up.

We really dig into the management team. We want to be totally confident that this team can deliver on the promises they have made. We do that by looking at their experience, by assessing how well they understand their industry and their customers. We want to know about their leadership in terms of the CEO and the heads of engineering, R&D, and marketing [or whatever the most important functions are for any given opportunity].

OD, USA

Execution is why the refrain 'management, management, management' is heard so often in venture capital circles. But what does great management look like, when viewed from up front, before events have unfolded? Is it about character? Chemistry? Drive or motivation? Perseverance in the face of adversity? Is it industry experience? Is it glib salespersonship? Is it technological expertise? Is it 'having done it before', as Louis Borders had done in book retailing before his ill-fated Webvan adventure?

❝what does great management look like?❞

In the research that led to this book, I learned that great management is about all of these things and something more. Do character, drive and perseverance matter? Sure. Is industry experience relevant? Of course. But not just as a line on a CV. Does the ability to sell matter? Absolutely: it's what successful entrepreneurs do with much of their time. But successful selling is not to be confused with a dynamic personality, as the naturally introverted Jeff Hawkins will attest. Most of these elements are like fitness to the athlete. Necessary, but not sufficient for greatness. What do astute investors look for?

What astute investors look for in people they back – and 'people', plural, is the right word here – is simple, really, but not always obvious to most aspiring entrepreneurs.

■ Investors want to know that the lead entrepreneur has identified and understands the CSFs in the industry they propose to enter, as well as the market and competitive environment they will encounter. A credible understanding of the seven domains can provide the evidence here. That's step one.

■ Step two, the crucial one, is that the lead entrepreneur has then assembled a team that can demonstrate – in past *deeds,* not words – that its players taken together can execute. 'On what?', you may ask. Execute on each and every one of the handful of CSFs that the venture's industry and strategy therein will require. Or, alternatively, and sometimes sufficiently, the entrepreneur has identified what's necessary and also what's lacking on their team and has acknowledged the need to fill that gap, perhaps with the investor's help.

Where key gaps in the team are present and unrecognised, however, the result is what I call an incomplete entrepreneurial team. The team may have a great idea, but if the ability to execute on one or more of the CSFs is missing, raising capital is likely to be extremely difficult. In my experience, it's one of the biggest reasons why many aspiring entrepreneurs never get to the starting line.

So, if you want investors' backing for your new venture, make the effort to understand the CSFs that your venture will face. If you've not worked in the industry you plan to enter, you'd better find someone who has. There are always just a few factors that are crucial. They're the ones that make the difference between who wins in your industry and who are the also-rans. Next, look in the mirror and ask what you – demonstrably, in past deeds, not just words – bring to the party. Finally, fill out your team with people who can deliver what you yourself do not have or cannot do. Fill it with people who are different from you – diverse teams generally perform better than look-alikes.

> **❝look in the mirror and ask what you bring to the party❞**

What (some) investors bring to the party

Building a great entrepreneurial team, one that can really deliver, isn't easy. Thus a role that early-stage investors often play is to provide skills, contacts and been-there-before experience and perspectives that an entrepreneur and his or her team will probably require but do not yet possess. If you are an investor reading this chapter, you might want to give some thought to the kinds of ventures, in market and industry terms, to which you could actually add value, based on what you've done before. Do you bring a useful network that might open key doors? Have you started or scaled a venture yourself, and thereby accumulated some scar tissue from which the next generation of entrepreneurs can learn? Have you started a business that crashed and burned? There are always lessons there. If you choose to do your investing where you can add real value, your entrepreneurs and their businesses will benefit, and you'll probably earn better returns, too.

Sadly, though, just about every early-stage investor, whether a seed-stage VC, an angel, or an accelerator, will at some point tell capital-starved entrepreneurs, 'If you just want money, I'm not your guy. But if you want added value apart from the funding, take your money from me.' The evidence, however, based on the disappointing performance of the vast majority of venture capital funds over their ten-year lives, suggests that *some* investors add value; many others do not.[42] So, if you're an entrepreneur, how might you secure an investor who brings more than money to the table? I believe the best answer is to find a way to generate a queue of investors outside your door. This puts you in a position to choose, and it will bring in your money on better terms, too!

And how might you generate such a queue, you ask? The most sure-footed path is to bootstrap your business – without investment capital – until customer traction has been clearly demonstrated, getting the cash you need from your customers when they pay. Once that's the case, you'll find no shortage of investors who will want to help you grow. We'll address how to do this in Chapter 12.

As a street-smart entrepreneur, though, you'll want to be sure to conduct careful due diligence on your prospective investors, just as they are sure to conduct on you. Calling the other CEOs in whom they've invested, especially the failures, is a great place to start, as is a look at what they've done before. Have they built a business – *themselves*? Have they ever had to find a way to 'make payroll' when there was no cash in the bank? Or are they bankers/consultants/advisers who just *think* they know how to help you build your business? Once you've taken their money, you're likely to get plenty of their help and advice, whether it's useful or not!

Lessons learned

As I noted in the first pages of this book, the majority of entrepreneurial ventures fail. They do so for many reasons, lots of which are opportunity-based. Some pursue poor markets. Others choose unattractive industries where almost no one can win. Some offer no real benefits to their prospective customers, or offer benefits no better than what is already available. Still others have no way to sustain their initial competitive edge or are stuck with an initial business model that simply doesn't stack up. At least some of these errors, however, can be overcome through effective execution.

If you were to ask the successful entrepreneurs whose case histories have graced the chapters in this book about the mistakes they have made, they would smile. Then they'd probably ask with a chuckle, 'How long have you got?' My research team and I chose each of the stories in this book to bring to life just one of the seven domains. In reality, though, most of these world-class entrepreneurs got more than just one domain right. They got most of them right, but not always on the first attempt, as we saw with Jeff Hawkins' Zoomer. But they would be the first to tell you that they also made lots of mistakes along the way. Having the right team – a team that can execute on the important things, the CSFs – is a crucial element in recovering and learning from those mistakes. Such learning is what today's lean start-up approach is all about, so if you are planning or thinking of investing in a start-up, assembling the right team – before you embark – is probably a very good idea.

Lessons learned from Palm Computing

In the case of Palm Computing, Jeff Hawkins not only knew what it took to succeed with a high-technology firm; he also made certain that his company had the right people to fulfil these necessary criteria. When Hawkins resolved that Palm would produce a simpler handheld, he knew 'the most critical employee to the project . . . was Ron Marietti'.[43] He needed an engineer of Marietti's calibre to write the operating system, otherwise the product simply would not work.

Earlier, Hawkins had agreed with his venture capital backers that he should hire a CEO to run the company. It took about a year, but when the time was right that's exactly what Hawkins did. Donna Dubinsky, Hawkins thought, could execute, and she could do things he could not.

To his credit, Hawkins knew his strengths and weaknesses, having never claimed to be a good manager.[44] He knew the CSFs that his business faced, and he built a team that could meet them. Execution mattered. Contrast Palm's execution with that of other early entrants into handheld computing – Apple's Newton and Microsoft's Pocket PC – which simply failed to understand the limits of the technology and to marry it with customer needs.

66 execution mattered – contrast Palm's execution with that of other early entrants into handheld computing 99

Hindsight tells us that, at least at its early stages, the handheld computing industry was a tough game to play. There were numerous entrants and quite capable substitutes – pen and paper, principally – that led most entrants to fail. Arguably, Palm's superior execution – Hawkins, Dubinsky, Colligan, Marietti and the rest of the team – made the difference.

Lessons learned from Schwinn

To be fair, the bicycle industry when Ed Schwinn took his family company's helm was not all that attractive. But there were segments – like mountain bikes – where the prospects were bright. But unlike the new mountain bike pioneers like Gary Fisher, Schwinn failed to respond to the trends sweeping the industry.

And, unlike Palm's Jeff Hawkins, Ed Schwinn seemed not to understand the importance of a good team. Instead of surrounding himself with the best and the brightest, he eliminated key veterans (flawed to be sure, but the newcomers didn't shine either) and replaced them with young relatives. Al Fritz, who latched on to the fitness trend, was demoted. Don Gillard, the bearer of bad news, was terminated. Family ties are no substitute for a team's lack of ability to execute on the CSFs.

Worse, Schwinn antagonised key partners – Giant and, later, China Bicycles – apparently not realising that one's team includes more than one's

> **❝one's team includes more than one's employees – bankers, suppliers and dealers count, too❞**

employees. Bankers, suppliers and dealers count, too. Arrogance, rampant at Schwinn, does not breed cooperation and team-work.[45] Business – as with entrepreneurship – is a team sport, and Ed Schwinn was not a team player.

As we'll see in the next chapter, there's one more dimension of every entrepreneurial team we've yet to deal with, and it addresses an important issue in completing your team. The team issues are crucial ones, especially if your venture requires external capital. As William Wordsworth noted in opening this chapter, it's in you and your *people* – not your *idea* – that investors will ultimately place their trust.

The new business road test: stage six – the 'can you execute?' test

■ What are the few – only a handful, please – critical success factors in your industry? What support can you provide to show that you've identified them correctly?

■ Can you demonstrate – in past deeds, not mere words – that your team taken together can execute on each and every one of these CFSs?

■ Alternatively, have you identified which CSFs your team is not well prepared to meet, for which you need help in filling out your team?

■ What risks, if any, do answers to the above questions add to your risk list? How might you mitigate them?

THE NEW BUSINESS ROAD TEST

If you open your *New Business Road Test* app, you'll find the above checklist reproduced there. As was noted in this chapter, if you are new to your industry, identifying your CSFs is likely to take conversations with a number of industry experts. The app makes it easy to keep track of your candidates for the factors that may eventually make up your CSF shortlist. It will undoubtedly be too long at the outset, as you gather more – and varied – input. But once you've got your shortlist trimmed to the handful of factors that you think are your real CSFs, the app also lets you then build a chart to help you size up yourself and your team to determine any gaps that need filling.

8

Your connections matter: which matter most?

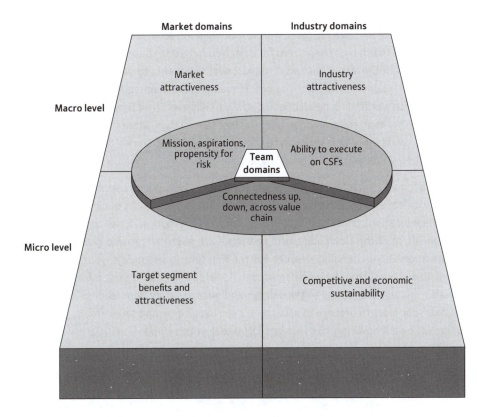

Littered with used oxygen tanks and rubbish, the Mount Everest base camp has played temporary host to the numerous climbers wishing to reach the summit of this 29,000-foot peak. Base camp serves many purposes, one of which is to acclimatise climbers to the high altitude.

Another purpose is to act as a central information hub for the climbing teams perched high above on this Himalayan monster. With the advent of wireless technology, climbers can stay in close contact with their base camp brethren. Not unlike an air traffic control station, climbers attempting to climb Everest can communicate with others at the base camp to learn of incoming inclement weather.

As a climber, communication with base camp can be a lifeline. Knowing that a storm is approaching can be the deciding factor for whether or not to attempt the summit. Not knowing that a storm is approaching can change a potentially successful ascent into a deadly adventure.

Put yourself in this situation . . . you and a team of climbers are perched at nearly 28,000 feet above sea level, with winds whipping around you and temperatures that haven't seen zero for days. You have just spent your thirtieth night on Mount Everest. It has taken you just over two weeks to get from base camp to this, your last overnight site before reaching the summit. You awaken at 5 a.m. with a pounding headache and spells of dizziness that have become the rule rather than the exception over the last several days. More than anything, you want to find your way to the summit and then quickly (albeit safely) make your way off this brutal mountain.

As has become the daily ritual, your team leader uses his satellite telephone to speak with base camp. Base camp is in contact with various teams of climbers at several locations on the mountain. Each team on the mountain has another vantage point of the cloud and storm systems. Each team can provide critical information about changing weather. For the first time in seven days, your team leader hears that the weather appears to be stable – for at least a few hours – enough time to get to the summit and back to safety. Your leader signals your team to prepare to ascend. You pack your gear and take off for what will be a long, tiring, but safe last 1,000 feet of this climb.

Entrepreneurial connections

It's not *what* you know; it's *who* you know.

Business wisdom from an unknown source

Choosing to communicate with base camp before attempting a summit seems like the obvious choice. With precious little oxygen and difficult climbing a given, why risk adding fierce weather to this already daunting mix? While lack of oxygen doesn't play much of a role in starting new ventures, the fierceness of competition can make you just as dizzy. The pace of technological change can create new markets in a heartbeat. Companies with strong networks of contacts having varied vantage points – including those of customers, suppliers and others in the industry and related industries – are more capable of anticipating and understanding forthcoming changes and are therefore better prepared to deal with them. Likewise, entrepreneurs who surround themselves with a strong network up, down and across the value chain are well positioned to gauge the ever-changing market and modify their offerings, operations, organisation and processes to meet the needs of a changing business climate.

Put another way, the ability to combine the tenacity for which entrepreneurs are legendary with a willingness to pivot – often due to new information that wasn't available earlier, including changes in the market or competitive environment – can make all the difference. Sometimes, such changes are favourable ones. Good luck can help an entrepreneurial venture. But good luck is most likely to pay off when those in charge have the right connections that provide the information required to help them respond to new information quickly and adroitly. Otherwise, it is unlikely that the company will be able to take advantage of good luck when it shows up. Without the information sources to tell you when pivots are necessary, all the willingness in the world will do you no good.

Thus, in order to be prepared, make the right pivots at the right time for the right reasons, both entrepreneurs and investors should ask how connected you and your team members are up, down and across the value chain as shown in Figure 8.1 – with suppliers and customers, as well as competitors in your industry or substitute industries – to address this concern. Connections with suppliers (up the value chain), with competitors (across the value chain) and with distributors, customers, consumers or end-users (all down the value chain) can provide crucial leading-edge information that could spell the difference between success and failure at an important juncture in the life of your business. If you're not yet sufficiently connected, start building your network now!

> **ff you should ask how connected you and your team members are up, down and across the value chain JJ**

In this chapter, we'll examine the case histories of two companies and take a more cursory look at a third. As we'll see, Virata's connections in the UK and Europe enabled it to change its business completely to take advantage of a new application for which its technology happened to be extremely well suited. Digital Equipment corporation, on the other hand, simply failed to

figure 8.1 Connections in all directions

adapt to several marketplace changes – including the PC revolution – and found its minicomputer business obsolete. Fuhu tanked, too. In all of these case histories we examine how just having connections is not sufficient – it's having the right ones and having the ability to understand and act on the new information, even if it's not what you want to hear. We then examine this domain from an investor's perspective, so that entrepreneurs may understand more of what investors will look for in an entrepreneurial team. Finally, the chapter closes with lessons to be learned from these two case histories for assessing your opportunity and the team you've assembled – or need to assemble – to pursue it.

Virata gets lucky. Why?[1]

Virata is not exactly a household name. We don't sip Virata coffee. We don't shop in Virata stores or ride in Virata cars. We don't talk on Virata telephones. Or do we?

If you dialled up your high-speed DSL connection today to check your Facebook feed, then your data probably passed through a Virata chip. If you bought a book from Amazon via a DSL connection, then you probably used Virata hardware and software. If you checked your email using a high-speed DSL connection, then it went a lot faster because of Virata.

Virata, a British company that grew out of technology developed in the research labs of Cambridge University, provides communications processors and the relevant software that enable the world's telephone companies to compete for the growing demand for high-speed digital access. But getting there wasn't easy.

With roots dating back to 1986, Virata was an offshoot of the Olivetti Research Laboratory in Cambridge, UK, where Andy Hopper and Hermann Hauser had been leading research into a new technology called Asynchronous Transfer Mode (ATM). ATM had what Hopper and Hauser thought was an important advantage over other competing technologies: it could simultaneously handle voice, video and data transmission over local area networks (LANs) and wide area networks (WANs), and it did so at high speed. With technology valued at $6 million and seed capital from Olivetti, 3i and private investors, Virata was spun out of the Olivetti lab in 1993. With premises in Cambridge,

> **❝Virata was an offshoot of the Olivetti Research Laboratory.❞**

it was given a chance to make its name developing and marketing equipment for LANs.

Ethernet, an older LAN technology that dated back to the 1970s, was not well suited to video and voice, since these time-dependent applications required information to be delivered in a constant stream. Ethernet separated data into packets that were distributed through different routes and reassembled at the receiving end. Ethernet worked fine for data in those days, but not for voice or video. Garbled conversations or jerky images were the result.

A better mousetrap

Hopper and Hauser thought the need for voice and video would grow, so their new company soon began marketing video servers, switches and network interface cards that together made up a complete ATM solution for LAN networks. Their ATM25 switch was the fastest in the world at the time, operating at 25 megabits per second compared with the 10-megabit products that the Ethernet providers offered. In 1994, with its new headquarters and sales office in California, to tap what was expected to be the first market for this new technology, Virata was off and running.

Like many technology companies, however, the cost of developing the technology outpaced the meagre early revenues. Thus, in 1995, with ATM all the rage in the venture capital community, Virata secured a first round of venture capital led by two prominent Silicon Valley firms, Oak Investment Partners and New Enterprise Associates, raising another $11 million for about 30 per cent of the company. As Hauser put it, 'Venture capitalists are basically "sector lemmings". When a sector is as hot as ATM was at the time, venture capitalists have got to have some ATM investments. We had one of the best ATM teams in the world and we had a product that was outstanding compared with all the other switches on the market.'[2]

With others developing similar technology, Virata staked its competitive advantage on its ability to enhance the software functionality of its ATM products. Unfortunately, however, by late 1995 it was clear that, in the words of Virata's Vice-president of Marketing, Tom Cooper, 'The dog was not eating the dog food – not just Virata's brand, no one's brand.' As one of Cooper's former colleagues from Hewlett-Packard pointed out, 'Tom, your problem is that you have a technology in search of a problem. No one has a problem yet.'[3] Tom's former colleague was right. The vast majority of traffic over LANs was data, not voice or video. Multimedia networking simply wasn't a mainstream application just yet.

But an absence of a real customer need was only part of the problem. Companies like 3Com, whose livelihoods were invested in Ethernet technology, were not about to let some upstart technology eat their lunch. These companies had deep pockets and large numbers of customers who had made significant investments in Ethernet networks.

> **❝companies like 3Com were not about to let some upstart technology eat their lunch❞**

These customers were happy to pay for upgrades and enhancements as further developments in Ethernet technology occurred. Even though Virata's ATM switches ran at more than twice the speed of Ethernet switches – at twice the price – customers just were not buying. 'It was the classic better mousetrap phenomenon,' said Cooper.[4] The better mousetrap, however, is not always the one that sells.

By 1996, morale at Virata was heading south. Virata's CEO tried to rally his troops, arguing that Virata was just slightly too early with its technology. He believed that, 'When this market takes off, Virata will be a leading player and will ride on its successes far into the future.'[5] Fortunately, there was continued faith among investors that ATM was a technology for the future. After all, ATM *was* a better mousetrap. As a result, Virata obtained another round of $13 million in June: $3 million from the original investors and $10 million from Oracle, whose CEO Larry Ellison had invested in another of Hauser's companies some years earlier. Ellison had faith in Hauser and it took only a 30-minute meeting to seal the deal.

Stay the course or change direction?

With a fresh injection of cash in hand, Virata renewed its efforts to sell its line of network products. Significantly, and as a result of connections built earlier in his career, Tom Cooper had had some success in licensing the software and semiconductors used in Virata's LAN equipment to companies interested in Virata's technology for applications in quite different areas. One recent approach had come from Alcatel, a French communications equipment company.

Alcatel was pioneering asynchronous digital subscriber line technology (ADSL), which it thought might make possible the upgrading of old-fashioned twisted-pair copper telephone wires to handle the growing interest in broadband applications. Alcatel wanted to use Virata's ATM LAN products as part of its ADSL demonstration, license the technology, and perhaps build it into its own hardware devices. These devices would handle high-speed data in the so-called local loop – the 'last mile' of copper that reached from telephone companies' facilities to their subscribers' homes and premises. As we saw in Chapter 4, the market for high-speed data applications like DSL looked promising even in 1996, and Virata's technology was worth a look, Alcatel thought.

Some at Virata were intrigued with the forecasts of rapid growth of online ADSL subscribers and wondered whether this market might be a more attractive one than the LAN markets Virata had been pursuing. But Virata's CEO would have none of this thinking: 'It would be disastrous to divert our attention to the licensing market as you suggest.'[6] The company soon found itself split into two camps and, barely one month after Virata received Ellison's cash, the CEO left the company.

In the summer of 1996, the Virata board asked Charles Cotton, the General Manager of the Cambridge operation since mid-1995, to become COO and acting CEO. Cotton's charge was to determine which direction Virata should take in the short term. Pulling his team together for a late summer strategic retreat in California's Napa Valley and fuelled by the California sunshine – and some of the world's finest wines – Virata management decided to pursue both directions concurrently, at least for the time being. It was too early to know whether the licensing strategy – or DSL itself, for that matter – would bear fruit, and it remained unclear whether the networking market might turn profitable. Although networking sales had grown to nearly $1.5 million per quarter, the direct selling and distribution costs exceeded the gross margin. Virata was burning cash rapidly and more would be needed soon.

That same month, Alcatel won a large contract with four regional Bell operating companies in the USA to deploy its DSL architecture. This broad-based deal covering a significant portion of the American telecom terrain focused the market on ATM-based ADSL solutions. At last, there was a light at the end of Virata's tunnel. In 1997, Virata licensed its technology to other telecom suppliers and to Com21Corporation, a leader in bringing high-speed data capability to American and European cable television operators, who also saw the potential for an ATM-based solution for their applications. Notwithstanding these deals, Virata's licensing revenues were still very small.

As the company pursued both the licensing strategy and the networking market, the Virata team remained badly divided. A new CEO – the third in just 15 months – was convinced that networking products – not DSL – were the bread and butter of Virata's future. The licensing business was just too different and required different skills. Licensing deals were sold to original equipment manufacturers (OEMs) that would add Virata's software technology and chips to their own products. Sales cycles were certain to be long and there was no assurance that the extensive selling effort required would actually result in purchase orders. The licensing business would also hitch Virata to the DSL wagon, and it was by no means clear that DSL would win the battle against other competing technologies.

Cotton and Cooper, however, were of the mind that Ethernet was going to win the battles *and* the war for networks, and that ATM – Virata's better mouse-trap – would lose. Licensing looked to them like the better bet. The debates over Virata's direction became increasingly divisive, and in September 1997, after only five months at the helm, the new CEO departed and Cotton was promoted into the position for good, this time. As he saw it, the two-pronged strategy was no longer tenable: 'We were straddling a chasm that was starting to widen. Sooner or later we had to jump to one side, otherwise we risked falling into the chasm never to recover.'[7] His first move was to dismiss Virata's entire networking product sales staff. The house would be bet on DSL.

❝Virata's better mousetrap would lose❞

The new direction required Virata to develop new capabilities in chip design. It also meant that Virata's customer base would shrink sharply in number, as it focused its efforts on large OEMs. By 1998, three customers accounted for 40 per cent of Virata's revenues, and its total customer base numbered less than 20. The long sales cycle also meant that Virata's cash continued to burn.

A happy ending

Fortunately, there was not a day that passed in 1998 when someone wasn't reporting the red-hot growth of the internet and its follow-on effect for broadband access. The internet frenzy enabled Virata to raise, with the help of Index Securities, a Swiss investment bank, another $31 million from existing and new investors to fund the company until a planned public offering in 1999. In November 1999, with Virata showing growth in the licensing business – no profits just yet, however, but declining losses – Virata shares started trading at $14 on NASDAQ and jumped to $27 by the end of the first day. Broadband access and the internet were hot. Virata's technology was playing a key role, and technology investors wanted to get on board. By early 2000, Virata's share price reached $100.

In the year after its IPO, in an effort to broaden its market and its technology base, Virata made four acquisitions. In doing so, it soon became evident that Virata was headed for a competitive collision with Globespan, an American fabless semiconductor company with a similar strategy. In December 2001, the two companies merged to create the world's leading provider of integrated circuits, software and systems designs for DSL providers.[8]

What endowed Virata's long struggle with its happy ending? To be sure, the coming of the internet age had a lot to do with it. Hermann Hauser's ability to raise a sorely needed $10 million from Larry Ellison in a 30-minute meeting didn't hurt either. But, as Hauser recalled, 'Without a doubt, the thing that carried us through was the quality of the team and all of its connections.' When Cooper told the story about Alcatel's interest in the Virata technology at a board meeting, 'The board seized upon the story and talked to some people that they knew. It turned out that the board had spotted an early trend, and this is where we made all of our money.'[9]

Virata's connections mattered. Call it luck or serendipity if you like. But Tom Cooper's connections down the value chain to potential customers in markets not then being served led to the Alcatel enquiry. The board's connections up and across the value chain – to suppliers and other players in related industries who could confirm what was happening with DSL – enabled Virata to place a very risky bet with more confidence than would otherwise have been possible. It's been said that lady luck comes to the well-prepared. As we've now seen, she also comes to the well-connected.

❝lady luck comes to the well-connected❞

Digital Equipment Corporation: missing the boat[10]

'Customers don't want a computer that sits on a desk. Customers want computers that sit on the floor.'[11] That's what Ken Olsen, co-founder of Digital Equipment Corp (DEC), said in a speech in the late 1970s. Most of us, of course, now have computers on our desks and others in our hands or laps or glued to our ears, with processing power that surpasses DEC's computers that sat on floors at that time. And DEC itself and most DEC computers are long gone, having been replaced in the 1980s and 1990s by PCs and servers from the likes of Dell, HP and Sun.

DEC founders Ken Olsen and Harlan Anderson set out in the late 1950s to provide functionality similar to large mainframe computers – mostly IBMs, in those days – but in a smaller, more bare-bones machine. In 1959, the company came out with its first computer – the Programmed Data Processor (PDP-1). Olsen described this computer as a console 'with all the instruments and lights, very much like you see in a power plant'.[12] The PDP-1 cost the customer $125,000–$150,000. By 1965, DEC had sales of $6.5 million, with profits of $807,000.

In 1966, DEC started selling the PDP-8. While considerably less expensive than its predecessor, each of these machines still sold for $18,000. DEC marketed the PDP-8, with its high-quality video display terminal, to businesses, universities, newspaper offices and publishers. It was also a particularly attractive computer for third parties who bought the PDP-8 machine from DEC, customised the hardware and software to meet the needs of their customers, and sold the enhanced computer as their own product. DEC's third-party business soon accounted for 50 per cent of its sales. By 1970, DEC was the most successful minicomputer manufacturer in the world.

Through the early 1970s, DEC remained a leader in the minicomputer industry. Olsen said, 'For many years we made the same two computers, the PDP-8 and the PDP-11. We kept that design consistently so that software the customers wrote would continue to work on newer models and the software we wrote would continue to work and get more and more robust.'[13]

Quite deliberately, rather than join the competition for the PC market as it emerged in the late 1970s, DEC avoided it and concentrated on networking issues: 'We made some PCs designed to be part of the networking but the general PC market was not for us. There were too many people in it . . . You could build them in your basement. That was not for us.'[14] The VAX was DEC's product line that offered networking capability. It connected several minicomputers in a LAN. One of the company's most popular networking products, the VAX 8600, allowed a system of minicomputers to function like a mainframe. But targeting the mainframe market, with its sales trend heading south, flew in the face of the rapid growth in the capability of PCs.

Finally, in 1980, DEC did begin developing personal computers, but Olsen insisted that the new machine be called an 'application terminal and small system' rather than a PC.[15] 'We believe in PCs. We encourage them. We network them. We use them in large numbers. But we still believe that most people in an organisation want terminals. With terminals you don't have to worry about data management, you don't have to worry about floppy disks. You just sit down and it does the work for you automatically.'[16]

DEC's late decision to enter the PC market, and to enter with three different product lines (Rainbow, Pro and DECmate), proved both confusing and damaging. In 1984, the effects began to show. In the third quarter of that year, earnings were down 72 per cent from the previous year. And that was only the beginning.

In 1988, Sun Microsystems introduced computers that ran the UNIX operating system. Hewlett-Packard soon followed with its own UNIX-based Apollo computers. All these systems had far more computing power than DEC's minicomputers and were much less expensive. Moreover, they ran on UNIX, which was rapidly becoming the de facto standard in operating systems, thereby encouraging third parties to write innovative software that would run on these platforms. Ironically, much of the UNIX software was developed on DEC machines. DEC, however, had been doing so well with its proprietary VMS operating system that it gave its UNIX offering little support. As UNIX took hold, no longer were DEC's minicomputers, with their proprietary operating system, the best alternative. They were no longer in the race.

By the dawn of the 1990s, DEC found itself in dire trouble. Tens of thousands of employees' jobs were lost. By 1994 DEC, once 126,000 people strong, was a company of only 63,000. Finally in 1998, DEC, by then no longer a computer maker, was sold to Compaq.

What did DEC miss?

There were many things that DEC did right in its heyday. It fared well for a quarter of a century – a veritable eternity in any high-tech industry. And, while it did post some impressive financial results along the way, it was plagued repeatedly by an inability to stay in front of the technology curve, missing the mark on some sweeping trends.

"it was plagued repeatedly by an inability to stay in front of the technology curve"

In the late 1960s, a group of DEC engineers led by Ed de Castro was assigned the task of designing a 16-bit computer that would replace the then-current 8-bit technology. Their final plan contained a basic 16-bit system that could be grown to 32 bits as well as a series of compatible products that would allow users to upgrade their existing machines rather than replace them. But what de Castro's group was suggesting amounted to scrapping the entire DEC product line and replacing it with the new 16-bit machines. DEC's management soundly rejected it. So in April 1968, de Castro and two other engineers left DEC, raised their own venture capital and started their own company, Data General Corporation, to produce 32-bit computers. By 1969, Data General was one of the hottest new companies in minicomputer manufacturing, tapping a market that could have been DEC's.

Then in 1972, a DEC team working on the PDP-11 recommended that DEC develop a product that combined a computer (the PDP-11/20) with a terminal and a printer. According to the PDP-11 group, this 'Datacenter' would appeal to a broad market of individual users, including scientists, technicians and others in administrative positions. DEC's leadership rejected this individual computer idea. Had DEC pursued the datacenter, could it have been the PC pioneer? We'll never know.

By 1980, with Apple and other personal computers beginning to make waves, and a year before IBM's PC introduction, DEC's product managers, those individuals who face the customer, suggested that DEC begin to play in the personal computer space. Olsen and his team refused. The rest is history.

Why?

Why did DEC repeatedly miss key changes in its marketplace? It's difficult to know with certainty without having been in DEC's meetings or inside Ken Olsen's head. The contrast with Virata, however, is striking. Virata had extensive connections up, down and across its value chain. When Virata got new information, it fanned out its other connections to help it interpret what it had heard. DEC, too, may have had some of these connections, but if it did, its top management wasn't very good at listening to them or leveraging other connections to take advantage of the information those connections provided. DEC leadership, like the ostrich, had its head in the sand.

❝DEC leadership, like the ostrich, had its head in the sand❞

The vibrancy of DEC's connections was perhaps encumbered by DEC's focus on and belief in its own technology and its faith that its solutions were superior to others. 'They believed [their] operating system was simply the best and would remain so into the new millennium,' said Jean Micol, a former DEC marketing executive.[17] If this is the case, why bother to develop connections for keeping track of external developments? Call it corporate arrogance or simply naïveté. DEC missed 16-bit computing. It missed PCs – not once, but twice! It missed UNIX. And now DEC is gone.

Markets and industries do change – especially high-tech ones. Success in changing markets requires well-developed connections to keep abreast of the changes, and it requires a top management team that's open-minded enough to consider changing course when conditions so indicate. Had Olsen spent time talking to and building a wider set of informational relationships – with DEC's sales channel and distributors, with its OEM manufacturers, even with its own marketing department – then he would have heard the resounding push towards PCs in the early 1980s and towards UNIX in the late 1980s. Hindsight suggests that the DEC team simply wasn't up to this task. Are you?

What investors want to know

Connections up, down and across the value chain are important to investors for a variety of reasons. In the short term, the team's connections with potential customers, especially large or strategically significant ones, enhance the likelihood that your new venture will meet its revenue targets. Connections up the value chain – with suppliers – enhance the likelihood that your new venture will be able to obtain the inputs it needs at favourable costs and on favourable terms. Connections across your industry and across potential substitute industries will enhance your understanding of the competitive situation that your venture will face, helping you differentiate and position your products in ways that will stand apart from those of your competitors. These short-run roles are important, and investors will want to know how your team measures up on such connections.

In the long term, however, the value of connections like these, whether brought to the business by the entrepreneurs or the investors, is more subtle. But it's extremely important, especially in the highly uncertain and changing markets where many entrepreneurial ventures play. Why? Investors know from experience that most of the money they've made has been made from plan B, not from plan A. 'Surprises are not deviations from the path. Instead they are the norm, the flora and fauna of the [entrepreneurial] landscape, from which one learns to forge a path through the jungle', says Saras Sarasvathy,[18] based on her research into entrepreneurial decision-making. But there's a problem here, because when an investor decides to invest in your venture, they do not really know what plan B will look like. How can investors insure themselves against the risk that your plan A will not work and that you might not come up with a suitable plan B? The best answer? Your and your team's connections.

> **"investors know from experience that most of the money they've made has been made from plan B, not from plan A"**

Without such connections, you may not have the market and competitive information that you'll need to revise your strategy when the need arises, as Virata was able to do at a crucial juncture but as DEC was not. You may not be able to take advantage of a favourable change in market needs that could benefit your venture substantially. You may not have the ability to judge quickly – and quickly may be important – which of several alternatives to a failing plan A ought to be your plan B. Whether your venture gets started on lean principles – where attention to the need for pivoting is top of mind – or otherwise, these are crucial investor concerns that will influence their view of the attractiveness of your opportunity and your entrepreneurial team, because they reduce the risk that your venture will fail. These concerns should be of similar concern to you. For a brief look at an investment that went bad very quickly, see Case Study 8.1

Fuhu: connections are not enough[19]

From the moment Robb Fujioka laid eyes on John Hui's ten-car garage with five Ferraris lined up inside, he knew that he wanted to emulate Hui, a self-made Chinese American entrepreneur and multi-millionaire. Hui and his brother Steve had co-founded PC maker eMachines and sold it to Gateway for nearly $290 million. A short time later, on a trip to Asia with the Huis, Fujioka got a glimpse into their high-rolling social circle, which included executives from Foxconn, a leading contract manufacturer of all things electronic. He wanted in.

The trio soon decided to launch a business together, developing software and licensing it to hardware manufacturers in the Huis' network. Fuhu would operate at a vastly larger scale compared to Fujioka's earlier small businesses in the tech marketing arena. As Fujioka was hardly a seasoned executive, the team recruited a former Accenture consultant, Jim Mitchell, as CEO. Mitchell, who had advised John Hui earlier, had the polish to get deals done on country club golf courses, in the founders' views. As the outward face of the company, Mitchell would do the deal-making, while Fujioka would develop products and run operations. The Huis would put up the initial capital and supply the necessary connections, including that with Foxconn, which invested $10 million in the young company.

Initially, all went well. Foxconn needed to unload a few thousand Android tablets, and Fujioka saw an opportunity. Fitting them with a child-friendly user interface and some child-friendly marketing, he and Mitchell convinced children's retailer Toys 'R' Us to stock them for Christmas. Toys 'R' Us sold them all, and a new category, mobile devices for kids, was born. Fujioka went all-in, introducing a range of Nabi kids' tablets, and sales reached $118 million in 2012, though gross margins, as was nearly always the case in hardware, were slim. Mitchell then signed licensing deals with Disney and Dream Works Animation, and convinced the latter to invest $10 million more. By late 2013, sales soared to $196 million.

▶

Could Fujioka do it again?

In the consumer electronics game, imitation happens fast, and the kids' tablet market was no exception. It was soon crowded with offerings from Amazon and Comcast's children's cable TV channel, Sprout, among others. Nabi sales went flat. Fuhu needed another big hit. A flurry of new products quickly followed, including the DreamTab, a fancy tablet that came loaded with cartoons and movies. Fujioka convinced Foxconn to make 150,000 of them, but by the summer of 2014 it became clear that the DreamTab was a dud. Unfortunately, this meant that Fuhu had stuck its distributor D&H with millions of dollars of unsaleable inventory, and Foxconn had not been paid for having made them. By the summer of 2014, Fuhu was haemorrhaging cash.

Fujioka knew he desperately needed another hit, and it would have to work this time. The Big Tab, a family-sized mobile tablet, was his answer. But it, too, flopped. By Christmas 2014, fewer than 4,000 units had been sold. 'It was a disaster launch,' admits Fujioka. Fuhu's 2014 sales totalled less than $70 million, off nearly 65 per cent from 2013.

The fallout thereafter got nasty: D&H sued, and in the autumn of 2015, Foxconn ran out of patience, cutting off Fuhu's supply and seizing its inventory. Fuhu's lenders then swept the company's remaining cash from its bank account, and the game was over. The company's assets were subsequently sold to Mattel in a bankruptcy fire sale for a paltry $21 million; the company's creditors were left holding a $110 million bag.

Why did Fuhu fail? The company's strategy seemed to have been based on little more than the Huis' connections, lots of smooth-talking, and blind faith in new products, with little regard for what consumers might actually buy. Connections are important, of course, and they allowed Fuhu to get started and to prosper for a short time. But they are not sufficient. Will Fujioka recover and live to fight another day? If so, it probably won't be with the same set of connections.

Lessons learned

The fact that connections matter will not surprise any astute entrepreneur. But some of the ways they matter, in both the short and long run, are issues to which many entrepreneurs give little thought. What can we learn from the case histories in this chapter to help you assess your opportunity or one in which you might invest?

Lessons learned from Virata

Virata was fortunate that a confluence of technological trends created a market – telecom providers seeking to provide dial-up broadband access to their telephone customers – for which its technology happened to be extremely well suited. It's been said many times that luck can play an important role in entrepreneurial success. Being in the right place at the right time, as Virata was, can turn a struggling company into a blockbuster.

The lesson from Virata isn't, however, about luck. The lesson is that connections – the right kind of connections – can deliver to an entrepreneurial firm three important outcomes:

■ Identifying fortuitous trends, new information or changes in the marketplace that the company might take advantage of;

■ Doing so early, before other would-be competitors can do so;

■ Obtaining a broad-based assessment of such a development, from a variety of perspectives outside the firm, in order that a decision to pursue it can be an evidence-based one rather than a risky guess.

With connections that deliver outcomes like these, your pivots – like the key pivot Virata made – are more likely to be grounded in evidence, which in turn should help you, whether you are an entrepreneur or investor, get comfortable with the change in strategy that the pivot entails.

What kind of connections will your venture or those you back want to have?

■ Connections *up* the value chain to suppliers who deal with the leaders in your industry and with firms in other industries that might serve as substitutes for the products you provide.

■ Connections *down* the value chain to potential customers – including distributors, consumers, and users – in target markets that you might serve one day in addition to the markets you plan to target at the outset.

■ Connections *across* your industry with competitors – and with firms from other industries that offer substitutes – so that you can gain some perspective to gauge accurately changes in market conditions. When your sales increase, it's good to know whether they are doing so because you are gaining market share or whether you are simply benefiting from a rising tide that floats all boats. The same is true when your sales are soft.

Connections across your industry also help you understand its CSFs, an important issue in helping you assemble an entrepreneurial team that can deliver the kind of performance most entrepreneurial ventures seek. These connections can also identify and build relationships with skilled people who know your industry and whom – now or later – you may wish to attract to your company.

Lessons learned from DEC

As we have seen, DEC failed to adapt to trend after trend in the computing industry: 16-bit computing, the rise of PCs and UNIX. The problem for DEC was not that they had no connections or that no one in DEC saw these things happening. Indeed, some did. Of the three outcomes listed above that the right kind of connections can deliver for an entrepreneurial firm, DEC's difficulties seemed to be with the third issue, i.e. obtaining a broad-based assessment of these developments from a variety of perspectives outside the firm. As a result, DEC's decisions not to pursue these developments in a timely and aggressive manner appeared to have been based on DEC's blind faith in its own products and solutions – arrogantly and naïvely, some would say – rather than on the basis of the marketplace evidence that was there to be seen and understood.

An inward-looking culture, especially in a rapidly changing industry like computing, adds additional risk to what we've seen is an always-risky game of entrepreneurship. As Andy Grove,[20] long-time CEO of Intel, wrote, 'only the paranoid survive'. The same is true for those assessing new opportunities. Yes, this means *you*. Being inward-looking, focused on your *idea* rather than on the market and industry where it might take root and on building the right team to help you achieve your dreams, is a pathway to impending disaster. Having a broad set of the right kinds of connections – *who* you and your investors know – does matter, not only in running your business once it starts, but much earlier as well, in assessing and shaping your opportunity as it evolves. Don't go too far without them. Entrepreneurial success is not just about *what* you know. It's about *who* you know and your ability to use your network productively.

Lessons learned from Fuhu

Fujioka concedes he had been out of his depth as a CEO. 'There was a bankruptcy of the business," he says, "but there was also a bankruptcy of the corporate culture.'[21] And he'd failed to attract and retain a solid management team. There were a lot of employees, he recalls 'Who just couldn't fulfill what they needed to fulfill,'[22] including numerous childhood pals in senior positions.

Not only did the company lack connections other than that to Foxconn, its team lacked the ability to execute on its industry's critical success factors, too, especially those relating to understanding consumers and meeting their needs and managing costs in the cut-throat hardware business. Executives in the finance department came and went, frustrated by the leadership's failure to come to grips with the numbers and a business model that simply was not working. Fuhu's slim product margins couldn't – and didn't – cover the overhead costs nor out-of-control spending. Worse, the profusion of products that Fujioka developed were never market tested, including the Dream-Tab and Big Tab, products on which Fujioka bet his company's survival.

After having examined the three team domains, and the four market and industry domains before them, "What's next?" you might ask. Grab your notes, as it's now time to put your learning to work, and to apply your lessons to your very own opportunity. To that task we turn next.

The new business road test: stage seven – the connectedness test

- Who do you and your team know, *up* the value chain in the companies that are likely suppliers to your proposed business and to your competitors? In suppliers to companies in other industries that offer substitute products for yours? Be sure you have names, titles and contact information.

- Who do you and your team know *down*, the value chain among distributors and customers you will target, both today and tomorrow? Names, titles and contact information, please.

- Who do you and your team know *across*, the value chain among your competitors and substitutes? Names, titles and contact information, please.

- Where are any key gaps in your teams' connections (to be added to your risk list), and how can you fill them?

THE NEW BUSINESS ROAD TEST

If you open your *New Business Road Test* app, you'll find the above checklist reproduced there. You might want to begin this stage of your road test by using the app to record an initial conclusion about just how connected you are – or are not – to others whose future information may help you pivot appropriately if necessary. The app provides a place to record that assessment, along with places to keep track of the new connections you make, organised into four categories: prospective suppliers, prospective customers or channel members, prospective consumers or end-users, and prospective competitors in the industry in which you plan to compete or in substitute industries.

9

Develop your opportunity: put the seven domains to work

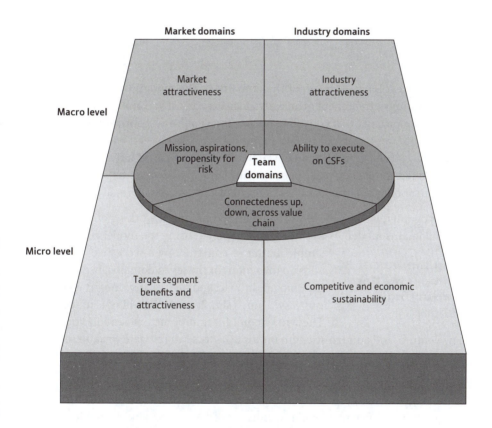

Market domains

Industry domains

Macro level

Micro level

Market
attractiveness

Industry
attractiveness

Mission, aspirations,
propensity for
risk

Ability to execute
on CSFs

Team
domains

Connectedness up,
down, across value
chain

Target segment
benefits and
attractiveness

Competitive and economic
sustainability

It's not simply a checklist

A moment's insight is sometimes worth a life's experience.

Oliver Wendell Holmes, writer (1809–94)[1]

We've now explored all seven of the domains in the model. Whether you are an aspiring entrepreneur or an early-stage investor, if you already have in mind an opportunity that you might pursue, then you've probably considered how well it fares in each of the seven domains as you've been reading this book. Most likely, your idea fared well in some domains and not so well in others. What should you make of this result? How should you interpret what you learn about your opportunity as a result of a seven domains analysis?

In this chapter, we grapple with the practical realities of working with the seven domains model. As was noted in Chapter 1, using the model is not a simple matter of constructing a scoresheet that adds up the scores for the seven domains, because the domains interact and their relative importance can vary. Thus, a simple checklist will not suffice. The wrong combination of factors can kill your new venture, and enough strength on some factors can mitigate weaknesses on others.

> **"using the model is not a simple matter of constructing a scoresheet"**

To help you interpret the results of a seven domains analysis, we first return to the fundamental purpose for doing a seven domains road test: answering the question, 'Why will or won't my idea work?' Next, we look at situations where things on the surface don't look so attractive, but where committed and insightful entrepreneurs can 'make lemons into lemonade'. It's important to understand the circumstances under which not-so-perfect opportunities can still be attractive. We then examine situations that are likely to be favourable for niche-market entrepreneurs who seek to start businesses having modest aspirations. Finally, we identify five common traps entrepreneurs and investors should avoid, where others before you have been led unwarily down a primrose path to disaster; and we explore how a seven domains analysis provides a guide to when and how to pivot in developing an opportunity that has potential, but hasn't yet been shaped quite right.

As is the pattern throughout this book, we close the chapter with some key things that investors should look for – issues that reach across the seven domains, including some red flags that can be the kiss of death if you don't address them carefully. Then we wrap up the chapter with several final lessons learned.

Why will or won't my idea work?

In Chapter 1, we raised a simple but all-important question that the best entrepreneurs ask regularly about their opportunities: 'Why will or won't my idea work?' Now that you understand all seven of the domains, it's time to apply this model to answer this all-important question. One way to use the seven domains framework would be to score your opportunity – say, from one to ten on the seven domains – and add up your opportunity's score, with 70 being perfect. But that's not exactly what I suggest you do. Score them, or rate them green, yellow or red if you wish, but don't add them up. (Actually, you should score or rate only six of them – you can skip the mission domain, for it's not really something to score.) Instead, do the following:

1 Consider your mission, aspirations and propensity for risk, so you'll know what sort of opportunity you are looking for. Take another look at the test at the end of Chapter 6 as you do so.

2 Look for the one domain (there may be more, but it's unlikely) where your opportunity's score is off the charts – a 12 on a 10-point scale. If you find one or two of these scores located in certain sectors of the model (see below), then you may have a high-potential opportunity. This is the 'moment's insight' that could make your life's experience! If you

> **❝ this is the 'moment's insight' that could make your life's experience! ❞**

are looking for a niche business, one that can fly under the competitors' radar, then this criterion is not so critical. Niche opportunities are a bit different and we'll address them explicitly later in this chapter.

3 Look for any domain where your score is low – say, five or below on a 10-point scale, and examine the list of risks that you've uncovered

in assessing each of the seven domains. Then, using what you'll learn in this chapter, ask yourself whether a strong score in another sector effectively mitigates this problem or any of the risks on your risk list. If so, that too can be another 'moment's insight' on which the feasibility of your opportunity is based. If not, then you'll have discovered that your opportunity probably needs more work. In this case, whether you are an entrepreneur or an investor, you'll need to put some effort into further developing and reshaping the opportunity, because you don't want to go to market with a crucial flaw in your opportunity. The sooner you make any necessary pivots, the better. If you can't mitigate this score by pivoting, then perhaps you should abandon it now and move on to something more attractive. Finding your Achilles' heel *before* you get started is not a bad outcome.

4   For the other domains with more intermediate scores, use what you'll learn in this chapter about how the domains work together to see whether some further pivoting may be required for these reasons.

Making lemons into lemonade

Some opportunities look unappealing on one or more of the seven domains, but they may nevertheless be attractive to certain entrepreneurs, given the presence of either:

■ Sufficient innovation that's meaningful to customers and is likely to cause a stagnant market to grow substantially;

■ Differentiation that is either proprietary or complex enough to provide sustainable advantage in spite of unfavourable industry conditions.

Sufficient strength in these micro-level domains – especially when combined with a strong, well-connected team – can offset weakness on the macro-level factors. Let's consider some examples.

Product innovation in stagnant markets

As we saw in Chapter 2, Phil Knight's passion for building a better athletic shoe, combined with his company's ability to differentiate its shoes on a seg-ment-by-segment basis through product design and effective marketing, even-tually made Nike a household name and one of the world's best-known brands.

Even more, it turned the previously boring athletic footwear industry into a growth machine. What Nike took advantage of – in the lower left corner of the seven domains model – was an opportunity so compelling, in terms of customer benefits (both tangible and psychological, as the Nike brand developed), that the benefits of building a better product (and doing better marketing) outweighed the then-stagnant market conditions, measured in macro terms.

Compelling customer benefits like Nike's can provide sufficient reason to proceed on an opportunity whose market looks otherwise unattractive. Another such example is Starbucks, where Howard

> **compelling customer benefits can provide sufficient reason to proceed on an opportunity whose market looks otherwise unattractive**

Schultz's insights into why customers might welcome a lively respite where they could enjoy better coffee led to rapid growth for more than 30 years, in spite of the fact that American coffee consumption had been declining in pre-Starbucks days. Here, innovation that produced an enjoyable customer experience and a better product, combined with effective execution, offset what might have appeared in the 1970s to be an unattractive market. Starbucks, by selling an experience, has achieved spectacular and very profitable growth.

Differentiation and careful market targeting in unattractive industries

A five forces analysis of the retailing industry would show that retailing is an unlikely setting in which to build a high-growth enterprise able to withstand imitation over the long term. Barriers to entry are simply too low, affording easy entry to imitators; supplier power, at least at the outset for a new entrant, can be high; and consumers usually have many choices of where to shop. This unfavourable industry structure is reflected in average industry profitability that ranks far lower than that of many other more attractive industries.

Zara, Wal-Mart and numerous others, however, have managed to build profitable, growing retail businesses whose competitive advantage has lasted, in spite of these unfavourable industry conditions. What did they see in the opportunities they pursued? Fundamentally, they saw opportunities to build competitive advantages – advantages that benefited customers and proved to be sustainable – over other retailers.

Zara, the Spanish apparel retailer with more than 2,000 stores throughout Europe and elsewhere, offered the latest styles of clothing in high-street locations at very competitive prices. By keeping its range and depth of apparel limited, changing its offerings rapidly, and keeping its supply chain short, Zara was able to consistently stay at the cutting edge of the latest fashion trends while achieving buying and operating efficiencies that it could pass on to consumers in lower prices.

In Wal-Mart's case, Sam Walton saw an opportunity to extend discount retailing to the small towns and cities of rural America and offer vastly superior selection at sharply lower prices than small-town, main-street merchants were able to offer. Unfortunately for the main-street merchants, Wal-Mart's relentless efficiency drove many of them out of business. This competitive advantage became sustainable over time, as Wal-Mart built complex, hard-to-imitate information and distribution capabilities (real-time sales data transmitted daily to headquarters via satellite, and low-cost cross-dock merchandise handling in its distribution centres, to name just two) that made it among the most efficient of retailers. Eventually, Wal-Mart put these capabilities to work globally and in doing so became the world's largest retailer.

It was the combination of three factors – genuine benefits to customers, clear differentiation for competitive advantage and teams that could deliver results – that enabled these retailers and others like them in other merchandise categories, such as Whole Foods in grocery retailing, as we saw in Chapter 3, to create successful entrepreneurial ventures in an otherwise daunting industry context. These companies and others have grown successfully for long periods of time. Amazon has done it, too, in online retailing. Thus, unfavourable industries – at the macro level – *need not be deal-killers, provided other pieces of the puzzle are strong enough.*

Opportunities for niche-market entrepreneurs

Not all entrepreneurs want to make their businesses large ones. Not all entrepreneurs want to exit. Many prefer to operate the business for many years or pass it on to subsequent generations of family or management. Local car dealers, small manufacturing firms, some franchised businesses and other businesses in fragmented industries or very small markets are examples. Can the seven domains model help these entrepreneurs assess and shape their opportunities?

❝not all entrepreneurs want to make their businesses large ones❞

Commonly, when such businesses are successful, it is partly because they fly below the radar of larger, more established firms, and target relatively small niche markets where larger companies choose not to compete. What makes a good opportunity for entrepreneurs having these kinds of objectives?

My research suggests that for those who want to build sustainable businesses of modest size, the macro-level factors aren't nearly as important as one particular micro-level factor: target segment benefits and attractiveness. If you can find a small market segment whose needs are not currently being served well, and – due to the sharply targeted nature of your business – you can deliver the benefits these customers need in a superior fashion, then that may be all you need to succeed. Thus, compelling customer benefits and clear differentiation in a carefully targeted market segment – in the lower left quadrant in the seven domains model – are the keys to assessing these kinds of opportunities.

Sometimes, as time unfolds, such niche businesses can grow into very large ones. Enterprise Car Rental, which focused for years on the neighbourhood market as opposed to serving business travellers at airports, is an example of one such business that grew relatively slowly but very persistently. Surprisingly to some, it's now the largest car rental company in the world, in spite of the modest early objectives of its founders.

Five common traps to avoid

In this section, we identify five common traps – common opportunity patterns revealed by my research – that look attractive by some criteria, at least at first glance, but often are fundamentally flawed. Whether you are an investor or an entrepreneur, if your proposed venture looks like it falls into one of these kinds of traps, you might think about pivoting now, or even looking for something entirely different.

Trap 1: the large market fallacy

Investors often hear entrepreneurs say something like this: 'My market is huge. If I get just 10 per cent of it (or 5 or even 1 per cent), we'll all be rich!' The problem with large markets, especially large markets that are growing fast, is that others like them too. Large markets attract competitors, often large established ones with deep pockets. Such markets can be very difficult places for entrepreneurs to play, especially in industries where the threat of entry is high. Equally importantly, if your product doesn't offer genuine benefits to your targeted consumers, then the largest market in the world will not save your business. Thus, serving a large market offers no assurance of entrepreneurial success.

❝the problem with large markets is that others like them too❞

For example, more than three decades ago, Nestlé's refrigerated foods division examined the American market for pizza, worth $18 billion at the time. They decided to enter this huge market with a refrigerated pizza product sold in supermarkets; they needed less than three-tenths of 1 per cent of the market to be successful.[2] Their entry failed. Why? Fresh-baked pizza, delivered for an easy family meal, was seen by consumers as superior in taste and was no more expensive than Nestlé's pizza. It was convenient too. Cheaper frozen pizza was adequate for a fast meal for the kids. Nestlé's refrigerated product offered no clear benefits to either market segment. Later high-quality entrants into the frozen pizza category did very well.

What's the lesson for avoiding this trap? For entrepreneurs and investors alike, large markets are good news only when the planned offering delivers genuine benefits for some clearly defined segment thereof. For new ventures serving large markets, it's generally far better to pursue a *large share* of a small but carefully targeted segment rather than a *small share* of the overall market. Nestlé failed to do that with its refrigerated pizza entry. In large markets, targeting is crucial. If entry into the initial segment provides entry to other segments later, so much the better.

Trap 2: the better mousetrap fallacy

Especially in technology-driven industries, entrepreneurs and investors who back them often try to capitalise on technology for its own sake. Doing so rather than asking what the technology can do that benefits some target segment of customers is a trap. Better technology – a better mousetrap – does not necessarily equal a better solution for the customer. The key question for technology entrepreneurs, where there's typically uncertain demand for the technology, is 'Who wants it and why?' Nestlé, as the story above shows, fell into this trap. Thus, the trap can occur in the low-tech world and in smaller markets too.

❝who wants it and why?❞

In 1999, a British start-up called Navigation Zone[3] developed a novel and patented method for searching and navigating very large websites. The market for search engines and Web navigation tools was large and growing rapidly, and the company was readily able to raise seed funding. A year after funding, the company had still not made any sales, and the money was running out. Crucially, the company had not identified exactly who wanted what they had to offer. Was it site owners, other search engine suppliers, or developers? While they had developed a technology that demonstrated small but real improvements over existing approaches, the gain was not sufficient to warrant any potential customer changing his or her current buying behaviour. The company was forced to downsize and survived only by refocusing entirely on the site developer market with a specific tool that improved the site developer's productivity by a factor of two.

Whether you are an entrepreneur or an early-stage investor, how can you best avoid this trap if your opportunity is technology-based? Re-read the case histories of OurBeginning.com in Chapter 2, Twilio in Chapter 3, Palm Computing in Chapter 7, and Virata and DEC in Chapter 8. Remind yourself that entrepreneurial success is not about you and your technology. It's about identifying the right customers and using technology to satisfy their needs. The lean start-up approach can be helpful in discovering, over time, exactly who the right customers are and their needs that you can most fruitfully address. But the sooner you can identify a customer segment that desperately wants something that you can offer, the better off you will be.

Trap 3: the no sustainable business model trap

Many failures during the dot.com bust had business models that were simply unsustainable. We've already seen the example of Webvan in Chapter 5. Pet supply e-tailers were another example.[4] While large, attractive markets of pet owners and compelling customer benefits were present (who likes carrying heavy bags of dog food home from the store?), the raw economics of acquiring new customers and shipping dog food one bag at a time were simply unsustainable. Put another way, the relationship between the two micro-level factors, i.e. benefits for which a group of target customers are willing to pay and a cost structure that makes the intended product or service economically viable, must be sustainable. If not, the business will not last long, as we saw in the demise of most pet supply e-tailers in 2000.

How, as an entrepreneur or investor, might you avoid this trap? Build your network so you understand your industry and its economics. Then do the mathematics on your opportunity. Grand concepts are no substitute for running the numbers, including those specified in Chapter 5 in the lower right corner of the seven domains model. Economic sustainability is a really big deal, and you can make lots of progress in determining whether you can expect to achieve it, *before* you get started!

Trap 4: the me-too trap

The combination of high threat of entry (a macro-level industry factor) and lack of sustainable advantage for new entrants (a micro-level industry factor) can cause a large number of competitors to pursue an opportunity, only to be winnowed in a hurry. In the early days of the Winchester disk drive industry, for example, so many me-too entrants entered the industry that capacity of more than 40 times the total market size was funded by venture capital investors.[5] Thus, the combination of low barriers to entry (revealed in the upper right corner of our model) and a lack of sustainable advantage (lower right corner) should be a red flag to would-be entrepreneurs. The only ones who should tolerate this combination are niche-market entrepreneurs who can fly below the competitors' radar.

> **❝the combination of low barriers to entry and a lack of sustainable advantage should be a red flag❞**

How to avoid this trap? This one's easy. If barriers to entry are low and you have nothing on which to sustain your initial advantage, stop before you start. If you are a prospective investor in such a deal, simply walk away! If you've already started or invested in such a venture, I suggest you sell now, unless you are happy to run a niche-market business in a market segment that does not compete with the big guys. That's what Jack and Andy Taylor did in starting Enterprise Car Rental. Hertz, Avis and the others couldn't be bothered with the neighbourhood segment, and the Taylors had it almost entirely to themselves.

Trap 5: the hubris trap

Some people build careers as serial entrepreneurs. They start venture after venture, seemingly always successfully. Those who are successful usually succeed by choosing opportunities without crucial flaws and by executing effectively. In Chapter 2, however, we saw Michael Budowski, a successful entrepreneur in his previous ventures, stumble with OurBeginning.com. Louis Borders stumbled with Webvan, in spite of his earlier success in bookstores, as we saw in Chapter 5.

> **❝having done it before does not obviate the need for attention to the seven domains❞**

How can you avoid this one, if you are an entrepreneur who has already done it before? Having done it before is a great advantage when it comes to fund-raising, but it does not obviate the need for attention to the seven domains. Don't rest on your laurels. Do your homework. Even *you* are not invincible!

When and how should you pivot?

Almost always, one's initial view of how an opportunity might best be conceptualised and pursued is off the mark, at least to some degree. Perhaps the initial target market isn't quite right. Perhaps the economics enshrined in the initial business model are not likely to work. Perhaps the entrepreneurial team, as initially assembled, lacks the ability to execute on one particular critical success factor. What should you, as the entrepreneur or as an investor who has come to the table, do in such an instance?

A rigorously prepared seven domains analysis will have identified a list of risks, and perhaps one or more domains that appear to be problematic. The risks and the difficult domains are the grist that can now be fed into the opportunity assessment and development mill in order to further develop – and alter – the opportunity in such a way that some risks are reduced or resolved and the challenging domains mitigated by strengths elsewhere in the seven domains model. The way these changes are made is what we now know as pivoting: changing some element(s) of the opportunity without changing the overall vision. Driving these pivots requires getting away from your desk and going outside the building to gather evidence – hard cold facts – about the risks you've identified and the domains that are seen as unattractive.

In the second half of this book, you'll find a collection of tools and techniques by which this evidence can be gathered or uncovered. The sooner you get out of the building to gather your evidence, the better! Hopefully, in fact, as you've gathered the evidence underlying your seven domains road test, you've stopped from time to time and perhaps pivoted already. The role of these pivots is to eliminate or mitigate the risks you've discovered and to enhance your opportunity's upside. The hypothesis-testing mindset that's entailed in the lean start-up process lies at the heart of this process. Test and learn. Test and learn.

What investors look for

Professional investors – those who invest for reasons other than that they love you – understand intuitively the seven domains, even though they, like entrepreneurs and the rest of us, do make mistakes.

❝professional investors do make mistakes❞

If you are a prospective investor in an early-stage start-up, what sort of mistakes are you likely to make?

■ You will confuse markets and industries, mistaking the attractiveness of one for the attractiveness of the other.

■ You'll overlook the distinctions between the macro and micro levels. As lemmings follow one another over the precipice, you'll perhaps follow other investors into large and growing markets, falling into the large market fallacy.

- You will fail to ensure that what your investees bring to market offers clear and differentiated customer benefits – falling into the better mousetrap trap.

- You'll forget to examine whether the initial advantage brought by those benefits can be protected and/or sustained.

- You will mistake personality, chemistry or a few lines on a CV for an entrepreneur's ability to execute on the CSFs. You'll forget to determine whether an entrepreneur has the necessary connections or not: up, down and across the value chain.

In short, early-stage investors, like the rest of us, are human. Nonetheless, professional investors – angels and venture capitalists – do know what they want in the deals they back. In general, they like to see:

- Large, growing markets supported by favourable macro trends;

- Attractive, competitively forgiving industries – four or five generally favourable forces;

- Market offerings that resolve real customer pain, by delivering clear and differentiated benefits not available elsewhere;

- Innovations that can be defended over time through patents or superior organisational processes and capabilities, having economically viable business models;

- Entrepreneurial teams whose missions, aspirations and propensities for risk are compatible with their own;

- Entrepreneurial teams who can execute on their industry's CSFs;

- teams well connected up, down and across the value chain.

Can they have it all in any particular deal? Exceedingly rarely, otherwise their success rates on individual investments would be far higher than the one or two in ten that most venture capital portfolios achieve. So, what do they do? They take risks in pursuit of greater rewards. They bet that a shortcoming on one domain or another will be compensated for by strength on another. That a strong enough team will meet the challenges that will inevitably be encountered. That others won't soon see the opportunity you and they see.

❝investors have identified certain red flags❞

In contemplating these risks, however, investors have identified certain red flags or warning signs that tell them when the risks are too great, regardless of how exciting the opportunity's other elements may appear. They've done this the hard way, through unpleasant experience. Among these signs are the following:

■ Lightweight (or even non-existent) market research. 'What are the customers saying?' asks Joseph Bartlett, a partner at Morrison and Foerster LLP. 'This kind of interchange has no substitute; it has to happen before you solicit money from venture capitalists.'[6] True, there have been a couple of periods when dot.com ideas scribbled on cocktail napkins somehow won funding. But those days are long gone.

■ Better than market research, even, are hard data that customers have actually bought or will buy. Actual orders from a website, letters of intent or other indications of real demand are powerful testimony. What people *say*, in a market research setting, is not necessarily what they will *do*.

■ Overly confident assessment of competition. 'It always puzzles me when I come across plans that claim they have no competition,' says Daniel Kim of Circle Group Internet.[7] Virtually every customer need is being satisfied presently, in some way, however imperfectly. Your competition may not look like you or what you plan to offer, but surely as day follows night, it's out there. If there's no competition, there's probably no market either!

Entrepreneurs who have carefully assessed the seven domains don't make the above mistakes because:

■ The research has been carried out;

■ Evidence of genuine demand has been gathered;

■ Competition – direct competitors as well as substitutes – has been identified and assessed.

❝ the seven domains analysis puts you and your investors on the same page ❞

Thus, if you are an entrepreneur in talks with prospective investors, the seven domains framework gives you the tools to speak their language of risk and reward. It takes you beyond blind faith – that everything is wonderful about your opportunity – and enables you to understand deeply your opportunity, warts and all. It enables you to answer for your prospective investors your two key questions, which happen to be their key questions, too.

■ Why *will* this work? What are the one or perhaps two domains that lend to your opportunity a compellingly positive story?

■ Why *won't* this work? Where do the risks lie, and what is there about your opportunity and your team that effectively mitigates them?

In short, the seven domains analysis puts entrepreneurs and their prospective investors on the same page. It aligns perspectives. It gives you a common language with which to discuss and debate the merits and flaws that each of you sees in the opportunity you wish to pursue. And, as we'll see in the next chapter, it provides a solid, evidence-based foundation on which to build a lean start-up or – if you must – write a compelling business plan.

Lessons learned

In this chapter, bringing together the seven domains, what additional lessons have we learned?

Not a checklist

As we've now seen, using the seven domains framework is not as simple as constructing a checklist and adding the scores. The seven domains work together in complex and sometimes surprising ways. Different entrepreneurs and different investors having different missions, aspirations and propensities for risk will reach different conclusions about opportunities that may be quite similar in market and industry terms. This point has important implications for developing your business, an implication we'll explore in the next chapter. It should now be clear, however, that assessing and shaping a market opportunity and pivoting when necessary is no simple task. It takes thought, evidence, hard work and insight.

> **❝assessing and shaping a market opportunity is no simple task❞**

The all-important micro-level domains

It should also be clear by now that, of the four market and industry domains, the most important, by far, in assessing an opportunity are the two micro-level domains. The importance of understanding customer needs and shaping the opportunity so that the offering delivers valuable and differentiated benefits to a clearly defined target market in a competitively and economically sustainable way is difficult to overstate. Unfortunately, though, in this internet age, many aspiring entrepreneurs (I trust you are not among them!) won't get out of their chairs and away from their computer screens to talk first hand with prospective customers to uncover the real problems inherent in their opportunities and to work out in advance how to resolve them. We'll have more to say in Chapters 10, 11 and 15 about how to conduct the research you must do, but surfing the Web is only step one.

Management, management, management

As we've now seen, there's an element of truth in this adage, though making the case for what you bring to the entrepreneurial party isn't as simple as updating your CV and turning on your charm. The lead entrepreneur – and more importantly the entrepreneurial team as a whole – is important. Get the team right. Entrepreneurship, if you're playing to win, is a team sport.

Lessons for the family and friends of aspiring entrepreneurs

As we've now seen, while most professional investors intuitively understand the ideas inherent in the seven domains, it's true that most investors – like the rest of us – do make mistakes. They do so more often than most like to admit. In researching this book and putting its principles to work for more than a decade, I have learned that most investors in young companies – business angels and venture capitalists alike – are still hungry for ways to think more clearly about their investment decisions. The same is true for informal investors including the three Fs – family, friends, but no fools among you, having read this far.

Informal investors may also find the seven domains model useful for dispensing, along with money, another kind of love – tough love, as it's sometimes called. Your objective, independent and dispassionate questions and an occasional moment's insight – in the words of Oliver Wendell Holmes, who introduced this chapter – for the entrepreneur you love are always welcome.

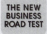 **THE NEW BUSINESS ROAD TEST** If you've been using your *New Business Road Test* app as you've read this book, you should now be in position to pull your thinking about all seven domains into a coherent and comprehensive picture of your opportunity, or perhaps more than one opportunity, warts and all. If that's the case, I suggest you step back and consider the totality of the data you've gathered – without the rose-coloured glasses you'd probably wear while writing a business plan. In Chapter 10, we'll suggest a concise way to do so, the customer-driven feasibility study. If you've not been gathering your data just yet, Chapter 10 will give you some ideas of how to get started, and it will address a question that may be on your mind, if like many entrepreneurs, you're an impatient sort who just wants to get on with it: 'Why bother?'.

10

What entrepreneurs and investors should do *before* pressing 'start'

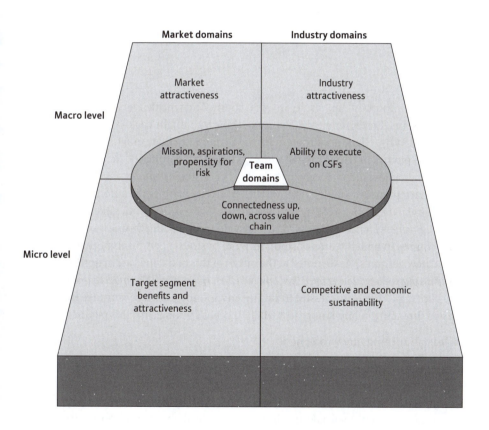

Why do most business plans raise no money?

Two roads diverged in a wood, and I — I took the one less traveled by.
And that has made all the difference.

Robert Frost[1]

Planning is important. But results are what count. And who delivers the results? Entrepreneurs. Entrepreneurs like you – or those you might back – can change the world. Why, then, does there remain so much fascination with business *plans* and pitches in the entrepreneurial community, despite the fact that the lean start-up movement has given the notion of business *planning* a firm shove off the entrepreneurial table? Why are there software packages to automate the business *planning* process? Why are there dozens of books with titles like *How to Write a Business Plan* and *How to Pitch*? Why do most leading business schools offer courses in which teams of students write business *plans* for hypothetical or real new ventures? As we noted at the outset of this book, the vast majority of business *plans – in whatever form they take, whether a plan, a business model canvas,*[2] *or a pitch deck* – are unsuccessful in raising any money. Of those ventures that do win financing, many if not most will fail. What's wrong with this picture?

At least four things are wrong here.

- First, most business plans of any variety are written for opportunities that are fundamentally flawed. Why write a business plan for a no-hope opportunity? If you're an aspiring entrepreneur, it's a waste of your very precious entrepreneurial time and talent. Instead, put your opportunity through a rigorous new business road test by doing the seven domains homework. If necessary, reshape your opportunity with one or more pivots or invest your time in finding a better one.

- Second, the inherently persuasive nature of business plans and their ilk, a principal purpose of which is often to raise money, forces their proponent entrepreneurs into the 'everything about my opportunity is wonderful' mode. As we saw in Chapter 9, the likelihood – even for attractive opportunities – is that *not* everything is wonderful but there may be one or two things that *are* quite wonderful that outweigh those that are not. The would-be entrepreneur who prepares and pitches an 'everything is wonderful' business plan – like the ones many business planning books and software describe – risks her credibility with investors, who know the real risks that entrepreneurial ventures entail. This naïveté makes it harder, not easier, to raise the money that's needed. Worse, such a positive slant risks blinding the entrepreneur to the very real risks that may lie in wait in one or more of the seven domains (even though a risk section in the typical plan identifies what might go wrong and explains why it won't).

■ Third, most business plans are focused on the entrepreneur and his or her idea. They are me-focused or my-idea-focused rather than customer-focused. People do matter – true – but investors don't really care very much about you and your idea, at least not at the beginning. What investors care about is solving significant customer problems or needs that offer significant profit and growth potential. If you have a solution to such a problem, then their ears will perk up. If you've shown that you can deliver results in solving this kind of problem, then you'll have their undivided attention. Thus, the importance of people lies in the context in which they operate. Set the context first. Let the people story – of you and your entrepreneurial team – close your sale.

■ Fourth, the unpleasant truth is that for almost every opportunity having meaningful potential, there's an abundance of uncertainty even *after* you've put time and effort into a rigorous seven domains analysis. And the greater the uncertainty, the less useful a business plan is likely to be, which is where the hypothesis-testing principles of the lean start-up movement come into play.

So what should you do before you get started on a seven domains journey, and before you launch even the leanest of start-ups, and way before you write your business plan or canvas, if you write one at all?

■ First, come up with an idea that you think might fly, one that solves genuine customer problems or needs, or offers consumers something delightful that they aren't getting now.

■ Second, assess and shape it, using the lessons of the seven domains framework with which you now are familiar. Doing so requires evidence, and lots of it, as we've seen.

■ Third, write what I call a customer-driven feasibility study – a memo to yourself, really – that lays out the conclusions you've reached from your evidence and analysis and, equally importantly, identifies the most crucial gaps in your knowledge – the risks, the reasons that arise in each domain about why your idea might not work.

In this chapter, and in the chapters that follow in the second half of the book, you'll find the nitty-gritty how-to that will begin to put in place the research foundation that will tell you just how attractive your opportunity is – or isn't. This chapter also addresses the sometimes blurry line that marks the divide where the feasibility study and its seven domains analysis end and the lean start-up journey begins. To do so, we outline what I call a customer-driven feasibility study – the output that your research journey will deliver. We examine the role of opportunity assessment in today's lean start-up world, and we compare and contrast a seven domains analysis with the business plan that you may, at some point, decide you'll need to write.

The chapter also examines some different approaches for tackling perhaps one of the toughest challenges for any entrepreneur – forecasting the demand you'll get for what you propose to sell. For the many entrepreneurs whose business plans are never funded, a whistle-in-the-wind forecast is what sends the ill-prepared pitch directly into the rubbish bin. Without a solid, evidence-based sales forecast, your investor pitch will be little more than a house of cards. The chapter then closes by addressing a couple of final, but crucial, questions – one for entrepreneurs, the other for investors.

■ Why bother? Is it really worth all this trouble? If you are an entrepreneur itching to get rolling on a new venture, why shouldn't you simply get started – whether that means launching your lean start-up or writing your business plan – without all the feasibility fuss?

■ What should investors be looking for in examining *a new venture* opportunity?

I'm not a market researcher – where should I start?

So, you've got an idea – a real opportunity, perhaps – and you've decided you'll assess it. But examining the seven domains seems daunting. Where should you start? First, give some thought to your mission, aspirations and propensity for risk. These factors will help you screen out lots of ideas that may not be right for you, given who you are and what you want to achieve. Once that's done, the four market and industry domains are the first to address – since knowing something about market and industry attractiveness tells you a lot about how differentiated your solution must be, and how important it is that your advantage be sustainable, in both competitive and economic terms.

The fastest way up the market and industry learning curve is to use what market researchers call secondary data – data that someone else has already collected and reported. All you have to do is find the data. There are three good places to look:

- Trade magazines and trade associations for your industry, usually the most direct route to relevant information;
- Business libraries with helpful librarians;
- The internet.

In most developed countries, secondary data are usually readily available and sufficient to assess quickly, at least in a preliminary sense, the macro-level domains – overall market and industry attractiveness. The questions your secondary data need to answer are those detailed in Chapters 3 and 4. Secondary data can also usually tell you something about competitors and substitutes, so you'll gain some idea about whether someone else is already doing what you propose to do.

If the secondary data don't kill your idea, the next step is to collect primary data that can answer the remaining questions to fill any gaps in your macro-level assessment and assess your market and industry at the micro level, as we examined in Chapters 2 and 5.

For readers who have not done research like this before, Chapters 11 and 15 outline a hands-on approach to the marketing research process from beginning to end. Doing much of the research yourself is a great way to build or extend your network. Doing so also adds considerably to your credibility and can help you answer the tough questions that prospective investors will throw at you later. The most important outcome, though, is that customer problems that your venture might solve – or the lack thereof – should become clear to you. The technique demonstrated in Chapter 11 may prove quite helpful in this regard. Without this kind of input, you can't shape your opportunity to maximise its potential,

> **❝doing much of the research yourself is a great way to build or extend your network❞**

you cannot prepare an evidence-based sales forecast, you cannot intelligently choose the best initial direction for a lean start-up, and you certainly cannot develop a compelling business plan. Your primary research should also enable you to identify your industry's CSFs, information you'll need to flesh out your entrepreneurial team.

So, don't hide behind your internet connection. Read the trade magazines. Get into the library. Get out in the field. Attend some trade shows. Crank up your confidence. There simply is no other way.

The customer-driven feasibility study

So, with opportunity in hand, your research gathered (the research never stops, actually, but at some point you'll have done enough of it to either abandon your opportunity or move forward with it) and an evidence-based sales forecast prepared, what else should an entrepreneur do before hitting 'Start'? If your conclusions about your opportunity's attractiveness are positive, then I suggest you document them in a customer-driven feasibility study that covers the seven domains (see Box 10.1). The discipline of making yourself actually write what you have learned is a good one, for it forces you to confront the clarity of the logic that underlies the attractiveness of the opportunity you have assessed. It's a concise memo to yourself or your team, no more than a page or so for each of the seven domains. Including an executive summary up front and a final summary and conclusion at the end, it need not exceed ten pages.

---

box 10.1

What's entailed in a customer-driven feasibility study?

1 Executive summary that briefly sets out what follows (tells the reader(s) – you and your team – what you are going to tell them).

2 Micro-level market assessment:

- target market and its pain identified; compelling benefits of your solution identified, with evidence that those in this segment are willing to pay a price that works;
- target market segment, size and growth rate;
- options to grow into other segments.
- unanswered questions (risks): why, from a customer perspective, might your idea not work?

3 Macro-level market assessment:

- overall market size and growth rate;
- macro-trends analysis to assess future market growth and attractiveness.

▓ unanswered questions (risks): why, from a macro-market perspective, might your idea not work?

4   Macro-level industry assessment:

▓ five forces analysis: whether or not the industry is attractive;

▓ likely changes therein going forward.

▓ unanswered questions (risks): why, from a five forces perspective, might your idea not work?

5   Micro-level industry assessment:

▓ Competitive sustainability

– any proprietary elements;

– any superior organisational processes, capabilities or resources identified that are not easily duplicated or imitated;

– competitors' offerings, their advantages, and yours

▓ economic sustainability of business model:

– revenue forecast;

– customer acquisition and retention costs, and time required to obtain a customer;

– gross margins;

– capital investment required;

– break-even analysis;

– operating cash cycle characteristics.

▓ unanswered questions (risks): why, competitively, might your idea not work?

▓ unanswered questions (risks): why might your business model not work?

6   Team assessment:

▓ team's mission, aspirations and propensity for risk;

▓ team's ability to execute on the CSFs in this industry;

▓ team's connectedness up, down and across the value chain.

▓ unanswered questions (risks): what are the gaps in your current team?

7   Summary and conclusions (tell the reader(s) the key highlights of what you've told them):

▓ why this opportunity is – or isn't – attractive and on what one (or, at most, two) domain(s) you rest your case.

Such a feasibility study is *customer-driven* because, unlike most organisation charts that put the entrepreneur or CEO at the top and the people serving the customer at the bottom (the me-first approach), the feasibility study begins with the target customer, without whom there will be no business. It begins in the lower left corner of the seven domains model, by identifying the target market and the customer pain you intend to resolve, and it examines the benefits you plan to deliver to your target market along with evidence that your market is willing to pay. It then proceeds clockwise through macro-level market and industry analyses; it assesses the sustainable advantage of the proposed venture, from both competitive and economic perspectives; and it closes with an examination of the entrepreneurial team and its dream: its mission, aspirations and propensity for risk; its ability to deliver results for the particular opportunity at hand; and its connections up, down and across the value chain.

Once the feasibility study is complete, you – provided you and your team are satisfied that the opportunity meets your mission and aspirations and is sufficiently feasible – will find yourself well along towards launching your start-up. You'll also find your understanding of the opportunity to have been sharpened by the analytical scrutiny to which it has been subjected.

❝once the feasibility study is complete, you will find yourself halfway towards crafting a business plan❞

On the other hand, if the feasibility study has identified obstacles or flaws that render your opportunity partially or fatally flawed, then you can ponder a pivot or, if necessary, mercifully put your perhaps half-baked idea to rest and move on to a better one.

The feasibility study, the lean start-up, and the business plan: how are they different?

In this entrepreneurial age, there's plenty of good advice available to entrepreneurs for how to write a business plan, including books, articles and software. (In my view, the best short article on this topic is Bill Sahlman's classic.[3]) And there's excellent advice about how to launch a lean start-up (thanks to books by Steve Blank and Eric Reis, and a growing set of online sources as well[4]), if yours is a venture that is conducive to that approach. Surprisingly, however, there has, until *The New Business Road Test* came along, been no widely accepted model for how entrepreneurs should assess opportunities *before* they launch lean start-ups or write business plans or prepare business model canvases. Such a model is the subject of this book, of course. But how do the seven domains model and the customer-driven feasibility study differ from what's in a good business plan, business model canvas or pitch deck? And where does a seven domains analysis fit in today's lean start-up world?

The role of opportunity assessment in today's lean start-up world

In some kinds of settings, the lean start-up process is an intelligent, efficient and disciplined way to get started on the pursuit of an attractive opportunity. It brings focus to that effort, and helps direct time and money to their most productive uses. All too often, however, we see aspiring entrepreneurs embarking on lean start-ups where, with a modicum of work to better understand the market and industry setting and what the entrepreneurial team brings – or does not bring – to the party, their effort would be better spent pursuing a more attractive opportunity that's actually worth the considerable effort.

To be sure, a seven domains analysis cannot resolve all the unanswered questions up front, and a lean start-up process is sometimes the best way to resolve some of them, particularly those about customer demand and the fit of the offering with what the customer needs and will pay for. But, because the lean start-up process, with its intensely customer-driven focus, largely ignores the industry and team issues that make up crucial portions of any seven domains analysis, it often leaves entrepreneurs vulnerable to industry- and team-based risks that could have been foreseen in advance.

Thus, the two tools – the seven domains analysis and the lean-start-up process – really complement one another, hand in hand. The lean start-up process is one of the best ways to definitively answer the unanswered questions that a marketing research-based analysis of the micro-market domain identifies (see again Box 10.1). The seven domains analysis examines the rest of the opportunity puzzle, and helps the entrepreneur decide whether or not to pursue the opportunity at all, whether in lean fashion or otherwise!

The seven domains analysis and the business plan

There is considerable overlap in the content of a customer-driven feasibility study and a business plan or canvas. In fact, all of the analyses we advocate are essential, though not sufficient, for crafting a thoughtful such plan.

So, what's new here? What's different?

■ *Customer focus:* The feasibility study is focused on the customer. As Peter Drucker wrote many years ago, the purpose of any business is to win a customer. The feasibility study homes in on that purpose, one quite different from that of most business plans – to win an investor. If there is no likelihood of there being customers, there will be no investors.

- *Fundamental economics:* The feasibility study addresses in a succinct manner the fundamental economics of the business, by identifying the key drivers of cash flow: revenue, customer acquisition and retention costs and timelines, gross margins, required capital investment, and the working capital characteristics of the operating cash cycle. If these drivers are satisfactory, then detailed strategies – for marketing, operations and financing – can probably be developed to make the venture economically viable, provided the market, industry and team elements are sufficiently attractive. If they are not, there's little point in wasting time developing such strategies and the spreadsheets that reflect them.

- *Mindset:* The customer-driven feasibility study asks the critical questions necessary to satisfy the entrepreneurial team's curiosity about the attractiveness of the opportunity itself, and makes it possible to answer these questions before developing the detailed strategy necessary for the completion of a business plan or a business model canvas. Thus, its mindset is to *ask* (and answer) questions, not to extoll the venture's merit. In contrast, a good business plan or canvas all too often starts with what is presumed to be an attractive opportunity, and then goes on to develop marketing, operating and financing strategies in an effort to *sell* the opportunity, in a sharply focused way, to investors and other stakeholders.

An evidence-based sales forecast: OK, but how?

A SWAG – a silly wild ass guess – or an evidence-based forecast? Which will you use to imagine the upside of your entrepreneurial dream? Without evidence to support that top-line number, any plan you eventually prepare will be worth little more than the paper it is written on. But how can you prepare an evidence- based forecast for something that doesn't even exist? Good question, and an important one. It's also a good test to see whether you have what it takes to reduce at least some of the overwhelming uncertainty inherent in your new venture into something more tangible that you and others can make sense of.

There are two kinds of forecast you'll probably want to do. The first is a forecast of market potential. Just how large is the market you'll serve, measured in different ways – number of units sold, revenue, numbers of customers? Secondary data and a little mathematics should get you here without great difficulty.

The second forecast – and the more difficult one – predicts how much you'll sell at the outset and going forward from there. Most often – but not always – forecasting a new venture's sales involves collecting primary data. How? Chapter 16 reviews the various approaches to creating evidence-based sales forecasts. As you'll see, doing so is by no means a perfect exercise, but it's far more credible than a SWAG, and it should bolster your confidence in the merit – or lack thereof – of the opportunity you will pursue.

But, hold on. You'll recall that what people *say* they will buy is not necessarily what they will *actually* buy, once they're asked to pull out their wallet or sign a cheque. This is why lean start-ups make so much sense, as they don't assume that the customer – even a well-researched one – will buy. Founders like you want evidence from the marketplace – real traction – that demand is genuine. We'll return to this challenge, from an investor perspective, later in this chapter.

Why bother with a seven domains road test?

'Is it worth the effort?' you might ask. Why shouldn't you, as a would-be entrepreneur, simply skip the feasibility study and proceed directly to preparing a business plan or, business model canvas or launching a lean start-up?

■ First, researching and preparing a customer-driven feasibility study gives you a chance to opt out early in the process, before investing the time and energy in preparing a more comprehensive plan. Thus, it can save weeks or months of time that might be wasted on a fundamentally flawed opportunity.

■ Second, for opportunities that do look promising, the feasibility study brings focus to a lean start-up. Your micro-market analysis identifies the most important unanswered customer questions – the leaps of faith, in lean language[5] – and tells you where to direct your efforts to develop and test hypotheses so that you can affirm or refute them – with real data from real customers about real goods or services.

■ Third, when you are (eventually) ready to develop a strategy to pursue an attractive opportunity that you've discovered, your seven domains analysis will jump-start the planning and modelling process, by providing a clear, customer-focused vision about why your proposed venture makes sense – from market, industry and team perspectives, viewed independently and collectively. It will identify the customer pain and how you'll resolve it, and the one or two domains that make the opportunity stand out. These factors become the key points that will underpin your strategy.

■ Fourth, by ensuring that all aspects of the opportunity are examined, your analysis reduces your risk of entering a fatally flawed venture.

Asking the feasibility questions with an open mind – deliberately, objectively and comprehensively – is an important first step that entrepreneurs ignore all too often. If you'd like to do the feasibility work in the company of others, Chapter 18 suggests a few ways you can find some support and perhaps some like-minded individuals as well.

No car-buyer would buy a new car without a road test, and that's a far less risky decision than the one you are about to make. A customer-driven feasibility study is the entrepreneur's new business road test. Entrepreneurs who proceed without doing one do so at their own risk.

What investors should look for in your seven domains analysis

To wrap things up, let's summarise some of the key things sensible, ambitious investors – the ones looking to make boatloads of money from *their* capital and someone's entrepreneurial efforts – should look for. Most of what follows you have read in earlier chapters, but it warrants repeating for those who will seek or provide capital.

■ Investors in early-stage companies are typically not very interested in your idea or technology *per se,* at least at the outset of their thinking about your new venture. Instead, they want to know that your business will offer differentiated solutions to real customer problems or pain, solutions that offer real competitive advantage. Better, faster or cheaper, please!

■ Investors love opportunities where market risk – whether or not customers will buy – has already been dealt with. If you have traction with customers, perhaps gained through the early stages of a lean start-up, then your feasibility study will be more solidly grounded. Thus, your feasibility study will evolve over time, as your venture moves forward and your real learning commences. There's no single point where the feasibility study is done with and the lean start-up takes over. Iteration is what's more likely to happen.

■ Investors generally look to invest in large and growing markets. Why? They want to know your venture can reach a sizeable scale, and they want to know your market is large enough to accommodate more than one successful new entrant.

■ Investors seek industries that are not competitively brutal; they like entry barriers to be high enough to make it difficult for others to enter.

■ Investors look for evidence that your initial advantage can be sustained. Why won't someone else steal your thunder?

■ Investors often look for business models that are capital-efficient, which means you can get farther on their money and also reduces the risk that you'll run out of cash.

■ Finally, sensible investors look for committed lead entrepreneurs and entrepreneurial teams who can deliver on the promises they make and whose mission, aspirations and propensity for risk are aligned with those of the investors. Life leading an entrepreneurial, venture-capital-backed company is simple really. Perform or move on. Having executed previously on the industry's CSFs, and being well connected enough to see the need to move to plan B – or, as we saw for Palm Computing in Chapter 7, plan Z – when conditions so dictate, are important indicators of this capability.

In the final analysis, an attractive opportunity begins and ends with the people – people who will understand and attract customers and deliver cash flow. They are the ones whose vision and hard work will turn any entrepreneurial dream into reality. It's no accident, then, that the team dimensions are placed squarely in the middle of the seven domains figure.

As we've seen in the case histories in this book, the entrepreneurs who have made our successful stories happen have been insightful, motivated and very capable people. And most of the time, like the American Poet Robert Frost, they took roads that were "less traveled by". [6] Once your venture gets started, people will make all the difference. But as Benjamin Franklin wisely observed, 'By failing to prepare, you are preparing to fail.'[7]

So, as you get ready to launch or bet on a start-up, do your seven domains preparation. You'll launch or invest smarter and wiser, to a better-targeted market, with a *more* viable product, rather than a perhaps *minimum* viable product. You'll probably save time and money, too. Will the venture still pivot? Of course! But your pivots are likely to be fewer and farther apart. I wish you good luck on your entrepreneurial or investment journey. Enjoy the ride!

If you've been using your *New Business Road Test* app as you've read this book, you should now have the data captured there to write a customer-driven feasibility study. If that's the case, start writing, and see what it tells you! If you've not been gathering your data just yet, there's no time like now to get started doing so. Bon voyage!

Part 2

A toolkit for your road test

11

How to learn what you don't know you don't know[1]

If you are an aspiring entrepreneur, despite your confidence in your nascent opportunity, there are – if you'll admit it – a few things you *know* you don't know about your idea and the customers who, if you are successful, will buy it.

What you *know* you don't know

What do you *know* you don't know about your idea and about customers' likely response? You probably know you don't *really* know at least a few important things:

- Whether customers, or enough customers, will buy what you propose to offer;

- Whether they will pay the price you think they will pay;

- Whether you've designed your goods or services in the best way to maximise their appeal, whether you have got the offering just right;

- Which target market is the most promising one – you probably lack the resources to go after everyone, so where should you start?

There's also lots of other information you know you don't know, above and beyond the customer issues, issues that are dealt with in other parts of this book. The focus in this chapter, though, is on customers and their needs. More specifically, this chapter will show you how to interview prospective users of whatever it is you plan to offer, whether a good or a service, to help you answer some of the key questions that you know you don't know, like those bulleted above. More importantly, though, you'll learn how to get customers to tell you *what you don't know to ask them*!

What you *don't know* you don't know

Why is learning what you don't know you don't know – or what your customers don't know *they* don't know – important? If customers already know they need what you plan to offer, they've probably already told someone about it, including your competitors. Many of the most exciting breakthroughs that entrepreneurs bring to market are innovations that customers haven't known they needed. 'Why didn't I think of that?' we hear, after such breakthroughs come to market.

Did anyone tell Steve Jobs that they needed a personal computer – or more recently, an iPod, iPhone or iPad? Did anyone tell Dan Bricklin and Bob Frankston, the developers of VisiCalc, the first spreadsheet application for PCs, that such an application for the Apple II was needed?[2] Ditto for the first word processor, for email, for the internet and so on. Did anyone tell British Airways, the original operator of the London Eye, the huge observation wheel – sort of a high-tech Ferris wheel – that's a magnet for tourists and London locals alike, that such an attraction would pack them in on the South Bank of the River Thames?

What most of these innovations have in common is that they resolved some sort of customer pain. That is, they made it much easier – or better or faster or more efficient – for customers either to do something they already did, perhaps quite differently (PCs, spreadsheets, word processors, email) or to do something they had not done before (bring information quickly and conveniently to one's desktop; or see London, a low-rise city for the most part, from a panoramic bird's eye vantage point).

Where was the customer pain that these innovations resolved? PCs, once relevant application software came along – word processors, spreadsheets and so on – made certain kinds of office work dramatically easier and faster and less frustrating to do and to revise. As Dan Bricklin later noted, 'VisiCalc took 20 hours of work per week for some people and turned it out in 15 minutes and let them become much more creative.' Email resolved, among other things, the customer pain of always getting people's voicemail and wasting time trying fruitlessly to connect with them. These sorts of innovations are painkillers in that their main reason for being is to resolve customer pain. Of course, email has now engendered its own customer pain, as it consumes increasing numbers of hours in people's workdays!

The internet and the London Eye, on the other hand, are enablers – innovations that enable people to do things they had not really been able to do previously.

One way to think about entrepreneurs' roles is as the developers of new pain-killers and enablers. In doing so, however, it helps if the entrepreneur really understands (for painkillers) the customer's pain. For enablers, the trick is to discern whether what's enabled is something that customers would actually embrace. One way to approach these issues, of course, is simply to launch your product or start-up and see whether people buy. Ultimately, this is the test you'll have to meet anyway, right? So why not just get started? The answer: cost. Most product launches and start-ups – at least those more ambitious than a simple app you can code in a few weeks – are costly, in time and effort, and often in financial terms, too. So for most start-ups, getting at least some understanding of what the customer wants and will pay for, before you build your first product and before you launch, makes intuitive sense.

> **❝one way is simply to launch your product❞**

Fortunately, there's a cost-effective technique that can be borrowed from the social sciences[3] that turns out to be a great way to get a good start gathering the insights you'll need. It's especially useful for entrepreneurs trying to find ways to solve customers' needs, including the kinds of needs that customers don't yet know they have, or cannot easily articulate. It's called the long interview, and this chapter will tell you how to do it.[4]

The long interview

You've probably already talked with lots of people about your idea for a new venture. If so, you're off to a great start. If you are like most entrepreneurs, though, chances are you've made one or more of the following mistakes that will have limited what you've learned from these conversations.

- You've let your enthusiasm show through. Doing so is great for selling, but it can limit the amount of honest feedback you'll get when your purpose is to learn rather than to sell. Most people don't like to disagree in the face of enthusiasm like yours.

- Rather than asking first about the customer's needs, any shortcomings or unmet or poorly met needs in the way they do things now, you've jumped right into 'me' or 'my idea'. Doing so too quickly can inhibit your learning about alternative solutions to the customer's problem, some of which might be slight tweaks of your idea or even something completely different, and perhaps even better than your initial idea.

- You've asked leading questions: 'Do you think this is faster?' The implication that it's faster will prompt some people simply to agree, whether they've really thought about it or not.

- You've asked questions that can be answered with a 'yes' or a 'no'. Such questions tend to close off the conversation, rather than keeping it open to see where it might lead.

The long interview technique we propose here addresses each of these problems. It serves two key purposes:

- It lets you seek answers about the things you *know* you don't know;

- But first, and more importantly, it encourages the customer to tell you things you do not know to ask and that they would not otherwise think to tell you, helping you learn what you *don't know* you don't know.

Let's use an example to bring the technique to life. Suppose you were an aspiring entrepreneur more than a decade ago. You loved yogurt and found it a healthy and delicious snack, good throughout the day whenever you needed a pick-me-up. You had been mixing yogurt with fruit juices and other nutritious ingredients and drinking it as a beverage, rather than eating it with a spoon. There might be a business here, you thought.

Planning the long interview

To conduct a fruitful long interview to better understand your prospective customers and their pain, you need first to construct an interview guide, which is easily done on a single sheet of paper. Doing so involves two steps:

- Reviewing what you think you *know* about your idea and its use;

- Reviewing what you know you *don't know.*

What do you think you *know* about your drinking yogurt? Your drinking yogurt is:

- delicious;

- nutritious;

- thick like a smoothie;

- convenient and easy to consume;

- easily combined with fruit or other flavours;

- good between meals;

- good for breakfast;
- good for dessert;
- loved by women;
- in need of refrigeration;
- and more.

What might you think you *don't know* about drinking yogurt?

- to whom it should be targeted;
- how thick or thin it should be;
- what flavours people will want;
- how it should be packaged;
- how you should price it;
- where it should be sold;
- how it should be pitched: thirst-quenching, as an energy source, as a party drink, like beer, as a between-meal snack;
- and more.

Preparing these lists serves two purposes. The lists will provide some structure for your interview, hence your learning. Further, by acknowledging what you think you know and don't know, they will help you remain distant enough from your own assumptions so you can learn. The lists will also help you identify aspects or relationships between yogurt and life that have perhaps not previously been addressed by the current marketers of yogurt in your market: drinking yogurt with herbal additives, for example.

❝ lists will provide some structure for your interview ❞

With these lists now in hand, you're ready to develop your interview guide. In fact, you are almost done, though you've barely started. Your interview guide will consist of five elements.

1 A brief introduction and some opening biographical questions to put the customer at ease.

2 A few (probably just two) 'grand tour' questions: broad, open-ended questions to encourage the respondent to tell you, from their own perspective, two things:

- Everything that's relevant *to them* about the occasions in which they might consume drinking yogurt – note, though, that this question is not about your product at all, it's about them, their attitudes, motivations and behaviour;

■ Everything that comes to their mind – not yours – about your drinking yogurt concept.

3   The third element consists of three 'floating' prompts for each of the interview drivers. There are three kinds of these floating prompts, which you can use at any point in the interview to get the respondent to say more about something they've just mentioned:

■ Raising your eyebrows following something the respondent has just said (maybe they've suggested that it would be good to be able to drink herbal supplements), a topic which you'd like them to go deeper into and tell you more about;

■ Repeating a word the respondent has just said – 'Herbal supplements?' – with a questioning tone.

■ Saying, 'What do you mean, herbal supplements?'

The purpose of these floating prompts is to get the respondent to tell you more about what they've just mentioned. It might be a topic that's already on your lists of what you think you know or don't know, but go ahead and listen to what they have to say, so they can either confirm or refute your current knowledge. Or it might be something not on your lists (e.g. herbal supplements). These are the nuggets of gold: things *you don't know you don't know.* You are hoping to glean from your interviews the one or two of these nuggets that might turn into revolutionary ideas that will reinvent your thinking, and perhaps the yogurt category (or the herbal category!)

4   The fourth element of your interview guide comprises your lists of what you think you know and don't know, determined earlier, preceded by the phrase 'What about . . . ' or occasionally 'What if . . . '. These are your 'planned' prompts. Here, the purpose is to get the respondent to talk about each of the topics about which you already think you know or don't know the answers. But here, at least, you know the questions to ask! You will use these planned prompts to cover any of these issues that the respondent does not touch upon as a result of your one or two grand tour questions, though many if not most of them will undoubtedly be addressed there.

5   Finally, to complete your interview guide, there are two other kinds of useful prompt, each beginning with 'What about . . . ' or 'What if . . . '.

■ *Contrast prompts.* Use these to ensure that all the alternatives are fully examined. The key word in contrast prompts is usually 'not'. For example, 'What if it's *not* for between meals?'

■ *Exceptional incident prompts.* Use these to explore non-obvious uses or situations where your idea may have utility. For example, 'What about not drinking it at all?'

Here the purpose is to get your respondent to stretch their thinking in ways neither you – nor they! – had previously thought of. You may find some more nuggets of gold this way, too, more things you don't know you don't know.

Let's now take a look at what a complete interview guide for the turn-of-the millennium drinking yogurt entrepreneur might have looked like (see Box 11.1).

---

box 11.1

Interview guide for drinking yogurt

Thanks for agreeing to speak with me today. As I mentioned on the phone, I'm studying what people do for drinks and snacks between meals these days, and I'd welcome your views. First, can we touch on a few biographical questions for my records?

What's the correct spelling of your name? _____

In what city or town do you live? _____

Do you sometimes eat between meals? _____

Enter gender and approximate age (observe, don't ask): Approximate age _____ Sex _____

Let's begin this way. Would you please tell me what your typical day is like between mealtimes?

Floating prompts

■ Eyebrow flash

■ _____?

■ What do you mean, _____?

Planned prompts

■ What about in meetings?

■ What about in your office?

■ What about at home?

- What about nutrition?
- What about health?
- What about convenience?
- What about thirst?
- What about hunger?
- What about energy?

Other prompts

- What about drinks and snacks at other times of day?
- What about meals, rather than between meals?
- What about weekends?

OK, thanks. Now I have a second broad question to ask you. It involves a concept for a new kind of yogurt you can drink. Here's a description of the concept. Would you take a look? (Let them read the concept statement. When they are finished, ask:) What's your reaction?

Floating prompts

- Eyebrow flash
- _____?
- What do you mean, _____?

Planned prompts

- What about taste?
- What about nutrition?
- What about texture?
- What about convenience?
- What about flavours?
- What about smoothies?
- What about between meals?
- What about breakfast?
- What about dessert?
- What about refrigeration?
- What about packaging?
- What about pricing?
- Where should it be sold?
- What about thirst?
- What about hunger?
- What about energy?

- What about parties?
- To whom should it be targeted?

Other prompts

- What about other uses?
- What about other occasions?

As noted above, the guide begins with a few biographical questions, simply to put the user at ease. You're really not trying to learn much here, though you should record the answers, in case a pattern develops among different kinds of respondents – older versus younger persons, or men versus women, for example.

Next comes the first grand tour question. I've phrased it very carefully to avoid the four mistakes interviewers often make. Note that:

- There's no enthusiasm for the drinking yogurt idea here – just an enquiry about the respondent's between-meal behaviour;
- In fact, there's no mention of the idea at all – that will come later, as the second grand tour question;
- It's not a leading question, and lets the respondent begin wherever they wish and wander as far afield as they like;
- The question cannot be answered with 'yes' or 'no'.

Then come the three kinds of floating prompts. These are here to remind you to use one of them when you hear something in the respondent's remarks that you'd like to explore further, perhaps something that's already on your list of planned prompts.

After that come some of your planned prompts, taken from your first two lists.

❝you won't end up using all of your planned prompts❞

You won't end up using all of your planned prompts, as the respondent will mention some – perhaps most – of them spontaneously. You may find it useful to tick them off as the respondent covers them, so you know which ones are left that you must ask.

Then come the contrast and exceptional incident prompts, to make sure you cover any non-obvious territory that the respondent has not yet mentioned.

Finally the process repeats itself, with the focus of attention now turned to your drinking yogurt idea itself. Note how open-ended the second grand tour question is: 'What's your reaction?' There's no overt enthusiasm or bias, no implied direction at all. In order to hear the respondent's reaction, however, you need to state your concept quite clearly and succinctly, yet comprehensively. One good way to do so is to write a succinct concept statement, perhaps including some nice graphics, if they help connote what you intend to offer. See Box 11.2 for what a concept statement might look like for drinking yogurt.

---

box 11.2

Concept statement for drinking yogurt

Refresh is a new concept in yogurt. Unlike yogurt you eat with a spoon, you can drink Refresh straight out of the bottle. It comes in a variety of flavours and sizes ranging from individual portions to containers to serve the whole family.

Note to the reader:

Note how succinct and factual the concept statement is. Since a key purpose of your interviews is to refine your concept, you do not want to hype it or describe it in excessive detail. You want your interviews to *give* you the detail. The version below is how *not* to do it.

Refresh is a delicious new concept in yogurt. Unlike yogurt you eat with a spoon, you can drink Refresh straight out of the bottle. It comes in a variety of scrumptious fruit flavours, plus coffee and chocolate flavours, and in sizes ranging from individual portions to containers to serve the whole family. It's tasty, nutritious and convenient for between-meal snacks or for when you have to eat on the run.

Don't forget that what you are doing is researching, not selling. The difference is crucial!

Conducting the long interview

With an interview guide now in hand, you are ready to pick up the phone and line up some appointments. But there are a few more questions you'll have to address in order to do so and to conduct the interviews.

- Who should I interview?
- Face to face or on the telephone?
- How many interviews should I conduct?

- How should I present myself in the interviews?
- Should I record the interview, or simply write very fast?
- Can I update my interview guide after I've done the first interviews and learned a few things?

Choosing respondents

'Should I interview my friends, or strangers?', you may ask. One problem with friends is that they are likely to tell you what they think you want to hear. Perfect strangers are better, and you want a very diverse pool, sampling as widely as possible, so you are more likely to hear diverging views. Should you interview experts or novices? In general, experts are *too* knowledgeable and too wedded to the way things are now. It's good to include a few experts in your sample, but they should not dominate it, unless your area of enquiry is so specialised that experts are the only realistic people to talk to.

Face to face or by telephone?

If you can get people to meet with you, that's far better. They'll talk longer than they will on the phone and you'll get their full attention. In my experience, an hour to an hour and a half is a common length, even from a short interview guide like the example shown here, which means you'll learn more than you would in a shorter phone call. But if the phone is the best you can get, take it. The technique – OK, not the raised eyebrows – will still work just fine.

How many interviews should I conduct?

Experienced researchers who use this technique find that the answers begin to get repetitive once the number of interviews gets into the teens. By about interview number 20, in my experience, you'll have heard virtually everything there is to hear. It's time to stop, draw your conclusions and get on with the rest of your seven domains analysis.

What about my interview persona?

Here's the hard part. You don't want to appear too clever, like you know all the answers – in fact, quite the opposite. Your interview persona should be benign and agreeable, not aggressive; accepting of whatever they say, but curious enough to ask your endless floating and planned prompts; a bit dim or naïve, to encourage them to enlighten you with all they know. With this sort of persona, you will present no danger that they will lose face in any way.

What about recording the interviews?

My experience is that people are happy to have you record what they say, as long as you tell them their remarks will remain confidential. Your smartphone won't be intimidating and will do nicely for this purpose.

Another way to go is to do your interviewing with a partner, where one person does the asking and careful listening and the other one writes.

What about updating my interview guide?

It's almost certain that, in your very first interview or two or three, your respondents will mention some things that you simply had not thought of. This is good news! You'll want to add some or all of these things to your list of planned prompts for the rest of your interviews, to allow you to get additional perspectives on them.

Consolidating your learning

Having completed your interviews, there are a few possible outcomes for each of your two grand tour questions. From your first grand tour and its subsequent prompts, you'll have learned much about how your idea might or might not fit into your intended users' current attitudinal, motivational and behavioural patterns. You might find your idea fits quite nicely. You might find some opportunities to adjust your concept, though you are generally on track. You might find there's a mismatch. You might also find there's something else the customers need more than what you were thinking about, which may prompt you to redirect your entrepreneurial efforts entirely.

From your second grand tour and its subsequent prompts, there are several likely outcomes. One is that the respondents will have widely turned 'thumbs down' on your idea. While this result does not necessarily mean you should abandon your idea entirely, it certainly does raise your risk! If this is what you hear, however, you may decide to pursue something else that looks more promising.

Another possible outcome is that you get concrete suggestions about how to improve your offering to give it more utility or appeal. You might, if you are lucky or especially insightful, get rave reviews that indicate you have a potential winner on your hands. While this is good news, it does not mean you are ready to go to market yet, for there are other questions raised in the seven domains for which you'll also want answers before you invest months or years of your life and lots of your and other people's money.

❝you might, if you are lucky or especially insightful, get rave reviews❞

If in your interviews you find enough promising regard for your concept, one good way to wrap up your learning is to edit your concept description to embrace the useful input you have obtained. Revise your offering to respond to what you've learned. It's never too soon to pivot, if the evidence tells you to do so. Rarely does an entrepreneur fail to get useful feedback from an exercise like this, feedback that can help further develop the offering.

Other uses for this long interview technique

Chapter 5 examined the likelihood that your proposed venture can develop sources of sustainable competitive advantage. As you saw, one element in doing so is ascertaining whether the business model you propose is viable. Long interviews can be useful for this purpose, too.

Chapter 7 addressed whether you and your entrepreneurial team can execute on the handful of critical success factors that prevail in your industry. Long interviews can be useful for identifying what these factors are for the industry in which you plan to compete.

THE NEW BUSINESS ROAD TEST

As you conduct your long interviews, you may find your *New Business Road Test* app a good place to keep track of what you're learning. As you do so, you should connect your lessons learned to your emerging conclusions about the attractiveness of your opportunity in micro-market terms (see Chapter 2), the economic sustainability of your business model (see Chapter 5), or your list of critical success factors on which you and your team will have to deliver (see Chapter 7). If you identify any key risks in your long interviews, the app has a place to keep track of them, too.

12

Who needs investors?

These days, people starting new ventures, whether inside large companies or in their garages, whether lean start-ups or otherwise, often assume that the first thing they must do is raise some seed capital to fund their start-up. A great idea plus some angel or venture capital and, voilà, we (and our investors) will soon be rich! Or so they believe. But that's not how things used to be, before venture capital investors captured the entrepreneurial financing limelight two generations ago. So, just maybe, is today's 'idea plus venture capital equals instant riches' notion misguided, or even fundamentally wrong? Is there a better source of seed capital for your new venture? And if so, if you're an early-stage investor, what are the implications for how you should invest? Let's consider some examples, then and now, and their implications for demonstrating the attractiveness and potential financing of a prospective new venture.

Coke re-enters India[1]

It was 1995, and the Coca-Cola Company had just re-entered India, after an aborted earlier effort, this time by acquiring the maker of Thums Up, India's leading cola. Along with the deal came a thick book describing each of the Thums Up bottlers' territories in plenty of legal jargon, but without a single map. Coke needed a way to find and understand its newly acquired territories.

Alas, no one had maps that could show Coke where its bottlers were located. Until the mid-1960s, maps had been banned for civilian use in India, and even 30 years later, a mapping culture and map-reading ethos simply did not exist, perhaps in part because there were very few accurate Indian maps.

Into the breach stepped Rakesh and Rashmi Verma, who had been licensing American digital mapping software to India's nascent map-making industry. The Vermas began to build a digital mapping business by scanning what rudimentary paper maps they could find and then overlaying demographic and other data to enable Coke – and soon other commercial customers – to do in India what they took for granted in other parts of the world. Cellular One, entering India as the country's telecommunications industry was liberalised, was their next client. 'Where should we put our cell phone towers?' Cellular One asked, from both a technical perspective (Where is the high ground? How do we achieve uncluttered line-of-sight coverage in a city of high rises?) and from a marketing perspective (Where are sufficiently dense concentrations of customers we can economically serve?).

A customer-funded business model

The Vermas didn't go out and raise venture capital for their venture. Instead, they identified customer after customer – even the Indian Defence Agency – that could benefit from digital maps, charging the customers fees to cover most of the development costs of creating additional maps or the costs of applying additional demographic or other information to maps they had already created. Over the next ten years, their mapping business grew slowly but steadily, funded by one customer assignment after another, and they became the dominant digital mapmaker in India.

Of course, venture capital of any kind hardly existed in India in 1995, so the Vermas probably had no other choice than to proceed as they did, using their customers' cash to finance the business as it got started and grew. Had they thought about it, though, they would have concluded that their approach wasn't a bad way to go, for several reasons.

First, there are significant drawbacks to raising capital too early (See Table 12.1):

- Raising capital demands a lot of time and energy, distracting entrepreneurs from building the actual business.
- Raising capital too early means *pitching* the merit of the business idea to potential investors, rather than *proving* its merit among customers in the marketplace.
- Raising capital early leaves the founder with a lower ownership stake, since most risks and unknowns are still unresolved.
- Raising capital early brings lots of baggage: tough terms and conditions that investors rightly require to offset the risks they take by backing the venture.
- Raising capital is almost always very hard, and may not always be possible, particularly in difficult economic conditions!

Table 12.1	Some drawbacks of attempting to raise capital too early
A distraction	Raising capital often requires full-time concentration, but so does starting an entrepreneurial business. One or the other will suffer when investment capital is sought. Why not raise money later when the business is less fragile?
Pitching vs. proving merit	Nascent entrepreneurial ideas, however promising, always raise numerous questions. *Proving* the merit of your idea, based on accumulated evidence and customer traction, is much more convincing than using your own wisdom and charm to *pitch* its merit.
Risk	The farther you progress in developing your business, the lower the risk, as early uncertainties become more certain. Less risk translates into a higher valuation and a higher stake for the founding team.
Baggage	The terms and conditions attached to institutional capital are onerous, as investors seek to protect themselves from downside risk. The farther along the path, the less onerous the baggage.
Difficulty	Raising capital, even in the best of times for the best of ventures, is a difficult task! Why make it even harder by trying to do it too early?

The Vermas got their funding in a different and arguably more sensible manner: from customers who had genuine needs for the digital maps which the Vermas offered. And, importantly, these customers were willing (and able) to pay for services to satisfy those needs. But is the Vermas' story an isolated incident, or could it become the new norm for start-ups?

Customer-funded business models: a typology

In an effort to better understand customer-funded business models, my research has uncovered five different types of models – each surprisingly familiar when you think about them carefully – through which founders have got their customers to fund their start-ups (See Table 12.2). You'll note that you don't see crowdsourcing mentioned there. Sure, you can post your idea

Table 12.2	Customer-funded business models – a typology	
Type	*Category-defining examples*	*Today's examples*
Matchmaker models	Real estate brokers, eBay, Expedia.com	Airbnb, Dog Vacay, Wonga
Pay-in-advance models	Consultants, architects	Dell, Via, easyFairs, Studenterbolaget
Subscription models	*Wall Street Journal,* Showtime	TutorVista, H. Bloom, Yammer
Scarcity-based models	Zara	Vente Privée, Gilt Groupe, Privalia
Service-to-product models	Microsoft	MapmyIndia, GoViral

on Kickstarter if you wish. But that's not very targeted and won't give you the benefits that arise from directing your focus to your prospective customers, as did each of the entrepreneurs whose stories make up this chapter. Further, I suspect it won't be long before we see a crowdfunding backlash, as those who've sought and won funding for their projects find themselves unable to deliver what they promised.

What is most striking about the five models in Table 12.2 is that each of them gives the company what accountants call negative working capital: that is, the company has the customer's cash in hand before having to produce or pay for the good (or service) it has sold. In exploring these models, we found that most of them work for selling both goods and services. Each of the following sections illustrates one of these types through a case study of a young company that got its start this way.

Matchmaker models

Some companies are in the business of matching up buyers and sellers – your local real estate broker, eBay or Expedia.com. Because they simply take the order, but never own the goods (somebody's home or junk from your attic) or services (air tickets or hotel rooms) that are sold, there's no need to tie up cash in inventory. The fees or commissions they earn from customers – whether from buyers or sellers or both – provide most or all of the cash to launch the business and grow it sufficiently to prove the concept. Consider the couch-surfing and home-stay phenomenon, Airbnb.

❝there's no need to tie up cash in inventory❞

Airbnb got its start in 2007, when founders Joe Gebbia and Brian Chesky noticed that San Francisco hotels were sold out with a big design conference coming to town. 'Why not let visitors to the conference have a more personal experience than they would get in a hotel,' thought the duo. So they offered space on a couple of airbeds on their floor, along with breakfast and local hospitality, to three intrepid conference goers unable to book hotel rooms. Two air mattresses and a thousand dollars later, they were in business.[2] The concept soon expanded – 'Why only conferences?' – and eventually took off, after the business got noticed during the Democratic National Convention in Denver in 2008.[3]

The most noteworthy aspect of Airbnb during this event in Denver might have been their 'hustle'. The business was in need of additional funding, so they came up with a creative – and customer-funded – scheme. Co-founder Joe Gebbia recalls: 'We made 500 of each [Obama O's and Cap'n McCains]. They were a numbered edition on the top of each box, and sold for $40 each. The Obama O's sold out, netting the funds we needed to keep Airbnb alive. The Cap'n McCains . . . they didn't sell quite as well, and we ended up eating them to save money on food.'[4]

Though this tactic had nothing to do with their core business – other than the second 'b' in its name suggesting they might deal in breakfast – it served its purpose of providing customer-funded cash to continue operations! And, their first investor, Y Combinator's Paul Graham, says that it was this story that convinced him that the Airbnb team had the hustle to do whatever it would take to make a successful business.[5] With the concept – and the team's gumption – proven, a small round of angel capital came in, followed by $7.2 million from two venture capital investors in 2010. But this investment never would have happened without the earlier funding from fees charged to happy Airbnb customers, along with judicious use of the founders' credit cards, and of course their creativity and willingness to do whatever it took, including selling cereal to cover expenses.

Matchmaker models, when effectively conceived, rarely need much cash to get started, so getting underway is often easy, especially if you bring in someone who can write code and develop a website, as the Airbnb founders soon did, adding techie Nathan Blecharczyk to the team.[6] Fast forwarding to 2017, Airbnb had raised some $3.4 billion in funding from several blue-chip VCs and others, and it lists more than 2 million properties in 65,000 cities in nearly 200 countries.[7]

The sharing economy, as many new companies like Airbnb have come to represent, is a fast-growing movement that enables sharing of under-utilised resources – powered by growing interest in conservation, increasing use of social media, and the need to economise. This trend is leading to matchmaker models serving all kinds of unlikely markets – from consumer finance (London's Wonga) to pet sitting (US-based DogVacay).

Pay-in-advance models

In some industries, customers traditionally pay the supplier in advance for at least part of the price of goods or services *before* receiving anything. Consultants, architects and other services firms are good examples. But entrepreneurs in other industries have also found ways to collect payment in advance. Consider Via, the fast-growing Indian B2B travel network that serves India's brick-and-mortar travel agents with real-time ticketing and other services.

In 2006, the travel industry in India was abuzz with the potential for online and mobile solutions that could revolutionise the industry there, as had already happened in much of the rest of the world. Starting in a small garage on 9th A Main Road in Bangalore in early 2006, Vinay Gupta saw a fragmented and inefficient travel industry that was ripe for change. But the change he had in mind was not what the rapidly growing number of online travel agents was pursuing.

On July 28, 2006, having secured IATA membership, Gupta launched Flight raja.com as a way to book air tickets via mobile phones, of which there were 170 million in India at the time.[8] Simultaneously, and out of the glare of industry publicity, Gupta was signing up local travel agents who previously had been unable to offer real-time ticketing to their customers because they had no real-time connections to airlines or aggregators to show which flights had available seats and which did not. In exchange for a rolling cash deposit against which tickets would be issued in real time, Gupta gave the agents a computer and connection that provided them with IATA-certified real-time ticketing capability – and better commissions, too. By September, his venture – funded by his customers' deposits – had signed up 110 travel agents in Bangalore and another 70 in Chennai, and was booking 200 tickets per day. Its progress was sufficient to convince angel investor and former India CEO for global travel giant Thomas Cook, Ashwini Kakkar, to take a small stake.[9] More important than his modest cash investment, however, were Kakkar's industry knowledge and connections.

By December, Flightraja had achieved break-even, and by June 2007, it had enrolled more than 3,000 agents in 290 Indian cities and was issuing 5,000 tickets per day.[10] Word had gotten around the Indian travel agent community that signing up with Flightraja was a good way to go. The company's rapid progress convinced venture capital investor NEA Indo US Ventures to come on board, with a $5 million investment to enable the company, renamed Via, to expand into hotel, rail and bus bookings.[11]

Via quickly established itself as the 'Intel Inside' of the Indian travel industry and was off to the races, while the burgeoning number of online players slugged it out for an online market that was proving slow to develop. Kakkar saw the problem. 'The issue here is that the total number of computer owners in India is 44 million; credit card owners 23 million; and broadband users 3 million. Though all these are necessary conditions for someone to book online, they do not have a mass appeal.' Travel was a cash and neighbourhood business in India, and Via's approach was right for the times.[12]

By 2017, thanks to its cash-efficient and customer-funded business model, along with some additional VC investment to fund expansion into new markets and travel categories, and its more than 100,000 travel agents and partners were serving some 2 million customers per day across 2,600 Via towns and cities in India the Philippines, Indonesia, Singapore, and the UAE.

Annual revenue was approaching $500 million, and Via had expanded into the Philippines and Indonesia.[13] Its initially customer-funded business model had served Via very well!

We've found pay-in-advance models popping up from Colombia (EasyFairs trade fairs) to Copenhagen (Studenterbolaget Friday beer parties in Danish student dorms) for both goods and services. Their potential appears limited only by entrepreneurs' imaginations – and, of course, by their ability to convince customers to pay in advance.

❝potential appears limited only by entrepreneurs' imaginations❞

Subscription models

In 2005, a cartoon showed an irate American father telling his son, 'No! You can't outsource your homework to Bangalore.'[14] Outsourcing the homework hasn't happened just yet, but outsourcing some of the learning has, thanks to the power of the internet and Krishnan Ganesh's observation that education – in mathematics, in particular – was suffering in the United States and elsewhere. In October of 2005, Ganesh took a small space in a business incubator in Bangalore; in November, he hired three Indian teachers, who began tutoring American students more than 9,000 miles away. With a headset and webcam at each end, a VOIP connection, and an 'erasable whiteboard' on their computer screens on which both teacher and student could write – one in red, the other in blue – TutorVista was born.[15]

Ganesh, who had already built and sold two successful companies in India, spent the first few months tinkering with the service. He hired an American educator to train his tutors on the application-based American pedagogy, which differs from the rote memory and repetition more common in India. Initially charging students an hourly rate, he soon discovered that a subscription model – $100 per month for all the tutoring you want, 24/7 – enhanced customer adoption, not to mention cash flow.

By June 2006, to keep pace with growing demand, Ganesh's roster of tutors had grown to 50, most of them working from their homes to serve 400 students, mostly in America. With this early success as evidence that he had discovered a huge opportunity, he raised $2 million in venture capital from Sequoia Capital to beef up his online marketing budget.[16] Growth took off, surpassing 2,000 students in 13 countries, served by 250 tutors, by December, at which point Sequoia and two other venture capital investors provided another $10.75 million to accelerate growth and fund forays into adjacent educational opportunities.[17]

Do students and tutors like the TutorVista experience? Isha Gulati of San Jose, California, age 8 – working on maths, science, geography and English four or five times per week with her tutor Bina Joseph – says, 'It's really fun. We always talk about things I really want to know.'[18] For Joseph, who has a master's degree in English and bachelor's degrees in science and education, it's a good deal. It gives her more time with her family than if she were teaching in an Indian school. And better pay, too.

TutorVista's subscription model makes the business itself highly capital efficient, since the subscription is paid for by the customer before the tutoring costs are incurred. And by leveraging the low cost of teaching talent in India, gross margins are healthy, too. New customers turn profitable almost instantly, so external capital is needed only to fund customer acquisition in order to grow the business faster.

"new customers turn profitable almost instantly"

There's nothing new about subscription models, wherein a subscriber pays for something – *The Wall Street Journal* or Showtime, for example – and the goods or services are then delivered over the ensuing period. But entrepreneurs like Ganesh – and others building subscription models in other settings from cut flowers (H. Bloom) to social networks for businesses (Yammer) – are using such models to prove their concepts with their customers' funding before raising capital to step on the accelerator.

In June 2009, Pearson plc, the world's largest education company, acquired a 17 per cent stake in TutorVista.[19] A year and a half later, in January 2011, it upped its stake to 76 per cent, buying out the early investors, giving them handsome returns. Pearson valued the company, with its 2,000 tutors serving 10,000 online students per month and a growing presence serving the Indian education system, too, at $213 million. Said Ganesh, 'We are the largest employer of teachers in India. Together with Pearson, we can make this happen even faster and help millions of students achieve their educational goals.'[20]

Scarcity-based models

Another way to build a customer-funded business is to use scarcity, rather than abundance, to motivate your customers to 'Buy (and pay) now!' in advance of when you must pay for what they are buying. Increasingly, retailers of various kinds are using scarcity-based models to achieve rapid inventory turnover that gives them negative working capital. Consider Zara, the Spanish-based originator of the fast-fashion concept in apparel retailing, whose parent, Inditex, has gone on to take its customer-funded fast-fashion model into other merchandise categories.

Each year, more than 10,000 Zara styles go from its in-house designers' studios to its 6,500 + stores in 88 countries in as little as two weeks.[21] Because customers know that next week's assortment won't be the same, if they see a dress they like, they buy it, long before Zara pays its vendor on 60-day terms. But Zara is merely the precursor to new scarcity-based models that are taking the retailing world by storm, where fashions, often women's fashions, are here today, gone tomorrow.

Consider Vente-Privee.com, the brainchild of Jacques-Antoine Granjon and seven partners, all with well-established roots in the distribution of manufacturers' overstock inventory, born in 2001 outside of Paris. Connecting the dots between the founders' prior experience of discreetly moving unwanted inventory for high-profile brands on the one hand, and the internet's ability to create a virtual store that could move volumes of discounted merchandise without disrupting the brands' carefully honed images on the other, Vente Privée's system was simple. Each day an email was sent to Vente Privée's members giving them 48 hours' notice of an upcoming 'sale event', which featured a lavishly produced video that not only presented the merchandise in the best possible way but also gave the brand confidence that its image was not being tarnished. Two days later, the merchandise, of which there was a limited quantity, went on sale, for just three to five days, at prices 50 per cent to 70 per cent below what the goods would have sold for on the Champs Elysées. When the sale ended, Vente Privée placed its order with the brand for what it had – already! – sold.[22]

Vente Privée's scarcity model is a unique combination of exclusivity, price and value-added merchandising. Success rests on Vente Privée's deep understanding of brands and their values and needs, more than selling on-the-cheap, and on the fact each event's scarcity – both in duration and in quantity – gives Vente Privée its eager customers' cash before it pays its vendors. It never has any of its suppliers' inventory on its own books. If the sales ran on forever, the system just wouldn't work. 'Nobody knows the wholesale business in Europe better than we do,' says Granjon. 'We are a medium for the brands. We are selling discount products, a product that people don't want. But we're selling it in a high-fashion way. That is the paradox. It's the key of our success.'[23]

❝it never has any of its suppliers' inventory on its own books❞

Because it received its customers' cash before it paid its vendors, Vente Privée grew steadily in its early years, without the need for institutional capital. In

2004, a successful lingerie event pushed Vente Privée into the limelight, and in 2005, its revenue quintupled. In 2007, as others began copying the Vente Privée formula, Granjon sold a 20 per cent stake to private equity firm Summit Partners to provide fuel for launching in seven other European countries. 'Vente-privee.com has created an entirely new channel for brands,' says Summit's Christian Strain.[24] In 2008, its invitation-only sales events attracted an average of one million unique visitors a day, with sales of some 40,000 items.[25]

But, as we've seen in Chapter 4, the flash sales industry has struggled, and consolidation has taken hold. In 2017, Vente Privee, which claims to be profitable, acquired its largest competitor, Privalia, which was the dominant player in Spain, Italy, and Latin America. Getting paid in advance is a good thing, for sure. But the business must make money, too!

Service-to-product models[27]

As we saw at the outset of this chapter, Rakesh and Rashmi Verma built a growing service business that grew by 2004 into what many regarded as India's premier source of navigable, accurate, detailed digital maps of all kinds. On a visit to the United States in that year, the Vermas observed that MapQuest had built a product it could offer online, wherein consumers or others could obtain maps anytime, anywhere, simply by going online. 'Could we do a MapQuest for India?' they wondered, and MapmyIndia was born.

Not content with developing a new customised mapping solution for each of its customers, as it had done in the past, MapmyIndia would 'productise" its mapping data, and let its customers – from retailers seeking to inform consumers where stores were located to consumers seeking location information of all kinds – do the work, zooming in for more detail, zooming out for the big picture, and more. A heretofore not very scalable services business would become a highly scalable product business.

Developing such a business would take capital, though, for algorithms, software development, GPS technology and much more. No longer was it realistic for customers to fund the growth of the business. MapmyIndia's first small round of venture capital was raised from California-based investors Kleiner Perkins Caufield & Byers and Sherpalo Ventures in 2006, valuing the still-small company – whose revenue in the prior year was barely $1 million – at about $7 million.

Three further rounds of capital at sharply higher valuations followed in 2007, 2008 and 2011, as MapmyIndia grew its product offering: consumer navigation devices for the auto aftermarket à la TomTom; fleet tracking solutions for the taxi and logistics industries in India; licensed content for automobile manufacturers' in-dash infotainment systems; locator content via the Web; and even a $50 app to turn your iPhone into a navigation device for India. And the original services business keeps humming along, too. One might think of the company today as MapQuest and TomTom or Garmin, for India, rolled into one.

But none of these products could have been developed had the customer-funded services business not created the raw material from which the subsequent products could be built. It's what Bill Gates did to build Microsoft on the back of a services contract to develop the operating system for IBM's first personal computer. GoViral, a Danish company with expertise in viral online video distribution, used its customers funds to grow from a bootstrapped start to a nearly $100 million exit to AOL.

Customer-funded business models in a lean start-up world

This book argues that it makes sense to assess the attractiveness of your opportunity *before* you embark on a start-up and *before* writing a business plan or pitching for funding. But the moment when a new venture comes into being is often unclear. When does research and analysis end and selling begin?

The essential idea underlying today's lean start-up thinking is that discovering what a customer will want to buy and pay for – often in an iterative and experimental fashion – is a critical step in the birth of any venture. If that's the case, why not get the target customer to buy *and pay* in a manner that can fund your venture, as the numerous entrepreneurs whose stories grace this chapter have done? As was noted at the outset of the book, not every venture can be built on lean principles, but if yours is one that can, and you can get the customer to fund it, go for it!

What customer-funded business models have in common

Regardless of type, our examples of companies having customer-funded business models share two attributes in common:

■ They required little or no external capital to get started.

■ All of them raised institutional capital eventually, and did so once the concept had been proven.

Further, these companies' stories tell us that, in almost every case, eventually there was a queue of VCs lined up, eager to invest. Contrast that with the length of the typical queue that an early-stage entrepreneur finds at his door: nil. Or, if he's really lucky and some investor shares his vision, one. Unfortunately for the entrepreneur, when there's a queue of one, it's the investor who calls the shots on the deal.

The pitfalls of pre-revenue investing

If you're an investor, you're probably wondering whether I'm arguing in this chapter that there's no room for you in the early-stage inn. In fact, I am, if 'early-stage' means prior to the time when the entrepreneur has secured a modicum of real revenues. Though too many entrepreneurs – and too many angels, too – have drunk the 'VC-or-Bust Kool-Aid', there's an important role here that you can play in helping your entrepreneur come to grips with the thesis of this chapter.

If you've been pitched a business that you like that you think has a chance to win customer-funding, what I hope you'll encourage your entrepreneur to do is do just that, perhaps with your help. Once some customer traction has been achieved, you and the entrepreneur will have learned a few useful and important things:

- That there appears to be at least some actual market demand. A possible pivot eliminated, and market risk down! That's good for your likely returns on this deal!

- That getting the business underway is likely to be capital-efficient. That, too, is likely to be good for your returns, as less dilution is likely in the future.

- That your entrepreneur doesn't just talk a good game at pitch time. He or she delivers progress, too.

- That your entrepreneur understands that building a great business is, first and foremost, about delivering what customers want to buy!

This chapter has only scratched the surface of customer-funding principles. For a more in-depth treatment, see my 2014 book, *The Customer-Funded Business.*[28] Particularly pertinent to early-stage investors, each chapter therein outlines the questions investors should ask about each of the five customer-funded models. Or if you prefer getting your content digitally, check out my Massively Open Online Course (MOOC) on Coursera.org, *How to Finance and Grow Your Start-up – Without VC.*[29]

The rest of the story

Whether you're an entrepreneur or an investor, there's more to this story than easier – albeit later – capital raised on better terms. First, waiting to raise capital forces the entrepreneur's attention toward his customers, where it should be. As we've just seen, customer focus and customer traction rank high on the list of what early-stage investors like to see. Customers matter, and as the late Peter Drucker noted, if there's no paying customer eventually, there's no business, either (the protestations of Twitter and some others to the contrary). And Winning customer orders often gives your customer a vested interest in your success , too. Second, making do with the modest amounts of cash your customers give you enforces frugality, rather than waste. Wasting investors' money is not a good recipe for cordial investor relations. Third, when capital is raised later, less of it is put at early-stage risk, meaning the terms and valuation are likely to be better, making the founder's stake – and perhaps control – more substantial, too. Perhaps, surprisingly, that's OK with investors, too. Less risk, even at the expense of higher valuation, is another thing investors like to see.

> **❝ wasting investors' money is not a good recipe for cordial investor relations ❞**

Finally, and perhaps best of all, focusing your fund-raising efforts on customers who are willing and eager to buy from your yet-unproven company is likely to mercifully put to rest a half-baked or not-quite-right idea that requires more development – one or more pivots – in order to hit the mark. Putting such ideas to rest, or altering them, earlier – thus failing early, and failing small – and moving on to better ideas, is a defining characteristic of many of today's most successful entrepreneurs. When a customer drives the pivot, and offers cash for doing so, it will be seen to make good sense, in sharp contrast to the willy-nilly flailing around that today's overemphasis on pivoting and starting a business – any business – over a weekend, sometimes entails. Customers, along with their cash, are, indeed, king.

So, if you are an entrepreneur working on the micro-market portion of your seven domains analysis, I suggest you consider whether one of the five customer-funded models might be applicable to your opportunity. If so, you could be up and running – with real customer traction – in no time, just as Joe Gebbia and Brian Chesky were with Airbnb. What better proof of your opportunity's attractiveness could there be, at least in micro-market terms, than having some customers happily and gratefully funding your business?

THE NEW BUSINESS ROAD TEST

As you talk with prospective customers, you may find your *New Business Road Test* app a good place to keep track of what you're learning about their willingness not only to buy, but also to pay with terms that could fund your venture. As you do so, you should connect your lessons learned to your emerging conclusions about the attractiveness of your opportunity in micro-market terms (see Chapter 2) and the economic sustainability of your business model (see Chapter 5). If you identify any key risks about your target customers' willingness to buy or pay in your long interviews, the app has a place to keep track of them, too.

13

Market analysis worksheet

This worksheet is intended to stimulate entrepreneurs' and investors' thinking about market size and growth rates and the various kinds of trends that are likely to influence demand for what you propose to offer. The points of this exercise are twofold:

■ to identify the extent to which the proposed venture can reach a sizeable scale or whether it's more likely to be a lifestyle business;

■ to identify the extent to which future demand is likely to grow or decline, based on trends that are likely to influence your customers' buying habits.

These trends may be in any of six broad categories.

■ *Demographic trends:* trends towards greater or lesser numbers of people (or businesses, for business-to-business offerings) in various demographic groups, based on age, income, gender, education, ethnicity, etc. Census data are useful in quantifying these trends. *Example: the trend towards an increasing number of people in older age groups in most developed countries.*

■ *Sociocultural trends:* trends towards greater or lesser numbers of people (or businesses) engaged in various lifestyle or other activities based on social or cultural trends. *Example: trends towards organic and vegetarian diets in some countries are creating increased demand for foods in these categories.*

■ *Economic trends:* changes in income levels, economic growth, interest rates and other economic indicators can have profound effects on demand for many kinds of goods and services. *Example: the rapidly growing purchasing power of families in many developing countries is creating increased demand for many kinds of consumer goods in Asia and elsewhere.*

■ *Technological trends:* developments in mobile telephony, biotechnology and a vast array of other technologies portend powerful effects on demand for many other kinds of goods and services. *Example: the falling cost of solar power and battery storage and the rise of autonomous driving technology may soon sound a death knell for the automobile industry as we know it.*

■ *Regulatory trends:* changes in laws and government policies affect demand in many ways. *Example: changes in legislation for how older people are housed and cared for in developed countries has spurred demand for new kinds of housing alternatives and other services for the elderly.*

■ *Natural trends:* global warming, the depletion of natural resources and other natural trends can influence some kinds of demand. *Example: demand for winter resort accommodation in the Alps is likely to decline if global warming makes Alpine snow sufficiently unreliable.*

The challenge for the entrepreneur – and for investors, too – is to identify trends in any of these categories that are likely to have a significant effect – whether favourable or unfavourable – on demand for what is proposed to be offered. The effects of such trends can be far more powerful than one might imagine.

> **the challenge for the entrepreneur is to identify trends in any of these categories that are likely to have a significant effect on demand for what is proposed to be offered**

The best places to look for such trends are in trade magazines and trade associations for your industry, government reports, consumer data sources like Key Note and Mintel in the UK and similar sources elsewhere, and in the general and business press. Finding objective sources of specific trends – and citing them – provides valuable indications to either support or detract from the viability of the entrepreneur's vision of how eager customers are likely to be to accept what is to be offered. Later, at business planning time, these data provide a powerful boost to the entrepreneur's credibility and can provide evidence-based support for the veracity of estimates of market potential.

So, here are the data that are needed to complete a comprehensive macro-level market analysis:

■ Market size, ideally measured in any or all of the following ways:

  – number of customers for the category of goods or services (athletic shoes or whatever) you will offer;
  – total spending in the category;
  – total units bought in the category;

- Recent market growth rate, measured in any or all of:
  - population changes;
  - total spending in the category;
  - total units bought in the category;

- Forecasted market growth rate from credible sources, measured in any or all of:
  - population changes;
  - total spending in the category;
  - total units bought in the category;

- Favourable trends, with sources cited, in any or all of the six macro-trend categories:
  - demographic;
  - sociocultural;
  - economic;
  - technological;
  - regulatory;
  - natural;

- Unfavourable trends, with sources cited, in any or all of the six macro-trend categories:
  - demographic;
  - sociocultural;
  - economic;
  - technological;
  - regulatory;
  - natural.

Overall conclusions result from answers to the following questions.

- Is this an opportunity for a lifestyle business or one that can reach sizeable scale?

- What few specific and crucial macro trends are important to the future of the venture? What are their implications for market attractiveness?

- Overall, based on the data you have gathered and cited, how attractive is the market you intend to serve?

THE NEW BUSINESS ROAD TEST

As you conduct your macro-market analysis, you may find your *New Business Road Test* app a good place to keep track of what you're learning – the size and growth of your intended market, and today's and tomorrow's macro trends that are likely to drive it going forward. As you do so, be sure to connect what you learn to your emerging conclusions about the attractiveness of your opportunity in macro-market terms (see Chapter 3). If you identify any important macro-market risks, the app has a place to keep track of them, too.

14

Industry analysis checklist[1]

This checklist is useful for asking the questions necessary to assess the attractiveness of the industry you propose to enter or in which you might decide to invest, based on Michael Porter's five forces framework.[2] Reading Porter's original article will broaden your understanding of this tool. The task here is to assess each of the five forces to determine whether their implications for industry attractiveness are favourable or unfavourable, and then to draw an overall conclusion based on all five forces taken together. Keep in mind that it is the *industry* (food retailing, software, restaurants or whatever) that you are assessing, not your proposed *venture,* without regard to whether you actually enter the industry.

❝keep in mind that it is your *industry* that you are assessing, not your proposed *venture*❞

In the discussion that follows, there's a chart showing the various drivers of each of the five forces. For example, in the first chart – threat of entry – you'll see that threat of entry is most severe when *all* of the drivers are at low levels. For an industry you are considering entering, you can rate each of the drivers as low or high, depending on the conditions that prevail given your examination of your industry.

If you find all the threat of entry drivers to be low (e.g. low economies of scale, little product differentiation and so on), that's generally bad news for you, as it indicates that your industry is marked by severe threat of entry. If you find all of the drivers to be high in your industry (e.g. lots of economies of scale, much product differentiation and so on), that's much better news, suggesting that, with regard to threat of entry, your industry is favourable.

Following each of the charts, you'll find an example of a particular industry that dramatises that force (i.e. one of the five) forces and its impact on industry attractiveness.

Threat of entry

In general, industries are more attractive when the threat of entry is low, meaning that competitors cannot enter easily to copy your initial success. This also means that it may be difficult for your venture to get started, but that's the price you pay for the ability to compete where others cannot easily follow.

Threat of new entrants into an industry is most severe when within the industry:	High	Low	Conditions for your industry (high or low)	Implications for industry attractiveness*
economies of scale are		XX		
product differentiation is		XX		
capital requirements are		XX		
companies' control of distribution channels is		XX		
companies' level of proprietary knowledge is		XX		
companies' control over access to raw materials is		XX		
government and legal barriers are		XX		
expected retaliation by established producers is		XX		
Summary evaluation				

* Indicate whether favourable (implying little threat of entry) or unfavourable (severe threat of entry).

Example: Threat of entry is extremely severe in the restaurant industry, since almost anyone can open a restaurant, perhaps in a fully furnished location vacated by a recently failed restaurant. For the restaurant industry, all factors in the chart above are low, except perhaps for product differentiation and expected retaliation, indicating severe threat of entry.

Now, consider the industry you propose to enter. Gather the information needed to complete the chart, and draw a conclusion about the threat of new entrants. Overall, is the threat of new entrants into your industry:

- Highly favourable;
- Moderately favourable;
- Moderately unfavourable;
- Highly unfavourable?

All conditions are not equal. Which, if any, of these conditions, singly or taken together, might make severe threat of entry a fatal flaw for your opportunity?

What specific obstacles, if any, will your venture have to overcome to enter this industry?

Supplier power

In general, industries are more attractive when their suppliers (of raw materials, labour, facilities and other necessary inputs) have little power to set the prices, terms and conditions under which you will buy. Here we are examining *your* suppliers, not you as a supplier to your customers.

Power of suppliers is strong when:	High	Low	Conditions for your industry (high or low)	Implications for industry attractiveness*
size and concentration of focal industry companies relative to supplier companies are		XX		
total volume or percentage of suppliers' products purchased by the focal industry companies is		XX		
product differentiation of suppliers is	XX			
switching costs for focal industry companies are	XX			
threat of forward integration by suppliers is	XX			
suppliers' knowledge about focal industry companies' cost structure is	XX			
extent of suppliers' profits is	XX			
cost savings for the focal industry companies from the suppliers' products are	XX			
importance of the suppliers' input to quality of the focal industry's final product is	XX			
cost of suppliers' products relative to the focal industry companies' total cost is	XX			
Summary evaluation				

* Indicate whether favourable (implying weak supplier power) or unfavourable (strong supplier power).

Example: Intel and Microsoft, both key suppliers to the personal computer industry, enjoy very strong power as suppliers to that industry, an unfavourable factor for personal computer makers.

Now, consider *your* industry. Based on your analysis of the drivers above, is supplier power in your industry:

- Highly favourable;
- Moderately favourable;
- Moderately unfavourable;
- Highly unfavourable?

All conditions are not equal. Which, if any, of these conditions, singly or taken together, might make strong supplier power (power of *your* suppliers, not you *as* a supplier) a fatal flaw for your opportunity?

If the power of suppliers in your industry is unfavourable, what activities (e.g. product differentiation, switching costs) could you or other potential entrants undertake to reduce their power?

Buyer power

In general, industries are more attractive when buyers (your customers) have little power to set the terms and conditions under which they will buy.

Power of buyers is strong when:	High	Low	Conditions for your industry (high or low)	Implications for industry attractiveness*
size and concentration of buyers relative to focal industry companies are	XX			
total volume or percentage of focal industry companies' products purchased by the buyers is	XX			
product differentiation by focal industry companies is		XX		
switching costs for buyers are		XX		
threat of backward integration by buyers is	XX			

buyers' knowledge about focal industry companies' cost structure is	XX	
extent of buyers' profits is		XX
cost savings for the buyers from the focal industry companies' product are		XX
importance of the focal industry companies' input to quality of the buyers' final product is		XX
cost of focal industry companies' product relative to the buyers' total cost is		XX

Summary evaluation

* Indicate whether favourable (implying weak buyer power) or unfavourable (strong buyer power).

Example: As customers of the tyre manufacturing industry, car manufacturers like Toyota and Ford have considerable buyer power.

Consider *your* industry. Overall, is buyer power of the customers served by your industry:

■ Highly favourable;

■ Moderately favourable;

■ Moderately unfavourable;

■ Highly unfavourable?

All conditions are not equal. Which, if any, of these conditions, singly or taken together, might make severe buyer power (power of *your* customers, not you *as* a customer) a fatal flaw for your opportunity?

If the power of buyers is unfavourable in your industry, what activities (e.g. product differentiation, switching costs, cost savings for buyers) could you or other potential entrants undertake to reduce their power?

Threat of substitutes

In general, industries are more attractive when the threat of substitutes is low, meaning that goods or services from other industries cannot easily serve as substitutes for your industry's products.

Threat of substitutes is most severe when:	High	Low	Conditions for your industry (high or low)	Implications for industry attractiveness*
buyer propensity to substitute is	XX			
relative price–performance relationship of substitutes compared with industry product is	XX			
Summary evaluation				

* Indicate whether favourable (implying little threat of substitutes from other industries) or unfavourable (severe threat of substitutes).

Example: Threat of substitutes is severe in the glass packaging industry, as numerous other industries produce packaging (aluminium can industry, paper and plastic packaging industries and so on) that can substitute for glass.

Overall, for your industry, is the threat of substitutes:

- Highly favourable;
- Moderately favourable;
- Moderately unfavourable;
- Highly unfavourable?

All conditions are not equal. Which, if any, of these conditions, singly or taken together, might make the severe threat of substitutes a fatal flaw for your opportunity?

If the threat of substitutes is unfavourable, what activities could you as a potential entrant undertake to reduce the threat's likelihood?

Competitive rivalry

In general, industries are more attractive when competitive rivalry is more genteel and less intense, meaning that competing companies do not undercut one another to win customers' business.

Intensity of competitive rivalry within the industry is most severe when:	High	Low	Conditions for your industry (high or low)	Implications for industry attractiveness*
number of companies or number of equally balanced companies is	XX			
industry growth rate is		XX		
fixed or storage costs are	XX			
product differentiation is		XX		
switching costs for buyers are		XX		
diversity of competitors is		XX		
exit barriers are	XX			
strategic stakes are	XX			
Summary evaluation				

* Indicate whether favourable (implying little competitive rivalry) or unfavourable (severe competitive rivalry).

Example: Rivalry in the aluminium can industry is severe, as can-makers compete aggressively for the business of the major beverage manufacturers. All the factors in the chart above are unfavourable, except perhaps for switching costs for buyers, since cans are typically manufactured on the beverage company's premises.

Overall, is competitive rivalry in your industry:

■ Highly favourable;

■ Moderately favourable;

■ Moderately unfavourable;

■ Highly unfavourable?

All conditions are not equal. Which, if any, of these conditions, singly or taken together, might make severe competitive rivalry a fatal flaw for your opportunity?

If competitive rivalry is unfavourable, what activities could a potential entrant undertake to reduce the level of rivalry?

Overall evaluation of industry attractiveness

Now, consider your industry on all five of the forces. If three or four of the five forces are unfavourable, then your industry is probably brutally unattractive. If only one or two are unfavourable, then industry conditions may be moderate, though if those one or two are severe enough, they could be sufficient to render the industry as unattractive in spite of the other more favourable forces.

Of the five forces, how many did you place in each category:

- Highly favourable;
- Moderately favourable;
- Moderately unfavourable;
- Highly unfavourable?

Based on the above analysis, what is your overall assessment of the attractiveness of your industry:

- Highly attractive industry;
- Moderately attractive industry;
- Moderately unattractive industry;
- Highly unattractive industry?

Which of the five forces impact most significantly on the overall structure of the industry, positively and negatively? What risks have you identified?

Does one of the forces single-handedly make the industry especially attractive? Which one? Why?

If severe threat of entry is a problem in your industry, is it reasonable to expect that you can enter and exit (by selling your business) successfully before subsequent entrants can catch up with you? Why? If not, or if such a strategy is not consistent with your entrepreneurial dreams, how will you resolve the threat of entry problem?

Based on your analysis, what changes do you anticipate in this industry – i.e. what trends will affect the five forces and make industry conditions better or worse? What can your venture do to take advantage of or influence these changes?

Finally, how might you shape or reshape your opportunity to cope with its industry setting? Is there another industry that's more attractive from which to pursue the market you seek to serve?

Please don't forget, though, that industry attractiveness at the macro level is but one of the seven domains. Just because your five forces analysis shows that your industry is unattractive does not necessarily mean that you should abandon your opportunity. As we noted in Chapter 4, it is possible, under the right conditions, to be successful in a bad industry.

THE NEW BUSINESS ROAD TEST

As you conduct your macro-industry analysis, you may find your *New Business Road Test* app a good place to keep track of what you're learning about each of the five forces. As you do so, be sure to connect what you learn to your emerging conclusions about the attractiveness of your opportunity in macro-industry terms (see Chapter 4). If you identify any key macro-industry risks as you do so, the app has a place to keep track of them, too.

15

Do-it-yourself marketing research for your new business road test[1]

You can do it. And you don't have to break the bank. If you are an early-stage entrepreneur, you may not have the resources to hire a professional marketing research firm to conduct the research that could be helpful in assessing your idea. Even if you had the resources, however, you might not choose to spend them this way, since the research may well show the idea to be a non-starter, a conclusion some are afraid to hear. So, if you've never done this before, how should you proceed?

Try the internet first?

Before diving into the kinds of more traditional research we'll outline in this chapter, you might want to think first about running a simple online test. If you've got the skills or the resources to assemble a website, perhaps on a platform where things like yours are sold – Etsy, Threadless, eBay, who knows? – you can put your offer out there, perhaps buy some ad words, and see if anyone bites!

It won't cost you much, and it can be a good place to start. If someone wants to buy, of course, you'll then face a dilemma. Do you make what the customer has ordered, or do you confess to your customer that your product isn't quite ready yet, and refund their money? Either way, you'll have learned something.

What does marketing research do?

Marketing research is the design, collection, analysis and reporting of research intended to gather data pertinent to a *particular* marketing challenge or situation. The word 'particular' is very important. Marketing research is intended to address carefully defined marketing problems or opportunities. Research carried out without carefully thought out objectives usually means time and money down the drain. Other portions of your research may address different objectives – identifying the CSFs in your industry, for example. Whether the research you need is marketing research or some other kind, however, the guiding principles are the same.

Let's begin with a model of the research process that sets forth the many decisions that must be made to conduct effective and actionable research. The steps in the research process are shown in Box 15.1.

---

box 15.1

Steps in the marketing research process: what can go wrong?

Steps	What frequently goes wrong?
1 Identify the managerial problem and establish research objectives	Management identifies no clear objective, no decision to be made based on the proposed research
2 Determine your data sources (primary or secondary) and types of data and research approaches (qualitative and quantitative) required	Primary data are collected when cheaper and faster secondary data will do. Quantitative data are collected without first collecting qualitative data
3 Design the research: type of study, data collection approach, sample, etc.	These are technical issues best managed by skilled practitioners. Doing these steps poorly can generate misleading or incorrect results
4 Collect the data	Collector bias: hearing what you want to hear
5 Analyse the data	Tabulation errors or incorrect use or interpretation of statistical procedures may mislead the user
6 Report the results to the decision-maker	Some users do not really want objective information – they want to prove what they already believe to be true

---

"the research process is fraught with numerous opportunities for error"

As this table shows, the research process is fraught with numerous opportunities for error. That's why it's so important for entrepreneurs to be well-informed and critical users of the information that results from marketing and other research studies.

To this end, we will now address each of the steps in the research process, in terms of the decisions that you, the researcher, will need to make.

Step 1: identify the managerial problem and establish research objectives

As for any other form of human endeavour, if you don't have clear objectives, any road will get you there. The same is true for conducting research. A good place to start is to ask what the managerial problem or question is that a proposed programme of research might address. For most entrepreneurs, in their initial enquiries about assessing an opportunity, there are numerous managerial questions to be answered. How large is the market? How fast is it likely to grow? What segments are most attractive? Is the industry attractive? Who are the key competitors, and what competitive advantages might they have and not have if we enter? What customer wants and needs are not currently well satisfied, for what groups of customers or consumers? How likely are consumers to buy the solution we propose to offer? How much might they be willing to pay?

Taking each of these managerial questions one at a time, and applying appropriate analytical frameworks to each of them – such as macro-trend analysis (see Chapter 3), Porter's five forces (see Chapter 4) and so on – provides clear guidance for the kind of information the researcher needs to obtain. The result is a set of research objectives (e.g. to determine market size and growth rate, to assess supplier power in this industry, to determine your target customers' likelihood to buy and so on) that will drive the research.

Step 2: determine data sources and types of data required

This step is critical in determining the cost-effectiveness and timeliness of the research effort. There are two key questions that the researcher must answer at this stage: should I gather data from primary or secondary sources? Whichever of these types of data source are called for, do I need qualitative or quantitative research to satisfy my research objectives, or both?

Primary data are data collected from individual research subjects – using observation, a survey, interviews or whatever – that are then gathered and interpreted for the particular research objective at hand. Secondary data already exist – on the internet, in government documents, in the business press, in company files or wherever. Someone has already done the primary data collection and placed the data where others can access them, whether easily or with difficulty, whether free or at some cost.

Which are better – primary or secondary data? *If* (and it's an important *if*) a research objective can be met using secondary data, that's usually the best course to follow. Why? Three reasons:

- First, it's usually *quicker* to find the data somewhere than to collect them from scratch – imagine having to collect demographic data without the census;

- Second, it's usually *less costly* simply to find existing secondary data than to collect them as primary data all over again;

- Third, secondary data are typically based on what people actually do, or how they behave – surveys, a common form of primary data, are based on what people *say* and the two are not the same, as we shall see in Chapter 16, on forecasting.

For entrepreneurs, secondary data, if they are available, should answer several important research questions, such as those on market and industry attractiveness at the macro level. To identify sources for the particular secondary data you will need, consult a business librarian. A resourceful one who knows where to look for what you need to satisfy the research objectives you specify can save you enormous amounts of time. To explore consumers' willingness to buy the solution you propose to develop, primary data may or may not be necessary.

Qualitative or quantitative data and research approaches?

Where secondary data are to be collected, the entrepreneur needs to decide whether qualitative data or quantitative data are required. Most secondary research studies require both qualitative (e.g. macro trends) and quantitative (e.g. market size) data. Fortunately, both are usually easy to find.

If primary data are necessary, a decision must be made about whether to collect the data using qualitative or quantitative research approaches.

> **the benefit of qualitative data is that they may yield deeper insights into consumer behaviour than are available from quantitative research**

Qualitative research usually involves small samples of subjects and produces information that is not easily quantifiable. The benefit of qualitative data is that they may yield deeper insights into consumer behaviour than are available from quantitative research. For this reason, qualitative research is often conducted first and then used to guide subsequent quantitative research. An important drawback of qualitative research, however, is that its generally small samples may not represent fairly the larger population. Most experienced marketing researchers would say, '*Never generalise* from qualitative research. Always follow up with a quantitative study to test the hunches developed in the qualitative study.' Such statements presume, however, that adequate research resources are available to conduct additional studies. Often, and particularly in entrepreneurial settings, such is not the case, and decision-makers are forced to rely, albeit tenuously, on small-scale qualitative studies.

Quantitative research collects data that are amenable to statistical analysis, usually from large enough samples so that inferences may be drawn with some confidence from the sample to the population from which the subjects in the sample are drawn. The principal benefit of quantitative research lies in its measurement of a population's attitudes towards or likely response to products or marketing programmes. Because of their larger sample sizes and quantitative metrics, greater confidence can be placed in quantitative studies, when conducted properly, using appropriate sampling procedures and statistical techniques. These issues are addressed in more detail below.

Qualitative research techniques

There are seemingly as many qualitative research techniques as there are stars in the sky.[2] The most commonly used ones, however, are focus groups and interviews of various kinds.[3] A focus group typically consists of 8 to 12 consumers from the marketer's target market brought together at a research facility to discuss a particular marketing problem, such as attitudes towards a proposed new product and various possible features thereof. A skilled moderator conducts the focus group, records the conversation on audio and/or video tape and writes a report of the findings. Typically, two or more groups are conducted for a single research project. Focus groups have significant limitations:

❝focus groups have significant limitations❞ they may be subject to data distortion caused by a dominant person in the group, their results are difficult to interpret and they are neither representative of nor generalisable to a larger population, due to their small sample size and convenience samples. They are a good way, however, to begin a research enquiry, or to gather at least some information when research budgets are tight.

Quantitative research techniques

In most quantitative research, questionnaires are used that enable the researcher to measure the subjects' responses on quantitative scales.[4] These scales allow the researcher to compare different product attributes, the responses of demographically different consumers, and other differences in order to better understand some crucial questions.

- What products or product attributes do your prospective customers prefer?
- Which product attributes are most important?
- How satisfied are the prospective customers with one product compared with others?
- How likely are the prospective customers to buy at different price points?

Where statistically significant differences are found, you can be relatively certain that the differences uncovered in the research reflect those actually found in the population as a whole. Examples of several kinds of quantitative scales commonly used in such research are shown in Box 15.2. Novice researchers, or those whose budgets are limited, can sometimes obtain useful market knowledge from small-scale research that begins with some qualitative research – perhaps several interviews – and concludes with a quantitative study using measures like those shown in Box 15.2.

---

box 15.2

Some commonly used types of scale for quantitative marketing research

Type of scale	Description	Example
Semantic differential scale	A scale connecting two bipolar words or phrases	How satisfied are you with your provider of cable TV? Not at all satisfied 1 2 3 4 5 6 7 Extremely satisfied
Likert scale	A statement with which the respondent shows the amount of agreement/ disagreement	I am extremely satisfied with my provider of cable TV Strongly agree 1 2 3 4 5 6 7 Strongly disagree
Quality rating scale	Rates some attribute on a scale from 'excellent' to 'poor'	My cable TV service, overall, is: Poor Fair Good Very Good Excellent
Importance scale, using semantic differential format	Rates the importance of some attribute	How important are the following criteria to your satisfaction with your cable TV provider?

How important are the following criteria to your satisfaction with your cable TV provider?

	Not at all					Extremely
Answers the phone quickly	1	2	3	4	5	6 7
Prompt repair service	1	2	3	4	5	6 7
Cleans up after installation	1	2	3	4	5	6 7
Service never goes dark	1	2	3	4	5	6 7

Intention to buy scale	Measures how likely the respondent is to buy at some price	How likely are you to sign up for the new InterGalactic Channel for an extra £4.95 per month?
		Definitely ☐
		Probably ☐
		Might or might not ☐
		Probably not ☐
		Definitely not ☐

Step 3: design the research

Designing secondary research is a simple matter of finding sources of information sufficient to satisfy the research objectives, and to ensure that the sources are credible ones. For primary qualitative research, such as focus groups or interviews, detailed guides must be prepared for conducting the research to specify what questions are to be asked. For primary quantitative research, research design is the most technical and most difficult step in conducting the research. It's a good place to get professional help if you can afford it. The key decisions to be made in primary research design are to determine the data collection method and prepare the research instrument, to determine how to contact the participants in the research and to design the sampling plan.

Determine the data collection method and prepare the research instrument

There are several methods of collecting qualitative primary data, of which the most common are observation, survey and experiment. Observation is just that: observing subjects doing something relevant to the objectives of the research. Typically, a form is prepared on which the observer records what is being observed. Many Japanese companies favour the use of observation to better understand not only consumers but also salespeople and distribution channel members.[5]

Surveys involve developing a questionnaire, which will include questions and either scaled answers (like those shown in Box 15.2) or spaces for open-ended answers, all of which are intended to capture whatever the researcher wants to learn. Demographic information about the respondent is also usually requested to aid in market segmentation and market targeting decisions. Constructing survey questions and formats for the answers is more difficult than one might expect, and is beyond the scope of this chapter, but several sources cited herein can help bring you up to speed on these tasks. Any business school marketing research text will have a chapter on questionnaire design.[6]

Experiments are studies in which the researcher manipulates one or more variables, such as price or product features, either within the context of a survey or in a laboratory or field setting, in order to measure the effect of the manipulated variable on the consumer's response. One common use of experiments is to examine the consumer's likelihood to buy a new product at different price points. Different respondents are given different prices for the product, and the researcher tests differences in consumers' likelihood to buy as the price changes. This procedure entails less bias than asking consumers what they would be willing to pay for a product, the real answer to which is probably 'As little as possible'.

> **one common use of experiments is to examine the consumer's likelihood to buy a new product at different price points**

Determine the contact method

Once a data collection method is chosen, the researcher must decide how to contact those who will participate in the research. Common choices include face to face (perhaps in a shopping mall or a public place), mail, telephone, fax, email and the internet. Box 15.3 shows some of the trade-offs that influence the choices you must make among these methods. A significant problem with survey research is that those who choose not to participate when asked ('We're eating dinner now, and please don't call back!') may differ from those who do participate. This non-response bias may distort the results of the research. Response rate can also be a problem, since many who are asked to participate will not do so. Response rates for mail surveys sent to consumers generally run around 15–20 per cent. Far lower response rates can be expected in business-to-business settings, which is one reason why qualitative research

---

box 15.3

Pros and cons of different contact methods for survey research

Method	Response rate	Cost	Timeliness	Non-response bias
Face to face	High	High	Slow	Low
Mail	Low	Low	Slow	High
Telephone	Moderate	Moderate	Fast	Moderate
Fax	Moderate	Low	Fast	High
Email	Low	Low	Fast	High
Internet	Low	Low	Fast	High

❝for a mail survey, five to six times the number of surveys as you hope to receive must be mailed❞

methods, which use smaller samples, are often used. The other types are better or worse, as shown in Box 15.3. Thus, for a mail survey, for example, at least five to six times the number of surveys as you hope to receive must be mailed.

Design the sampling plan

Selecting a sample of participants for observational, survey or experimental research requires that three questions be answered.

1 Who is the population (or universe) from which the sample of respondents will be drawn?

2 What sample size is required to provide a level of confidence in the results that is acceptable to the decision-maker who will use the results of the research?

3 By what method – probability sampling (also called random sampling) or non-probability sampling (such as convenience sampling) – will the sample be selected?

Let's discuss each of these issues briefly. (For more on sampling, see the relevant chapter in any business school marketing research text.[7]) First, the population from which the sample is to be drawn must be specified clearly. Typically, this consists of the target market, defined in demographic or behavioural terms, although excluding current non-users might not be a good idea for an entrepreneur who hopes to expand the market.

Second, the sample must be large enough to provide confidence, in a statistical sense, that statistical data, such as mean responses to survey questions, are truly within some narrow enough range, sometimes called the margin of error. In general, the larger the sample size, the smaller the margin of error. Box 15.4 provides rough approximations of the margin of sampling error associated with different sample sizes.

Third, the idea behind probability or random sampling is that every person in the population has an equal chance of being selected. If non- probability samples, such as convenience samples, are used, then the sample may be biased. As a practical matter, convenience samples are used quite often for marketing research, because true random samples are more difficult and costly to obtain. Arguably, the non-response problem makes almost all samples potentially biased in the same way. An astute user should always ask what the sample selection method was. If the method is not random, then the user should enquire in detail about how the sample was selected to look for any obvious source of bias that might distort the research results.

---

box 15.4

Margin of error associated with different sample sizes

Assume a poll of eligible voters is taken to determine which candidate is in the lead. Suppose the results are that Jones has 45 per cent of the voters in her corner, Smith has 41 per cent and 14 per cent are undecided. Can we conclude that Jones leads Smith? It depends, in part, on the sample size of the poll.

Sample size	Approximate margin of error for 95 per cent confidence level	Implications for the Jones and Smith race
100	10 percentage points	Jones has 45% plus or minus 10%, or 35% to 55%. Smith has 41% plus or minus 10%, or 31% to 51%. Smith could be leading by as much as 51% to 35%.
500	4.5 percentage points	Jones has 45% plus or minus 4.5%, or 40.5% to 49.5%. Smith has 41% plus or minus 4.5%, or 36.5% to 45.5%. Smith could be leading by as much as 45.5% to 40.5%.
1000	3 percentage points	Jones has 45% plus or minus 3%, or 42% to 48%. Smith has 41% plus or minus 3%, or 38% to 44%. Smith could be leading by as much as 44% to 42%.

What will the headlines say? Probably that Jones leads Smith, 45 per cent to 41 per cent. If the sample size is 1000, typical in national or statewide political polls, is this a fair conclusion?

Source: Based on What is a Margin of Error?', American Statistical Association Section on Survey Research

Step 4: collect the data

By now, the hardest parts of the research process are complete, but the most time-consuming parts have just begun. Unfortunately, the data-collection process contributes more to overall error than any other step in the process. In some cases, especially where entrepreneurs conduct marketing research themselves instead of contracting with a third party, these errors are magnified. There are several common kinds of error in face-to-face or telephone surveys that entrepreneurs should guard against:

- Selection errors by the interviewer (i.e. selecting respondents who are not members of the specified population);

- Collector bias: this occurs when the person collecting the data – inadvertently perhaps, in their enthusiasm for the opportunity – biases the respondents, so they tell the researcher what they think he or she wants to hear;

- Interpretation and recording of answers: in their zeal to obtain research results that support the feasibility of their opportunity, entrepreneurs sometimes have difficulty in interpreting their data objectively; in the end, the only people they fool are themselves;

- In surveys conducted by fax, email or over the internet, an additional problem is that the researcher does not really know who actually replied to the survey.

The data collection effort for surveys like these can be substantial. To complete 100 surveys with randomly selected homes using random-digit dialling, several hundred phone numbers and more than 1,000 calls will likely be required.

Step 5: analyse the data

When the data have been collected, the completed data forms must be processed to yield the information that the project was designed to collect. The forms must be checked to see that instructions were followed, that the data are complete and that the data are logical and consistent within each respondent's form. Typically, the data are then entered into computer files, percentages and averages are computed and comparisons are made between different classes, categories and groups of respondents. Often, sophisticated statistical analyses are required. If you lack the skills to do these things, you may wish either to obtain professional help or to find some marketing research students at a nearby university to help you with this phase – or any of the phases, for that matter – of your research.

Step 6: report the results

This is where the rubber meets the road. If the research study began with clearly defined research objectives, then reporting the results simply returns to those objectives and reports what was found. Where research is carried out without clear objectives – as is sometimes the case, unfortunately – reporting can be difficult, as no clear conclusions may be available. Including a report of the results of a well-designed marketing research study in a business plan or pitch deck can be a source of credibility for the writer and a powerful differentiator against other business plans. Perhaps the most common shortcoming of pitches that are rejected summarily by funding sources is that they lack any marketing research to provide support for the conclusions they draw. Wishful thinking and optimistic hand-waving are not enough.

❝ including a report of the results of a well-designed marketing research study can be a source of credibility ❞

What users of marketing research should ask

The research process described in this chapter makes clear where many of the potential stumbling blocks lie in designing and carrying out marketing research. Whether you conduct the research yourself or whether you hire someone to do it for you, an informed and critical user of marketing research, whether entrepreneur or investor, should ask the following questions to ensure themselves that the research is unbiased and the results may be relied upon. These questions should be posed before the implementation of the research and again before its completion. Prospective investors who are presented with the supposed results of one or more marketing research studies should ask them, too.

1   What are the objectives of the research? Will the data to be collected meet those objectives?

2   Are the data sources appropriate? Are cheaper, faster, secondary data used where possible? Is qualitative research planned first to ensure that quantitative research, if any, is on target?

3   Are the planned qualitative and/or quantitative research approaches well suited to the objectives of the research? Qualitative research is better for deep insights into consumer behaviour, while quantitative research is better for measurement of a population's attitudes and likely responses to products or marketing programmes. For most entrepreneurs, the first of these purposes is the more important.

4   Is the research designed well? Will questionnaire scales permit the measurement necessary to meet the research objectives? Are the questions on a survey or in an interview or focus group unbiased? ('Isn't this a great new product? Do you like it?') Do the contact method and sampling plan entail any known bias? Is the sample size large enough to meet the research objectives?

5   Are the planned analyses appropriate? They should be specified *before* the research is conducted.

Rudimentary competence: are we there yet?

A key objective of this chapter is to provide entrepreneurs with at least a rudimentary level of competence in designing and carrying out marketing research studies, and investors with some basics to watch out for. Entire courses dealing with marketing research are offered in nearly every business school curriculum, and this brief chapter does little justice to the detail and technical expertise involved in this important craft. Nonetheless, by reading this material and a few of the cited reference sources on particular research techniques, any entrepreneur should be able to conduct at least some useful research for a new venture. Such research, despite its limitations, will yield greater insights into the opportunity's attractiveness than will hunches alone.

THE NEW BUSINESS ROAD TEST

As you conduct your marketing research, you may find your *New Business Road Test* app a good place to keep track of what you're learning about each of the seven domains. As you do so, be sure to connect what you learn to your emerging conclusions about the attractiveness of your opportunity, domain by domain. If you identify any key risks as you do so, the app has a place to keep track of them, too.

16

Evidence-based forecasting[1]

I know of no manager or entrepreneur who has ever seen a forecast that came in exactly on the money. Some forecasts turn out too high, others too low. Forecasting is an inherently difficult task because no one has a perfect crystal ball. The future is inherently uncertain, especially in today's rapidly changing markets. Consumer wants and needs change, buffeted by the winds of ever-changing macro trends. Competitors come and go. New technologies sweep away old ones.

Some forecasts are based on extensive and expensive research, others on small-scale enquiries, still others on uninformed hunches. Forecasting plays a central role in all kinds of planning and budgeting in all kinds of businesses and organisations. For entrepreneurs and their prospective investors, forecasting can be crucial because it's the foundation on which every business plan is based. The forecast drives the level of expenses that will be required to operate the business. It drives the level of investment needed to produce the sales. And it tells the entrepreneur whether there's enough revenue to be had from the opportunity to make it worthy of pursuit.

> **for entrepreneurs, forecasting is crucial because it's the foundation on which every business plan is based**

The lean start-up school argues that forecasts made too early are probably baseless, and rightly so. But eventually, if your opportunity looks like it might pan out, the time will come when you want to prepare a forecast, for your benefit, or at others' request. But how?

A forecaster's toolkit: a tool for every forecasting setting

Before choosing a method to prepare a forecast, the entrepreneur must know first what is to be estimated or forecasted. First, there's market potential, i.e. the likely demand from all actual and potential buyers of a product or product class. An estimate of market potential often serves as a starting point for preparing a sales forecast, about which we'll talk more later.

Prospective investors will want to know how large the potential market for your goods or services will be in the coming years, measured perhaps in several ways: in numbers of potential users, numbers of units to be purchased and in pounds sterling, dollars or even Tanzanian shillings, if you are in Tanzania. There's also the size of the currently penetrated market – those who are actually using goods or services like those you propose to offer. Investors will also want to know these figures – the size of the potential and penetrated markets – for the market segments you intend to serve, i.e. your target market. Clearly, though, you will not win a 100 per cent share of this market. You'll probably also need to prepare a sales forecast, perhaps for three to five years going forward, if you get to writing a business plan or preparing a pitch. How might you do all these things?

In established organisations, there are two broad approaches for preparing a sales forecast: top-down and bottom-up. Under the top-down approach, a central person or people take the responsibility for forecasting and prepare an overall forecast, perhaps using aggregate economic data, current sales trends or other of the methods described shortly. Under the bottom-up approach – a common approach in decentralised firms – each part of the company prepares its own sales forecast, and the parts are aggregated to create the forecast for the firm as a whole. Either of these logics may be useful in preparing a sales forecast for your new venture.

> **there are two broad approaches for preparing a sales forecast: top-down and bottom-up**

For example, using the bottom-up logic, you can break your anticipated demand into pieces – either market segments or product lines – and add up the components to create the summary forecast. There are numerous advantages to using this approach. First, it will force you to think clearly about the drivers of demand for each market segment or product line and thus understand better the real potential of your opportunity and the parts thereof. Second, you will be forced to make explicit assumptions about the drivers of demand in each category, assumptions you can debate – and support with evidence gathered from your research – with prospective investors and that you and they can verify later as the business unfolds. Third, such an approach facilitates 'What if . . . ?' planning. Various combinations of market segments and/ or product lines can be combined to build a plan that looks viable.

So, what forecasting methods or tools can you choose from? There are six major evidence-based methods for estimating market potential and forecasting sales: statistical methods, observation, surveys, analogy, judgement and market tests. A seventh method, not evidenced-based – the SWAG – is not condoned here, though there is little else to support the forecasts of far too many entrepreneurs!

Statistical and other quantitative methods

Statistical methods use past history and various statistical techniques, such as multiple regression and time-series analysis, to forecast the future based on an extrapolation of the past. Is this method useful for entrepreneurs or new product managers charged with forecasting sales for a new product or new business? Often not, for there is no history in their venture on which to base a statistical forecast. Your business may not even exist yet.

In established firms, for established products, statistical methods are extremely useful. When Michelin, the tyre maker, wants to forecast demand for the replacement car tyre market in Europe for the next year, it can build

> **" in established firms, for established products, statistical methods are extremely useful "**

a statistical model using factors such as the number and age of vehicles currently on the road in Europe, predictions of GDP for the region, the last few years' demand and other relevant factors to forecast market potential, as well as Michelin's own replacement tyre sales for the coming year. Such a procedure is likely to result in a considerably more accurate forecast than other methods, especially if Michelin has years of experience with which to calibrate its statistical model.

As with all forecasting methods, there are important limitations of statistical methods. The most important of these is that statistical methods generally assume that the future will look very much like the past. Sometimes this is not the case. US WEST, the regional Bell telephone company serving the Rocky Mountain and northwest regions of the USA, ran into trouble in the 1990s when its statistical models used to predict needs for telephone capacity failed to allow for the rapidly increasing use of computer modems, faxes and second lines for teenagers in American homes. Suddenly, the average

number of lines per home skyrocketed, and there was not enough physical plant – cable in the ground, switches and so on – to accommodate the
growing demand. Consumers had to wait, sometimes for months, to get
additional lines, and they were not happy about it.[2] Similarly, if product
or market characteristics change, then statistical models used without adequate judgement may not keep pace. When tyre makers began producing
car tyres that would last 80,000 miles instead of 30,000 to 50,000 miles, the
annual demand for replacement tyres was reduced. If car manufacturers were
to change the number of wheels on the typical car from four, then the old
statistical models would also be in trouble.

A variety of other quantitative forecasting methods, especially for new product forecasting, have also been developed. These include methods to model
mathematically model the diffusion of innovation process for consumer durables,[3] and conjoint analysis,[4] a method to forecast the impact upon consumer
demand of different combinations of attributes that might be included in a
new product. For entrepreneurs who are so inclined, these methods are worth
a look.

Observation

Another method for preparing an evidence-based forecast is to observe
or gather existing data directly about what real consumers really do in the
product market of interest. Like statistical methods, observation-based forecasting is attractive because it is based on what
people actually do. To the extent that behavioural
or usage data can be found from existing secondary sources – in company files, at the library or on
the internet – data collection is both faster and
cheaper than if a new study has to be designed
and carried out. For new-to-the-world products,
however, observation is typically not possible and
secondary data are not available, since the product often does not exist yet,
except in concept form. Market tests, discussed later, are one way to get real
purchase data about new-to-the-world products.

❝ like statistical methods, observation-based forecasting is attractive because it is based on what people actually do ❞

Surveys

Another common way to forecast sales or estimate market potential is to
conduct surveys. These surveys can be done with different groups of respondents. Consumers, after being shown a statement of the product concept[5]

or a prototype or sample of the product, can be asked how likely they are to buy it. Buyers can also be asked about their current buying behaviour: what they currently buy, how often or how much they use. The salesforce can be asked how much they are likely to sell. Experts of various kinds – members of the distribution channel, suppliers, consultants, trade association executives and so on – can also be surveyed.

❝there are important limitations of surveys, however❞

There are important limitations of surveys, however.

■ What people *say* is not always what people *do*. Consumer surveys of buyer intention are always discounted heavily to allow for this fact. For one common approach to doing so, see Box 16.1.

---

box 16.1

A survey of buyers' intentions: what people *say* is not what they *do*

When Nestlé's refrigerated foods division in the USA was considering whether to acquire Lambert's Pasta and Cheese, a fresh pasta maker, it wanted to forecast the likely first-year sales volume if the acquisition were completed. To do so, Nestlé used a concept test in which consumers were asked, among other things, how likely they were to try the fresh pasta product. The results were as shown in the first two columns in the table below.

Purchase intent	Percentage response	Rule of thumb reduction for forecasting purposes	Percentage of market deemed likely to actually buy
Definitely would buy	27%	Multiply by .8	27% x .8 = 21.6%
Probably would buy	43%	Multiply by .3	43% x .3 = 12.9%
Might or might not buy	22%	Count as zero	
Probably or definitely would not buy	8%	Count as zero	
Totals	100%		21.6% + 12.9% = 34.5%

Even though 70 per cent of consumers surveyed indicated they were likely to buy, Nestlé's experience indicated that these 'top two box' percentages should be cut sharply: 'Definitely' responses were reduced by 20 per cent, while 'Probably' responses were reduced by 70 per cent. 'Maybe' responses were considered as 'No'. These adjustments, shown in columns three and four, reduced the 70 per cent figure by more than half, to 34.5 per cent.

▶

> Most consumer product manufacturers who employ concept tests use similar rules of thumb when interpreting purchase intent data for forecasting purposes, because they have learned that what people *say* they will buy exceeds what they will *actually* buy. Similar logic is useful in a variety of forecasting situations.
>
> *Source:* Based on Marie Bell and V. Kasturi Rangan, 1995, *Nestlé Refrigerated Foods: Contadina Pasta and Pizza*, Harvard Business School Publishing, Boston, MA.

- The people who are surveyed may not be knowledgeable, but if asked for their opinion they will probably provide it.

- What people imagine about a product concept in a survey may not be what is actually delivered once the product is launched. If consumers are asked whether they will buy an 'old-world spaghetti sauce with home-made flavour', they will surely provide a response. Whether they will actually *like* the taste and texture of the sauce that the lab develops is another story.

In general, statistical and observational methods, where adequate data or settings are available in which to apply them, are superior to survey methods of forecasting, because such methods are based, at least in part, on what people have actually done or bought (e.g. the number of old cars actually on the road), while survey methods ('Are you likely to buy replacement tyres this year?') are based on what people say, a less reliable indicator of their future behaviour.

Analogy

An approach often used for new product forecasting where neither statistical methods nor observations are possible is to forecast the sales or market potential for a new product or new venture by analogy. Under this method, the product is compared with similar products that were introduced earlier, for which historical data are available. When Danone, the French marketer of yogurt, plans to introduce a new flavour of packaged yogurt, its managers will likely look at the sales history of earlier introductions to forecast the sales for the newest flavour. This method is also used for new-to-the-world high-technology products, for which product prototypes are often either not available or are extremely expensive to produce.

> **❝ an approach often used for new product forecasting where neither statistical methods nor observations are possible is to forecast the sales or market potential for a new product or new venture by analogy ❞**

Rather than conduct surveys to ask consumers about their likelihood of buying a product they can hardly imagine (what would someone have said in 1978 about their likelihood of buying a personal computer?), forecasters consider related new product introductions with which the new product may be compared. Early forecasts for high-definition television (HDTV) were done this way, comparing HDTV with historical penetration patterns for colour TV, video recorders, camcorders and other consumer electronic products.[6]

As always, there are limitations. First, the new product is never exactly like that with which the analogy is drawn. Early video recorders penetrated their markets at a much faster rate than did colour TV. Which analogy is more applicable to HDTV? Why? Second, market and competitive conditions may differ considerably from when the analogous product was launched. Such conditions need to be taken into account.

Judgement

While we hesitate to call this a forecasting method of its own, since capable and informed judgement is required for *all* methods, forecasts are sometimes made solely on the basis of experienced judgement or intuition. Some decision-makers are intuitive in their decision processes and cannot always articulate the basis for their intuitive judgements.

Said a footwear buyer at Nine West Group, 'Trend forecasting is a visceral thing that cannot be trained. I rely on my sense of colour and texture, but at times I cannot explain why I feel a certain way . . . I just know.'[7] Those with sufficient forecasting experience in a market they know well may be quite accurate in their intuitive forecasts. Unfortunately, it is often difficult for them to defend their forecasts against forecasts prepared by evidence-based methods when these forecasts differ. Nonetheless, the importance of experienced judgement in forecasting, whether it is used solely and intuitively or in concert with evidence-based methods, cannot be discounted.

Market tests

Market tests of various kinds are the last of the commonly used forecasting methods. Used largely for new products, market tests may be carried out under controlled experimental conditions in research laboratories, on the internet or in live test markets with real advertising and promotion and real distribution in real stores. In one sense, market tests are what lean start-ups are all about, albeit on a very small scale. In large companies, though, use of test markets has declined over the past few decades for three reasons:

- They are often expensive to carry out, since usually significant quantities of the new product must be produced and marketing activities of various kinds must be paid for;

- In today's data-intensive environment, especially for consumer products sold through supermarkets and mass merchants, competitors can buy the data collected through scanners at the checkout and learn the results of the test market without bearing the expense to conduct it;

- Competitors can engage in marketing tactics to mislead the company conducting the test, by increasing sampling programmes, offering large discounts or buy-one-get-one-free promotions, or otherwise distorting normal purchasing patterns in the category.

The coming of the internet has made possible a new kind of market test: an offer directly to consumers online, as we saw in Chapter 15, or through a crowdfunding campaign. Offers to chat rooms, interest groups or email lists of current customers are some of the approaches that are commonly tried. Entrepreneurs' use of such techniques will likely continue to increase, due to their ability to carry out such tests quickly and at low cost.

Mathematics entailed in forecasting

Regardless of the method used, the ultimate purpose of forecasting is to generate numbers that reflect what the entrepreneur believes is the most likely outcome – or sometimes a range of outcomes, under different assumptions – in terms of future market potential or for the sales of a product, a product line or a new venture. The combination of judgement and other methods often leads to the use of either of two mathematical approaches to determine the ultimate numbers: the chain ratio calculation or the use of indices. Boxes 16.2 and 16.3 offer examples of how to apply these mathematical approaches to arrive at sales forecasts.

---

box 16.2

Chain ratio forecast: trial of fresh pasta

Once Nesté's research on fresh pasta had been completed (see Box 16.1), it used the chain ratio method to calculate the total number of households that would try their fresh pasta. The chain ratio calculation went like this.

Research results for:	Data from research	Chain ratio calculation	Result
Number of households in target market	77.4 million		
Concept purchase intent: adjusted figure from Box 16.1	34.5% will try the product	77.4 million x 34.5%	26.7 million households will try if aware
Awareness adjustment: based on planned advertising level	48% will be aware of the product	26.7 million x 48%	12.8 million households will try if they find product at their store
Distribution adjustment: based on likely extent of distribution in supermarkets, given the introductory trade promotion plan	The product will obtain distribution reaching 70% of US households	12.8 million x 70%	9.0 million will try the product

Similar chain ratio logic is useful in a variety of forecasting settings.

Source: Based on Marie Bell and V. Kasturi Rangan, 1995, *Nestlé Refrigerated Foods: Contadina Pasta and Pizza*, Harvard Business School Publishing, Boston, MA.

---

box 16.3

Estimating market potential using indices

In most developed countries there are several published indices of buying behaviour, including the 'Annual Survey of Buying Power' published by *Sales and Marketing Management,* for the USA.

The buying power index (BPI) is a weighted sum of a geographical area's percentage of national buying power for the area, based on census income data (weight .5), plus the percentage of national retail sales for the area (weight .3), plus the percentage of national population located in the area (weight .2). If this calculation comes to 3.50 for a given state or region, one might expect 3.5 per cent of sales in a given category (toys, power tools or whatever) to come from that geographical area.

Category development indices (CDIs) are similar indices that report the ratio of consumption in a certain *category* (say, restaurant sales) to population in a defined geographical area. Trade associations or trade magazines relevant to the category typically publish such indices. Ratios greater than 1.0 for a particular geographic area, say metropolitan Manchester, indicate that the area does more business than average (compared to the country as a whole) in that category.

Brand development indices (BDIs) compare sales for a given *brand* (say, PizzaExpress restaurants) to population. Companies that use BDIs typically

> calculate them for their own use. The ratio of the BDI to the CDI for a given area is an indicator of how well a brand is doing, compared to its category overall, in that area.
>
> These various indices are useful for estimating market potential in defined geographic areas. They are, however, crude numbers, in that they do not consider differences in consumer behaviour from region to region. The CDI or BDI for snowmobiles in Austria is far higher than in Spain, for example. Attempting to rectify this imbalance by increasing the snowmobile advertising budget in Spain would be difficult!

Note that both mathematical approaches begin with some kind of an estimate of market potential (the number of households in the target market in Box 16.2; the national market potential for a product category in Box 16.3). The market potential is then multiplied by various fractional factors that, taken together, predict the portion of the overall market potential that one firm or product can expect to obtain. In Box 16.2, which shows the more detailed of the two approaches, the factors reflect the appeal of the product to consumers, as measured by marketing research data, and the company's planned marketing programme.

Cautions and caveats in forecasting

Keys to good forecasting

There are two important keys to improving the credibility and accuracy of forecasts of sales and market potential. The first of these is to make explicit the assumptions on which the forecast is based. This way, if there is debate or doubt about the forecast, then the assumptions can be debated and data to support the assumptions can be obtained. The resulting conversation is far more useful than stating opinions about whether the forecast is too high or too low.

The second key to effective forecasting is to use multiple methods. Where forecasts obtained by different methods converge near a common figure, greater confidence can be placed in that figure. Where forecasts obtained by multiple methods diverge, the assumptions inherent in each can be examined to determine which set of assumptions can best be trusted. Ultimately, however, entrepreneurs and especially investors should remember that any forecast is almost certainly wrong.

❝ entrepreneurs should remember that any forecast is almost certainly wrong ❞

Don't be silly: the problem with assumptions

We've just noted the importance of making any assumptions underlying a forecast explicit. Actually, there's an even bigger problem here: the presence of any 'assumptions' at all! Instead of assumptions, I'd rather you find real evidence to support the forecasts you make. So when you're playing with Excel in creating your forecasts, I suggest that each time you need to decide on an 'assumption' to use, stop in your tracks. Get out of the building and collect some real evidence, using the toolkit in Part 2 of this book, to support the number you're going to put into that cell. Investors, you should expect nothing less!

Biases in forecasting

Entrepreneurs should recognise several sources of potential bias in the forecasts they make. First, forecasts often fall prey to what Dan Lovallo and Daniel Kahneman call the planning fallacy, a tendency to base forecasts on delusional optimism rather than on a rational weighting of possible gains and losses and the probabilities thereof. They suggest, as an alternative, the systematic use of multiple analogues, using the actual outcomes of other similar offerings, laid out from best outcome to worst, then positioning the proposed project in that distribution.[8]

Second, capacity constraints are sometimes misinterpreted as forecasts. Someone planning to open a car wash that can process one car every seven minutes would probably be amiss in assuming sufficient demand to actually run at that rate all the time. A restaurant chain that hopes to turn its tables twice each night, on average, must still do local market research in order to ascertain how much volume a new restaurant will really produce. Obviously, putting similar 30-table restaurants in two different trade areas with different population make-up and density with different levels of competition will result in different sales levels.

Finally, unstated but implicit assumptions can overstate a well-intentioned forecast. While 34.5 per cent of those surveyed (after adjustments, as shown in Box 16.1) may indicate their willingness to buy a new grocery product, such as fresh pasta, for such a forecast to pan out requires that consumers are

❝ entrepreneurs should not assume 100 per cent awareness and distribution coverage ❞

actually made aware of the new product when it is introduced, and that the product can actually be found on supermarket shelves. In forecasting the likely sales of consumer goods and others to be marketed on the internet or through distribution channels, entrepreneurs should not assume 100 per cent awareness and distribution coverage.

Actual awareness and distribution levels should be estimated based on the planned marketing programme for the product and factored into the forecast via the chain ratio method (see again Box 16.2). The difficulty in doing so with any degree of certainty is one of the reasons why many investors in early-stage companies view forecasts built in bottom-up fashion, or those based on close analogues, as more credible than other approaches.[9]

If you've been using your *New Business Road Test* app as you've read this book, you may want to make note there of the forecasts you prepare. Your forecast of market potential will be useful for assessing the macro-market domains. Your forecast of your sales in the first or early years will be useful in considering the economic sustainability of your business model in the micro-industry domains.

17

Have you got what it takes?[1]

These days, it seems, almost everyone fancies being an entrepreneur, if not today, sometime in the not-too-distant future. If you're reading this book you are probably among them. As you ponder your aspirations to become an entrepreneur, or as an early-stage investor you consider whether an entrepreneur you might back 'has what it takes', you might want to give some thought to the surprising and not simply *unconventional* – but somewhat *counter-*conventional – ways in which these characters we call entrepreneurs behave and the ways in which entrepreneurial minds typically work.

Over the better part of twenty years, I've worked closely with hundreds of entrepreneurs and studied more than 40 of them in considerable depth. More often than not, I find, they exhibit six ways of thinking and acting that lie at the very heart of their entrepreneurial endeavors.

'Yes, we can'

Sao Paolo's Arnold Correia had a dilemma.[2] His small company had been producing events – sales conferences, motivational events, campaign launches and more – for some of Brazil's fastest growing companies during Brazil's economic renaissance in the mid-1990s. At an event for Walmart, the company that had been hired alongside Correia's company to produce a video of the event failed to show up, so Correia was asked if he could do it. 'Sure, we can,' was his reply, though he'd neither shot nor edited a video in his life. Correia frantically began calling his friends to find someone who could record the video. 'Forty minutes later,' he recalls, 'I found someone who could help, but in the strangest place. I had to pick him up at the cemetery, as it was the Day of the Dead, a Christian holiday in Brazil,

> **'Sure, we can,' was his reply, though he'd neither shot nor edited a video in his life.**

which commemorated the faithful departed.'[3] Video production soon became a key element in Correia's core offering.

In 2004, following a visit to the United States, Correia spotted an opportunity to produce and distribute training and other video content for his increasingly far-flung multi-location retail clients. Doing so, however, meant not just producing video content, something his ten-person team had learned how to do; it would also require mastering satellite distribution of video content, sending staff to install video equipment all over Brazil, and making a considerable investment. Correia's staff wondered whether he'd hit his head on something during his trip to the USA, and posed all kinds of reasons why a move into 'corporate TV' was simply too risky. Once again, Correia's view was simple. 'Yes, we can.' And, they did.

Several years later, after the global financial crisis which very nearly put his company under, in 2009 Correia realised that being a 'cost' to his customers wasn't good enough. 'I want to be part of the revenue for my customers,' he recalled.[4] The way to do so, he decided, was to produce and distribute customer-oriented content to be broadcast to his retailers' selling areas, which, when interspersed with ads, would generate advertising revenue that could be shared with his retail store clients. 'Yes, we can' produced copious amounts of suitable content. 'Yes, we can' learn to sell in-store advertising to advertising and media agencies, something his company had never done before. 'Yes, we can' licence additional content to fill the schedules. Correia's business was completely reinvented yet again. Today, his business, Atmo Digital Media, is one of Brazil's largest digital out-of-home media companies with some 18,000 screens in more than 1,000 'points of sale', like retail stores, and 'points of wait', like doctor's offices and fitness centres.

'Yes, we can,' when you've never done something before isn't just unconventional thinking. It runs counter to conventional managerial wisdom which holds that one should 'stick to one's knitting'[5] and only pursue opportunities for which the necessary competencies[6] are in hand. Not so for entrepreneurs like Arnold Correia. First they say, 'Yes, we can.' Then they figure out how.

Beg, borrow or steal

In 2009, Toronto's Mimi Naghizada was planning her wedding.[7] In preparation for the wedding, she started thinking about how she wanted to style her hair. She decided that she wanted to use hair extensions – something becoming increasingly popular with both celebrities and her friends. However, after going to the local mall with her sister Leyla, she came home quite frustrated. While she found hair extensions, she was not able to find what she was looking for. The amount included in any one package was not quite right; one $150 package was not going to be enough, but she didn't really need the full second pack. The colour selection was also really limited, and the quality was not what she had expected. She had then gone online to see whether there was anything better she could order. There wasn't.

Her fiancé, Alex Ikonn, had been looking for an opportunity to start his own business. 'Is this an opportunity the two of us should pursue?' he wondered. Ikonn had already gained some digital marketing and social media experience working in a start-up, so starting an online business seemed the right way to go. 'But what about resources,' he asked. He logged onto Alibaba.com and found Chinese manufacturers who could supply the hair extensions, and would do so in the package sizes and colours that Alex and Mimi thought the market wanted. He found a logistics provider who would receive, hold and ship the goods to consumers. He found an e-commerce template with which he could build a rudimentary website that could display the hair extensions and process orders. And, thanks to the offers that seemed to arrive weekly in his mailbox, he even found most of the money he needed to pay for the first shipment from China via credit card offers of new accounts with six months' free interest on cash advances.

'We've got six months to make this work,' he said to Mimi as he boldly ordered $20,000 worth of hair extensions. Meanwhile, Mimi began building a following on YouTube with a series of videos addressing hair styling questions which women were typing into their Google search boxes.

By 2016, a mere six years on, Mimi's videos had been viewed by some 3 million loyal subscribers, and their company, Luxy Hair, was selling millions of dollars' worth of hair extensions annually, with a workforce of only four employees. In many companies, the unspoken assumption underlying any new product or new market initiative is that the requisite resources should be rare, valuable, inimitable and owned and controlled, not borrowed.[8] Though the Ikonns didn't really beg (Well, OK, they did ask Alex's Mom for some start-up funding, to supplement their credit card funding), nor steal, in essence they 'borrowed' (and continue to borrow) virtually every resource they needed – from factory to warehouse to cash and more – to start and grow what is has become a thriving business.

Think narrow, not broad

In August of 2007, Brian Chesky and Joe Gebbia (whom we also met briefly in Chapter 12) were struggling to come up with the rent soon due on their San Francisco apartment.[9] Drawing on the 'creativity can solve problems' mantra they'd learned in college, they came up with an idea that might solve their cash crunch. A large design conference was coming to town, and San Francisco's hotels were booked solid. Chesky recalls, 'We thought we could make some money if we rented out our place and turned it into a bed and breakfast. We got three airbeds and created a website called Air Bed and Breakfast. People signed up to rent the airbeds, and we cooked them breakfast every morning and acted like tour guides.'[10]

Of course, the design conference wasn't the only such event headed their way, so over the next few months, they repeated the process, targeting conferences for which San Francisco's hotel capacity was insufficient. Conferences, nothing else, were their target, met by booking their own airbeds as well as spare rooms and couches of others they commandeered. Sometimes they had success, sometimes not, as getting the word out proved difficult. In early 2008, a much larger and more visible conference was looming, the Democratic National Convention in Denver, at which 100,000 people were expected to attend, putting a strain on Denver's 30,000-room supply of accommodation. Perhaps this was an opportunity to turn their fledgling venture into something more, they thought.

❝ Conferences, nothing else, were their target, ❞

To make a long story short, a quirky stunt, in which they bought 500 boxes of Cheerios, packaged as 'Obama O's', and sold them at $40 per box, and another 500 boxes of another cereal packaged as 'Cap'n McCain's' (though these boxes didn't sell very well to the Democratic crowd!), got Gebbia an interview on CNN. That interview, together with lots of publicity that getting a hotel room in Denver was practically impossible, began putting their still-fledgling company, Airbnb, on the map.

In 2009, the duo managed to get accepted into the winter cohort at the elite business accelerator Y Combinator. Venture capital funding soon followed, and the business widened its previously narrow focus on conference-goers to travellers worldwide. The rest, of course, is history. By 2017, Airbnb had more than 3 million listings in nearly 200 countries and was valued at more than $50 billion. Its founders' narrow focus on conferences in the company's early days had enabled it to build a beach-head and a small platform from which it could grow.

In many of today's established companies, opportunities to serve narrow markets such as conference attendees are handily rejected. 'Too small; won't move the needle,' they say.[11] But an incredibly narrow target market at the outset – one that would scarcely have 'moved the needle' for a larger company – has served Airbnb very well.

Problem-first, not product-first logic

Far too often I hear this from aspiring entrepreneurs. 'My new idea is to sell Product X to Customer Y.' Not so fast. The much more important question is whether Customer Y has a compelling problem that Product X can resolve. Consider Mexico's Simon Cohen, who in 1996, fresh out of university, was working to build up the international side of his family's textile business.[12] But he had a problem. 'The service from the freight forwarding company was very poor. My first order was sending 14 cubic meters of goods to Costa Rica. We didn't know anything about timing because they didn't keep us updated, the goods got damaged, and we hadn't been advised about insurance, so we lost money. This company had been recommended to us, but it was terrible. I tried 10 others, but they were all bad.'[13]

Cohen reasoned that other importers and exporters must be struggling with similar service issues, and he wondered whether doing freight forwarding better might be an opportunity to do something independent from what the rest of the family was doing and solve a real problem, too. After an introduction to two Germans who owned a freight forwarding business in Mexico City, Cohen began learning the ropes and, using his sales skills and his network, he soon secured four shipments to handle. He then proposed to the Germans to set up a joint venture in Monterrey to do what the Germans were doing in Mexico City.

From the beginning, Cohen focused on differentiating through quality service. He did not strive to be the cheapest freight forwarder, but aimed to offer the best service. Providing information was key; this involved keeping customers updated on the status and location of their shipments. Cohen worked hard to keep on top of developments: 'In the early days, I took advantage of the time differences across the world. Each night, I set my alarm for 2 AM, and spent an hour or so replying to emails, to give instructions to the shipping lines, talk to my agents, get cargo updates, and let customers know where their goods were. Then I would go back to sleep until the morning. For shipments from China, this meant I gained a day.'[14]

Cohen's quest to offer superior service played out in a variety of ways. For one, a shipping line would typically charge 'demurrage' fees for its containers, starting from seven days after arrival at the port. This meant that the customer needed to unload and return the container to port as quickly as possible. Anticipating that there could be delays during a shipment's inland phase, Cohen negotiated with carriers a longer period in which its customers could unload their containers. He was often able to push the deadline back to 15 days – sometimes even 28 days – after arrival, potentially saving his customers thousands of dollars in fees. He also provided a service whereby clients could leave empty containers in the destination city, rather than paying for their return to port. He would usually fill the container with exporters' goods for the return journey. This saved the customer approximately 40 per cent of inland freight costs.

By solving importers' and exporters' problem of poor service, Cohen's company, Henco Logistics, has grown to become one of Mexico's largest freight forwarders and is expanding its presence across Latin America. Solve genuine problems and your business will thrive! As the prominent venture capital investor Vinod Khosla famously remarked, 'To me, any big problem is a big opportunity. It's very simple. Nobody will pay you to solve a non-problem.'[15]

‟Nobody will pay you to solve a non-problem”

'No' is something waiting to be turned into 'Yes'

Thomas Knobel had shown entrepreneurial tendencies since he was a child, having sold fresh eggs to his Swiss neighbours, even selling his toys while on family vacations to earn pocket money.[16] While in college in the USA, he decided to put to work the fruits of a study he and a classmate had done on the phone card industry. He bought a vending machine and filled it with phone cards, after having made a deal with a Florida-based carrier which would carry the calls. One week later, his supplier went bankrupt and the phone cards stopped working!

Knobel was devastated, having poured all his savings into the new venture. His supplier's lawyer told him he was at the back of the queue and would never get his money back. Desperate to survive, Knobel remembered a lesson one of his American classmates had taught him about the value of persistence. 'No' is something waiting to be turned into 'Yes'. He began a campaign. Every day, he left at least one voicemail message on every phone at his supplier's offices. 'Nobody was answering their phone. I would call and leave a message on extension 101, and then I'd call back and dial extension 102, until there were no more extensions to dial. It was a fight for survival,' he recalled. His calls became increasingly emotional. 'I'm a student. I have no money. You've taken away my business. I hope your sons and daughters aren't ever treated in this way.'[17] After only a week, the lawyer called back and said Knobel would receive his money if he stopped the voicemails. His money was returned.

In much of today's business world, there are processes for this, procedures and systems for that, and for good reason, too. Eventually, even the most successful entrepreneurial ventures must be 'professionalised'.[18] But the best entrepreneurs, for better or worse, often simply cut to the chase. For them, breaking the rules of 'how things are normally done' is part of the landscape and 'No' is not an acceptable answer. They find a way to turn 'No' into 'Yes'.

> **❝But the best entrepreneurs simply cut to the chase❞**

Ask for the cash and ride the float

In the fourth quarter of 2007, the global financial crisis suddenly landed with a thud on the desk of Rud Browne, a Vancouver-based entrepreneur who'd built a thriving business dealing in used and refurbished mobile computing devices.[19] These devices, like the ones every FedEx driver carries or your local supermarket clerk uses to reorder more groceries, go through technology cycles, with old versions and their accompanying software regularly being updated to newer-faster-better versions.

Browne's insight was simple. Not everyone wanted the newer-faster-better model. If a company operated a fleet that was growing, for example, thereby requiring additional devices, sometimes what they wanted was more of the 'old' devices, rather than having to upgrade the entire fleet to the new model and the software and systems that went with it. So his company, Ryzex, would buy outdated equipment when companies upgraded – for a song, as it was no longer needed by its previous owners – and refurbish and resell it to companies who needed it – for a premium price, of course, as Ryzex was typically the only source that could provide the discontinued model.

Browne financed his company's growth by asking for 90-day terms when he bought no-longer-needed equipment and by getting his customers to pay him on delivery, even sometimes in advance. Riding the float between when he received his customers' payment and when he paid his suppliers enabled Ryzex, with no outside investment, to reach $75 million in revenue, with five offices around the world and 360 employees. When economic confidence stalls, however, IT spending is the canary in the gold mine. Thus, when the crisis hit, companies stopped upgrading their IT, and Ryzex's sales and margins took a hit.

> **❝IT spending is the canary in the gold mine❞**

Browne sprang into action, further improving his already impressive business model. He switched his maintenance contracts from monthly and paid in arrears to annually, paid in advance. He suggested that customers buying new systems (which Ryzex was also offering by then) lease them, at historically low financing rates, rather than buying. This meant he'd get paid by the leasing company in 72 hours, but he wouldn't have to pay the vendor that made the gear for 45 or 60 days. These and other tactics enabled Ryzex to weather the storm. Despite a fall of 25 per cent in sales and 50 per cent in margin dollars, Ryzex went from having $3 million in debt to a $6 million cash surplus in just 17 months.

Does riding the float by getting paid on delivery (or even in advance) and paying suppliers on generous terms make more sense than giving up a stake in your business to access investment capital or relying on bankers with their covenants? Surely, it does. And it's vastly cheaper capital, too![20]

So, what about you?

The good news is that great entrepreneurs are almost always made, not born. If you are an aspiring entrepreneur, that means you too can learn from the lessons of this chapter. Just as Arnold Correia learned to repeatedly do what his company had not done before, and Thomas Knobel learned from a college classmate the power of persistence, so too can you learn to think and act like an entrepreneur. Can you too do new things and assemble – but not bother to own – the resources you'll need, and not take 'No' for an answer? Can you find a narrow target market having a compelling problem you can solve? Can you 'ride the float' and use your customers' funding to start or grow, as did Rud Browne, and as we explored in Chapter 12? Yes, you can!

18

Getting help with your road test

There you have it. Ten chapters of what you as an entrepreneur or a thoughtful investor need to know to road test an idea for a new venture (or otherwise, for that matter!), and seven chapters of hands-on tools and ways of thinking and acting to help you get the job done. The good news is that, as an entrepreneur, you are not alone, not with 2 million others in the UK, another 10 million in the USA, and similarly large numbers wherever else you may be, doing like-wise. There's plenty of company for early-stage investors, too, thanks to the burgeoning number of business angel networks all over the world.

But if you haven't yet built your entrepreneurial team or found some like-minded angel investors, road testing an idea can seem like a lonely task. Fortunately, there are lots of places to network with others on similar paths – people in the throes of testing an idea for a new business, getting a business started or working to get their growth curve pointing skywards.

A good place to start looking for someone to accompany you on your seven domains journey is on the internet, where communities of start-up aficiona-dos, bloggers and early-stage investors are building networks, some of them global in scope.[1]

For more hands-on support, every summer the entrepreneurship faculty at the London Business School runs an Entrepreneurship Summer School, where several dozen participants from around the world come to work on their new business ideas, each under the guidance of a mentor from the school's exten-sive entrepreneurial network. There are summer programmes of various kinds at other schools, too. For those who would like to travel the road in the com-pany of others on similar journeys, this is a good way to do it if the season fits. For details of suitable programmes for you, check the websites of the leading business schools.

In whatever manner you carry out your own road test, know that you'll have plenty of company. Tens of thousands of readers of this book's four previous editions have travelled this path before you. For many, the road test has put the brakes on a venture that was found to be fatally flawed, saving countless weeks or months of time – precious time for entrepreneurs – not to mention the money that would likely have been wasted. Time that those same entrepreneurs could then spend putting their efforts into ideas that *could* fly. Time that, with hard work and perhaps a little luck, just might lead to a thriving venture that employs others, that brings business to suppliers and that delivers great solutions to customers to resolve their pain. Tomorrow's new jobs depend on people like them – and like you – because it's the community of entrepreneurs who drive the engine of economic development. Whether you are an entrepreneur or an early-stage investor making it possible for someone's start-up to launch or to grow, you're on a noble and exciting path. May your journey be a fulfilling one!

Appendix
Research methodology

As a three-time entrepreneur with a win, a loss and a draw to my name, I've long been curious about what was for me a burning question: what is it that makes the difference between new ventures that succeed and those that fail? Eventually, I grew curious enough about this question that I moved on from my 20-year business career, went back to school to earn a PhD and began teaching and learning about entrepreneurship in a more systematic way. Not having to fight the daily fires I'd fought as an entrepreneur gave me the time to think carefully about this question, and working with bright MBA students and entrepreneurs still in the trenches challenged my thinking further.

In 2000, while on sabbatical at the London Business School, one of the world's top institutions in the teaching, research and practice of entrepreneurship and a remarkably entrepreneurial place in its own right, and amid the unravelling of the dot.com boom, I undertook an extensive effort to shed new light on my question. I began my research with a careful reading of the varied literature that had something to say about opportunity assessment – literature in entrepreneurship, strategic management, marketing, finance and economics. What had the world's best academic minds learned about what makes an opportunity a good one? I then formulated a series of open-ended questions that I would ask of experienced venture capital investors and serial entrepreneurs, people who, in my judgement, must be skilled at the opportunity assessment task out of necessity. In their lines of work, assessing opportunity poorly would lead quickly to failure. Their real-world perspective was essential, I knew.

I then conducted a series of qualitative interviews – typically ranging in duration between one and two hours and based on the research methodology described in Chapter 11 – with 24 serial entrepreneurs and venture capital investors in the USA and the UK – from Cambridge and London to Silicon Valley in California. My research assistants and I prepared transcripts of the interviews and analysed the results. As a final check, I then discussed and debated the results with my London Business School colleagues and others.

Finally, I provided a draft of my conclusions to a subset of those I had interviewed, and asked two questions: 'What's wrong, inaccurate or incomplete here?' and 'What, if anything, do my findings add to what people who start or fund new ventures already know?'

The key result of this research was the seven domains model that makes up the intellectual and pragmatic core of this book. To make the seven domains come alive, I worked with a talented former student – now a successful businesswoman in her own right – to identify examples of companies whose stories would show how the seven domains play out in practice. Researching these companies completed the analysis. These case histories bring the seven domains to life far better than my own words ever could.

Then, in 2005, 2009, and again in 2013, I revisited the book and its case histories, bringing all of the companies' stories up to date. In 2013 I also linked the book's focus on opportunity assessment and its seven domains model to some of the emerging literature that was changing the face of entrepreneurial practice, much as the first edition of this book did a decade earlier. That literature, characterised herein as the lean start-up movement (or approach, methodology, mindset, or some other suitable noun) has more or less finished the job of demolishing the idea that the business plan is the centerpiece of entrepreneurial thought and practice. And appropriately so. Where and how, I wondered, does a seven domains analysis fit into this new lean start-up culture? The fourth edition delivered the answer.

Taking things one step further in this fifth edition, I've again updated the case histories, of course, and dropped a few of them. Significantly, I've also added a handful of compelling new ones to bring this edition bang up to date and to reflect the digital and online nature of the ventures which many of this book's readers will be working on. And because I've found over the years that many early-stage investors use the seven domains framework as a guide to their investment decisions, I've placed additional emphasis on the investor's perspective in nearly every chapter in Part 1 of this fifth edition. A new subtitle reflects this emphasis.

As readers might imagine, my colleagues and I – and a growing number of entrepreneurship faculties around the world – regularly use the seven domains model in our business school classrooms, most notably in the Entrepreneurship Summer School at the London Business School. There we help a typical group of 60 aspiring entrepreneurs each summer put their ideas through the seven domains tests, under the guidance of mentors from the school's global entrepreneurial community (see www.london.edu/summer_school for more information). We've also used the model in executive programmes in the venture capital and private equity industries on five continents, and found that it consistently opens eyes. Markets and industries really *are* different, and that difference matters. Both macro and micro levels merit careful scrutiny. Entrepreneurs can't be assessed adequately by simply reading their CVs or examining their character and entrepreneurial drive. The model is comprehensive, yet simple and parsimonious. It not only helps an entrepreneur or early stage investor assess opportunities, but develop and shape them, too. It is straightforward to understand and apply. It captures the key elements of opportunity attractiveness. And it works to answer the aspiring entrepreneur's most fundamental question: why will or won't my idea work?

Entrepreneurs and others who've used the seven domains framework have also discovered that it serves as a useful diagnostic check-up at virtually any point in a growing company's history. It's a good way to see what's changed in the environment in which the business operates, what hasn't, and whether any of the assumptions that have guided the business need to be altered or updated.

As luck would have it, the model also works to provide new insights into investors' own portfolios and the patterns inherent in their portfolios' successes and failures. Are angel investors and venture capitalists serial mistake-makers, the victims of recurring patterns of errors that make their overall success dependent on the one or two in ten investments that hit the big time? Or are other patterns at work? There's much yet to learn!

Notes

Chapter 1

1   Quoted in 'Venture capital has gone from one unreality to another', *Knowledge at Wharton,* http://knowledge.wharton.upenn.edu/
2   For those interested in reading more about what makes for a successful entrepreneur, see Chapter 2 in David A. Kirby, 2002, *Entrepreneurship,* McGraw-Hill, Maidenhead.
3   See Steven Gary Blank, 2005, *The Four Steps to the Epiphany,* Quad/Graphics, Wisconsin; and Eric Ries, 2011, *The Lean Startup,* Crown Business, New York.
4   We distinguish between *market* opportunities – those brought about by the confluence of market and competitive factors – and *financial* opportunities, such as those where arbitrage or underpriced assets provide the primary basis for economic gain.
5   The short blocks of italicised text in this and subsequent chapters are quotations from the interviews that make up the research on which this book is based.
6   Such environmental assessments are explained in further detail in the environmental analysis chapter of any textbook on marketing management, such as Chapter 3 in H. Boyd, O. Walker, J. Mullins and J.-C. Larréché, 2005, *Marketing Management: A Strategic Decision Making Approach,* McGraw-Hill/Irwin, Burr Ridge, IL.
7   A useful process for discovering what customers really want and will pay for is provided in *The Four Steps to the Epiphany* (see note 3).
8   For more on real options, see Avinash K. Dixit and Robert S. Pindyck, 1995, 'The options approach to capital investment', *Harvard Business Review,* May–June; and Rita Gunther McGrath, 1999, 'Falling forward: real options reasoning and entrepreneurial failure', *Academy of Management Review,* January.
9   For details on how to conduct a five forces analysis, see Michael Porter, 1979, 'How competitive forces shape strategy', *Harvard Business Review,* March–April.
10 For more detail on these ideas, see the chapter on resources and capabilities in any strategic management textbook, such as Chapter 5 in R.M. Grant, 2004, *Contemporary Strategy Analysis,* Blackwell, Oxford.
11 For more on operating cash cycle characteristics and their impact on a firm's ability to grow, see Neil C. Churchill and John W. Mullins, 2001, 'How fast can your company afford to grow?', *Harvard Business Review,* May.
12 For a systematic process for getting from plan A to plan B, see John Mullins and Randy Komisar, 2009, *Getting to Plan B: Breaking Through to a Better Business Model,* Harvard Business Press, Boston.
13 For some better approaches to getting a new venture started – after conducting a seven domains analysis of the opportunity, of course! – see Mullins and Komisar (see note 12) and Eric Ries (see note 3).
14 See note 3.

Chapter 2

1   Peter Drucker, 1967, *The Effective Executive,* Harper & Row, New York, p. 53.
2   Danny Bradbury, 2001, 'WAP could get a shot in the arm from iMode', *Computer Weekly,* 1 February, p. 46.
3   Figures from Census of Japan, http://jin.jcic.or.jp/stat/index.html
4   Yaeko Mitsumori, 2000, 'NTT's iMode paves the way for wireless data services', *Radio Communications Report,* 28 February, p. 108.
5   Preliminary FY1999 Statistics on Telecommunications Market in Japan, Telecommunications Carrier Association, 31 August, 2000, p. 5.
6   www.nua.ie/surveys/?f=VS&art_id=905357352&rel=true
7   Bien Perez, 2000, 'DoCoMo boosts iMode reach; Japanese mobile operator exports version of home services while moving to create fit with partners' systems', *South China Morning Post,* 12 December.
8   See note 4.
9   Catherine Ong, 2000, 'iMode a success thanks to HTML', *Business Times (Singapore),* 10 June.
10   'Why i-Mode is successful in Japan', www.nttdocomo.com/html/imode02_4.html
11   Clive Keyte, 2001, 'Learn mobile lessons from Japanese', *Computer Weekly,* 9 August, p. 18.
12   Jamie Smyth, 2000, 'I-mode set to take Europe by storm', *Irish Times,* 6 October.
13   *Communications Today,* 2000, 'Wireless industry prospers, except 3G, execs say at Wireless 2000', 29 February.
14   See note 11.
15   *ISP Business News,* 2001, 'Japan's NTT turns i-Mode toward American markets', 28 May.
16   *Japanese News Digest,* 2004, 'Japan NTT DoCoMo I-Mode Service Overseas Subscribers at 3.0 Mln End-June 2004', 12 July.
17   See note 17.
18   Kevin J. O'Brien, 2007, 'Forerunner of mobile Internet, i-mode is fading in Europe', *New York Times,* 17 July. DOCOMO announcement reported on https://www .telegeography.com/products/commsupdate/articles/2016/11/04/docomo-to-phaseout-i-mode-phones-by-year-end/, accessed 13 January 2017
19   Greg Farrell, 1994, 'Lite weight no longer', *Brandweek,* 31 October, p. 18.
20   Fran Brock, 1985, 'Brewers need drinkers for their low-alcohol beer', *AdWeek,* 18 March.
21   Stratford Sherman, 1985, 'America's new abstinence', *Fortune,* 18 March, p. 20.
22   Figures from 'Population and housing characteristics of baby boomers 26 to 44 years old: 1990', http://www.census.gov/population/censusdata/cph-1-160h.txt
23   Bart Barnes, 1983, 'Survey indicates sports play a major role in our lives', *Washington Post,* 16 March.
24   William Oscar Johnson, 1988, 'Sports and suds: the beer business and the sports world have brewed up a potent partnership', *Sports Illustrated,* 8 August, p. 68.
25   See note 21.
26   Tony Schwartz, 1981, 'Light beer ad can be heavy work', *New York Times,* 10 December.
27   Mike Littwin, 1985, 'They're all-stars at play; the mood is light; the product is lite; results are heavy', *Los Angeles Times,* 4 February.
28   'Shakeout in the brewery industry', http://www.beerhistory.com/library/holdings/ shakeout.shtml
29   See note 26.

30   Robert E. O'Neill, 1986, 'No stopping the light brigade (1986 supermarket sales manual – beer and wine)', *Progressive Grocer,* July, p. 49.

31   James E. Causey, 1997, 'Nation's beer drinkers see the light', *Milwaukee Journal Sentinel,* 1 June.

32   The Top 20 Top Selling Domestic Beers, HuffPost Food, 2 April 2013, http://www.huffingtonpost.com/2012/09/03/top-selling-domestic-beers_n_1846582.htmlslide=1454255

33   Brewers Association, 'Small and Independent Brewers Continue to Grow Double Digits', 22 March 2016, https://www.brewersassociation.org/press-releases/small-independent-brewers-continue-grow-double-digits/, accessed 27 January 2017.

34   Dave Infante, 'The Great Craft Beer Sellout', *Thrillist,* 13 October 2016, https://www.thrillist.com/drink/nation/craft-breweries-selling-out-big-beer-companies, accessed 27 January 2017.

35   Scott Cendrowski, 'China's New Craft-Beer Bully', *Fortune,* 15 March 2017, pp 90–96.

36   Information on Nike's case study was taken from the Nike, Inc. website at http://www.nike.com/nikebiz

37   Geraldine E. Willigan, 1992, 'High-performance marketing: an interview with Nike's Phil Knight', *Harvard Business Review,* July–August.

38   Kristin Kovacich, 2012, 'Why Nike's a Model Digital Brand', 6 September. http://www.digiday.com/agencies/why-nikes-a-model-digital-brand/

39   'Nike Soho Debuts the Future of Sport Retail', *Business Wire,* 9 November 2016, http://www.businesswire.com/news/home/20161109006188/en/Nike-Soho-Debuts-Future-Sport-Retail, accessed 13 January 2017.

40   Phil Knight, *Shoe Dog: A Memoir by the Creator of Nike,* 2016, Scribner, New York.

41   NIKE, Inc. Reports Fiscal 2016 Fourth Quarter and Full Year Results. 28 June 2016. http://news.nike.com/news/nike-inc-reports-fiscal-2016-fourth-quarter-and-full-year-results, accessed 13 January 2017.

42   http://www.usna.com/news_pubs/publications/shipmate/2000/2000_04/brides.htm

43   *Business Wire,* 1999, 'OurBeginning.com revolutionizes wedding invitation industry with launch of first complete online sales and services site', 12 April.

44   Kathleen Kelleher, 2001, 'Birds and bees; so there are more single people, but it's still a couple's world', *Los Angeles Times,* 12 February.

45   'Communications and information technology', statistical abstract for the USA, http://www.census.gov/prod/2001pubs/statab/sec18.pdf

46   Nancy Pfister, 1999, 'Marketing the frou-frou to growlin' football fans', *Industry Wrapups,* 3 December.

47   Ellen Zavian, 2000, 'Women score first down as Super Bowl ads debut', *Brandmarketing,* February.

48   *Business Wire,* 2000, 'OurBeginning.com reports record quarter following Super Bowl XXXIV debut', 25 May.

49   Traffic figures in this paragraph are from Neilsen/NetRatings survey, as reported in Greg Farrell, 'Bailing out from the Super Bowl ad binge', 2000, *USA Today,* 7 June.

50   Barnet D. Wolf, 2000, 'Money can't buy name recognition on the internet', *Columbus Dispatch,* 11 June, p. 1H.

51   See note 52.

52   See note 47.

53   See note 52.

54   Kim Girard, 2002, 'Crash and learn', *Business 2.0,* June.

55   Jeffrey D. Zbar, 2001, 'Marketing agencies have learned how to handle Dot-Com phenomenon', *Sun-Sentinel,* 19 January.

56   See note 50.

57   Sandeep Junnarker, 2000, '"Dot Coms" look to score from Super Bowl ads', CNET News.com, 21 January, http://www.news.com.com/2100-1017-235943.html

Chapter 3

1   William Shakespeare, *Julius Caesar,* Act IV, Scene iii.

2   Miguel Helft, The Wizard of Apps: How Jeff Lawson Built Twilio into the Mightiest Unicorn, *Forbes,* 14 September 2016, at http://www.forbes.com/sites/miguelhelft/2016/09/14/the-wizard-of-apps-how-jeff-lawson-turned-twilio-into-the-mightiest-unicorn/#4f508e3ccbf7, accessed 23 January 2017.

3   Bruce Rogers, 'Jeff Lawson's Twilio Disrupts Telecom Industry', *Forbes,* August 12, 2013, http://www.forbes.com/sites/brucerogers/2013/08/12/jeff-lawsons-twilio-disrupts-telecom-industry/#67072bf03dc6, accessed 15 December 2016.

4   http://www.phonemyphone.com/

5   See note 2.

6   Om Malik, 'From Zero to Half a Billion: CEO Jeff Lawson Writes the Perfect Story for Twilio', *Gigaom,* 8 June 2013, https://gigaom.com/2013/06/08/from-zero-to-half-a-billion-ceo-jeff-lawson-writes-the-perfect-story-for-twilio/, accessed 23 January 2017.

7   Heather Clancy, 'Why Voice and Messaging Specialist Twilio Thinks Communications Should "Disappear"', *Fortune,* 4 May 2015, http://fortune.com/2015/05/04/twilio-customer-conversations/, accessed 15 December 2016.

8   Nick Hughes, 'Why Twilio Will Kill AT&T', *So Entrepreneurial,* 5 January 2012, https://soentrepreneurial.com/2012/01/05/why-twilio-will-kill-att/, accessed 24 January 2017.

9   Heather Clancy, 'Why Voice and Messaging Specialist Twilio Thinks Communications Should "Disappear"', *Fortune,* 4 May 2015, http://fortune.com/2015/05/04/twilio-customer-conversations/, accessed 15 December 2016.

10   Om Malik, 'Got a Twilio-Based App? Get Some Investment Dollars', *Gigaom,* 23 September 2010, https://gigaom.com/2010/09/23/got-a-twilio-based-app-get-some-investment-dollars/, accessed 24 January 2017.

11   Nick Hughes, 'Why Twilio Will Kill AT&T', *So Entrepreneurial,* 5 January 2012, https://soentrepreneurial.com/2012/01/05/why-twilio-will-kill-att/, accessed 24 January 2017.

12   See note 2.

13   See note 2.

14   Timothy Green, 'Why Twilio Stock Crashed 47% in October', 9 November 2016, http://www.fool.com/investing/2016/11/09/why-twilio-stock-crashed-47-in-october.aspx, accessed 23 January 2017.

15   Twilio, Inc., https://www.google.com/search?q=twilio+stock+price&ie=utf-8&oe=utf-8&client=firefox-b, accessed 24 January 2017.

16   Barry Janoff, 1999, 'Supermarkets go au naturel', *Progressive Grocer,* vol. 78, issue 3, p. 75.

17   Dennis Roth, 2000, 'America's fascination with nutrition', *Food Review,* January–April, p. 32.

18   S.C. Gwynne, 1998, 'Thriving on health food' *Time,* http://www.time.com/time/archive/preview/0,10987,987856,00.html

19   http://www.wholefoodsmarket.com/products/list_preparedfoods.html

20   Steve Dwyer, 1997, 'The right prescription for maturing', *Prepared Foods,* February, p. 12.

21   Buck Jones, 'Deli update 1997', *Progressive Grocer,* vol. 76, issue 4, p. 131.

22   See note 35.

23   Press release, 2012, 'Consumer-driven U.S. organic market surpasses $31 billion in 2011', 23 April. http://www.organicnewsroom.com/2012/04/us_consumerdriven_organic_mark.html

24   http://www.wholefoodsmarket.com/investor/AR00_letter.html

25   Erin Kelly, 2000, 'Health-food chains spar for baby boomers', *Fortune,* 3 April, p. 56.

26   Chairman's Letter, 2008 Annual Report, http://www.wholefoodsmarket.com/company/pdfs/ar08_letter.pdf; and Rachel Wharton, 2008, 'Whole Food tries to shake "whole paycheck" image with free value tours', *NY Daily News,* 8 August.

27   'Whole Foods quarterly sales hold up, shares soar', 25 July 2012. http://www.reuters.com/article/2012/07/25/us-wholefoods-results-idUSBRE86O1O520120725

28   '365 by Whole Foods zeros in on Millennial organic shoppers'. 21 August 2015, http://www.mintel.com/blog/food-market-news/365-by-whole-foods-zeros-in-on-millennial-organic-shoppers, accessed 15 January 2017.

29   *Reading Post,* 2012, 'Pride of Reading Entrepreneur Award', Reading Post, 29 November. http://www.getreading.co.uk/news/special_features/pride_of_reading/s/2124864_pride_of_reading_entrepreneur_award; http://en.wikipedia.org/wiki/Ella's_Kitchen; http://www.ellaskitchen.com/; Jon Yeomans, 'Ella's Kitchen sold to US giant Hain Celestial', *The Grocer,* 3 May 2013, http://www.thegrocer.co.uk/companies/ellas-kitchen-sold-to-us-giant-hain-celestial/343012.article

30   https://www.bcorporation.net/what-are-b-corps

31   Paul Hemp, 2001, 'Managing for the Next Big Thing: an interview with EMC's Michael Ruettgers', *Harvard Business Review,* January, p. 132.

32   Daniel Roth, 2002, 'Can EMC restore its glory?', *Fortune,* 22 July, pp. 107–110.

33   EMC, 2002a, 'A brief history of EMC through 1998', http://www.emc.com/about/emc_story/brief_history.jsp

34–35 See note 52.

36   http://www.emc.com

37   See note 52.

38   See note 50.

39   EMC, 2002b, 'EMC profile', http://www.emc.com/about/corp_profile/index.jsp?openfolder=all

40–41 See note 52.

42   See note 50.

43   See note 58.

44   EMC, 2001, 'EMC Symmetrix named "Product of the Year" by *Network Magazine*', http://www.emc.com/about/news/press/us/2001/20010418-876.htm

45   Nelson D. Schwarz, 1999, 'The tech boom will keep on rocking', *Fortune,* 15 February, p. 72.

46   David Kirkpatrick, 1999, 'Storage! Storage! Storage!', *Fortune,* 15 February, p. 72.

47   See note 50.

48   Daniel Lyons, 2001, 'What's eating EMC?', *Forbes,* 26 November, pp. 62–65.

49   Steve Hamm, 2005, 'From the Brink to the Big Leagues', *BusinessWeek* European Edition, 15 August, pp. 60–61.

50   See note 68.

51   Andy Reinhardt, 2004, 'Can EMC find growth beyond hardware?' *BusinessWeek* European Edition, 1 November, pp. 62–63.

52   EMC Corporation, *BusinessWeek,* http://investing.businessweek.com/research/stocks/earnings/earnings.asp?ric=EMC

53   Dina Bass, 2012, 'EMC Weighs Using $5.65 Billion Cash on Security Startups', 15 August. http://www.bloomberg.com/news/2012-08-15/emc-weighs-using-5-65-billion-cash-on-security-startups.html

54   'Historic Dell and EMC Merger Complete; Forms World's Largest Privately-Controlled Tech Company'. 7 September 2016, https://uk.emc.com/about/news/press/2016/20160907-01.htm, accessed 15 January 2017.

55   Gary Taubes, 1995, 'The rise and fall of Thinking Machines', *Inc. Technology,* issue 3, p. 61.

56   Joshua Hyatt, 1985, 'Breakthrough: start-up fever may return to computer industry', *Inc.*, August, p. 15.

57   *Omni,* 1992, 'Danny Hillis: interview', October.

58–59 See note 75.

60   *The Economist,* 2001, 'Rethinking machines', 24 March.

61–62 See note 75.

63   Michael E. Knell, 1994, 'Cuts for computer maker Thinking Machines goes Ch.11', *Boston Herald,* 16 August, p. 27.

64   John Markoff, 1992, 'Company news: super-duper computer; it may be faster than anyone wants', *New York Times,* 10 June, p. D3.

65   See note 50.

Chapter 4

1   Quoted in Herb Greenberg, 2002, 'How to avoid the value trap', *Fortune,* 10 June, p. 194.

2   Michael Porter, 1979, 'How competitive forces shape strategy', *Harvard Business Review,* March–April.

3   *Public Citizen,* 2001, 'Drug industry most profitable again', http://www.citizen.org/congress/reform/drug_industry/corporate/articles.cfm?ID=838

4   *San José Mercury News,* 1993, 'Study: drug profits excessive', 26 February, http://www.ibiblio.org/pub/academic/medicine/public-health/drugs3.Feb93

5   David Noonan, Joan Raymond and Anne Belli Gesalman, 2000, 'Why drugs cost so much', *Newsweek,* 25 September, p. 22.

6   *US Business Reporter,* 2001, 'Pharmaceuticals industry', 15 December, http://www.activemedia-guide.com/pharmaceutical_industry.htm

7   Anita M. McGahan, 1994, 'Industry structure and competitive advantage', *Harvard Business Review,* November–December.

8   Perry L. Fagan, 1998, 'The pharma giants: ready for the 21st century?', Harvard University Note 9-698-070, 6 May.

9   See note 7.

10   See note 5.

11   *Chemical Week,* 1984, 'A prudent boost in spending', 11 January, p. 3.

12   Alfred A. Sagarese, 1989, 'Fine chemicals: ripe for takeover', *Chemical Week,* 3 May, p. 24.

13   See note 7.

14 Elisa Williams and Robert Langreth, 2001, 'A biotech wonder grows up', *Forbes,* 3 September, p. 118.

15 American Health Line, 2005, 'Industry Profits Unlikely Until Decade's End, Report Says', 1 June.

16 Sam Cage, 2009, 'Roche's $46.8 billion Genentech deal outshines others', 12 March, http://www.reuters.com/article/topNews/idUSTRE52B1DN20090312

17 See note 14.

18 Geoffrey Carr, 1998, 'Survey of the pharmaceutical industry', *The Economist,* 21 February, p. 16.

19 Amgen, Inc., *Business Week,* http://investing.businessweek.com/research/stocks/earnings/earnings.asp?ric=AMGN.O

20 See note 18.

21 See note 8.

22 Henry Dummett, 2003, 'New FDA Generics Regulations Take Effect', *WMRC Daily Analysis,* 19 August.

23 See note 18.

24–25 See note 8.

26 William C. Castagnoli, 1995, 'Is disease management good therapy for an ailing industry?', *Medical Marketing & Media,* January.

27 See note 5.

28 Ken Lacey, 2000, 'Under transformation: the pharmaceutical industry reinvents itself', *Pharmaceutical Technology Europe,* December.

29 John Chave, 2011, 'Free movement of prescription drugs hampers regulation', 28 June, http://www.bbc.co.uk/news/uk-northern-ireland-13938961

30 Robert Pear, 'U.S. to Compare Medical Treatments', February 15, 2009, *The New York Times,* http://www.nytimes.com/2009/02/16/health/policy/16health.html.

31 Pharmafile. Seven pharma trends for 2017. 22 December 2016. http://www.pharmafile.com/news/512053/seven-pharma-trends-2017

32 See note 18.

33 See note 8.

34 See note 28.

35 See note 8.

36 See note 18.

37 Fleming.Team, '8 pharmaceutical trends of 2016 to set your course for 2017',*Fleming,* https://fleming.events/library/article/8-pharmaceutical-trends-of-2016-to-set-your-course-for-2017, accessed 27 January 2017.

38 Market Realist. 'Drug Patent Expirations: $190 Billion Is Up for Grabs', 3 March 2016, http://marketrealist.com/2016/03/drug-patent-expirations-190-billion-sales-grabs/. Accessed 27 January 2017.

39 Congressional Budget Office, 1998, 'How increased competition from generic drugs has affected prices and returns in the pharmaceutical industry', http://www.cbo.gov/showdoc.cfm?index=655&sequence=1

40 *Fortune,* 2001, 'Most profitable industries: return on assets', http://www.fortune.com/indexw.jhtml?list_frag=list_f5_ind_mostprofit_asset.jhtml&channel=list.jhtml

41 'How the industries stack up', *Fortune,* 17 April, 2006, p. F–26.

42 *Fortune,* 2009, 'Top industries: Most profitable', http://money.cnn.com/magazines/fortune/global500/2009/performers/industries/profits/assets.html

43 CSI Market, http://csimarket.com/screening/index.php?s=roa&pageI=1&fis=#tableind, accessed 4 February 2017.

44 https://www.crunchbase.com/organization/groupon#/entity, accessed 5 February 2017.

45 Alice Truong, 'Groupon is still the fastest company to reach a billion-dollar valuation', *Quartz,* 15 May 2015, https://qz.com/398090/groupon-still-the-fastest-company-to-reach-a-unicorn-billion-dollar-valuation/, accessed 27 January, 2017.

46 Alexia Tsotsis, 'Groupon IPO Shares Pop 40% on First Trade, Debuts at $17.8B Market Cap', *TechCrunch,* 4 November 2011, https://techcrunch.com/2011/11/04/groupon-ipo-shares-pop-40-on-first-trade-debuts-at-17-8b-market-cap/, accessed 27 January 2017.

47 https://www.crunchbase.com/organization/livingsocial#/entity, accessed 5 February 2017.

48 https://twitter.com/rakeshlobster/status/307291700919934977, accessed 5 February 2017.

49 http://investor.groupon.com/results.cfm 3Q16 Earnings Release, accessed 5 February 2017.

50 Brad Tuttle, 'Why Daily Deals Sites Are Giving Up on Daily deals', 12 November 2013, http://business.time.com/2013/11/12/why-daily-deal-sites-are-giving-up-on-daily-deals/, accessed 5 February 2017.

51 Venture Deal, 'Venture Deal M&A Analysis', November 2016, http://www.venturedeal.com/Reports/pdf/MA_Report_-_Nov_2016.pdf, accessed 5 February 2017.

52 Bob Zider, 1998, 'How venture capital works', *Harvard Business Review,* November–December, p. 133.

53 The British Venture Captial Association, the European Venture Capital Association and the National Venture Capital Association in the USA all publish directories that identify the investing preferences of their member firms. *Pratt's Guide to Venture Capital,* available in many business libraries, provides similar information.

54 Stephanie Hoi-Nga Wong, 'Selfie Generation Turns Make-Up Chain Ulta into Rare Retail Star', 27 January 2017, https://www.bloomberg.com/news/articles/2017-01-27/ulta-shines-as-rare-bright-spot-in-retail-as-makeup-demand-soars, accessed 5 February 2017; Phil Wahba, 'More than Skin Deep', 15 September 2016, *Fortune,* pp. 120–126

Chapter 5

1 Philip Van Munchen, 1998, 'The devil's adman', *Brandweek,* 15 June, p. 30.

2 Joan Holleran, 1997, 'Craft brews, a beer rabbit?', *Beverage Industry,* January, p. 8.

3 Jim Collins, 2000, 'Best beats first', *Inc.*, August, pp. 48–51.

4 Institute for Brewing Studies, 1997–1998, *North American Brewers Resource Directory 1997–1998,* Institute for Brewing Studies, Boulder, CO; National Restaurant Association, 2001, *Restaurant Industry Operations Report,* National Restaurant Association, Washington DC.

5 Constantinos C. Markides and Paul A. Geroski, 2005, *Fast Second: How Smart Companies Bypass Radical Innovation to Enter and Dominate New Markets,* Jossey-Bass, San Francisco, CA.

6 See note 3.

7   Joel Dreyfus, 1983, 'SmithKline's ulcer medicine "holy war"', *Fortune,* 19 September, p. 129.

8   See note 7.

9   Leon Jaroff, 1995, 'Fire in the belly, money in the bank', *Time,* 6 November, p. 56.

10   William E. Sheeline, 1989, 'Glaxo's goal: new wonder cures', *Fortune,* 6 November, p. 101.

11   See note 9.

12   Brand Finance, 2008 and 2012, BrandFinance Global 500, March each year.

13   McKinsey Quarterly. 'Nokia's Next Chapter'. December 2016, accessed 3 February 2017. http://www.mckinsey.com/industries/high-tech/our-insights/nokias-next-chapter, accessed 3 February 2017.

14   Andrew Tausz, 2001, 'Still the one to beat; Nokia strives to maintain its lead in the wireless handset market', *Telephony,* 13 August.

15   Christopher Brown-Humes and Robert Budden, 2004, 'Nokia begins to get the message', *Financial Times,* 6 May.

16   Techtree News Staff, 2009, 'Nokia Targets Low Cost Segment in India', 20 August, http://www.techtree.com/India/News/Nokia_Targets_Low_Cost_Segment_in_India/551-105688-547.html; S. Kamakshi, 2012, 'Nokia Continues To Reign Supreme', 6 March, http://www.techtree.com/content/news/784/nokia-continues-to-reignsupreme.html

17   Adam Ewing and Kasper Viita, 2013, 'Nokia Investors Approve Phone Units Sale to Microsoft', 20 November, http://www.bloomberg.com/news/2013-11-19/nokiainvestors-approve-phone-unit-s-sale-to-microsoft.Html

18   BBC News. 'Microsoft to buy Nokia's mobile phone unit'. 3rd September 2013, accessed 3 February 2017. http://www.bbc.co.uk/news/business-23940171, accessed 3 February 2017.

19   See note 13.

20   Yves Doz, Jose Santos and Peter Williamson, 2001, *From Global to Metanational: How Companies Win in the Knowledge Economy,* Harvard Business School Press, Boston, MA.

21   Dan Steinbock, 2001, *The Nokia Revolution: The Story of an Extraordinary Company that Transformed an Industry,* American Management Association, New York.

22   See note 19.

23   Jonathon, D. May, Paul Y. Mang, Ansgar Richter and John Roberts, 2001, 'The innovative organization', *McKinsey Quarterly,* Spring, p. 21.

24   Tracy Sutherland, 2000, 'The Finn formula', *The Australian,* 28 November, p. 32.

25   Nokia, 2001, 'Nokia expands ventures organization with new tool for corporate innovation', http://www.press.nokia.com/PR/200112/842293_5.html

26   Alexandra Chang, 2012, '5 Reasons Why Nokia Lost Its Handset Sales Lead and Got Downgraded to "Junk"', 27 April, http://www.wired.com/gadgetlab/2012/04/5-reasons-why-nokia-lost-its-handset-sales-lead-and-got-downgraded-to-junk/

27   McKinsey Quarterly. 'Nokia's Next Chapter'. December 2016, accessed 3 February 2017. http://www.mckinsey.com/industries/high-tech/our-insights/nokias-next-chapter, accessed 3 February 2017.

28   Christopher A. Bartlett, 1985a, *EMI and the CT scanner (A),* Harvard University Press, Boston, MA.

29   David J. Teece, 2000, *Managing Intellectual Capital,* Oxford University Press, Oxford, p. 93.

30   Christopher A. Bartlett, 1985b, *EMI and the CT scanner (B),* Harvard University Press, Boston, MA.

31   Pier A. Abetti, 1989, 'Technology: a key strategic resource', *Management Review,* February, p. 37.

32–33 See note 28.

34   *BusinessWeek,* 1976, 'Can Britain's EMI stay ahead in the US?', 19 April, p. 122.

35   *BusinessWeek,* 1980, 'GE gobbles a rival in CT scanners', 19 May, p. 40.

36   Rita Gunther McGrath, 'Transient Advantage', *Harvard Business Review,* June 2013, p 4.

37   Rita Gunther McGrath, 'Transient Advantage', *Harvard Business Review,* June 2013, p 7.

38   Rita Gunther McGrath, 'Transient Advantage', *Harvard Business Review,* June 2013, p 10.

39   Daniel Eisenberg, 2001, 'Why are these CEOs smiling?', *Time,* 5 November.

40   eBay, 2002, 'Fee changes', 16 January, http://www2.ebay.com/aw/marketing .shtml#011602232649

41   '2004 Annual Report', eBay, http://investor.ebay.com/annual.cfm

42   See note 34.

43   Whit Andrews, 1998, 'Investors betting on eBay to maintain its auction lead', *Internet World,* 5 October, p. 72.

44   Rick Spence, 2000, 'The eBay economy', *Profit,* February–March, p. 6.

45   Robert D. Hof, 2001a, 'The people's company', *BusinessWeek,* 3 December, p. EB14.

46   Michael Rappa, 2002, 'Business models on the Web', http://www.digitalenterprise .org/models/models.html

47   Tom Gardner, 1999, 'The eBay model: powerful networks', http://www.fool.com/ portfolios/RuleMaker/1999/RuleMaker990128.htm

48   *Business Wire,* 2005, 'eBay Inc. Announces Second Quarter 2005 Financial Results', 20 July.

49   See note 43.

50   Gene G. Marcial, 2001, 'eBay – for hard times', *BusinessWeek,* 3 December, p. 63.

51   eBay Financial Releases 2008–2016. https://investors.ebayinc.com/financial_releases .cfm, accessed 3 February 2017.

52   Online Retailing UK. Mintel. July 2016, accessed 3 February 2017.

53   eBay Annual Report, 2016, at xxx, accessed 3 February 2017.

54   Saul Hansell, 2001, 'Online grocery goes to the checkout lane', *Milwaukee Journal Sentinel,* 10 July, p. 1A.

55   John Case, 2001, 'Food for thought: the on-line grocery business just keeps growing. So why can't anybody make any money at it?', *Inc.,* September, pp. 44–46.

56   Carol Emert, 2000, 'Webvan sees sales surge 136%', *San Francisco Chronicle,* 28 July, p. B1.

57   Dana Canedy, 1999, 'Need asparagus? Just click it; on-line grocers take aim at established supermarkets', *New York Times,* 10 September, p. C1.

58   Carolyn Said, 2000, 'Webvan sees revenue losses grow', *San Francisco Chronicle,* 14 April, p. B1.

59   *Los Angeles Times,* 2001, 'Online grocers hurt by delivery costs, apathy', 22 May, Business Section, p. 7.

60   Monica Soto, 2001, 'When a company fails to deliver', *Seattle Times,* 7 May, p. A1.

61   See note 54.

62   Vanessa Hua, 2001, 'Running out of gas; Webvan's efforts to keep on truckin' not likely to succeed, analysts say', *San Francisco Chronicle,* 27 April, p. B1.

63   'Tesco launches online grocery shopping in Slovakia', 8 October 2012, http://www
      .tescoplc.com/index.asp?pageid=17&newsid=688

64   Glynn Davies, 2011, 'Online food retail – case studies from Tesco to Migros', 27
      July, http://www.just-food.com/management-briefing/online-food-retail-case-
      studiesfrom-tesco-to-migros_id116104.aspx

65   Tescoplc.com, 'Our History', http://www.tescoplc.com/index.asp?pageid=11

66   Dave Chaffey, 2008, 'Tesco case study & Tesco.com case study for E-commerce
      & Internet marketing', September, http://www.davechaffey.com/E-commerce-
      Internetmarketing-case-studies/Tesco.com-case-study

67   See note 52.

68   IGD, 2011, 'Online grocery shopping to be worth £11.2bn in 2016 – almost double its
      current value', 18 October, http://www.igd.com/index.asp?id=1&fid=6&sid=25&tid=
      90&cid=2177

69   Alex Lawson, 2012, 'Tesco close to 50% of internet food sales', 29 February, http://
      www.racplus.com/news/tesco-close-to-50-of-internet-food-sales/8627120.article

70   See note 60.

71   Mark Vandevelde, 'Tesco offers 3-hour online order collection'. *Financial Times*. 24
      August 2016, https://www.ft.com/content/73349392-6a08-11e6-ae5b-a7cc5dd5a28c.

72   '29% of UK online grocery shoppers are shopping for groceries more online now than
      a year ago'. Mintel. 14 April 2016, http://www.mintel.com/press-centre/retail-press-
      centre/29-of-uk-online-grocery-shoppers-are-shopping-for-groceries-more-online-
      now-than-a-year-ago.

73   'Tesco to deliver in an hour'. IGD Retail Analysis. 17 January 2017, http://retailanalysis
      .igd.com/Hub.aspx?id=13&tid=1&rid=24&nid=16185.

74   Colleague Interview with Dave Lewis and Alan Clark. Tescoplc.com. 5 October 2016,
      https://www.tescoplc.com/media/391669/interims-16-17 transcript.pdf.

75   For the whole enchilada on the incredibly pragmatic fruits of that research and on
      building better business models, see John Mullins and Randy Komisar, 2009, *Getting
      to Plan B: Breaking Through to a Better Business Model,* Harvard Business Press, Boston.

76   Alexander Osterwalder and Yyes Pigneur, 2010, *Business Model Generation,* Wiley,
      New York.

Chapter 6

1   Indira Gandhi, 1982, *Indira Gandhi: My Truth,* Grove Press, New York.

2   Quoted from Edmond Rostand, 'La Princesse Lointaine', 1980, *The Oxford Dictionary of
      Quotations,* 3rd edn., Oxford University Press, Oxford, p. 410.

3   Howard Schultz and Dori Jones Yang, 1997, *Pour Your Heart into it: How Starbucks Built a
      Company One Cup at a Time,* Hyperion, New York.

4   Howard H. Stevenson, H. Irving Grousbeck, Michael J. Roberts and Amarnath Bhide,
      1999, *New Business Ventures and the Entrepreneur,* McGraw-Hill/Irwin, Burr Ridge, IL.

5   Most of what follows is based on Schultz and Yang (1997), see note 3.

6–8   See note 3.

9   Alex Witchel, 1994, 'Coffee talk with: Howard Schultz; by way of Canarsie, one large
      cup of business strategy', *New York Times,* 14 December, p. C1.

10   See note 3.

11   Matt Rothman, 1993, 'Into the black', *Inc.*, January, p. 59.

12–17 See note 3.

18 Dori Jones Yang, 1994, 'The Starbucks enterprise shifts into warp speed', *BusinessWeek,* 24 October, p. 76.

19–20 See note 3.

21 Stanley Holmes, 2002, 'Planet Starbucks', *BusinessWeek,* 9 September, pp. 100–110.

22 'Starbucks Corporation Fiscal 2004 Annual Report', http://www.starbucks.com/aboutus/investor.asp

23 *Fortune,* 2005, '100 Best Companies to Work For', 24 January.

24 See note 21.

25 Andy Serwer, 2009, 'Starbucks fix: Howard Schultz spills the beans on his plans to save the company he founded', *Fortune,* 18 January.

26 Claire Cain Miller, 2011, 'A Changed Starbucks. A Changed C.E.O.', 12 March, http://www.nytimes.com/2011/03/13/business/13coffee.html?pagewanted=all&_r=0

27 See note 26.

28 Starbucks Newsroom, 2009, 'Starbucks Posts Strong Third Quarter Fiscal 2009 Results', 24 July, http://news.starbucks.com/article_display.cfm?article_id=249

29 'Starbucks CEO Howard Schultz on first roastery in Italy', *Bloomberg,* 28 February 2017, https://www.bloomberg.com/news/videos/2017-02-28/starbucks-ceo-howard-schultz-on-first-roastery-in-italy, accessed 6 March 2017.

30 Maggie McGrath, 'Howard Schultz Stepping Down as Starbucks CEO', *Forbes,* 1 December 2016, https://www.forbes.com/sites/maggiemcgrath/2016/12/01/howard-schultz-stepping-down-as-starbucks-ceo/#21e03d0f2534, accessed 6 March 2017.

31 Liz Welch, 'Busting Out', *Inc.*, November 2016, pp. 84–95.

32 See note 3.

33 From a speech given at Stanford University, 23 October 2002.

34 See note 3.

35 Scott S. Smith, 1998, 'Grounds for success (interview with Starbucks CEO Howard Schultz)', *Entrepreneur,* May, p. 120.

36 See note 3.

Chapter 7

1 From William Wordsworth, *The Prelude,* book xi, 1.11.

2 Howard Schultz and Dori Jones Yang, 1997, *Pour Your Heart into it: How Starbucks Built a Company One Cup at a Time,* Hyperion, New York.

3 Andrea Butter and David Pogue, 2002, *Piloting Palm: The Inside Story of Palm, Handspring and the Birth of the Billion Dollar Handheld Industry,* John Wiley & Sons, New York.

4–8 See note 3.

9 Paul E. Teague, 2000, 'Father of an industry', *Design News,* 6 March, p. 108.

10 See note 3.

11 See note 9.

12 Rae Dupree, 2001 'Words to live by from an apostle of simplicity', *U.S. News and World Reports,* 15 January, p. 35.

13 Katie Hafner, 1999, 'One more ultimate gadget', *New York Times,* 16 September, p. G1.

14–16 See note 3.

17 David A. Kaplan, 1997, 'The cult of the Pilot', *Newsweek,* 21 July, p. 35.

18 See note 3.

19   Joanna Pettitt, 1998, 'Palm Computing hangs on to control of handheld market', *Computer Weekly,* 16 April, p. 21.

20   See note 3.

21   Kim Clark, 2004, 'Round two at Palm', *U.S. News and World Reports,* 1 November.

22   'Palm Reports Q4 and FY 2009 Results,' http://files.shareholder.com/downloads/ PALM/755201276x0x302996/fc5f86a8-8a30-4c60-93ca-347e9d3797b9/ PalmReportsQ4AndFY09Results.pdf

23   Tricia Duryee, 2009, 'Former Apple Exec Jon Rubinstein Replaces Ed Colligan as Palm's CEO', *moconews.net,* 10 June, http://www.washingtonpost.com/wp-dyn/content/ article/2009/06/10/AR2009061003344.html

24   'HP to Acquire Palm for $1.2 Billion', April 2010, http://www.hp.com/hpinfo/ newsroom/press/2010/100428xa.html

25   Daniel Eran Dilger, 2011, 'HP kills webOS, spins off PC business to focus on software', 18 August, http://appleinsider.com/articles/11/08/18/hp_to_spin_off_pc_business_to_ focus_on_enterprise_software.html

26   Nilay Patel, 'HP emerges as big winner in webOS sale, and LG doesn't rule out a phone', *The Verge,* 25 February 2013, http://www.theverge.com/2013/2/25/4027814/ hp-emerges-as-big-winner-in-webos-sale, accessed 6 March 2017.

27   Micah Singleton, 'Palm could be coming back to life — as an Android phone from Alcatel', *The Verge,* 31 December 2014, http://www.theverge.com/2014/12/31/7474965/ hp-sells-palm-acatel-one-touch-tcl, accessed 6 March 2017.

28–29   See note 3.

30   Michael Treacy and Fred Wiersema, 1993, 'Customer intimacy and other value disciplines', *Harvard Business Review,* January–February, pp. 84–85.

31   See note 29.

32   The details in the case study that follows were reported in Judith Crown, Glenn Coleman and Drew Wilson, 1993, 'The fall of Schwinn', *Crain's Chicago Business,* 11 October.

33   See note 31.

34   Based on 'Bicycle makers: kids' stuff', *The Economist,* 3 June 1989, p. 101.

35   Jennifer Foote, 1987, 'Two-wheel terrors', *Newsweek,* 28 September, p. 72.

36–41   See note 31.

42   John Mullins, *The Customer-Funded Business,* Jersey City: Wiley, 2014, pp. 25–26.

43–44   See note 3.

45   See note 31.

Chapter 8

1   This case study is taken from Lloyd *et al.* (2001a, 2001b). See notes 2 and 7.

2   Julian Lloyd, Eileen Rutschmann and John Bates, 2001a, 'Virata (A)', London Business School.

3–6   See note 2.

7   Julian Lloyd, Eileen Rutschmann and John Bates, 2001b, 'Virata (B)', London Business School.

8   3i, 2005, '3i backs Virata vision', at www.3i.com/ourportfolio/successstories/ss_virata. html

9   Quoted from an interview with Hermann Hauser on 7 April 2000.

10   This case study is taken from David Allison, 1988, 'Ken Olsen interview', http://www .americanhistory.si.edu/collections/comphist/olsen.html

11 John C. Whitney Jr and Bruce C. Greenwald, 1987, *Invisible barriers to successful marketing in new environments,* Working Draft, University of Wisconsin.

12 Allison (1988), see note 10.

13–14 See note 10.

15 Jones Telecommunications and Multimedia Encyclopedia, 'Digital Equipment Corporation (DEC)', http://www.digitalcentury.com/encyclo/update/dec.html

16 See note 10.

17 Interview with Jean Micol on 12 September 2002.

18 Saras Sarasvathy, 2001, 'What makes entrepreneurs entrepreneurial', working paper, University of Washington.

19 Lindsay Blakely and Burt Helm, 'Game Over', *Inc.,* September 2016, pp. 134–145.

20 Andy Grove, 1996, *Only the Paranoid Survive,* Currency/Doubleday, New York.

21 Lindsay Blakely and Burt Helm, 'Game Over', *Inc.,* September 2016, pp. 134–145.

22 Ibid.

Chapter 9

1 Quoted from Oliver Wendell Holmes, 'The Professor at the Breakfast Table', 1980, *The Oxford Dictionary of Quotations,* 3rd edn., Oxford University Press, Oxford, p. 253.

2 V. Kasturi Rangan and Marie Bell, 1995, *Nestlé Refrigerated Foods: Contadina Pasta and Pizza (A),* Harvard Business School Press, Boston, MA.

3 See www.navigationzone.com for details.

4 Harper W. Boyd Jr, Orville C. Walker Jr, John Mullins and Jean-Claude Larréché, 2002, *Marketing Management: A Strategic Decision Making Approach,* McGraw-Hill/ Irwin, Burr Ridge, IL.

5 Bob Zider, 1998, 'How venture capital works', *Harvard Business Review,* November–December.

6 Kopin Tan, 2002, 'USA: venture capitalists still detect red flags in lots of proposals', *Wall Street Journal,* 7 August.

7 See note 6.

Chapter 10

1 And most of the time, like the American Poet Robert Frost, they took roads that were "less traveled by".6

2 See Alex Osterwalder and Yves Pigneur, *Business Model Generation,* Jersey City: Wiley, 2010 for a useful pictorial method of planning a new venture.

3 William H. Sahlman, 1997, 'How to write a great business plan', *Harvard Business Review,* July–August.

4 Steven Gary Blank, 2005, *The Four Steps to the Epiphany,* Quad/Graphics, Wisconsin; Eric Ries, 2011, *The Lean Startup,* Crown Business, New York.

5 Leaps of faith are beliefs you hold about unanswered questions despite having no evidence that these beliefs are true. For more on how to determine whether your leaps of faith are actually true, see Chapter 1 in John Mullins and Randy Komisar, 2009, *Getting to Plan B,* Harvard Business Press, Boston; or Chapter 5 in Eric Ries, 2011, *The Lean Startup,* Crown Business, New York.

6   See note 1.

7   http://quotationsbook.com/quote/30474/

Chapter 11

1   Adapted from a working paper of the same title, John W. Mullins, 2005, London
     Business School. Later revised and published by John W. Mullins, 2007, 'Discovering
     "Unk-Unks"', *Sloan Management Review,* Summer.

2   Mary Bellis, 'Inventors of the Modern Computer, The First Spreadsheet – VisiCalc – Dan
     Bricklin and Bob Frankston', http://inventors.about.com/library/weekly/aa010199.htm

3   See Grant McCracken, 1988, *The Long Interview,* Sage Publications, Newbury Park, CA.
     Much of this chapter is based on McCracken's interviewing methodology.

4   Another useful source, one that nicely complements this chapter, will help you figure
     out how best to ask customers questions without having them lie to you. It's a won-
     derful little book by Rob Fitzpatrick, *The Mom Test* (London: CreateSpace, 2013).

Chapter 12

1   This section is based on an interview with Rakesh, Rashmi and Rohan Verma,
     24 June 2012.

2   Airbnb corporate homepage, http://www.airbnb.com/home/story

3   Chris Velazco, 2012, 'Airbnb, Brit + Co, TaskRabbit, and Lyft Founders Share How
     They Nabbed Their First 10K Users', *TechCrunch,* 10 September, http://techcrunch.
     com/2012/09/10/airbnb-brit-co-taskrabbit-and-lyft-founders-share-how-theynabbed-
     their-first-10k-users/

4   Fred Wilson, 2011, 'Airbnb', *AVC,* 16 March, http://www.avc.com/a_vc/2011/03/airbnb.
     html

5   Om Malik, 2011, 'What Every Startup Can Learn From Airbnb', *GigaOM,* 22 February,
     http://gigaom.com/2011/02/22/airbnb/

6   See note 5.

7   Craig Smith, "98 Amazing Airbnb Statistics and Facts (July 2017), DMR, at https://
     expandedramblings.com/index.php/airbnb-statistics/.,

8   Regina Anthony, 2007, 'Real journeys, but it's still virtual profit for online travel
     firms', *LiveMint,* 6 June, http://www.livemint.com/2007/06/06001946/Real-
     journeysbut-its-still.html

9   Sudipto Dey, 2006, 'Ashwini Kakkar trains sights on travel start-ups', *The Economic
     Times,* 18 September, http://articles.economictimes.indiatimes.com/2006-09-18/
     news/27460036_1_start-ups-majority-stake-sms-platform

10   Gayatri Vijaykumar, 2007, 'Flightraja now Via, announces US$ 5 million VC', *Express
     Travel World,* July, http://www.expresstravelworld.com/200707/aviationworld15.shtml

11   See note 10.

12   See note 8.

13   Via website at https://in.via.com/about?type=Us.

14   Narayan Krishnamurthy, 2006, 'Log in and Learn: More and more teachers are
     learning that it pays to move into the virtual classroom', *Outlook Money,* 16 January,
     http://www.tutorvista.com/press/mediacover/outlookmoneyjuly.php

15   Stephen David, 2006, 'Teachers in India help students in the West master maths and science through Internet tuitions', *India Today,* 15 July, http://www.tutorvista.com/press/mediacover/indiatodayjuly.php

16   Michelle Tsai, 2006, 'TutorVista Gets $2M To Teach American Kids Online', *Dow Jones,* 2 June, http://www.tutorvista.com/press/mediacover/djjuly.php

17   B.M. Thanuja, 2006, 'Sequoia to put in $3 million in TutorVista', *The Economic Times,* 20 December, http://articles.economictimes.indiatimes.com/2006-12-20/news/27439188_1_sequoia-capital-india-online-coaching-jv-partner

18   Vanessa Hua, 2006, 'One for the books – tutoring gets outsourced', *San Francisco Chronicle,* 22 October, pp. A1, A10.

19   Heather Timmons, 2009, 'Pearson Acquires Stake in 2 Indian Education Companies', *The New York Times,* 24 June, http://www.nytimes.com/2009/06/25/business/global/25rupee.html?_r=1&dbk

20   *Times of India,* 2011, 'Pearson takes control of TutorVista', 19 January.

21   Graham Ruddick, "How Zara became the world's biggest fashion retailer" The Telegraph, October 20, 2014, http://www.telegraph.co.uk/finance/newsbysector/retailandconsumer/11172562/How-Inditex-became-the-worlds-biggest-fashion-retailer.html.

22   vente-privee.com, 2012, Wikipedia, http://en.wikipedia.org/wiki/Vente-privee.com

23   Ben Rooney, 2011, 'Vente Privee: The Art of Trading Discounted High-End Goods', *The Wall Street Journal,* Tech Europe, 16 September, http://blogs.wsj.com/tech-europe/2011/09/16/vente-privee-the-art-of-trading-discounted-high-end-goods/

24   Jennifer L. Schenker, 2008, 'Vente-privee.com Refashions Closeouts', *Bloomberg Businessweek,* 11 January, http://www.businessweek.com/printer/articles/298192-vente-privee-dot-com-refashions-closeouts?type=old_article

25   See note 24.

26   Natasha Lomas, "Vente-Privee buys Spanish fashion ecommerce site Privalia for ~$560M", TechCrunch, https://techcrunch.com/2016/04/14/vente-privee-buys-spanish-fashion-ecommerce-site-privalia/.

27   The remainder of the MapmyIndia story is based on an interview with Rakesh, Rashmi and Rohan Verma, 24 June 2012.

28   John Mullins, *The Customer-Funded Business: Start, Finance, or Grow Your Company with Your Customers' Cash,* Jersey City: Wiley, 2014.

29   https://www.coursera.org/learn/startup-financing-without-vc

Chapter 14

1   Adapted with permission from the work of Professors Robert McGowan and Paul Olk of the University of Denver.

2   Michael Porter, 1979, 'How competitive forces shape strategy', *Harvard Business Review,* March–April.

Chapter 15

1   Adapted from *Marketing Management: A Strategic Decision Making Approach*, 8th edition, McGraw-Hill Companies, Inc (Mullins, J., Walker, O.C., Boyd Jr, H.W 2013) Chapter 6, Copyright (c) 2013 McGraw-Hill Education.

2   For additional qualitative research techniques, see Abbie Griffin, 1996, 'Obtaining Customer Needs for Product Development', in M. D. Rosenau, ed., *The PDMA Handbook of New Product Development,* John Wiley & Sons, New York; and Gerald Zaltman, 1997, 'Rethinking marketing research: putting people back in', *Journal of Marketing Research,* November, pp. 424–437.

3   The definitive guide to conducting in-depth interviews is Grant McCracken, 1988, *The Long Interview,* Sage Publications, Newbury Park, CA. Chapter 11, the first of the toolkit chapters in this book, is based on McCracken's approach.

4   For a useful guide to conducting surveys and interpreting their results sensibly, see www.whatisasurvey.info

5   Malcolm Gladwell, 1996, 'The Science of Shopping', *New Yorker,* 4 November, pp. 66–67; and Gary Hamel and C. K. Prahalad, 1991, 'Corporate Imagination and Expeditionary Marketing', *Harvard Business Review,* July–August.

6   See, for example, Nigel Bradley, 2013, *Marketing Research: Tools and Techniques,* Oxford University Press, Oxford.

7   See note 6.

Chapter 16

1   Adapted from *Marketing Management: A Strategic Decision Making Approach*, 8th edition, McGraw-Hill Companies, Inc (Mullins, J., Walker, O.C., Boyd Jr, H.W 2013) Chapter 7, Copyright (c) 2013 McGraw-Hill Education.

2   Deborah Solomon, 2000, 'Local phone companies put customer service on hold, critics charge', *Wall Street Journal,* 6 July, p. B1.

3   Frank M. Bass, 1969, 'A new product growth model for consumer durables', *Management Science,* January, pp. 215–227; Trichy V. Krishnan, Frank M. Bass and V. Kumar, 2000, 'Impact of a later entrant on the diffusion of a new product/service', *Journal of Marketing Research,* May, pp. 269–278.

4   Robert J. Dolan, 1990a, *Conjoint Analysis: A Manager's Guide,* Harvard Business School Publishing, Boston, MA.

5   Robert J. Dolan, 1990b, *Concept Testing,* Harvard Business School Publishing, Boston, MA.

6   John Mullins and Randy Komisar, 2009, *Getting to Plan B,* Harvard Business Press, Boston, MA, p.17.

7   Colin Welch and Ananth Raman, 1998, *Merchandising at Nine West Retail Stores,* Harvard Business School Publishing, Boston, MA.

8   For details of their method, see Dan Lovallo and Daniel Kahneman, 2003, 'Delusions of Success,' *Harvard Business Review,* July.

9   For more on the use of analogues and antilogues in entrepreneurial settings, see Chapter 1 in John Mullins and Randy Komisar, 2009, *Getting to Plan B,* Harvard Business Press, Boston, MA.

Chapter 17

1   This chapter is adapted from John Mullins, 'The Counter-Conventional Mindsets of Entrepreneurs', Working paper, London Business School, 2016.

2   A more complete story of Arnold Correia and the business he developed may be found in Alessandro Ananias, Brian Forde and John Mullins, 'SubWay Link (A) and (B)',

London Business School cases CS-13-002 and CS-13-003 (London: London Business School, 2013).

3   SubWay Link (A), page 3.

4   SubWay Link (B), page 3.

5   For more on the logic behind playing to one's dominant strength, see Geoffrey Moore, 'Strategy and Your Stronger Hand', *Harvard Business Review* (December 2005).

6   C.K. Prahalad and G. Hamel, 'The Core Competence of the Corporation', *Harvard Business Review* (May–June 1990).

7   A more complete story of Alex and Mimi Ikonn and Luxy Hair may be found in Benjamin Hallen and John Mullins, 'Big Beautiful Hair', London Business School case CS-16-015 (London: London Business School, 2016).

8   For more on resources, see Chapter 5 in Rob Grant, *Contemporary Strategy Analysis,* (Jersey City: Wiley, 2016).

9   A more complete story of the origins of Airbnb may be found in Chapter 3, John Mullins, *The Customer-Funded Business,* (Jersey City: Wiley, 2014).

10   E.B. Ekiel, 'The Entrepreneur Questionnaire: Brian Chesky, Co-Founder of Airbnb', April 8, 2011, Greylock Partners, http://greylockvc.com/2011/04/08/the-entrepreneur-questionnaire-brian-chesky-co-founder-and-ceo-of-airbnb/

11   For more on the importance of market size in new product development thinking, see Robert G. Cooper, 'The Stage-Gate Idea-to-Launch Process–Update, What's New and NexGen Systems', *Journal of Product Innovation Management* 25-3 (May 2008), pp 213–232.

12   A more complete story of Simon Cohen and the business he developed may be found in D. Gubbins, J. Walker, and J. Mullins, 'Simon Cohen (A), (B), and (C)', London Business School cases CS-11-012, CS-11-013, and CS-11-014 (London: London Business School, 2012).

13   Simon Cohen (A), page 2.

14   Simon Cohen (A), page 6.

15   Vinod Khosla, 'Any Big Problem Is a Big Opportunity', Stanford Technology Ventures Program, April 24, 2002, http://ecorner.stanford.edu/videos/26/Any-Big-Problem-is-a-Big-Opportunity

16   A more complete story of Thomas Knobel and the business he developed may be found in Elizabeth Philp and John Mullins, 'Nobel (A) and (B)', London Business School cases CS-15-003 and CS-15-004 (London: London Business School, 2015).

17   Nobel (A), page 6.

18   For more on professionalising entrepreneurial ventures to enable them to scale up, see Ranjay Gulati and Alicia DeSantola, 'Start-Ups That Last', *Harvard Business Review* (March 2016), pp 53–61.

19   A more complete story of Rud Browne and Ryzex may be found in Chapter 1, Mullins, *The Customer-Funded Business.*

20   For more on the cost of equity capital for entrepreneurial ventures, see Chapter 7 in J. Christopher Leach and Ronald W. Melicher, *Entrepreneurial Finance* (Mason, Ohio: South-Western Cengage Learning, 2015).

Chapter 18

1   Among the networks and blogs I respect are One Million by One Million (www.1mby1m.com) and the Fred Wilson (www.avc.com) and Mark Suster (www.bothsides@upfront.com) blogs.

Index